MURDER

MURDER
An Analysis of Its Forms, Conditions, and Causes

by
Gerhard Falk

WITH THE ASSISTANCE OF
CLIFFORD FALK

McFarland & Company, Inc., Publishers
Jefferson, North Carolina, and London

British Library Cataloguing-in-Publication data are available

Library of Congress Cataloguing-in-Publication Data

Falk, Gerhard, 1931–
    Murder, an analysis of its forms, conditions, and causes / by
Gerhard Falk.
        p.   cm.
    [Includes index.]
    Includes bibliographical references.
    ISBN 0-89950-478-7 (lib. bdg. : 50# alk. paper) ∞
    1. Murder. I. Title.
HV6515.F35   1990
364.1'523–dc20   89-13571
                                                            CIP

Manufactured in the United States of America

McFarland & Company, Inc., Publishers
  Box 611, Jefferson, North Carolina 28640

In loving memory of my parents,
Leonhard Falck and Hedwig Cibulski Falck,
and to the love of my life, Ursula Adler Falk,
and to our children
and to the many victims
of murder described in this book
"Non omnis moriar; I shall not be dead forever"

Acknowledgments

First, and most of all, I wish to thank my son, Clifford Falk, whose invaluable assistance and hours of work improved this book considerably. This is true because of his great expertise in the use of the computer and word processor, which made it possible to use that device to its fullest possibilities.

I am also grateful to Sister Martin Joseph Jones, of the Society of Martin of Nemour, archivist/librarian of the Butler Library at the State University College at Buffalo for collecting the archives of the Buffalo, N.Y., Courier-Express and organizing them in such an efficient manner. She and the staff at the Butler Library have always been my support and mainstay in all my years of research and publication.

Particular thanks also go to Barbara Metivier, Daniel Occiolo and Paul Reynolds of the Computer Services Department at the State University College for their endless patience in teaching me Word Star 2000 and SuperCalc 3.

Finally I owe a debt of gratitude to Professors Carl Backman and Thomas Weinberg for helping me in the preparation of Chapters Two and Three of this book.

Table of Contents

Introduction

"And it came to pass, when they were in the field, that Cain rose up against Abel his brother, and slew him." So the Bible describes the first murder in Genesis 4:8.

Whether this murder story is taken literally or viewed as an allegory, we cannot overlook that murder is seen as a heinous crime everywhere and by everyone, at all times and in all places. This is true for two reasons: First, because the only possession any of us truly have is our lives, and second, because the murder of some people by others exists almost everywhere. We cannot, of course, speak for all societies. However, we do know that murder has plagued humanity as long as history has been written, i.e., for at least 4,000 years.

It is also true that the number of murders is not the same in all places and among all peoples. On the contrary: There are some societies which have rarely experienced any homicide, while others such as the United States near the end of the 20th century are victimized by an exceptional amount of murder. To illustrate the word "exceptional," it is well to compare the murder rates of several countries with those of the United States. Dane Archer and Rosemary Gartner show in their book, *Violence and Crime in Cross National Perspective* (New Haven: Yale University, Press, 1983), that homicides vary considerably from one society to another.

For example, the state of Georgia had 167.3 homicides for every 1,000,000 inhabitants at the time of Archer and Gartner's investigation, while Massachussetts had only 13.6 murders per year for every 1,000,000 persons living there.

In England and Wales the homicide rate was yet lower with only 4.8 murders for every 1,000,000 inhabitants.

International variations in homicide rates show that the amount of murder found in any community is an outgrowth of that community's lifestyle and not an accident.

I should also add that the alleged relationship between any human behavior and the phases of the moon does not exist and that therefore there is no connection between homicide and the full moon, as is widely believed. This has been well established by James Rotton and I.W. Kelly in their review of 37 studies of the relationship between phases of the moon and homicide, suicide, "lunacy," crime and a host of other forms of human conduct (James Rotton and I.W. Kelly, "Much Ado

About the Full Moon: A Meta-Analysis of Luna-Lunacy Research," *Psychological Bulletin*, 97, No. 2, 1985, pp. 286–306).

Thus, an overview of homicide rates as published by the United Nations illustrates these differences and indicates that the United States is not only among those countries which exhibit a large number of killings but is in fact the most homicidal industrialized country. Other industrialized nations, such as Great Britain, West Germany and Japan, have far smaller homicide rates than we have. The following table illustrates this:

Homicide Rates for Selected Countries, 1980

(for every 100,000 inhabitants)

From: *United Nations Demographic Yearbook 1983*, p. 21

Country	Rate	Country	Rate	Country	Rate
United States	9.9	Hong Kong	1.6	Japan	1.0
Guatemala	7.7	Italy	1.6	Greece	0.8
Bulgaria	3.4	Austria	1.5	Ireland	0.7
Australia	1.9	W. Germany	1.2	England	0.4
Israel	1.8	France	1.0		

As already noted, differences such as these also exist within the United States because life is not the same in every part of this country, nor is it the same at all times. This is well illustrated by comparing the homicide rates of black Americans to those of white Americans and the homicide rates of American males to that of American females. Such a comparison is vitally important because nothing determines life chances and lifestyle more than race and gender.

Homicide Rates in the United States by Race and Sex, 1960–1983

(for every 100,000 inhabitants)

From: *Statistical Abstract of the United States*, 1987

Year	All	Black		White	
		Male	Female	Male	Female
1960	4.7	36.7	10.4	3.6	1.4
1970	8.3	67.6	13.3	8.3	2.1
1975	9.9	69.0	14.9	9.0	2.9
1976	9.0	61.6	13.4	8.2	2.6
1977	9.1	59.1	12.9	8.6	2.9
1978	9.2	58.1	12.8	9.0	2.8
1979	10.0	63.8	13.5	9.9	3.0
1980	10.7	66.6	13.5	10.9	3.2
1981	10.3	64.8	12.7	10.4	3.1
1982	9.6	59.1	12.0	9.6	3.1
1983	8.6	51.4	11.3	8.6	2.8

The table on the previous page clearly demonstrates the great disparity of homicide rates between the sexes and races in the United States as a whole.

These disparities are also true in Erie County, New York, and this author will establish that the detailed study of homicide in that county (Part I) is representative of any urban county in the United States despite small individual differences between regions and epochs, areas and times. The findings shown are drawn from one newspaper – the now-defunct *Buffalo Courier-Express* – over a span of 40 years, and present a reliable picture of what we can expect to find if we were to study every American urban county relative to homicide over a long period of time.

Murder is a form of human relationship. This means that every murder takes at least one killer and one victim, although some murders involve large groups of both murderers and victims. This book, therefore, seeks to exhibit these various relationships and further seeks to show the forms which murder has taken in the course of many years in the United States and elsewhere.

The book begins with murder in Erie County, New York, not because that county is unique in exhibiting this crime, but on the contrary, because it has had a very typical American urban murder history. As will be shown, it is reasonable to assume that murder in Erie County followed and continues to follow patterns of criminal homicide which also exist in other American urban centers. Therefore, the first three chapters and the final statistical appendix are a good and sufficient explanation of murder case histories, relationships between killers and their victims, the conditions under which murder takes place in the United States, and the disposition of murder cases by the American criminal justice system. In short, I contend that what is true of Erie County with reference to murder is also true in the United States as a whole.

It is further my contention that the conditions, circumstances and relationships reflected in the homicide statistics and case histories concerning Erie County during the 40 years here presented continue to be true in 1990 despite the many social changes which have occurred in recent years in Erie County and elsewhere in the United States.

Murder is not only confined to homicide which is defined as the killing of one person by another in the course of every-day experiences. In addition to homicide, mankind has also been plagued by multicide, which is the killing of many people either by the same killer or by groups of killers. Multicide can involve genocide (the mass murder of whole nations or peoples on grounds of religion, race or nationality). Chapter Four discusses the genocide of the Armenian Christians, the European Jews and the native Americans. Genocide is usually organized by governments. There are, however, also individuals who commit multicide. Such killers are known either as serial killers, like Ted Bundy, or as mass murderers, such as Leslie Lowenfeld. These killings are the subject of Chapter Five.

Chapter Six deals with assassinations. Assassination refers to the deliberate murder of another person for either fame or gain. Thus, there have been Americans who have deliberately murdered United States presidents and other famous persons in order to attract attention to themselves and gain notoriety or fame. In addition, organized criminals have always resorted to murder as a means of eliminating their business rivals. These are often called assassinations for gain, rather than fame.

In more recent years, political terrorists have murdered utterly innocent persons in order to promote their cause. Many of these terrorists have used airplane "hijackings" and bombings in the mistaken notion that this would advance their political fortunes. Such murders are the subject of Chapter Seven.

Chapter Eight deals with the death penalty. This chapter is called "Murder by Death," because this author is a firm opponent of the death penalty. Nevertheless, the discussion exhibits both sides of this eternal argument. Eyewitness accounts of capital punishment by electrocution, hanging, gassing and injection are presented. There is also a discussion of the legal ramifications of this punishment and a discussion of the current status of the death penalty in the United States.

Chapter Nine is a detailed sociological analysis of murder. Here I have presented the principal reasons for murder of every kind. Beginning with the current state of murder in the United States, I show that the amount of murder differs from region to region in this country because social conditions differ. The thrust of my argument is that murder has a sociological explanation which is to be sought in social conditions such as the American frontier of past centuries, urbanization, religious attitudes, racial and ethnic experiences, frustration tolerance and relative deprivation, the use of drugs and social class. This is a very important chapter because it demonstrates that the cause of murder is to be sought in social, not psychiatric conditions.

Chapter Ten deals with the meaning of murder and therefore also contributes to our understanding of its causes. Here the contribution of family violence to murder is discussed. Also discussed are the consequences of emotional stress on Americans, and how emotional stress is not only a psychiatric, but also a social condition derived from reducing human relations to so low a level that people view each other as objects, not persons. My argument is that the murder of another person viewed as an object is much easier than the murder of someone viewed as another human being.

The book ends, as it begins, with a presentation of murder in Erie County. A detailed analysis of the relationship of various social factors related to one another and involved in the 912 killings give the reader an opportunity to understand just how various conditions in the physical environment, such as temperature, and the social environment, such as the Christmas season, affect the murder rate. Not everyone may wish to read this statistical analysis. It is, however, of the greatest importance to those who have a professional interest in understanding murder in particular, and the influence of social conditions on human relations generally.

This is a unique book. Unlike any other book concerning murder, the material regarding homicide in Erie County has been taken entirely from newspaper accounts. Other studies of this kind are derived from police reports. The advantage of newspaper accounts of murder is that the reporters who write about murder do so immediately after the killings have taken place and therefore present a primary source of information to the researcher which police reports cannot present.

This book is unique in that it deals with all kinds of murder except suicide. Suicide is, of course, a form of killing which is widespread in the United States and elsewhere, taking at least 20,000 lives in this country each year. However, suicide has different motives, different social origins and follows different patterns than the murder of others. A discussion of suicide would therefore require a good deal more space, perhaps even an entire book.

The psychiatric approach to murder is hardly mentioned in this book. That is so because the author is an educationist and sociologist, and is not qualified to discuss psychiatric findings. In addition, it is my view that psychiatry cannot explain more than a few cases, because murder is the product of social conditions despite its evident psychiatric overtones.

This book, therefore, fills an important gap in the current literature on the subject. It seeks to cover all forms of murder while acknowledging that much more research lies ahead. I have written in the field of criminology for over 30 years and have made numerous in-depth studies of homicide, rape, the criminal justice system, aggression and other related topics. These studies have led me to the conclusion that the present book will not only contribute to our understanding of murder and its possible reduction, but will also stimulate others to study this phenomenon in the future so that more research and more understanding will benefit all of us.

Part I

Homicide

1. Case Histories

The following case histories of murder are illustrative of the kinds of murder encountered by reading about 912 such killings which occurred in Buffalo and Erie County, New York, during the 40 years ending in 1983. The first example, a so-called "gang killing," is taken from public testimony included in a book entitled *Juvenile Delinquency* by Martin R. Haskell and Lewis Yablonski. Although this murder did not take place in Buffalo but in New York City, it illustrates the extent to which gang violence can permeate any urban area.

MURDER BY YOUTH GANGS

This illustration of a homicidal assault by the "Egyptian Kings," an extremely violent gang, on two boys in New York's Central Park, led to the death of one boy and the wounding of another. A description of the assault given by some of the gang members and one of the victims, Roger McShane, who, though badly stabbed, survived the attack, follows. The other victim, Michael Farmer, a polio victim, was killed.

> *McShane:* "It was ten thirty when we entered the park. We saw couples on the benches, in the back of the pool, and they all stared at us, and I guess they must 'ave saw the gang there—I don't know, they were fifty or sixty feet away. When we reached the front of the stairs, we looked up and there was two of their gang members on top of the stairs. They were two small ones, and they had garrison belts wrapped around their hands. They didn't say nothin' to us, they looked kind of scared."
>
> *First Egyptian King:* "I was scared. I knew they were gonna jump 'em an' everythin', and I was scared. When they were comin' up, they all were separatin' an' everythin' like that."
>
> *McShane:* "I saw the main body of the gang slowly walk out of the bushes, on my right. I turned around fast, to see what Michael was going to do and this kid came runnin' at me with the belts. Then I ran, myself, and told Michael to run."
>
> *Second Egyptian King:* "He couldn't run anyway, 'cause we were all around him. So then I said, 'You're a Jester,' and he said, 'Yeah,' and I punched him in the face. And then somebody hit him with a bat over the head. And then I kept punchin' him. Some of them were too scared to do anything. They were just standin' there lookin'."

3

Third Egyptian King: "I was watchin' him. I didn't wanna hit him at first. Then I kicked him twice. He was layin' on the ground lookin' up at us. I kicked him on the jaw, or someplace; then I kicked him in the stomach. That was the least I could do, is kick 'im."

Fourth Egyptian King: "I was aimin' to hit him, but didn't get a chance to hit him. There were so many guys on him—I was scared when I saw the knife go into the guy, and I ran right there. After everybody ran, this guy stayed, and started hittin' him with a machete."

First Egyptian King: "Somebody yelled out: 'Grab him. He's a Jester.' So then they grabbed him. Magician grabbed him, he turned around and stabbed him in the back. I was . . . I was stunned. I couldn't do nothin'. And then Magician— he went like that and he pulled . . . he had a switchblade and he said, 'you're gonna hit him with that bat or I'll stab you,' so I hit him lightly with the bat."

Second Egyptian King: "Magician stabbed him and the guy he . . . like hunched over. He's standin' up and I knock him down. Then he was down on the ground, everybody was kickin' him, stompin' him, punchin' him, stabbin' him, so he tried to get back up and I knock him down again. Then the guy stabbed him in the back with a bread knife."

Third Egyptian King: I just went like that, and I stabbed him with the bread knife. You know, I was drunk, so I just stabbed him. (Laughs) He was screamin' like a dog. He was screamin' there. And then I took the knife out and I told the other guys to run, so I ran and the rest of the gang ran with me. They wanted to stay there and keep on doin' it."

Fourth Egyptian King: "The guy that stabbed him in the back with the bread knife, he told me that when he took the knife out o' his back, he said: 'thank you'."

McShane: "They got up fast after they stabbed me. And I just lay there on my stomach and there was five of them as they walked away. And as they walked away . . . the other big kid came down with a machete or some large knife of some sort, and he wanted to stab me too with it. And they told him: 'No. Come on. We got him. We messed him up already. Come on.' . . . And they took off up the hill and they walked up the hill and right after that, all of them turned their heads and looked back at me. I got up and staggered into the street to get a cab. And I got in a taxi and asked him to take me to the medical center and get my friend and I blacked out."

An example of gang violence in Buffalo leading to murder was described in the *Courier-Express* in 1972 when Judge Joseph Mattina said in court, "teenage gangs have infiltrated a large portion of our city and are creating havoc and fear in the area" (June 10, 1972).

He was referring in particular to the murder of 14-year-old Lawrence Lewis who had been killed by a blast from a sawed-off shotgun on July 13, 1971. Lewis had become the victim of a gang war between the so-called "Allah-Turks" and the "49rs" of which he was a member. Milton Marshall and Donald Dennis, 16 and 17 years old respectively, were convicted of this murder. The murder was deliberate and planned, since Lewis was shot from an automobile as he stood on the porch of his house on Brunswick Street.

The same fate awaited Cleobie Ridgeway who was shot to death in a restaurant on Fillmore Avenue in November of 1972, a result of gang warfare. Again the

"Allah-Turks" were mentioned as the gang to which Ridgeway belonged. On that occasion police arrested 17-year-olds Donald K. Jones and Kevin E. Delk. Both were convicted of manslaughter by a jury. Jones was sentenced to 20 years and Delk to 15 years for the killing of Ridgeway. This killing was motivated by revenge because Ridgeway had been accused of killing Leonard "Fat Jack" Miles the night before.

In May of 1973, eight members of a fraternity called "Sigma Psi" were arrested for killing Joseph Thompson who belonged to another fraternity called "Kappa Psi." In addition to those held directly responsible for this murder, seven more members of "Sigma Psi" were arrested later for conspiracy to commit murder. This murder climaxed a feud between these two "fraternities" composed of street gangs whose members had dropped out of area high schools. The attackers stabbed, beat and clubbed Thompson with a rifle butt because he belonged to another fraternity.

Nine of the youths arrested were given "youthful offender" status by the courts and therefore were able to seal their records from public scrutiny. The only participant in this murder old enough to be tried as an adult, Norman Mack, 20, was placed on probation for five years. Thus, a 17-year-old lost his life in a senseless feud whose substance even the participants had long forgotten.

That murder kills teenagers and young adults more than any other age group in the United States is well illustrated by the death of John Bogumil who was stabbed fatally aboard a public-transit bus in December of 1972 when he was 16-years-old. A junior in computer science at Hutchinson Technical High School, Bogumil had been in no trouble in school nor was he known to have been involved in fights or other difficulties. On the contrary, his teachers and fellow students agreed that his conduct was always good and that he was a "quiet" boy. But John Bogumil was forced to ride a bus to and from school each day and that is what killed him. Constant fights on these buses between students from different schools led to the use of knives by some of them and finally led to the indiscriminate stabbing of Bogumil by John McIver who was later convicted of this crime and sentenced to 20 years in prison. Of course, McIver was eligible for parole after six years and eight months, i.e., after serving one third of his sentence behind bars.

MURDER BY ADULT GANGS

In September of 1958, the murders of Fred Aquino and his brother, Frank, made headlines in both of Buffalo's daily newspapers. Fred was found in a car in Lackawanna and Frank's body in an open field in the town of Tonawanda.

It was obvious to the police and everyone else that the Aquino brothers had been murdered deliberately as their bodies had been mutilated. Thus, the *Courier Express* on September 18, 1958, reported that, "Fred Aquino must have been tortured to death. His vengeful killer poured some type of acid over the top of the body from the shoulders up." Further, the *Courier* reported, "Fred was tortured to death by someone who not only wanted to kill him, but to erase the swarthy features that made him good looking to women." Earlier that week Frank Aquino had been found with a rope and also wire marks around his neck, plainly showing that he had been choked by a wire contrivance. In addition, he had been shot in the back. Both of these methods of killing have been used repeatedly on the victims of organized crime.

The killers of the two Aquinos were never found. However, such clues as were available to the police by reviewing the life stories of the two victims plainly showed that both were associated with organized crime, particularly in the area of gambling. They were, in newspaper parlance, "small time hoods."

Similar conclusions were drawn from the double murders of Vincent St. Angelo and Angelo Palestine in August of 1961. Both were found in the town of Lancaster at Bowen Road near William Street, their bodies hidden in tall grass in that area. Both bodies showed severe beatings and ropes tied tightly around their necks. At the time of the killings police questioned then-reputed Mafia boss of the Niagara frontier, Joe Di Carlo, concerning these murders. However, no arrests were ever made in these cases as was also true in murders of other "underworld" connected killings. Instead, the *Courier* reported that in these killings, "Police are running into the blank wall of silence," just as they do whenever a murder victim is killed by organized criminals.

Both St. Angelo and Palestine had a police record and both had been convicted or had been charged with of a number of crimes. In fact, St. Angelo had been acquitted of a murder charge sometime earlier and Palestine had served five years in the Elmira reformatory on a larceny charge.

Similarly, John C. Cammilleri was gunned down in front of a West Side Buffalo restaurant, the Roseland, in 1974. Evidently, a car stopped briefly in front of the restaurant as Cammilleri was about to enter. "A man got out," wrote the *Courier-Express*, "fired a volley of shots at Cammilleri, leaped back into the car and the car sped around the corner and south on Chenango street." Cammilleri also had a long police record. His killers were never found, and a great deal of evidence showed his connection to organized crime in the Niagara border area. At the time of that killing it was believed that the motive for the killing of Cammilleri on his 63rd birthday was "a power struggle within Laborers Local 210." He had been one of the four lieutenants in the western New York crime family of the late reputed crime chieftain Stefano Maggadino (*Courier-Express*, May 8, 1974).

In 1978, Edward L. Cicero was tried for the murder of James Harper, whom Cicero allegedly killed in 1971 in the company of Joseph Gugino. Gugino had participated in the killing of the 17-year-old Harper and then testified against his accomplice Cicero in February of 1978. The evidence showed that Harper was killed because he meant to reveal what he knew about a burglary committed by Cicero. Gugino and Cicero drove Harper to the Cattaraugus Indian Reservation. There, Cicero shot Harper in the face and then, with Guginos' help, buried the body in a dumping area. Sentenced to a term of 25 years to life by Judge Frederick M. Marshall, who called him "Western New York's foremost executioner," Cicero was tried again on July 20, 1979, for the murder of Lester E. Speaker. This trial was declared a mistrial because of a *Buffalo News* article detailing the defendant's background, thus making it impossible to select an impartial jury.

Gang-style killings related to organized crime continued in Erie County into the

'80s. Most dramatic of these murders was the killing of William M. "Billy" Sciolino on March 7, 1980. This killing, too, was never solved and has been attributed to organized crime rivalries. Coupled with the murder of Carl J. Rizzo at about the same time, it was speculated then that both murders had been related to the Laborers Local 210 and the lucrative steward's position Sciolino held there.

The circumstances of these murders were as follows: On March 7, 1980, a car drove into a parking lot off Main Street, where Sciolino was then staying inside a construction trailer used in connection with the building of the subway. A second car followed immediately. Stopping in front of the trailer, three men left the first car, carrying guns. All three were masked. As one of the masked men opened the door of the trailer, all three fired into the trailer at Sciolino. They then jumped into the second, "getaway," car and were never seen again. The first car, left at the murder site, had been stolen.

Carl Rizzo was murdered on or about March 6, 1980 when he was first reported missing by his family. On April 10 of that year his body was found in the trunk of a leased car parked on Taunton Place. His body was badly decomposed then and it was evident that he had been murdered by garroting. This method of murder is accomplished by binding the victim's hands behind his back, tying his legs at the ankles and knotting the same rope around the throat. Consequently, the victim throttles himself to death as his legs become tired and he is forced to lower them, thus tightening the rope around his throat. This gruesome method of murder is commonly used by organized criminals and was also used in the Nazi concentration camps. Both Rizzo and Sciolino had been arrested numerous times and had "done time" after a number of convictions. Of course, neither murder was ever "solved."

RAPE-MURDER

Rape-murder shocked the Buffalo community in February of 1950 when Mrs. Marion Little Frisbee was found dead in a ditch alongside North Harris Hill Rd., in the town of Clarence.

Since Frisbee belonged to a so-called "socially prominent" family, the murder created a media sensation in that a tremendous amount of news space was devoted to it and its aftermath. (It is worth noting that newspapers and other media do not devote an equal amount of space or time to all killings. The social position, prestige and income of the victim and/or the killer is very much related to the coverage a murder receives. Thus, many killings in Erie County have received very little coverage, such as one and a half column inches in one edition of the *Courier-Express*, if the killer and the victim were both poor and black.) In any event, a short time after the murder of Mrs. Frisbee, Harley George La Marr was arrested and convicted of this crime. La Marr, then 19-years-old, was eventually executed for this murder since New York still had the death penalty at that time.

Only a few weeks earlier, on January 8, 1950, George La Marr's mother had murdered her second husband and was serving a 15-year sentence at Westfield State Farms.

Son of a native American father and a Caucasian mother, Harley La Marr had been raised under all those circumstances which just about guarantee a dreadful outcome of a short life. The murder of Frisbee occurred in the following manner: the victim was sitting in her car in front of the Campanile Apartments on Delaware Avenue at Bryant Street. La Marr was walking on the sidewalk carrying a loaded rifle. On seeing Frisbee in her car, La Marr forcibly entered the car, and at gunpoint forced Frisbee to drive to the Harris Hill location. There he ordered Frisbee to disrobe on the front seat. Frisbee partially disrobed but then attempted to prevent a sexual attack by the six foot tall La Marr. His gun went off at that point, either by accident or design, killing her. La Marr then dragged Frisbee's body into a nearby ditch where it was later found.

In May of 1980, Johnny K. Moore was sentenced to a prison term of 25 years to life for the rape-strangulation murder of Virginia E. Malecki. Moore had been convicted of killing the 60-year-old vice president and treasurer of a meat packing firm which bears her name. Her body was found in a car in an empty parking lot of a department store located at Main and Eggert. The car had been parked there since the previous afternoon. Moore had beaten Malecki on the head, then raped, and strangled her. At the time of that killing, Moore was awaiting trial on charges that he had raped two other women and also killed Judith A. Marchese, who had been his neighbor. Her body was found in a field in March of 1979.

While rape-murders are not common in Erie County and constituted only a small percentage of the 912 murders discovered to have taken place in the 40-year period ending in 1983, it is believed that such murders occur far more than is reported. This discrepancy between actual occurrence and the number reported in the media, particularly during the epoch studied here, is related to the race and social standing of the victims.

PARENT-CHILD MURDER

Murders between parents and children and vice versa are known everywhere because they are by no means uncommon. Of course, the murder of a child by his own parent would seem so extreme an action and so repulsive a crime that its relative frequency may be hard to believe. Yet, there are a number of such cases in our group of 912 homicides.

James Watts, Jr., died on January 29, 1978, in Children's Hospital from a blood clot in the brain, caused by a blow he received from his mother's boyfriend the day before. The boyfriend, Oliver Kinder, was thereupon convicted of first degree manslaughter and sentenced to 15 years in prison. The mother of young James was sentenced to a term of four years in prison as she was found guilty of criminally negligent homicide. Examination of the boy's dead body indicated not only the results of blows to the head but also numerous black and blue marks to the body as well as burns on the buttocks made by cigarettes. The torture of this child had been systematic over some time. Watts' mother, who is white, had left her husband earlier and moved into an apartment with Kinder, who is black.

On September 19, 1959, Henry L. Kingston was convicted of fatally beating four-year-old Ronald Zelasko, who had been placed in the Kingston home as a foster child by Catholic Charities. The boy's mother, Dorothy Zelasko, told the *Courier-Express* that she had repeatedly complained to Catholic Charities that her child was being beaten in the Kingston home. She made this complaint because she noticed severe bruises on his back for several months. No action was taken by Catholic Charities, however, because they claimed that "the boy may have been punished before but we have no complaints that it was excessive punishment."

Sentenced to a prison term of three to five years, Kingston was released under a "Certificate of Reasonable Doubt." When the Court of Appeals upheld Kingston's conviction, County Judge Jacob Latona suspended his sentence and placed him on probation.

Lamont F. Reukauf was described by his neighbors as a "model father." This label did not prevent him, however, from stabbing and strangling his four-year-old son to death in December of 1980. After committing this murder, Reukauf stuffed the body of the child into a plastic bag and left it on top of a junked clothes dryer in front of his home. Divorced from his wife, Cindy, Reukauf had not worked for some time because he was disabled. Subsequent to the killing Reukauf was described by neighbors as "lonely and deeply depressed." Court testimony revealed that he had taken a utility knife, cut the boy on the neck several times, and then strangled him with a scarf. This admission prompted Erie County Judge John R. Dillon to accept a plea of "Not Guilty by Reason of Mental Disease or Defect." Five psychiatrists had agreed, after examining Reukauf, that he was a "paranoid schizophrenic" and was therefore not criminally responsible at the time of the murder. This plea became possible after the state of New York amended the insanity statute in September of 1979 (*Courier-Express*, January 2, 1981).

Another Erie County father who killed his child was Arthur J. Pinkel, who admitted on August 12, 1956 that he murdered his infant daughter by pounding her head with his fists. This resulted in a skull fracture of which Sandra died at the age of 6 weeks. Sentenced to a minimum of two-and-one-half years in prison, Pinkel claimed that the child fell from his hands and that her death was accidental.

Mothers as well as fathers have killed their own children. Janet Groblewski was charged with second degree murder in November of 1974 when she smothered her eight-month-old infant son with a pillow. Under police questioning Groblewski described how the infant was annoying her with his crying until she killed him. The deliberate nature of this killing is best understood by the description of the murder as related to the police. In that statement Groblewski said that she held a pillow over the face of the child for 40 minutes. When the child was still breathing after all that time, she placed the pillow over his head again until the child was completely quiet. In view of psychiatric testimony, Janet Groblewski was found innocent by reason of insanity and sent to an institution.

In July of 1978, the *Courier-Express* headlined the stabbing to death of four young children by their mother, Gail Trait. The horror of these murders was augmented by the fact that the arms and legs of two of the children had been hacked off and the eyes of one of the children had been gouged out. The children were eight, six, four and two years of age. A veteran homicide detective was quoted by the *Courier-Express* concerning this scene. "This is the worst thing I have ever seen," was his comment.

Similarly, Carol Quinn murdered her seven-year-old daughter Eileen in February of 1967 by stabbing her through the heart. She also attacked her son Michael who was then ten years old and her daughter Kathleen, but did not succeed in killing these children. Both Gail Trait and Carol Quinn were found innocent by reason of insanity, particularly since Quinn had been a patient in three mental institutions in earlier years.

Perhaps no child murder by her own parents so agitated the people of Erie County than the killing of five-year-old Deborah Schwartzfigure in July of 1962. This bizarre story revolved around the death from malnutrition of the five-year-old victim, whose father weighed 320 pounds but was only 5'9" tall. Mary Schwartzfigure, the mother, less than five feet tall, weighed 92 pounds. This contrast became particularly important when Schwartzfigure repeatedly testified that he could not intervene in Mary's failure to feed Deborah because he was afraid of her.

Mary Schwartzfigure kept the child in an upper bedroom of their house and then refused anyone admission to that room. She did not feed Deborah, who weighed only 21 pounds when she died. Both parents, who also had six other children were indicted and tried. Mary Schwartzfigure was sent to the Mattewan Hospital for the Criminally Insane, and Joseph was sentenced to a minimum of three-and-one-half years in Attica prison.

CHILD-PARENT MURDER

On February 11, 1974, Michael Sielski, spattered with blood, ran from the premises of the National Printing Company storefront at 761 Fillmore Avenue, a knife stuck in his belt. He had just killed his father by stabbing him at least 21 times. A graduate of Canisius College and a teacher, Sielski had evidently planned this murder since he took the butcher knife with him from home, traveling to his father's shop on a bus. The victim, Thaddeus Sielski, was 64 years old; the killer, his son, was 28. The attack by the younger Sielski upon his father was obviously "prolonged, brutal and frantic" (*Courier-Express*, February 13, 1974). Diagnosed as a paranoid-schizophrenic, Sielski was sent to the Buffalo Psychiatric Center after having been found innocent "by reason of mental disease or defect." On February 23, 1975 Michael Sielski walked away from the Psychiatric Center. That afternoon he was found dead after having been run over by a freight train in the William and Queen streets area. His death was ruled a suicide.

Also declared insane was Michael McKinley, who stabbed his father to death and seriously wounded his mother in February of 1976. The stabbing took place after the younger McKinley was asked to leave the family home.

The best remembered and most dramatic case of child-parent murder, however, was the killing of William Fitzsimmons, 64, and his wife, Pearl, 60, by their son George. George Fitzsimmons murdered his parents on January 12, 1969, by using "karate." George claimed that his father tried to hit him because he refused to go to church with his parents. George Fitzsimmons was 31 years old at the time. In an effort to defend himself, he hit his father on the head several times and then beat his mother until she too was dead. Thereafter, he drove to Rhode Island in his father's car. Apprehended and tried for this double slaying, Fitzsimmons was sent to the Buffalo Psychiatric Center from which he was released in 1973 on the grounds that psychiatrists testified that "he is without danger to himself and others."

Having inherited $123,000 from his parents, Fitzsimmons went to Potter County in Pennsylvania to stay with his aunt and uncle, both 80 years old. Shortly thereafter he stabbed both Euphrasia Nichols, his aunt, and De Alton Nichols, his uncle, to death with a hunting knife. Previously he had been convicted of assaulting his wife.

CHILD MURDERS AND CHILD MURDERERS

When a ten-year-old boy killed his baby-sitter with his mother's loaded shotgun, the killing of Frances Drozdzak was ruled an accident. The gun was loaded and accessible, thus becoming one more "empty" gun which killed just the same. Judged a juvenile delinquent for the unlawful possession of a loaded gun, the child-murderer was given an 18-month sentence to a state training school. This occurred in January of 1982.

In March of 1974 the *Courier-Express* reported that a 16-year-old girl had been charged with manslaughter because she drowned her newborn baby in a bathtub to stop its crying. Mary Joanne Kline had given birth to the baby in the bathroom of her home in order to hide the birth from her mother and father, who later claimed that they knew nothing of Mary Joanne's pregnancy. After the drowning Mary Joanne took the dead infant and wrapped it in towels. She then placed the body in a plastic bag and then threw the bag with the child into the bank of the Cazenovia Creek. Some boys subsequently found it there. Thereupon the Homicide Bureau asked area hospitals to give them information concerning women who had received postnatal care without having a child in evidence. This turned up Mary Joanne Kline, who was then at Mercy Hospital.

A hearing before Judge Julian F. Kubiniec resulted in his decision to release Mary Joanne into the custody of her parents on the grounds that "she had never been in any kind of trouble" (*Courier-Express*, March 30, 1977).

An enormous amount of newspaper space was devoted to the murder of three-year-old Andrew Ashley whose body was found in Delaware Park Lake on June 25, 1961. Kidnapped from his home two days earlier, the child was found tied with nylon stockings and partially nude. Intensive police investigation identified a 15-year-old girl, Cheryl Joles, as the kidnapper and killer of little Andrew. In addition to this crime, Cheryl Joles was also accused of kidnapping two other children from the north Buffalo area. Both escaped unharmed.

In view of a history of mental illness, Cheryl Joles was committed to Mattewan

State Hospital in 1962 after a long and detailed psychiatric report by Dr. Samuel Yochelson declared her "insane." In 1969 all charges against Cheryl Joles were dismissed on the advice of psychiatrists who deemed her unfit to stand trial. In January of 1971, Cheryl Joles, then 25 years old, was released from St. Lawrence Hospital in Ogdensburg to which she had been transferred a year earlier.

In April of 1977, a fifteen-year-old boy was accused of killing Mrs. Linda Wilson, whose body was found in a field in the town of Concord about two miles from her home. She had been abducted by an acquaintance of the family who had strangled Wilson with a scarf. The boy, whose name was not reported because of his age, had been living in a foster home near the Wilsons for six years. His natural parents had been adjudicated "neglectful" when he was five. Since the "McKiever Decision" makes a jury trial optional for a child, the judge conducted a fact finding hearing and determined to subject the boy to five years of supervision by the State Division for Youth as punishment for his crime.

In November of 1971 a three-year-old child who suffered from cerebral palsy and could not walk was found strangled to death in his crib in Children's Hospital. A lie detector test cleared his 24-year-old father of this crime. The mother, then also 24 years old, took a lie detector test as well. That too proved inconclusive. Thus, no one was ever charged with the homicide of Davie James, son of Jimmie and Bonnie James, who was murdered in a place where, as a patient, he should have been most safe.

His mother, Bonnie, was in the hospital at the time of the murder.

SPOUSE MURDER

Years of domestic fighting usually precede the murder of a spouse. This was the case when Bernard W. McDonald murdered his wife, Shirley, in their West Seneca home by repeatedly striking her with a hammer. He pleaded guilty to a reduced charge of second degree manslaughter and was subsequently sentenced to 5 to 12½ years in Attica Correctional Facility. The mother of four had been so severely beaten that she died of brain injuries. Her body was found wedged between a bed and the wall in a second floor bedroom. McDonald was initially sent to Mattewan Hospital for the Criminally Insane for one year and subsequently on to Attica.

When Paul S. Lewczyk, then 41 years old, ax murdered his wife Joanne in November of 1978, police officer Donald Sutz, the first officer on the murder scene, commented to the *Courier-Express*, "It was the bloodiest mess I have ever seen." Officer Sutz found Mrs. Lewczyk, 37, dead in the living room with a long-handled ax embedded in her skull. Sutz had been called because the two daughters of the couple reported smelling gas on approaching the kitchen through the garage entrance. (Paul had injured himself and turned on the gas in an effort to commit suicide after the murder. In this he failed.) Subsequently, the father of seven children was sentenced to 8⅓ to 15 years in prison.

According to police, a long history of domestic quarrels preceded the following bloody deed. The deliberate, cold blooded, planned murder of John Yuhas led to the conviction of James F. Butler in November of 1976. Described by police as a hit man, Butler was employed by the victim's wife, mother-in-law, sister-in-law and Butler's girlfriend to commit this murder. Yuhas was stabbed eight times, beaten with a cut-down pool cue and shot three times. His body was then stuffed into the trunk of his car on a shoulder of the State Throughway in West Seneca, N.Y. Butler was sent to prison for 25 years to life on his murder conviction, in addition to 8⅓ to 25 years for conspiracy to commit murder. His girlfriend, Linda Smith, was sentenced to 8⅓ to 25 years for conspiracy. The victim's sister-in-law, Margaret Alvey, drew the same term for criminal solicitation and criminal facilitation.

JEALOUSY MURDER

In August of 1971, Rodney Haymes was sentenced to an indeterminate term of up to 18 years in prison for killing Frank Jurczak as he was leaving the home of Yvonne Haymes. The latter had been separated from Rodney Haymes. Haymes had been a codefendant with Jurczak in a previous rape case. After Haymes shot Jurczak on the front porch of the Haymes home, he was told that Jurczak was still alive. He thereupon shot Jurczak a second time in a deliberate manner. Haymes then waited for the police to arrive and gave himself up without any struggle or dispute. Later, however, while being held in the Erie County Penitentiary, Haymes escaped in the company of four other convicts. Recaptured, he was convicted and sentenced to prison.

In 1979, Edward Belica of West Seneca was sentenced to seven years in prison after pleading guilty to first degree manslaughter in the strangulation death of Thomas Banes, whom he had found in the apartment of June Sevard on May 11, 1975. Although married, Belica had become the rival of Banes for the affection of June Sevard. Six feet tall and weighing 220 pounds, Belica used the key Sevard had given him and found Banes with Sevard at 2:00 A.M. that morning. Seeing Banes asleep in Sevard's bed infuriated Belica. He attacked Banes, beat him severely and then strangled him. The father of two children, Belica had been a foreman at the Chevrolet plant in Buffalo.

MURDER OF A WOMAN FRIEND

The murder of women friends by their male friends is as common as the murder of wives by their husbands and is the outcome of the same "machismo" attitude which precipitates both kinds of homicide. Thirty-seven such cases were found among the 912 killings we investigated. Here are a few examples: On November 17, 1980, Roger Barber, at that time 27 years old, stabbed and beat to death 17-year-old Victoria Kelly. Only hours before her death, Victoria Kelly had filed a complaint on a charge of harassment against Barber, who was then arrested but released almost at once. Barber, however, had practically advertised his intention of killing Kelly. Nevertheless, he was released because no adequate grounds for keeping him existed. This is still a common occurrence, because there is no easy way to distinguish between an idle and a real threat. So far, no mechanism exists which will protect the public from such a sudden attack or predict an attack before it happens.

Dennis Trembly murdered Lisa Beth Daniels in her home in Amherst, N.Y. He was her "boyfriend." Trembly stabbed her several times with a butcher knife from her own kitchen. After this murder became public it was reported by the *Courier-Express* that Trembly had a history of assault upon women and was considered "especially dangerous" by the police (*Courier-Express*, January 16, 1979). In view of the ambition and intelligence which Lisa Beth Daniels displayed in college and the popularity she enjoyed with her friends, it seemed incongruous that she should spend time with a man known for his violent outbursts and uncouth conduct.

The same may be said for Linda Schaus of Cheektowaga, who was stabbed 40 times in the chest, back and head by Leon Brown, an east-side man who at that time was 32 years old. Evidently, Brown had broken into Schaus' bedroom through an upstairs window. This followed Schaus' abandonment of Brown, with whom she had been staying and had a nine-month-old daughter. Brown had threatened repeatedly that he would kill Linda Schaus while she was still living with him. Linda Schaus had brought the child with her to her mother's house, where Brown caught up with her. Having killed her, he then assaulted her mother, and ran out the back door of the house as police arrived at the front.

There is a tendency on the part of some women to lend themselves to this kind of violence from brutal men. Such a man was William Callahan who allegedly fatally shot his girlfriend, Josephine Hannah, in June of 1977. At the time of the slaying Callahan was on parole for killing his wife. Thus, not only his girlfriend but also the court trusted him to live in society despite his past history. While Callahan had killed his wife with a carving knife, he reportedly used a gun to kill his girlfriend. Nevertheless, Callahan was found "not guilty" by a jury who tried him.

MURDER OF A WOMAN STRANGER

Attacks on women and female children by men whom the victims do not know are examples of sudden murders in Erie County and elsewhere.

In 1973, a 17-year-old girl was found dead and naked in a snowbank. She had been murdered by Morris A. Stevens, whom she had met in a tavern near the parking lot where her body was found.

The victim, Cathy Edmiston had evidently come to the Red Pepper tavern on her own volition. It was Christmas night, and Cathy Edmiston arrived with a girlfriend at the tavern at about 9:30 P.M. Throughout the evening, Cathy talked to a number of men and in the course of such conversation became acquainted with Morris Stevens. She was seen exiting the tavern with a man, leaving her coat and purse behind. Her friend then waited for her until 4:00 A.M., but when she did not return to the tavern, the friend accepted a ride home from one of the other tavern patrons. When Cathy Edmiston was finally found, dead in a snowbank, it became evident that she had become the victim of a vicious assault. "Her body bore multiple bruises," wrote the *Courier-Express*, "she had deep abrasions across the chest and her ears had been partially torn from her head." Finally, death was caused by strangulation and the breaking of a bone in the larynx, which had been cracked by the killer. On March 21, 1975, Stevens was sent to prison for 15 years to life for the brutal deed he committed on December 25, 1973.

In a similar situation, Diane Snell, at that time 20 years old, was murdered by Harry G. Skinner after she refused his sexual advances. Skinner beat Snell to death on June 22, 1975, and threw her body into a ditch in the town of Amherst, N.Y.

MURDER BY REASON OF INSANITY

Two women, Bertha Lee Johnson and Sarah Johnson, were standing on the sidewalk in front of 230 William Street on November 5, 1964. They were talking to each other when Rufus Lee accosted them concerning a wallet he said he had lost. When both women denied knowing anything about the wallet, Lee shot them on the spot. For this double murder Lee was sent to the Buffalo State Hospital Psychiatric Center and committed "by reason of insanity." In 1973 he was released under Section 330.20 of the State Code of Criminal Procedure which provides for such releases.

When Donald Strongren was sent to Mattewan State Hospital for the Criminally Insane he too was declared "not guilty by reason of insanity." This decision was made by a jury which considered the murder of Daniel Strongren, Donald's father, whom Don had murdered by beating him to death with a hammer. This occurred on January 4, 1985. Verdicts such as these have come under a great deal of criticism and have been vigorously disputed since an English jury first excused Daniel McNaughton from the consequences of murdering the secretary of Sir Robert Peel, then the British Prime Minister. McNaughton falsely assumed he was shooting at the Prime Minister. He was found "not guilty by reason of insanity" in 1843.

ACCIDENTAL MURDER

There is no doubt that a good number of killings by firearms do indeed occur as a result of accidents involving either the belief that a gun is not loaded or failure to take elementary precautions while using a gun.

Such a case was the February 1977 murder of Bruce Schatz, who was visiting the home of his friend Ronald Ess on North Forest Road in Amherst. Using a .22 caliber rifle for target shooting practice in Ess' basement, Ronald Ess shot Schatz "while firing from the hip" (*Courier-Express* February 17, 1977). After his arrest, Ess told police that Schatz was screaming and bleeding from the mouth and that he, Ess, lost his temper and fired six more shots from the rifle into his friend, who thereupon died. Ess then secreted the body of Schatz in a crawlspace above his bedroom where it was finally found on April 20, 1977, two months after being placed there. It was the smell of the decomposing body which led Ronald Ess' parents to trace the location of the body and discover the murder. Convicted and sent to prison for five to fifteen years, Ronald Ess admitted the use of drugs and alcohol since an early age.

In the early morning hours of July 5, 1960, James Batcho shot his wife to death. Batcho "thought that the safety catch was on" when he pointed his loaded rifle at his wife. Batcho had been drinking and thought it humorous to celebrate the Fourth of July by throwing a firecracker under his wife's bed. Tried on murder charges, Batcho was discharged when the jury could not reach a verdict. The Batchos had two children and Mrs. Batcho was pregnant at the time of her death.

"Patsy" Purpora was not as fortunate as Batcho. He was sentenced to a term of two to four years in prison after being convicted of the murder of Ellis Maynard when his sawed-off shotgun went off "accidentally" in front of the home of the victim's sister in January of 1979. Purpora said that he was Maynard's friend and that the gun used in the killing belonged to Maynard, who had at that time just been released from serving a 90-day jail term.

ARSON MURDER

Arson-murder is an unusual crime — my study listed only 11 such cases in a total of 912 killings. This is true mainly because arson-murder is too uncertain a method of murder for a determined killer. Instead, arson-murder is more likely to be the unanticipated consequence of deliberate arson, a very common crime.

On January 7, 1975, Lt. Burton W. Winspear of the Buffalo Fire Department died in the course of fighting a fire at 951 Genesee Street. Winspear was crushed under a roof and walls of a derelict building which fell on him as the building burned. Subsequently, Joseph Horton, at that time 19 years old, and 18-year-old Ronald Bader were arrested for murder because they had sprinkled gasoline inside the building and set it on fire. Labeled "mentally retarded" and "emotionally disturbed," both offenders were sentenced to maximum terms of ten years in prison after pleading guilty to the charges. Bader had been arrested for arson two years before. Since both arsonists had been released from institutions for the mentally ill, they lived at Transitional Services, an agency which provided living quarters to persons "in transition" from institutions to the general community.

MURDER OF AND BY POLICE OFFICERS

Nothing is viewed by some as better evidence of the injustice of the criminal justice system than the differential treatment received by those who kill the police and the members of the police force who kill an innocent citizen. Two excellent examples of this difference in treatment are the cases of Efrain Rodriguez and Richard Long.

Rodriguez, a 21-year-old migrant worker, was convicted for the September 1978 killing of sheriff's deputy William R. Dills and went to prison for 25 years to life.

Just one year later, on September 27, 1979, three of six police officers, all members of the Buffalo Police Department, kicked an innocent young man, Richard Long, to death, because he "cut them off" while driving along Hertel Avenue. They followed him to his house, dragged him out of his car, and murdered him. Yet, three of the perpetrators were not even indicted by a grand jury, while the other three were given the lightest possible sentences after their conviction. One of the killers was in fact reinstated on the force.

The murder of Edward Prather, at that time only 18 years old, did not even lead to an indictment by the grand jury in 1979. "Absolved of any 'wrong-doing,'" as the *Courier-Express* called it, were two police officers, Matthew Parsons and Norman Siewic. The same grand jury cleared police officer Dennis Adams in the murder of John J. Russell, who was gunned down at the age of 21.

MURDER IN THE COURSE OF A ROBBERY

Robbery is one of the most frequent motives for murder in Erie County and elsewhere. Several examples will serve to illustrate the nature of these crimes.

It is no exaggeration to say that nothing ever so enraged the citizens of Collins, N.Y., as the murder of Harold J. Ross on October 13, 1956. On that day, Ross, a six foot, 210 pound man, attempted to chase four men from his property when he mistook them for hunters trespassing there. The four were, however, not hunters. They were thieves whose had just stolen a strongbox from Ross' home, a fact he did not know. The four, Salverio Silvagnia, 23, Joseph Silvagnia, 19, Salvatore T. Lo Faso, 18 and Louis Pisa, 19, attacked Ross with two large sledgehammers when he caught them outside his house. Ross was found later with multiple depressed skull fractures, brain lacerations and intercranial hemorrhages. It soon turned out that all four killers had been convicted on numerous previous occasions. Salverio Silvagnia had been sentenced for burglary, grand larceny and other offenses, had served in a penitentiary, and had been on probation several times. Pisa had also been repeatedly charged and Lo Faso had been accused of shooting Robert C. Dillmore earlier that same year. That charge was declared an "accident" in connection with a target-shooting practice. All were sentenced by Judge Jacob Latona to prison terms ranging from ten to twenty years.

Although sentenced to death in the electric chair, Joseph B. Hughes survived because the governor of New York, Nelson Rockefeller, commuted that sentence to life in prison. He did so on the recommendation of the jury which had heard the case against Hughes whom they had convicted of the murder of Vincent Spinaci. Hughes shot Spinaci during a holdup in Spinaci's delicatessen on Oak

Street because Spinaci had refused to give Hughes any money. Shot on November 20, 1957, Spinaci lived until January of 1958 when he died of his wounds in Emergency Hospital. Justice Fisher sentenced Hughes to die despite the jury's recommendation for mercy, because Fisher believed that the death penalty would deter others from committing the holdups and murders which were then plaguing Buffalo almost daily.

Henry "Snow" Flakes and Walter T. Green were not as fortunate as Hughes. They were electrocuted on May 19, 1960, for the killing of Joseph Friedman on November 7, 1958. Both men were 33 years old. They were convicted of a $96 holdup of Friedman's Lackawanna clothing store. Brutally beating Friedman on the head with their pistols, they killed him in front of his wife. Before fleeing the store, they fired two shots at Mrs. Friedman but missed. De Witt Lee was the third defendant in this crime. The driver of the get-away car, he was sentenced to life in prison.

The 1977 reversal of the conviction of Dominic "Dim" Tascarella, Leonard Mordino and Robert Brocato for killing Ing "Sam" Wing in 1971 was sensational news at the time. This reversal came about as the result of a press conference given by the F.B.I. and the local police concerning that killing. This press conference was "condemned in the strongest terms" by the appellate judges, Reid S. Moule, Richard D. Simons, Stewart F. Hancock and Harry D. Goldman. The conference was deemed to have prejudiced the case against the defendants. All three had robbed and murdered Wing, who had been the operator of a laundry in the Grant Street area for 30 years.

This case was particularly difficult to unravel as it took the Buffalo Police Department three years to "crack" this murder, which had taken place on June 10, 1971. At that time the Erie County Medical Examiner, Dr. Edmond Gicewicz, ruled that Wing had died of asphyxiation because he had a T-shirt stuffed in his mouth. Adhesive tape had been used to keep the gag there and the victim had been tied hand and foot as well as blindfolded.

The motive for this brutal murder was undoubtedly robbery as Wing was known for displaying large bank rolls in area taverns. In 1975, all three defendants (Tascarella, Mordino and Brocato) were convicted of this murder and sentenced to 20 years to life in prison by Judge Frederick M. Marshall. Upon reversal of these convictions by the Appellate Division of the New York State Supreme Court, a new trial was held. Dominic Tascarella and Leonard Mordino were again found guilty and sentenced once more to 20 years to life, their original sentences. Robert Brocato, however, was not tried again. He was given immunity under the Federal Witness Protection Program because he had turned government informant against the other defendants.

It is most unusual for a woman to be convicted of armed robbery-murder. Carla Leach, however, gained this status when she was convicted of fatally shooting a deaf mute man in a tavern holdup. The killing and robbery took place on January 22, 1964, and sentence was pronounced on July 13, 1966. Leach was sent to the Westfield State Farm for Women for a period of ten to 20 years. The murdered man, John Jonkins, was unable to hear the command by Leach to get out of the way during a holdup at 699 Broadway. Leach had spent almost all her life in state institutions after her parents had been charged with neglect. Her codefendant, Robert Hayes, had a similar background. He had come to Erie County with her from Ohio and was sentenced to five to ten years in the State Penitentiary at Attica.

Robert Mulkerrin, at that time 42 years old, attacked Arthur Salzman on the front porch of Salzman's home at 270 Georgia Street at 11:15 P.M. on a Monday. During the ensuing fight, Salzman and Mulkerrin reached Salzman's lawn adjoining the house where Mulkerrin severely beat Salzman and then stomped on him several times, resulting in Salzman's death. Mulkerrin then took Salzman's wallet and fled towards the Emergency Referral Center for Alcoholics at 202 Niagara Street where police arrested him a short while later. The argument and fight resulting in Salzman's death began when Salzman helped the owner of the La Salle Delicatessen evict Mulkerrin from that store because Mulkerrin was drunk and causing a disturbance. Mulkerrin then followed Salzman to his nearby home. Following his conviction on the murder charge, Mulkerrin was sentenced to a minimum prison term of eight years and a maximum of 25 years.

In April of 1979, Curtis Kelly was convicted of shooting and killing Robert E. Campbell who was sitting in his car after shopping in a grocery store on East Ferry Street. Without provocation, Kelly entered Campbell's car, shot him in the forehead, right elbow and right knee and then stole his wallet and his watch. He also tried to slide his wedding ring from his finger but did not succeed.

On being arrested, it turned out that Kelly had been convicted of four other robberies. His motive in all five of these crimes was drug addiction. He needed money. Consequently, Kelly was sent to prison on four separate terms of six to twelve years for the four robberies and additionally to 20 years to life for the robbery-murder of Robert E. Campbell.

In a dramatic turnaround, David Kwiatkowski and Douglas R. Page were both killed by jewelry store owner Donald Pallas when they held up his store in February of 1980. Page, who had a record of 18 arrests with 32 charges including robbery and felony assault, and Kwiatkowski, who had a record of four arrests including felony assault, rape and sexual abuse, operated an auto collision shop together.

They had entered the jewelry store wearing Halloween masks and carrying two .38 caliber revolvers and a crowbar. Upon entering they smashed a display case holding jewelry and diamonds when Pallas fired at them five times. Despite their "bullet proof" vests both men were dead within minutes. Kwiatkowski died in the store and Page fell dead minutes later in the parking lot as he attempted to reach his getaway car which was parked nearby. No charges were placed against Pallas who was deemed to have acted in self defense.

Lack of evidence led to the dismissal of murder charges against James B. Walker and Fred Norris who were accused of beating and robbing Russell Turner in his apartment on Genesee Street in September of 1971. The dismissal of the murder charges was the direct result of the refusal of Anthony Jeffries, a key prosecution witness, to testify in court despite being charged with criminal contempt of court. Jeffries was at that time already serving a term for narcotics possession. Consequently, Walker and Norris were convicted on a guilty plea of attempted second degree assault, despite the death of their victim, Russell Turner, four days after the beating. The two assailants were 22 and 23 years old, Turner was 56 when he died.

The murder of Esther Normille, only 24 years old at her death, was particularly horrible. A part-time cashier at the Bell grocery store at 765 Elmwood Avenue, she had just returned from maternity leave when she was gunned down. She was killed by Michael Falzone, then 20 years old, and Joseph Cordova, 19 at the time. Both had held up the store for the cash and lottery tickets held in the office. The two robbers forced Normille to the office at gun point. There they shot her in the back with a .38 magnum, killing her instantly. Thereafter, the Peter J. Schmitt Company, owners of Bell stores, set up a trust fund for the benefit of Normille's daughter, Sara Marie, who had just been born in 1979 when her mother was murdered.

Equally hideous was the murder of Edward D. McFarland in November of 1979. He was mugged in the Rochester area by Jackie Johnson and Gerald Brockton. Johnson and Brockton then drove to Buffalo with their victim. There they stretched McFarland on the ground after knocking him unconscious. They placed his head against a road delineator post and then crushed his head against the marker with the bumper of their automobile. They then threw the body of McFarland into a throughway drainage ditch. Convicted of this gruesome murder, both Johnson and Brockton were sent to prison for 25 years to life.

MURDER IN THE COURSE OF ARGUMENTS AND FIGHTS

This category of homicide constitutes one of the most frequent kinds of murder. This is very significant because it represents an attitude concerning people's relationship to one another. United States culture promotes the view that violence is a means by which people may legitimately deal with each other. The belief that violent behavior is legitimate is fostered particularly with respect to the education of boys and men in the "machismo" attitude that masculine dignity and honor is dependent on aggression and an exhibition of power over other men and women. It is, in this author's view, no accident that "machismo" type killings are particularly frequent among our black population, due to the above-stated cultural beliefs.

The table concerning "Homicide Rates in the United States by Race and Sex" presented on page xii reveals this difference dramatically. Thus, the black male homicide rate for every one of the 11 years cited in that table is at least six times greater and rises to over ten times the white male homicide rate in three of those years. This discrepancy is also true if we compare black female homicide rates to white female homicide rates. White female homicide rates appear to be only one-third of white male homicide rates, while black female homicide rates are more than four times the white female rates.

These differences are the product of American culture. Homicide rates, therefore, reflect the needs which different members of our society satisfy by killing others. Most Americans learn the view that violence is to be held in high esteem. However, all do not need violence to the same degree or the same extent. There are those who never use violence because they never need it. This is particularly true of high-status white men who gain their prestige, social honor, money and power from holding high status occupations, gaining election to public office or exhibiting wealth so as to show their ascendancy over others by conspicuous consumption.

This is, however, not possible for the poor, particularly blacks and other minorities. Therefore, lower status men, particularly black men, are more likely to act upon the prescriptions of our culture and choose violence as a means of dealing with others, because violence seems, to many people caught in the cycle of poverty and racism as the only means available to validate one's existence. The causes of murder are not the trivial arguments or incidents that appear on police blotters or in newspapers. Instead, the causes of murder are the beliefs that Americans have about the maintenance of self-respect in a competitive culture which insures not only that some are winners, but of necessity, that therefore so many others are losers.

Several examples of such seemingly senseless killings are available. For instance, on November 12, 1972 the *Courier-Express* reported that Homer Burke, then 38 years old, was shot to death in the home of a lady friend. Burke had become involved in an argument with the lady's brother, John Jackson. In the heat of the dispute, Jackson killed Burke with a .22 caliber rifle. On appeal of his murder conviction, Jackson showed that he had acted in self defense; the conviction was overturned. It is significant that the dispute between Burke and Jackson had reached such violent proportions that Burke tried to use a knife and that both men had weapons available with which to carry their dispute to such extremes.

This example indicates that many Americans believe they have a right and an obligation to use and therefore possess weapons. "One man was shot and killed and two others were wounded in an exchange of gun fire in a house at 15 Hill Street, at 7:40 P.M. Monday," reported the *Courier-Express* on November 17, 1980. No greater motive for this killing could be found than the anger of one assailant against the three victims.

Similarly, a spilled drink led to the murder of Robert Plaetzer, who was stabbed in the heart and died outside an Allen Street tavern in March of 1982. Arrested for this murder were Donald Shoe, at that time 16 years old, and James Vickerd, who was then 18. The circumstances of this murder are a good example of the frivolous reasons for homicide in so many instances. According to Joan Myers, a barmaid at Mickey's Grill, a dispute began in the bar between Jeannette Shoe and Gartha McCollough, both customers. She was accompanied by her son, Donald. Shoe accused McCollough of deliberately spilling a drink on her. In this she was supported by her son. McCollough, however, was not alone in her screaming defense. Robert Plaetzer, a porter in a nearby tavern, had entered the bar for a brief visit. He chose to defend McCollough, although he had never met her before. At the conclusion of the argument between the two women, Plaetzer walked McCollough home. Donald Shoe and his friend, James Vickerd, followed Shoe and McCollough into the street and continued the argument about the spilled drink. When all of them reached the corner of Allen and North Pearl streets, Donald Shoe attacked Plaetzer with a large hunting knife, stabbing him. Plaetzer fell to the ground and bled badly in the street. He died that night at about 10:15 P.M. (the *Courier-Express*, March 13, 1982). It would be hard to decide whether a 75-cent bottle of wine was yet a lesser reason to take two lives than an argument over a spilled drink.

In any event, Willie Troy Simms and Robert Lawrence both died at 4:00 A.M. on September 8, 1958, as Lawrence Evans "stormed through the door" of the Rhythm Grill on Michigan at Eagle Street and "sprayed six bullets from a .38 revolver into the place" (the *Courier-Express*, September 8, 1959).

On New Year's Eve, 1975, Michael Milburn was walking under a Walden Avenue railroad viaduct. There he met Eugene Racey who was returning from a nearby liquor store. An argument ensued between them and ended with the death of Milburn at Racey's hands.

These are just a few of the 165 killings whose motives are called "sudden anger" in this study. These killings are indeed senseless, not only because their precipitating motives are so negligible, but also because there appears to be no gain for the killer in committing these murders except self assertion and a desire to dominate the opponent. These motives are taught in American life and are not only the property of the murderers depicted here but of almost all Americans. There is good reason, therefore, to call our culture one of aggression and violence. This does not mean that every American is aggressive and violent. It does mean however, that violence is as much part of our civilization as driving automobiles or speaking English. Therefore, we cannot look for the causes of murder in the area of abnormal psychiatry, but must look for such causes in the anticipated consequences of our life style and teachings.

SELF-DEFENSE MURDER

Numerous killings in Erie County have been attributed to self-defense over the years. Typical of these was the killing of Willie Folmar, who was shot to death by Reginald Williams while he and his companion Paul Thornton were in the process of robbing Williams' apartment. Williams came home unexpectedly and was accosted by the two robbers at the door of his apartment. Williams fled inside, seized his rifle and shot both robbers as they came to assault him.

MURDER BY UNKNOWN KILLERS

In November of 1978, James Walters, a Missouri salesman, was found dead in his room at the Statler-Hilton Hotel. Despite the fact that signs of a struggle were found in Walters' room and bloodstains were found on his bed, the police never discovered who killed the salesman.

A similar fate befell Professor Thomas J. Clifton. A music professor at the University of Buffalo, he was found stabbed 29 times on Buffalo Beach in the town of Evans on June 15, 1978. Unable to find a single clue identifying the killer, the police turned to a so-called "psychic" for help without success.

One of the most unusual and peculiar cases of murder occurred in Buffalo in September of 1979. In this case a suspect was charged with murder although the victim could not be found. The police charged Wayne R. Lankey, a homeless man, with the murder of a victim whose body was found in the Scajaquada Creek near the Elmwood overpass. The victim, however, who had a fractured skull and had been drowned, disappeared from the bank of the creek shortly after the police found it. The body was never identified.

Parler Edwards, a cab driver, was found in the trunk of his taxi at about 11:00 A.M. on October 8, 1979. He had been killed with a blunt object. Head and body injuries revealed that the killers had savagely beaten him and that he had "a deep long slash to the left breast" (*Courier-Express*, October 9, 1979). No one was ever arrested in connection with this brutal killing. The motive was evidently robbery since Edwards carried at least $1,000 on his person at all times.

"No Clues in Bandit Killing of Bar-keep" was the headline on December 5, 1980, as the *Courier-Express* described the murder of Kenneth Prouty, a 33-year-old bartender at Bruno's Lounge on Genesee Street in Buffalo. Prouty was killed with a shot to the back of the head at around 2:00 A.M. inside the tavern he managed for his father-in-law. In this case robbery was also the motive as $300 were missing from the cash register. No one was ever arrested, no killer was ever found.

Numerous citizens have been murdered in Erie County and elsewhere in the United States whose killers have never been found. A random check on killings since 1956 demonstrates this clearly.

Anthony Pacello was stabbed to death that year at Swan and Seymour streets in Buffalo. Pacello was accosted by a stranger while he and Josephine Swigonski were walking to her home at about midnight. At a railroad underpass the stranger accosted Pacello without provocation and killed him by stabbing. The murderer was never found.

In March of 1975 Gilbert Davenport, financial secretary of a local United Auto Workers union, was found dead at the desk of his office. He had been shot five times and stabbed 11 times. Since nothing was taken from the union office, robbery was ruled out as the motive. Despite the offer of a reward and a number of "leads," no one was ever apprehended in connection with this killing.

The same fate befell Harold Goldman, who was murdered by an unknown person in August of 1976. In this case, robbery was clearly the motive. Goldman operated a smelter business at 127 Fillmore Avenue. The business had been in the family for over 70 years. Goldman kept a good deal of cash in his possession during business hours, a fact that must have been known to his assailant. Goldman was killed just after he arrived at his establishment at 7:00 A.M. and before his employees arrived at 7:30 A.M. No one was ever charged with this murder.

Renee Bahleda was ax murdered in her Hamburg, N.Y., home on November 21, 1977. "She was lying in bed," the *Courier-Express* reported, "turned in towards the center of the bed and the wall." The body was discovered by Bahleda's seven-year-old daughter who then called her father at work. Bahleda had been separated from her husband. An autopsy showed that she had been killed by about seven blows to the face with an ax. Since the house was not disturbed in any way and even her bedroom was in perfect order, it would appear that Bahleda knew and trusted her killer, as it appeared she admitted that person to her house.

Innumerable additional examples of murder by unknown killers could be given. Suffice it to say that there are those who do indeed "get away with murder."

MURDER BY REPEAT KILLERS

Unknown killers are not the only ones who "get away with murder." Even persons who are known to have a history of murder sometimes escape punishment and are therefore free to murder again. Such is the case of Freddie Washington, who was charged with the murder of a 67-year-old woman in January of 1982. He had been convicted of a previous murder of a 60-year-old man and an assault on a 91-year-old man.

In 1982, Washington had killed Dora Manuel by stabbing her in the left eye and into the chest with a steak knife. Police described Washington as being motivated by "a depraved indifference to human life." At his arraignment, Washington claimed that Mayor Griffin of Buffalo and former President Jimmy Carter told him to murder Manuel. Washington had been confined to the Buffalo Psychiatric Center, also known as Buffalo State Hospital, for three months as a result of his earlier convictions on murder and assault. However, he was released when his behavior was deemed "stabilized" by the resident psychiatrists.

A similar situation developed around Larry Campbell, who had been released from Mattewan State Hospital for the Criminally Insane where he had been confined for several crimes of an aggressive and assaultive nature. Upon his release he enrolled at Buffalo State University College under a program for disadvantaged students. There he met several students who shared an apartment on nearby Elmwood Avenue. Invited to visit there, Campbell turned on his hosts in a "reign of terror." He bound all four students hand and foot, then strangled Rhona Eisman and Thomas Tunney and slashed Michael Shostick and Teresa Beynart. Convicted of these two murders as well as assault and rape, he was sent to prison for 75 years. Nevertheless, Campbell will be eligible for parole in 1992.

Samuel Robinson, who was convicted of murder in 1972 at the age of 15, was charged with two more murders only one year after his release from the Training School at Industry, N.Y. He had killed Carroll M. Davis and Gile Morton within days of each other. Previously, Robinson had used a broken glass jar to stab his mother and slash her across her left eye, blinding her. He, too, was released to murder again.

"WHITE COLLAR" MURDERS

A "white collar" crime was defined by the late Professor Edwin Sutherland as a crime committed by a high status person in the course of his ordinary business dealings. Normally then, the term applies to such practices as drug use or sales by medical personnel or embezzlement committed by bankers and lawyers.

Murder can also be a "white collar" crime. The following example does not meet Sutherland's criterion that the crime must be committed by a high status person or a group of persons. However, the killing of Bobby Cunningham for the sake of a possible profit fits the description of "white collar" criminality in all other respects, as first proposed by Sutherland at his inaugural address upon assuming the presidency of the American Sociological Association in 1939.

In 1974, two youths, one age 15 and the other 16, were arrested by Buffalo police for killing Bobby Cunningham, whom they had fatally shot the day before. Police said that the two had been hired by the victim to shoot him in the legs in order to collect disability insurance afterwards. Murphy Davis, the 15 year old, missed the legs of Cunningham and killed him by shooting him in the head. Adjudicated a youthful offender, Davis' record was sealed.

A more specific case of "white collar murder" was the killing of Ida Holden, an 83-year-old widow. Holden froze to death when the heat in her apartment was shut off by an oil company because her landlord had not paid the bill on previous oil delivered to the building in which she was a tenant. After four days without heat in extremely cold weather, Holden died in 11-degrees-below-zero temperatures. The results of a police investigation into the death of Holden were turned over to the district attorney's office in Buffalo, but nothing came of this effort to indict those responsible.

MULTICIDE

There are three kinds of multicide (the killing of many persons): genocide, mass murder and serial murder. No cases of genocide were found in Erie County. This is to be expected, since genocide is usually organized by governments or by other large institutionalized groups. Mass murder did occur in two instances among the 912 killings reviewed in this study.

On April 5, 1975, five senior citizens were found stabbed and hacked to death at 236 Pine Street in Buffalo. Afterwards the house had been set on fire so that the victims were first found by fire fighters who responded to an alarm. The killer evidently collected more than $1,000 in Social Security checks and welfare payments. No one has ever been arrested for these murders. The former chief of the Buffalo Police Department's homicide bureau said in a 1978 interview with the *Courier-Express*, however, that an unnamed suspect in that crime had himself been killed during a robbery attempt in 1976.

In that same year, four people were murdered by four killers in connection with the sale and use of drugs. Alexander Clark, Edward McKnight, Dennis McKnight and Sylvester West murdered Ralph Butler, George Washington, Rubeana Hacket and Marie Vigorito when the first three victims were unable to pay money owed from the sale of drugs and the fourth victim became an inadvertent witness to the killing of the other three. All four killers were arrested, tried and sentenced to prison terms of 25 years to life by Justice William Ostrowski. The four murderers and their victims had long histories of drug abuse and arrests.

No murder so agitated the city of Buffalo and the people of Erie County than the serial killings committed by Joseph Christopher in the course of 1980. Christopher, at that time a soldier stationed at Fort Benning, Georgia, used his leave to murder 14-year-old Glenn Dunn, 30-year-old Emmanuel Thomas and 32-year-old Harold Green. He killed all three in sudden, unprovoked attacks while the victims were either walking on the street or sitting in a car. In addition, Christopher had murdered Joseph L. McCoy of Niagara Falls, N.Y., and was later found guilty of several murders in New York City.

On his return to Fort Benning, Christopher was jailed on suspicion of murder concerning another soldier. While in the camp stockade, he bragged about the killings he had committed during his leave. Thereupon he was tried in Buffalo and New York City and upon conviction sent to prison for life. All of Christopher's victims were black.

So ends the recitation of numerous cases of murder which actually occurred in Erie County during the 40 years ending in 1983. All of these cases were taken from the *Courier-Express* where they were published immediately after they occurred. These cases are representative of the 912 cases found in the pages of the *Courier* over those years. It is now time to turn to an analysis of the conditions under which these 912 cases of homicide were perpetrated. This will give the reader an opportunity to understand the circumstances that lead to murder, the situation in which murder most often occurs and the outcome of such murders, at least from the judicial point of view.

2. Who Kills Whom, How, and Why

METHODS

This study is based on 912 cases of homicide which occurred in Erie County, N.Y., and which were reported in the *Courier-Express*, a daily newspaper published in Buffalo until September 1983, when it closed its doors. All of the homicides included here occurred between 1916 and 1983 and were found in the archives of the *Courier-Express*. These archives included very few cases of homicide before 1943. This does not, of course, mean that there were no murders before that year, but rather that the archives of the *Courier-Express* do not contain information concerning homicide before 1943 except for a few cases in the 1920s and the 1930s and one case in 1916. Information concerning these 912 homicides was gathered by copying from newspaper accounts six principal areas of concern:

Demographic variables. This included the number of inches of newspaper space devoted to each homicide. This was done to discover whether the social position of the killers or the victims had any influence on the extent of coverage given the murder reported. The date, day of the week, hour of the day and political subdivision of Erie County where the killing took place are also listed. This helps to distinguish between killings in the city of Buffalo and killings in the various suburbs and rural areas constituting Erie County. The concentric zone model of city organization as first developed by Park, Burgess and McKenzie in their 1925 book *The City* was used here.

Next, information was gathered concerning the actual locations of each murder included in this study. Whether the killing took place indoors or outdoors, and beyond that, whether in the street, a park, a car or other outdoor locations is noted. If indoors, the room in the house or apartment in which the killing took place and also the distinction between a private and a public accommodation, is mentioned. Finally, the average temperature for each day on which a murder had occurred is given. This information was gathered from material published by the United States Department of Commerce.

Characteristics of the murderer. Here information about the ethnicity, age, sex and address of the offender, followed by marital status, occupation, mental condition and arrest record was gathered.

27

The relationship of the killers to their victims. Whether they were relatives, neighbors, friends, casual acquaintances, strangers or law enforcement officials was investigated.

The circumstances pertaining to the murder scene. Here the weapons used, such as handguns, rifles, shotguns, knives, switchblades, stilettoes, axes, hatchets, clubs, icepicks, motor vehicles and "other" are dealt with. The latter category of killing instruments turned out to be mostly beatings.

Information as to the presence of alcohol at the murder scene, sexual involvement and motives for murder was also collected. Motives ranged from victim precipitation to jealousy, drug dealing, business deals, organized crime, gang wars and racial antagonism. Divorce was also listed as a motive for murder. However, the most frequent cause of homicide appeared under the category "other," because sudden outbursts of anger were listed there.

Disposition of the cases. Here are included dismissal before trial, trial by judge or jury and the penalties imposed on those found guilty.

After collecting the above information, all material was coded and then entered into a computer. Data was not available in every category for every case because the *Courier-Express* did not report the same material or characteristics for every homicide. In fact, the nature of any newspaper story about a killing was determined by the writer and the editors at the time of the report. Thus, it was fashionable in some years to inform the readers of the room in the house or the place in an apartment in which a killing had taken place. In other years, this information was not given. At other times, the occupation and place of employment of the offender and victim were mentioned, a feature utterly absent in some years.

Consequently, this author was able to obtain information in all of the categories of interest to us, but was limited to those items reported in each instance of homicide. I am satisfied, however, that the number of times that an attribute of the homicide situation was listed was sufficient in every area to make this study valid.

Upon obtaining the results of this study from computer analysis, conclusions were drawn based mostly on questions resulting from *Patterns in Criminal Homicide* by Wolfgang et al. during the past 30 years. This study, therefore, represents a description of these questions and the answers this study has obtained. Produced here is an exhaustive study of the social characteristics of homicide in Buffalo and Erie County, N.Y. Its conclusions are applicable to all American homicides. A copy of the form used to collect this information is attached in the appendix.

FINDINGS

The influence of geographic conditions on crime has been studied for over 100 years by numerous scholars in the United States and abroad. Thus, the French civil servant Guerry de Champneuf collected some data regarding crime rates in 86 different French departments, showing differences in various geographic areas with reference to the number of persons accused of crimes.[1]

In 1904 Dexter published an extensive study of weather influences on crime and in 1911, the fourth volume of Lombroso's *Criminal Man* appeared in English translation, including a study of seasonal crime rates based on the work of Guerry in England and France and that of Curcio in Italy.[2]

Additional studies of this kind were made by Enrico Ferri in Italy, William Douglas Morrison in England, von Ottingen and Aschaffenburg in Germany and von Mayr in Austria. In the United States, H.C. Brearly dealt with seasonal variations in the homicide rate in 1932 and Joseph Cohen published *The Geography of Crime* in 1941. In addition, a number of books concerning crime have published at least some material concerning crime and weather conditions.

This book explores this subject anew, dealing however not only with temperatures and other weather-related events but also with the date, the day of the killing, the hour of the day on which the murder took place, and the district in the county as well as the location as to its occurrence outdoors or indoors. The room in the house in which murder occurred, and the number who were killed outdoors are also listed. Finally, the temperature as a factor influencing killings throughout the year is noted, along with the number of murders by the day of the week for the epoch beginning with 1916 and ending in 1983.

Following is a table showing the results of the study over this period of time. This table is based on information concerning 908 homicides as reported by the *Courier-Express*. Information concerning the day of the week on which four of the 912 homicides occurred was not available.

Table 1
Homicide by the Day of the Week
Erie County, N.Y., 1916–1983

Day	# of Homicides	Percent	Cumulative %
Friday	137	15.1	– – –
Saturday	198	21.8	36.9
Sunday	139	15.3	52.2
Monday	113	12.4	64.6
Tuesday	106	11.7	76.3
Wednesday	101	11.1	87.4
Thursday	114	12.6	100.0

This table indicates that homicide in Erie County, during the time considered, was principally concentrated upon the weekend. Thus, 52.2 percent of the 908 homicides occurred at the weekend, from Friday night through Saturday night. The fewest homicides occurred in the middle of the week (Wednesday).

This concentration of homicides on the weekend plainly supports the view that homicide is a social event. This means that the situation in which the killing of a human being occurs is an important aspect of that event. Human behavior is largely determined by culture, that is, the man-made environment. Since the expectations and social configurations of the weekend in American society differ from behavior expected during the week, homicide patterns also differ. The cycle of activities during the weekend is different for most Americans than the cycle of activities during the working week. Weekends lend themselves to the development of conduct that leads to homicide more often than is true in work situations. In addition to the pattern of homicide related to the day of the week, it is evident from this study that homicide is also related to the hour of the day. The time of killing in 504 of our 912 cases was determined, which led to the establishment of the degree of danger for each hour of the day.

Work and leisure relationships which were true during the years here studied continue to be true in 1990. Thus, Americans generally continue to spend their days in the manner which was also true between 1916 and 1983. The following table indicates the rank order of danger of murder by hour of the day.

Table 2
Homicide by Hour of Occurrence

The degree of danger at each hour

Time		%	Cumulative Percent	Time		%	Cumulative Percent
Midnight to	1:00 A.M.	6		Noon to	1	3	50
1	2	4	10	1	2	3	53
2	3	8	18	2	3	2	55
3	4	6	24	3	4	4	59
4	5	5	29	4	5	4	63
5	6	3	32	5	6	4	67
6	7	2	34	6	7	4	71
7	8	2	36	7	8	4	75
8	9	2	38	8	9	5	80
9	10	3	41	9	10	5	85
10	11	4	45	10	11	6	91
11	Noon	2	47	11	Mdnt.	9	100

This table indicates that 11:00 P.M. to midnight is the most dangerous hour of the day relative to murder as 9 percent of all homicides took place then. A close second in degree of danger is the hour of 2:00 A.M. to 3:00 A.M., when 8 percent of homicides occur. The other degrees of danger are visible by inspecting the table. Inspection of both tables, dealing with homicide by the day and by the hour, reveals that the hour of 11 to midnight on Saturday is the most dangerous hour of the week.

Tables revealing the frequency with which homicide occurs either indoors or outdoors, and showing the locations where the killings were reported to have occurred, appear next.

Table 3
Location of Homicides

Indoors

Public Accommodations	Number	Percent (of 912 murders)
1. Bars, taverns, restaurants or hotels	51	6.0
2. Stores, offices and warehouses	50	6.0
3. Recreation centers	5	*
4. Theaters	1	*
5. Banks	2	*
6. Police stations	1	*
7. Plants	1	*
8. Schools	2	*
9. Hospitals	1	*
10. Bus and train depots	1	*
11. Churches	1	*
Totals	116	12.0

Private Accommodations (House or apartment)	Number	Percent
1. Room not specified	212	24.7
2. Bedroom	83	9.6
3. Living room	42	4.9
4. Kitchen	26	3.0
5. Hallway	20	2.0
6. Bath	10	1.0
7. Basement or cellar	6	*
8. Dining room	6	1.8
9. Garage	3	*
10. Closet	1	*
Totals	409	47.0
Total number of indoor homicides in which location was reported	525	61.0

*Less than 1 percent.

These tables indicate that more than 60 percent of all homicides included in this study occurred indoors, and that of these, more than three times as many took place in a private home or apartment than in a public accommodation. This supports the frequent finding that large numbers of homicides are committed by relatives and friends of the killer—persons who live with the victim or visit in each other's homes.

The large number of killings in bars, taverns and restaurants as well as hotels are also easily understood and by no means a surprise. Alcohol related killings are common particularly because alcohol impairs good judgment and is related to sudden anger, a frequent cause of homicide.

Robbery often causes homicides which are unplanned, but nevertheless occur in the course of holdups of stores, offices, warehouses and other places of business. It is remarkable that only one bank holdup led to one murder among the 912 cases. Holdups of banks are more frequent now than they were in earlier years. However, they succeed less often because security concerning them is so great and banks are generally known to have federal protection, in that the F.B.I. is charged with investigating these federal offenses. Obviously, private places of business have far fewer security arrangements, are seldom as well protected by armed guards as are banks and are not as often so located as to attract immediate attention if robbed.

Turning now to those homicides which took place outdoors, the following table depicts the locations of these killings, indicating that over 70 percent of these murders took place in the street. Street killings usually happen outside a bar or tavern and are the consequence of altercations which began inside a "watering hole," and are then continued directly outside the place in which they began.

Table 4
Homicides Occurring Outdoors

Location	Number	Percent
Street	237	27.7
Car	36	4.3
Parking lot	15	1.8
Backyard	10	1.2
Playground	8	*
Park	7	*
Field	7	*
Porch	5	*
Driveway	3	4.0
Wooded area	2	*
Cabin	1	*
Farm	1	*
Totals	332	39.0
Total number of indoor homicides in which location was reported	525	61.0
Total number of indoor and outdoor homicides in which location was reported	857	100.0

*Less than 1 percent.

Inspection of this table reveals that murders in automobiles occur more than twice as often as the next frequent category, murders in a parking lot. Together, these killings occupy 8.1 percent of all outdoor homicides. It is most important to remember that only 39 percent of all murders occur outdoors and that 61 percent of murders in this study occurred indoors. This is undoubtedly due to the cold weather in Erie County, which makes outdoor social interactions difficult for at least five months of each year. In addition, the number of killings within the circle of friends and family adds to the indoor killings because family in particular will meet each other at home. The same explanation refers to the high number of killings in automobiles. Normally, family members have much more access to each other's cars than is true of strangers and even friends.

Extreme cold discourages homicide somewhat. This appears to be the evidence when inspecting the number of homicides taking place in Erie County during the years here considered.

Table 5
Homicides and Temperature

Average temperature range	Percent of days per year in temperature range	Percent of homicides in temperature range
Below 32 degrees	25%	21.5%
32–63 degrees	50%	51.5%
Above 63 degrees	25%	27.0%

This table indicates that homicide rises significantly, but not radically, with an extreme rise in temperature. The average annual temperature for Erie County is 47.6 degrees Fahrenheit, and the average annual temperature at which murder occurs is 48.2 degrees Fahrenheit. Therefore, murder occurs at temperatures slightly higher than are expected.

The best explanation for this phenomenon is that more people move about, visit, travel and are available as victims during moderate and hot temperatures. Homicide rises somewhat with the temperature in the summer months and falls in the winter. It is of course important to recognize that earlier studies which claimed more extreme variations were conducted before modern heating and air conditioning devices were in use. These devices have created totally different social conditions than existed before their invention, thus leveling the degree of interpersonal relationships between summer and winter, spring and fall, and therefore also leveling somewhat the amount of homicide to be expected throughout the seasons of the year.

The relationship between race, ethnic origins, religion and homicide is well established and has been reported by every homicide study published. This means that homicide does not occur at random, but that some groups of people are more likely to kill one another than other groups. This an important finding which may seem "old hat" to some, but needs to be understood by readers not familiar with homicide patterns.

At first glance, any comment attributing more homicides to some groups than to others may provoke the belief that such a finding is motivated by racial or ethnic bigotry or has other motives. However, the findings in this matter are certain and need exposition and explanation, not because we seek to enhance or diminish one ethnic group or another, but because those most affected by homicide have a right to know the facts and to protect themselves.

The ethnicity of 714 murderers was established in the study of 912 homicides. This was determined by using the description of the killer in the *Courier-Express*, or by studying the picture of the accused if one was provided, or by assuming the race or ethnic origins of the accused according to his name and address. Buffalo and Erie County are segregated by race as are almost all United States cities. It is almost certain, therefore, that anyone living in the so-called "Fruit Belt" area of Buffalo is black. This area of the city has many streets named after fruits, such as "Orange" or "Apple," etc. By the same token, names or persons which are distinctly of non–English but European origins, such as Polish or Italian names, lead to the conclusion that the bearer is white, particularly if he lives in a neighborhood with a predominantly ethnic population or if he lives in the suburbs. Keeping in mind these methods of determining race and ethnicity, six categories were used in this connection as follows:

Table 6
Ethnicity of Murderer

Ethnic group	Frequency	Percent
White	257	36.0
Black	425	59.6
Hispanic	24	3.4
Native American	3	.4
Asian	1	.1
Other	4	.5
Total known ethnicity	714	100.0

The foregoing table shows that almost 60 percent of all homicides in Erie County were committed by blacks. Since only ten percent of the population of the county is black, this constitutes an over representation of six times the murder rate to be expected from that population. Exactly the same finding was discovered by other researchers working in other cities and at other times.[3]

Wolfgang, in *Patterns in Criminal Homicide*, concludes that "there is a significant association between criminal homicide and the race and sex of the offender and the victim." This significant association of the victims' ethnicity and homicide is well illustrated by the findings in our study, seen in the following table:

Table 7
Ethnicity of Victim

Ethnicity of victim	Number	Percent
White	390	47.4
Black	401	48.8
Hispanic	26	3.2
Native American	3	.4
Asian	1	.1
Other	1	.1
Totals	822	100.0

Black victims of homicide are also very much over represented, as nearly half of all victims in this study were black. This constitutes a victimization rate six times greater than expected. This is in agreement with Wolfgang and others, who have made similar studies in other American urban areas.

Two more factors were added in the attempt to establish a profile of the American murderer and his victim—age and gender. Table 8 looks at age. The ages of 746 killers were discovered in the study, along with the ages of 889 of the 912 victims involved.

It is clear from these findings and the tables presented here that the age group 15 through 33 had disproportionate amounts of homicide in each age, that age 19 with 43 killers involved leads all other ages in dangerousness and that fully 59.1 percent of all killers were between the ages of ten and 30. Eighty-two percent of all killers were 42 years old or less, with the youngest being age ten. After the age of 42 the number of killers declines sharply. The oldest killer was 84 years old, but he was the only one of his age appearing in the study. There were seven killers in their seventies, 20 in their sixties, and 49 in their fifties. Obviously, advancing age reduces the inclination to kill.

Table 8
Age of Murderer

Age	Frequency	Percent
10	1	*
14	1	*
15 to 30	439	58.8
31 to 42	170	22.9
43 to 49	58	7.8
50 to 84	77	10.3
Totals	746	100.0

Statistically insignificant.

When the ages of the murderers are compared with the ages of their victims, it is apparent that the distribution of victims' ages is greater than is true of murderers because the youngest children can be victims but cannot very well commit murder. Similarly, very old people are victims but, as already stated, do not commit murder very often.

Nevertheless, the bulk of victims are also about 15 to 46 years old. This confirms that murder is a social affair between people of the same ethnicity and age. It appears that murder occurs between people who share certain social situations because they have a great deal in common, as do all people who share social situations.

The following table illustrates the ages of murder victims and demonstrates, as does the previous exhibit on ethnicity, that people kill those who are near and dear to them much more often than those who are strangers.

Table 9
Age of Victim

Age	Frequency	Percent
Less than one year	1	0
Fourteen or less	52	6
Fifteen–nineteen	84	9
Twenty–twenty-nine	229	26
Thirty–thirty-nine	189	21
Forty–forty-nine	134	15
Fifty–fifty-nine	87	10
Sixty–sixty-nine	67	8
Seventy–ninety	46	5
Totals	889	100

It is evident from the above that 62 percent of all victims fall into the age category of 20 to 49, and that 418 of the victims are between the ages of 20 and 39. Thus, fully 47 percent of the victims are 20 to 39 years of age, which is also the age at which most murders are committed.

Once more, however, it is necessary to remember that the range of victims' ages is a good deal greater than that of the perpetrators. Turning now to the issue of gender in the murder relationship, 87.8 percent of all murderers included in this study were men, and only 12.2 percent were women. This involves only 909 of the cases, as the gender of the murderer in 3 cases was not determinable.

Table 10
Gender of Murderers and Victims

	Frequency		Percent	
Gender	Killer	Victim	Killer	Victim
Male	799	648	87.8	71.0
Female	110	264	12.2	29.0
Total	909	912	100.0	100.0

The evidence here is that males had a homicide rate more than seven times that of females in the group we studied. This is a universal finding. All studies of homicide reveal this, leading Wolfgang to comment in his study, *Patterns in Criminal Homicide*, that "Blacks and males have homicide rates many times greater than whites and females." Several reasons for this discrepancy can be advanced. Surely, anyone familiar with American lifestyles is aware that gender is not only a biological condition but also a social status, here and in all cultures. Therefore, it is reasonable to expect different performances in all areas of life for both sexes. This is reflected in the homicide rate.

Aggression is taught to young boys in the United States and in many other countries with murderous results. This is not to say that every boy who has been taught that aggression is an admirable male attribute becomes a killer. There can be no doubt, however, that the constant repetition of the "macho" theme together with the belief taught to boys and men that aggression is a means of dealing with frustration, promotes murderous attacks by men.

While males constitute almost 88 percent of all killers, only 71 percent of victims are men. This is true because the number of women murdered is so much greater than the number of women who kill. In fact, women are victims of homicide two and one-half times more often than they are murderers. Nevertheless, men are killed two and one-half times more often than women, because both sexes are more likely to kill men.

An earlier study (Falk "Status Differences and the Frustration-Aggression Hypothesis") has revealed that homicide, subsequent to frustration, is the product of social standing, both with reference to sex, and also with reference to such other indicators of status and role as occupation, income and residence.

In fact, residence or the zone of a city in which an American lives, may well be considered one of the most important indicators of social standing that we have. Therefore, the address of every killer and his victim was listed, and then these addresses were located on a map of Buffalo and Erie County in order to determine the zone of the city in which both lived.

Using the work of Park, Burgess and McKenzie,[4] the city was divided into five zones and a sixth one, "out of town," was added. The five zones listed by the above authors are: 1) the downtown area or inner city; 2) the industrial area surrounding downtown; 3) the residential and business area uptown within the city limits; 4) nearby suburbs; 5) wealthier and far removed suburbs; and 6) this author's contribution—other towns and places not in Erie County or incorporated separately from Buffalo, if in Erie County.

Using these six zones, it was found that of the 912 homicides described in this study, the residence of 823 killers (90 percent) was established. The following table reveals the relationship between place of residence and proclivity to murder and clearly shows that some areas in Erie County and the city of Buffalo have far more killers in residence than is true of other areas.

Table 11
Residence of Murderer

Zone	Number of murderers	Percent
One	86	11
Two	496	60
Three	98	12
Four	52	6
Five	43	5
Six	48	6
Total	823	100

It is evident from this table that 582, or 71 percent of all killers included in this study, lived in the inner city or in an area immediately adjoining the inner city. In fact, zone two, the zone with the largest black population in Buffalo, is the place of residence for the largest proportion of all killers involved here. This, therefore, verifies what has already been said about race and homicide, and once more indicates the great association of homicide with poverty and other conditions produced by racial segregation and its consequences.

Turning now to the place of residence of the victims of murder, the findings are that they too live in those areas of the city and county which are also the principal areas of residence for their killers. That this should be so is of course not surprising. Most killings are intraracial, that is, occuring within the same race. Hence, in racially segregated U.S. cities, homicide, like all interaction, occurs almost entirely within the group who live in the same area. In addition, many killers are either related to their victim or otherwise closely associated with them. This also contributes a great deal to the physical proximity of killer and victim. Following is a table showing the zones in Buffalo and Erie County, where 905 of the victims discussed in this study were located.

Table 12
Residence of Victim

Zone	Number of Victims	Percent
One	110	12
Two	468	52
Three	131	14
Four	107	12
Five	51	6
Six	38	4
Total	905	100

In addition to ethnic or racial origins and place of residence, occupation is undoubtedly an excellent indicator of social class and status-role. In fact, sociologists generally agree that occupation is probably the best indicator of social class in America, as shown by any inspection of the leading sociology texts now in use.

Once more, a listing on the following page of the occupations of the killers in this study promotes my original hypothesis that persons with lower-class occupations are most likely to be involved in homicide both as perpetrators and as victims.

The occupations of 216 killers were obtained from the over 900 included in this study. This reflects the failure of newspapers, at least the *Courier-Express* in this case, to mention the occupation of murderers in more than 75 percent of the cases. Nevertheless, the characteristics of 216 murderers suffice to provide a reliable source for an analysis of occupations of murderers.

If those occupations which take a good deal of education and earn a relatively high income are separated from those which pay an hourly wage and earn relatively less, it then becomes evident that only 15 murderers had a managerial and or professional status. That constitutes only seven percent of all murderers.

It is also significant that only 27 unemployed persons were involved in the sample of murderers. If to this number is added the two murderers on welfare, there are

Table 13
Occupations of Murderers

Type of Occupation	Number	Percent
Laborer	61	28
Service worker	36	17
Operative	11	5
Craftsman-foreman	19	9
Clerical-sales	7	3
Managerial	9	4
Professional	6	3
Housewives	2	1
Unemployed	27	13
Student	29	13
Professional criminal	3	1
Petty criminal	4	1
Welfare recipient	2	2
Total	216	100

only 29, or 13 percent of all murderers who suffer the ignominy of lacking employment. Occupations which are generally frustrating and very much under the control of bosses, such as laborer, service worker (waiter, etc.) or operator of a machine, are as likely to promote the kind of anger and sudden rage that is so typical of so many murder situations.

The same type of occupational distribution was discovered in an earlier study which tested the frustration-aggression hypothesis. Turning to the victims of murder and looking at their occupations, it is apparent that the distribution of occupations is larger than is true among perpetrators. This means that higher status occupations are much more prevalent among the victims, particularly because robbery-inspired murders so often involve shop and store owners and others who have valuables to steal.

Thus, among killers, the three hourly paid occupations (laborer, service worker and operative) constitute 50 percent of the sample. Among victims however, these three occupations only constitute 38 percent of the sample. This is still a very high number and is indeed a plurality. Nevertheless, the distinction is striking as the table on the following page illustrates.

One hundred and twenty-eight of the 336 victims whose occupations are known are clustered in three categories—laborers, service workers and operatives. This resembles the occupations of murderers to some extent. However, clerical, managerial and professional workers, who are victimized by killers in almost a third of our cases, far exceed the proportion of killers who have such occupations.

In fact, only 22 of the killers were in those occupational categories, constituting only 10 percent of all killers whose occupations were determined. This discrepancy is obviously the result of the attraction which persons with higher earnings present to robbers and others, since such persons are frequently in charge of a good deal of money and other valuables.

Table 14
Occupation of Victims

	Number	Percent
Laborers	62	19
Service workers	48	14
Operatives	18	5
Craftsmen/Foremen	10	3
Clerical workers	24	7
Managerial employees	58	17
Professionals	25	8
Housewives	7	2
Retirees	5	1
Unemployed	22	7
Students	42	13
Welfare recipients	3	.8
Professional criminals	7	2
Petty criminals	5	1.2
Totals	336	100.0

A similar difference exists in the category "Housewives." Only one percent of our killers are listed by that occupation, but two percent of the victims are housewives, usually having been murdered by their own husbands.

This leads to a discussion of the marital status of both the killers and the victims in this study. The marital status of 404 of our murderers was obtained, and the distribution was found to be as follows:

Table 15
Marital Status of Murderers

Status	Number	Percent
Single	233	57
Married	151	37
Divorced	9	2.5
Separated	9	2.5
Widowed	2	1
Totals	404	100.0

If the divorced, separated and the widowed are added to the single group in this sample, then fully 63 percent, or 253 of all the killers in this study, were not living in a marital state. There is evidently a very high correlation between living in a single state and becoming involved in homicide.

This does not mean that failure to be married is the cause of homicide. However, it does mean that persons living in the marital condition are less likely to get into situations that can and often do result in murder, possibly because the marital state includes more satisfactions and more contentment than the single state. There is less frustration in the marital condition than in the single condition and this is largely due to the elimination of competition for sexual favors, the steady influence of marital friendship and the increased recognition and social standing of the married American as compared to the single person. The following table examines the marital status of murder victims:

Table 16
Marital Status of Victims

Status	Number	Percent
Single	309	53.0
Married	214	37.0
Divorced	23	4.0
Widowed	25	4.3
Separated	6	1.7
Totals	577	100.0

If the divorced, the separated, the widowed and the single victims are added together, they constitute about two-thirds of all the sample. Thus, of the 577 victims of homicide whose marital status is known, 364, or 63 percent, were not married or living in a marital arrangement. Both killers and victims were living in a single state twice as often as in a married state. The conclusion is that the murder situation, whether experienced as killer or as victim, is far more often derived from the single life style than from married life. It can be said that single people are more likely to be present in bars, to fight more and to be less self-controlled than the married. It is, however, also possible that those who drink a good deal of alcohol or are more interested in displaying a "macho" type of behavior are less likely to be married than those who do not drink much and do not enter bars.

This raises the question as to the mental state of killers and that of their victims. A large number of persons believe that murder is the result of so-called "insanity," and are also convinced that the presence of alcohol has a great deal to do with violence and killings. Therefore, statistics were developed concerning "mental disability" and or alcohol presence in both our killers and their victims, particularly because alcohol can and does often lead to "victim precipitated homicide."

The review of the 912 murders included here reveals that only 47 killers involved were labeled mentally ill by the reporters who wrote the news stories from whence the data was derived. While this does not mean that a good number of psychiatrically disturbed people could not have been involved in killing others without coming to the attention of a *Courier-Express* reporter, it is nevertheless significant that amidst hundreds of killers only a few were so described by reason of a history of earlier commitment to a mental institution. Among victims, the number of persons identified as being mentally ill was even lower, as could have been expected. Only six victims were so labeled.

In a previous publication, this author discussed the so-called "insanity" defense at length and concluded that this is a very weak and dubious defense against homicide, not only because so few persons are truly mentally ill, but also because that "illness" is so poorly defined, vague and hard to identify.[5]

It is for that reason that psychiatrists on both sides of a trial involving violence, and particularly homicide, are likely to argue both for and against the proposition that the defendant was or was not mentally ill, or insane at the time of the offense.

By and large, the United States is fed up with various forms of insanity defenses, as evidenced by the public outcry against John Hinckley who shot President Reagan, and other atrocious and well-publicized killings and attempted killings.

It is this author's contention that even if it can be shown that a killer is insane, psychotic or otherwise incompetent, a jury or judge should still find such a person guilty of a crime that he evidently did commit, since the public must be protected, particularly from persons who are not responsible for their actions. Furthermore, someone who has been found guilty of homicide but is definitely a psychiatric case should not be sent to prison, but be institutionalized elsewhere, that is, in a hospital. The establishment of guilt is very important and no one should be adjudicated "not guilty by reason of insanity."

Table 17
Prior Convictions of Murderers

Type of Crime	Number	Percent
Violent	84	42
Property	21	11
Violent and property	11	6
Public order	18	9
Violent and public order	7	3
Property and public order	5	2
All three	13	7
Convicted, but offense not known	12	6
Convicted of minor offense	27	14
Totals*	198	100%

*The 162 killers previously committed a total of 198 crimes.

While the number of persons who kill because they are mentally ill is very few, there is a good deal of evidence that killers have been involved in previous violent crimes. This means that murder is often the culmination of a violent career and that some murderers have killed a number of persons. A later chapter discusses multicide, which is the killing of several or even thousands of people. The prior conviction records of 162 of the 909 murderers included in this study were obtained. Remember that there were 912 victims but only 909 killers, because three of the victims included here were killed by someone who also killed others in this victim group.

In any case, of these 162 murderers, 84, or 52 percent have been reported as convicted of violent crimes on previous occasions. It is reasonable to assume that the news reporters on whose stories this study is based did not always report or even know about previous violent acts by those convicted of killing someone at the time the report was published in the *Courier-Express*. This author believes, therefore, that prior violence was much greater among this sample of murderers than can be determined now.

In addition to crimes of violence of which these 162 killers had been convicted, many of them had also been convicted of yet other crimes. The table on the preceding page illustrates the kinds of offenses for which convictions were obtained concerning these 162 killers.

Please note that in the table, the offenders who committed more than one type of offense are counted repeatedly. Thus, the total is meant to include only those killers whose previous convictions are known, even if they were convicted more than once.

3. The Conditions and Dispositions of Homicide

Homicide is a social act. This means that killing another human being is a form of social interaction just like other forms of interaction, derived from the meaning which people give to the events that occur in their lives. Sociologists speak of "symbolic interactionism," meaning that humans are the only earthly creatures who give meaning to signs, like words, or symbols such as a cross or a star, or even facial expressions and body movements. It is, therefore, not surprising that homicide is so often the result of close relationships between the killer and his victim. The relationship between these two actors in the homicide drama in 735 of the 912 cases of homicide was discovered, constituting 81 percent of the murders, a very reliable finding.

The analysis of this data reveals that 21 percent of all killings in this study occurred between relatives. Seventy-four of the 155 relatives who killed one another were husbands or wives, and 81 were otherwise related. This would mean, at least superficially, that people who live in a marital relationship are almost as likely to kill their spouse as people related by blood ties are likely to kill one another.

However, if the category "lovers" is added to that of spouse, and thereby include persons of both genders living together in a manner which resembles a marital household, then a total of 111 killings occurred under such circumstances, exceeding other relatives by 30 cases among those whose relationship is known. In addition, a category of relationship between the killer and the victim, "friend," is listed without reference to gender. Almost all of these cases refer to killings between men. "Friends" constitute 120 of the 735 known relationships, thus adding another 16 percent to those closely associated with one another when murder occurred.

The table on the following page illustrates how a large proportion of killers are well known to their victims and thus constitutes an excellent argument for the view that murder is a family and friendship affair.

This table illustrates that fully 70 percent of all the killers and victims among those whose relationship was identified knew each other, and that only 30 percent of killers and victims did not know each other, with the assumption that the 15 law enforcement officers who were all victims were not known to their killers. This could not be determined. In the table showing "Occupation of Victim" (p. 40) law

Table 18
The Relationship of the Killer to the Victim

Relationship	Number	Percent
Spouses	74	10
Lovers	37	5
Relatives	81	11
Friends	120	16
Neighbors	46	6
Co-workers	24	3
Casual acquaintances	132	19
Sub-total (killers known to the victims)	514	70
Strangers (not law enforcement)	206	28
Law enforcement officers	15	2
Totals	735	100%

enforcement personnel were included in the 58 managerial employees listed there. The category "casual acquaintance" generally refers to people who met each other briefly in a bar, restaurant or other place of amusement, recreation or entertainment. It is significant that almost all those 119 killings, which involved the use of alcohol, were killings between persons categorized as "casual acquaintances."

Let us now turn to the use of alcohol and other drugs, which do indeed constitute one of the conditions of homicide. There was mention of the presence of alcohol and other drugs in only 140 of the 912 killings used in this study, constituting only 15 percent of all murders included here. Therefore, this author's comments concerning the influence of drugs including alcohol on homicide may seem inconclusive to some readers. It should be remembered however, that scientific data are generally held reliable even if they are derived from a sample of only ten percent. The following table concerning the presence of alcohol and other drugs is presented with the clear understanding that any of these drugs could of course have been present in many other cases in this study, but that the *Courier-Express* failed to mention this because the reporter involved did not know whether or not drugs were present or found it not worth mentioning.

Table 19
The Presence of Alcohol or Other Drugs at the Murder Scene

Type of Drug	Number	Percent
Alcohol	119	85
Alcohol and other drug	4	3
Heroin and opiates	2	1
All other drugs	15	11
Totals	140	100

The other drugs include LSD, PCP, amphetamines, and drugs not specified in the newspaper report. It is significant, however, that heroin plays a very small part in murder and that alcohol, and only alcohol, is a dangerous drug with reference to this study. This author contends that the relative absence of drugs in the murder situation as revealed here is probably quite accurate for all of the United States. Murder is not caused by drug or alcohol addiction, but by the social situations that develop between relatives and friends. While no doubt a few murders may have come about because alcohol beclouded the judgment of some drinkers, it is in accord with the evidence that it really makes little difference whether or not alcohol is present at the murder scene.

The death of almost anyone leaves survivors behind who must then cope with the loss of a loved one. This is particularly difficult in cases of murder because such a loss, unlike death by disease, is very sudden, like an auto accident. Death by murder is hard to tolerate and difficult to accept for the survivors who cannot really explain such a death to themselves. Murder seems so unnecessary and senseless a crime that it can hardly be given an adequate explanation. There are those, of course, who argue that murder is the result of handgun ownership, and therefore seek gun control laws which they hope will reduce the number of killings and maimings experienced in almost all American communities over the years. This study reveals that handguns were used in 27 percent of all the cases of 874 victims whose mode of death was ascertainable.

This will be interpreted by some to mean that the 232 killings by handgun included in this study would not have happened if only no handgun had been present. However, it is just as reasonable to hold that at least one-half of the homicides committed by handgun would have been achieved by some other method as it is to hold that they would not have been done at all. Now, if shotguns and rifles are added to the handguns used to commit murder, this still represents just 47 percent of all murder methods in evidence. Therefore, it cannot be inferred that handgun control will necessarily reduce the murder rate, any more than firearms control in general will cause a reduction. It is just as reasonable to argue that the absence of firearms is responsible for homicide as it is to argue the opposite, since 55 percent of all the murder cases here discussed were not committed by firearms.

In fact, there is at least one western-style, technologically advanced society in which handguns are carried by a yet greater proportion of the population than the American population. That society is Israel. The Israeli murder rate, however, is far lower than it is in the United States as already noted in the Introduction. The table on the following page examines the distribution of murder methods used against 874 of the 912 victims discussed here, keeping in mind that the method of inflicting death was ascertained in 96 percent of all killings reported in the Courier-Express during the 40 years ending in 1983.

The methods of murdering, other than firearms, knives or hands, include such techniques as using an axe, an icepick, a screwdriver or a hammer. Some people use motor vehicles and others kill with poison or scald or strangle the victim to death. Arson is rarely, but sometimes, fatal, and drowning is also used on a few occasions to kill the victims. Please note that some killers use more than one method to get rid of the victim. They evidently want to make certain the victim is really dead and therefore use several methods to murder him. This multiple effort to kill

Table 20
Methods Used to Kill Murder Victims

Methods	Number		Percent	
Handguns only	218		25	
Handgun and hands	4			
Handgun and club	5		2	
Handgun and knife	4			
Handgun and axe	1			
Total handguns	232		27	
Rifles or shotguns	158		18	
Total firearms		390		45
Kitchen knife	96			
Switchblade or stiletto	145			
Knife only		241	28	
Handgun and knife	4			
Hands and knife	11		2	
Club and knife	10			
Knife and other weapon		25		
Total knives		266		30
Hands and knives	11			
Hands and club	4			
Hands only	123			
Total hands		138		16
Other methods		80		9
Total number of murders in which weapons or methods were known		874		100%

occurred in 39 out of 874 murders in which the method of killing is known, constituting only four percent of all these murders.

In sum, murder is not caused by the presence of this or that object, substance or tool. Instead, murder is caused by social conditions which promote attitudes toward human life leading some people to kill others because they see their fellow man in a light that permits them to kill him. The motives for killing vary, and of the apparent motives for 695 homicides in which the motive was discussed by the *Courier-Express*, 15 categories were drawn up.

It is, of course, true that every action anyone takes is in a sense so personal that it has its own and private motives known only to the actor. Nevertheless, it is apparent that by observing each other, conduct can be seen to have at least enough similarities, and occur under circumstances which are so similar, that there is good reason to believe that murderers have similar motives.

For example, a good number of the killings here discussed came about because the killer was engaged in the hold-up of a store. These killings were together under the heading of "other crimes." The same is true of the other motives that were seen repeatedly, and which resemble each other in general, even if not in detail.

Following is a table showing the 15 principal motives for murder which were identified. Motives were determined in 76 percent, or 695 of the 912 cases. The reasons for homicide in Erie County, N.Y., can be spoken of with some certainty, therefore. There is every reason to believe that these motives are very common in all of the United States, because they have been discovered in so many other areas of this country over a long period of time.

Table 21
Apparent Motive for Murder

Motive	Number	Percent
Other crime	194	27.9
Sudden anger	166	23.9
Victim precipitation	78	11.2
Jealousy	75	10.8
Business dealings	50	7.2
Insanity	23	3.3
Gang war	19	2.7
Organized crime	17	2.4
Drug dealing	15	2.2
Accident	11	1.6
Divorce situation	10	1.4
Racism	8	1.2
Revenge	7	1.0
Refusing sex	2	.3
Other	20	2.9
Total	695	100.0

This table clearly shows that murder is very often the result of unexpected conditions derived from the commission of such crimes as assault, rape or robbery, or from outbursts of sudden anger mostly stemming from a perceived attack on the killer's feeling of self worth.

In the first chapter, several case histories involving holdups which led to the death, usually by shooting, of a store owner or clerk were presented. In one case the two would-be robbers were killed by the storeowner. Obviously, assault often turns into murder. In fact, the difference between assault and murder is frequently the speed with which an ambulance arrives at the scene of an assault or the skill of an emergency surgeon who first sees the assault victim. Thus, a slow-arriving ambulance or a traffic tie-up during an attempt to deliver an assault victim to the hospital can turn a beating into a killing. Sudden anger is very much related to assault, but was listed separately in this study because it led to the immediate death of the victim.

Sudden anger cases are also described in the first chapter. In these situations, murders that come about when the killer feels his honor is demeaned are generally confronted. Sometimes this occurs in an argument over the attentions of a woman. In other cases the killer feels that he must assert himself "like a man" even if the argument in which he has become entangled deals with an issue of no particular importance. Thus, when one man kills another over who is to get 40 cents' change on a bar counter, the killing is not truly related to the amount of money involved but to the question of who is dominant. Sociologists call this kind of need to dominate at any cost "existential validation." This comes from the Latin word *valeo*, i.e, strong. Many men, in particular, validate (or test their strength) by killing an opponent and gaining a sense of power in a world in which they feel they have no power at all. Killing compensates some people for their constant feeling of helplessness and powerlessness and at least once in their lives makes them, the killers, the boss over life and death.

Turning now to the disposition of homicide, the final outcome of murder both for the killer and society in general will be examined. The first concern is with the trial phase of a homicide accusation, which indicates how the courts in Erie County dealt with the accused. The following table exhibits these dispositions in 528 cases in which it was determined how the courts acted concerning homicide defendants.

Table 22
Disposition of Homicide Cases

Method	Number	Percent
Dismissed before trial	52	9.8
Trial by judge	223	42.2
Trial by jury	250	47.4
Innocent by reason of insanity	2	.4
Sent to juvenile court	1	.2
Totals	528	100.0

Please note that almost 90 percent of all homicide cases in this study were tried by either judge or jury and that very few were dismissed before trial by reason of insanity. This means that police work in these cases was done very well and that hardly anyone is brought to trial on homicide charges unless the charge is well prepared and documented. It also means that the popular belief that anyone can easily get away with murder by claiming insanity is not true.

It is also significant that the number of defendants who choose to be tried by a judge alone is about the same as the number who choose to be tried by a jury. There are defense attorneys who believe that judges are more likely to find a defendant innocent and there are those who think juries are easier to influence in favor of the defense. Objective studies of this issue have, however, shown that "the odds for acquittal are far better with a jury than with a judge."[1]

In fact, Kalven and Zeisel report that in their study, the conviction rate by judges as opposed to juries was 83.3 percent and 64.4 percent respectively.[2] The next question is, whether or not murder defendants are convicted, and how often they are convicted. In short, can one really get away with murder in Erie County? The answer has to be an emphatic "no" for those 528 cases which were in fact dealt with by the Erie County courts during the years of this study, 1940 to 1983. Evidence suggests that this is still the case.

While this study was only able to discover how 528 cases were dealt with by the courts in order to reach a decision in their case, a total of 639 verdicts concerning murderers in this study were made. This author was not able to determine how 111 of the verdicts came about or whether a judge or a jury reached a verdict in those 111 cases, because the *Courier-Express* did not report this in those 111 instances.

Table 23 shows whether or not a conviction was obtained among the 639 homicide cases whose disposition is known.

Table 23
Conviction of Defendants Accused of Homicide

Disposition	Number	Percent
Convicted	528	83
Pled guilty	25	4
Not convicted	72	11
Not known	14	2
Totals	639	100

An overwhelming number (83 percent) of all defendants who were tried on homicide charges were convicted and another four percent pled guilty. Thus, only 11 percent of those so charged were not convicted.

This is a very important finding, since charges other than homicide usually lead to guilty pleas on reduced charges. About 92 to 95 percent of all cases prosecuted by United States prosecutors end in "plea bargaining," a situation which permits the defendant to accept punishment for a lesser charge than the one facing him, giving prosecutors a far higher conviction rate than they could otherwise obtain. Conviction, however, does not always carry the same punishment. In fact, one of the great weaknesses of the criminal justice system in the United States is that so many convicts are given totally different sentences even though they have committed the same crime.

This disparity in sentencing is based largely on the observed evidence that crimes that appear the same, are not necessarily the same. For example, a woman who kills her husband because he beat her incessantly would receive a different sentence if convicted of murder than someone who deliberately killed a relative after becoming the beneficiary of the victim's insurance policy. Therefore, four kinds of punishment have been used in Erie County during the period under consideration. In addition, some cases are reversed on appeal, and the accused is either dismissed or retried. The sentences handed out to 524 murderers included in this study could be determined. Table 24 exhibits the sentences given them.

Table 24
Type of Sentence Handed to Persons Convicted of Homicide

Type of Sentence	Number	Percent
Death	11	2
Prison	445	85
Psychiatric hospital	28	5
Probation	37	7
Reversed on appeal	3	1
Total	524	100

The above table obviously points out that people should be primarily concerned with the use of prison as punishment for murder, since death constitutes only two percent of all sentences. This is true not only because the death penalty was abolished in New York, but also because New York and other states never used the death penalty as much as imprisonment even when it was in use.

Furthermore, only five of the 11 murderers sentenced to death in this study were actually executed. The others had their sentences commuted to life imprisonment, or reversed on appeal. Only seven percent of all convicted killers were given probation and only five percent sent to a psychiatric hospital. These two categories, therefore, constitute a negligible number of convicts among those convicted of homicide.

The following table shows the number of prison sentences that were determined in 439 cases available to this study, together with the length of the minimum prison terms to which those convicted were sentenced.

Table 25
Length and Frequency of Prison Sentences

Length of sentence (in years)	Number	Percent
1 to 2	46	11
3 to 4	46	11
5 to 6	56	13
7 to 8	43	10
9 to 10	43	10
11 to 14	6	1
15 to 16	60	14
17 to 18	4	0
19 to 24	49	11
25	56	13
30 to 35	7	1
35 to 100	23	5
Total	439	100

This information shows that the typical person convicted of homicide in this study served less than ten years in prison (median), a figure which is about the same for most of the United States. In fact, the median number of years served in American prisons for murder is ten years, and the mean is 14.7 years.

Thus, it is evident that homicide in the United States, depite its relative frequency compared to other countries, is generally not considered a capital crime. Americans, in other words, do not usually choose to inflict the death penalty on those convicted of murder, nor do murderers normally kill themselves after having killed someone else. In fact, among the 355 cases in which such information was available, only 20 killers killed themselves after killing their victim. No doubt, many more suicides occur in the United States every year, and surely in the course of 40 years. In fact, there are about 20,000 suicides in America every year, but not because 20,000 people who murdered their fellow citizens or relatives killed themselves thereafter.

SUMMARY AND CONCLUSIONS

The previous discussion leads to the following conclusions concerning homicide in Buffalo and Erie County and the United States as a whole. It remains this author's contention that the conclusions herewith presented have been corroborated by other studies and can be viewed as being representative of American homicide in general. Some of these other studies are: "Homicide Trends in Atlanta" by Robert Munford, Ross S. Kazar, Roger Feldman and Robert R. Stivers, in *Criminology, 14, no. 2, August 1976; "Patterns in Criminal Homicide in Chicago" by Harwin L. Voss and John R. Hepburn in The Journal of Criminal Law, Criminology and Police Science, 59; Homicide in an Urban Community* by Robert C. Bensing and Oliver Schroeder; "Homicide in Detroit" by Joseph S. Fisher in *Criminology, 14, no. 3, November 1976; and Patterns in Criminal Homicide* by Marvin Wolfgang. There are of course several others.

The conclusions regarding homicide in Buffalo and Erie County during the 40 year period ending in the fall of 1983 are these:

The Geography of Homicide

1. Sixty-one percent of all killings occur indoors, and of these, over three-quarters occur at home.

2. Thirty-nine percent of all killings occur outdoors, and of these, 70 percent occur in the street.

3. Most homicides occur in moderate temperatures.

4. Eighty-three percent of all killers and 78 percent of all victims live in the city and only 17 percent live in the suburbs.

5. Sixty percent of all killers and 52 percent of all victims live in zones one or two, that is, downtown or adjacent to downtown. This includes the black ghetto.

6. Overcrowding is directly related to murder.

Ethnicity

1. Sixty percent of all murderers are black in an area (Erie County) which has a black population of only eight percent. Therefore, blacks are seven-and-one-half times overrepresented among killers.

2. Nearly one half of all murder victims are black; nearly one-half of all victims are white and the rest are Hispanic or native Americans. Thus, blacks are also overrepresented among victims while whites are underrepresented.

3. Whites are more often victims than offenders.

4. Only 36 percent of all killers are white in a population in which almost 92 percent of all residents are white.

Age

1. Nearly 60 percent of all killers are between 15 and 30 years old.

2. Nearly 82 percent of all killers are between 15 and 42 years old.

3. There is a decline in the number of killers as age advances.

4. The age range of victims is greater than that of killers. Thus, victims can be small babies or very old people.

Gender

1. Men kill eight times more often than women. Eighty-eight percent of all killers are men.

2. Seventy-one percent of all homicide victims are men, because both genders kill men more often than women.

Marital Status and Relationships

1. Fifty-seven percent of all killers and 53 percent of all victims are single.

2. Seventy percent of all killers and their victims know each other.

3. Ten percent of murders involve spouses.

4. Two percent of murders involve law enforcement officers.

Prior Violations

1. Forty-two percent of all killers were arrested for earlier violence.

Occupations

1. Fifty-nine percent of all killers are employed in working class, hourly occupations, i.e., laborers, operators or service workers.

2. Only 13 percent of all killers are unemployed and only seven percent are professionals or managers.

3. Thirty-eight percent are employed in working class occupations but 25 percent are professionals or managers.

Drug and Alcohol Use

1. Very few murder scenes involve drugs other than alcohol.

2. Alcohol is present at murder scenes as much as anywhere else and therefore plays no significant part in murder.

Methods of Killing

1. Twenty-seven percent of all killings are by handgun.
2. Firearms kill 45 percent of all victims.
3. Thirty percent of all killings are by knife.
4. Sixteen percent of all killings involve beatings.
5. Some killers use several methods at the same time.
6. Gun control cannot reduce the murder rate.

Motives

1. Sudden anger (24 percent), victim precipitation (11 percent) and jealousy (10 percent) constitute 45 percent of all murder motives.
2. Robbery and other crimes provoke 28 percent of all murders.
3. "Insanity" is present in only three percent of all murders.

Conviction and Disposition

1. While about 42 percent of apprehended killers are tried by a judge alone, and 47 percent are tried by judge and jury, only ten percent are dismissed for lack of evidence and a small fraction are considered "insane."
2. Eighty-three percent of all accused in a murder trial are convicted and four percent plead guilty, thus making a total conviction rate of 87 percent.
3. Eighty-five percent of all people convicted of murder are sent to prison.
4. Seven percent of people convicted of murder are placed on probation and five percent are sent to a psychiatric hospital.
5. Before the abolition of the death penalty in New York, only two percent of those convicted of murder were executed.
6. On the average (median), ten years are spent in prison for murder in Erie County, N.Y., and in the United States. Nevertheless, the mean prison sentence for murder in the United States is 14.7 years, and in Erie County it is 15 years. This includes some extremely long sentences given to a few convicted of murder.

Having presented a good deal of information concerning one-on-one homicide, multicide is dealt with in the next chapter. This concerns the killing of numerous persons by one killer either at once (mass murder), or over a prolonged period of time (serial murder), or by a number of persons systematically, a practice called "genocide."

Part II

Multicide

4. Genocide

So far, this book has dealt only with one-on-one homicide. By using the example of one American county, Erie (N.Y.), for a period of 40 years and showing how over 900 people were killed there during those years, this author has shown the typical American homicide situation. The conclusions this study arrived at also apply to any other urban area in this country; and since most Americans now live in urban areas or are heavily influenced by urban events through the media, there is every reason to believe that this review depicts the typical American murder situation.

This belief is strengthened because the other urban homicide studies mentioned at the end of the previous chapter reached similar conclusions regardless of the area in which they were made. These studies were conducted in Philadelphia, Cleveland, Houston, Detroit, and Chicago at different times and in geographically and socially widely different communities. Yet, homicide in all of these areas, and over all of the years studied, always follows a pattern very much resembling what was found to be true of Erie County, N.Y.

There is, however, a type of murder which follows no such pattern and which cannot be explained by the means so far used. That type of murder is called "multicide," the murder of numerous victims. This type of murder does not always have the same motive, nor are the same methods used in all cases. In addition, it is evident that both the killers and their victims differ by social background, depending on the kind of multicide involved. There are three distinguishable types of multicide: genocide, serial murder and mass murder. While mass murder and serial killing have been extensively practiced in the United States, genocide is best illustrated by the non–American example of the Holocaust, the murder of the European Jews and others, between 1933 and 1945.

An example of genocide in the United States is the murder of the native Americans. As will be discussed in a later chapter, their murders do not really resemble the type of genocide practiced in Europe, despite the atrocities they represent.

Meanwhile, in order to understand genocide in its fullest measure, the Holocaust will be summarized, not only because it is the most outstanding example of deliberate killing of innocent persons in history, but also because the background and organization of that genocide follows all those principles which explain genocide in general; the Holocaust allows people to understand other forms of genocide as well. The Holocaust is a model for genocide everywhere because, unlike any other genocide (such as the killing of the Armenian Christians by the Turks between 1915 and 1922), the Holocaust encompasses every sociological variable associated with this kind of event. Whoever understands the Holocaust can then understand related genocides as well.

The word Holocaust is of Greek origin and means "whole fire." This word has since then been used to refer to innumerable other events that are far from the catastrophe to which the term originally attached. Many people now use the term "holocaust" to refer to any event that may be disconcerting to them or that may indeed be catastrophic to some. This overuse of the word tends to erase the special character of the European holocaust, which some call the Jewish Holocaust.

This author contends that it is a mistake to refer to these events as "Jewish," not only because millions of non–Jews were also murdered in the various camps set up for these purposes by the German Nazis, but also because the phrase "Jewish" makes it appear that only Jews need consider this problem. Genocide is a universal horror which should be addressed by everyone.

It is a matter of historical record that one-third of the world's Jewish population was murdered during the epoch 1933–1945. It is undoubtedly true, therefore, that in proportion to all others who were not Jewish and were also murdered, the Jewish population bore the brunt of these horrors. Nevertheless, these events dare not be consigned to Jewish history alone, not only because this would permit non–Jews to ignore these events, but also because of George Santayana's famous dictum: "Those who cannot remember the past are condemned to repeat it."[1]

In attempting to relate the story of these murders which collectively make up the Holocaust, this author relied, in the main, upon *The Holocaust* by Gilbert as well as similar books by Davidowicz and Levin.[2]

THE HOLOCAUST

Multicide on the scale perpetrated by the Nazis and their followers between 1933 and 1945 has not been equaled before or since. There may be those who now quibble over whether or not 11,000,000 people were actually murdered, or whether only nine to ten million met such a fate. Such arguments may be of concern to some but are not at issue here. The concern here is to describe the murders then committed and to use eyewitness accounts as much as possible so that the descriptions contained here are based on the dictum of the famous German historian Leopold von Ranke, who taught that history should be written "Wie es eigentlich gewesen ist" (as it actually happened).[3]

Shootings, Stabbings and Other Methods

On March 18, 1933, six weeks after the Nazi election victory in Germany, a baker's apprentice in Berlin by the name of Siegbert Kindermann was taken to Storm Trooper barracks there and "beaten to death. His body was then thrown out of a window into the street, a large swastika having been cut into his chest."[4]

Kindermann had openly agitated against the Nazi gangs which had beaten him before they were elected, and he had also taken them to court where they were convicted of assault. Upon reaching power, the Nazis took their revenge by committing the murder just described. From this example it would appear at first that only those who were known opponents of the government were murdered. However, that is far from the truth.

Hitler and his followers believed that anyone who had any Jewish background whatsoever should be murdered. Tens of thousands of Christians, therefore, who were in no way Jewish, were also murdered because they had Jewish parents or grandparents who had converted to Christianity and had raised them as Christians. To the Nazi mind that made no difference. Hitler had defined a "Jew" as anyone with so-called Jewish blood, meaning anyone who could never be a true "German" because he was not racially pure. In an orgy of hate, the Nazi party and their followers burnt synagogues, burned books by Jewish authors, beat and whipped innocent Jews in public and tore apart Jewish religious books and articles all across Europe.

At the beginning of World War II in September 1939, the Nazi invaders of Poland carried their hatred for Jews into that land, which at that time had a Jewish population of 3,000,000. This constituted ten percent of the Polish population. The brutality of these killings was unprecedented. For example, "at the village of Widawa, home of 100 Jewish families, the Germans ordered the local rabbi to burn his Holy Books. When he refused they burned him publicly with the scroll of the Holy Torah [Five Books of Moses] in his hands.... At Mielec, another Polish village, 35 Jews were taken to the local slaughterhouse and there burned alive. Another 25 were burned alive in the synagogue."[5]

Another example of such private brutality: ". . . a few Germans came upon the scene and began to beat their victim with rubber truncheons. They called a cab and tried to push him into it but he resisted vigorously. The Germans then tied his legs together with a rope, attached the end of the rope to the cab from behind, and ordered the driver to start. The unfortunate man's face struck the sharp stones of the pavement, dying them red with blood."

Other methods of torture and murder were invented. For example, in the winter of 1939–1940, the German invaders forced the Jews of Poland to transfer cakes of ice from one place to another without wearing gloves. "The terrible cold pierced the flesh," wrote one observer. Having moved the ice cakes under these horrible conditions, the palms of the hands of the victims became so frozen that their hands had to be amputated."[6]

It was however, hunger which killed more Jews in the Polish ghettos to which they had been confined by the Nazi invaders than anything else. A large number of Jews died of starvation while many others committed suicide to escape their torturers. Weakened by hunger, Jews could hardly defend themselves, for in addition to the German murderers they were hunted and brutalized by the native populations amidst whom they had been born.

When the Germans invaded Rumania, local Rumanian "Iron Guard" members, a Nazi organization, carried out some horrible murders which were described as follows: ". . . hundreds of Jews were taken to slaughterhouses and killed according to [Jewish] ritual practices in slaughtering animals. The bodies of those so murdered were then hung on meat hooks in the slaughterhouse with placards around them announcing 'Kosher Meat.'"[7] In Dubossary, 600 elderly Jews were driven into that town's eight synagogues. "Completely surrounded by Germans, the synagogues were then set afire. All 600 died an agonizing death."[8]

Many Jews were taken to execution in open pits as described by Schutzstaffel (SS) General Karl Wolff who recollected a visit by the head of the SS, Heinrich Himmler, to the "Operations Center" in Minsk. He recollected how Himmler, "asked to see a shooting operation." Here is his account of that operation:

> An open grave had been dug and they had to jump into this and lie face downwards. And sometimes, when one or two rows had already been shot, they had to lie on top of the people who had already been shot and then they were shot from the edge of the grave. And Himmler had never seen dead people before and in his curiosity he stood right up at the edge of this open grave – a sort of triangular hole – and was looking in.
>
> While he was looking in, Himmler had the deserved bad luck that from one or the other of the people who had been shot in the head he got a splash of brains on his coat, and I think it also splashed into his face, and he went very green and pale . . . ;

An organized massacre of Jews selected by German SS troops and Lithuanian police from a Polish ghetto was recorded by Dr. Helen Kutorgene:

> [A]t the Fort the condemned were stripped of their clothes, and in groups of 300 they were forced into the ditches. First they threw in the children. The women were shot at the edge of the ditch, after that it was the turn of the men. Many were covered while they were still alive. All the men doing the shooting were drunk. . . .
>
> One of the Lithuanians boasted . . . that he had dragged small Jewish children by the hair, stabbing them with the edge of his bayonet, and throwing them half-alive into the pits . . . the smallest children he just threw into the pit alive, because to kill all of them first "is too much work."[9]

Hermann Graebe was a German engineer who saw a death pit near the small Ukrainian town of Dubno and described it as follows:[10]

> Without screaming or weeping these people undressed, stood around in family groups, kissed each other, said farewells, and waited for the sign from the SS man who stood beside the pit with a whip in his hand. During the fifteen minutes I stood near, I heard no complaint or plea for mercy. I watched a family of about eight persons, a man and a woman both about 50, with their children about 20 to 24, and two grown up daughters about 28 or 29. An old woman with snow white hair was holding a one-year-old child and singing to it, tickling it. The child was cooing with delight. The couple were looking on with tears in their eyes. The father was holding the hand of a boy about ten years old and speaking to him softly; the boy was fighting his tears. The father pointed to the sky, stroked his head and seemed to explain something to him.
>
> At that moment the SS man at the pit started shouting something to his com-

rade. The latter counted off about 20 persons and instructed them to go behind the earth mound. Among them was the family I have just mentioned. I well remember a girl, slim with black hair, who, as she passed me, pointed to herself and said, "twenty-three." I walked around the mound and stood in front of a tremendous grave. People were closely wedged together and lying on top of each other so that only their heads were visible. Nearly all had blood running over their shoulders from their heads. Some of the people shot were still moving. Some were lifting their arms and turning their heads to show that they were still alive. The pit was nearly two-thirds full. I estimated that it already contained about a thousand people. I looked at the man who did the shooting. He was an SS man who sat at the edge of the narrow end of the pit, his feet dangling into the pit. He had a tommy-gun on his knees and was smoking a cigarette. The people, completely naked, went down some steps which were cut in the clay wall of the pit and clambered over the heads of the people lying there to the place to which the SS man directed them; some caressed those who were still alive and spoke to them in low voices.

Testimony concerning these mass murders was taken from some of the top commanders of the killing squads who accompanied the German army during its invasion of Poland in 1939 and again during and after the Russian campaign in 1941. These killing squads were called "Einsatzgruppen" by the Nazis, a word which means approximately "Special Commitment Group"—a group of persons particularly devoted to a cause. (The testimony referred to here was taken at the numerous war crimes trials beginning in 1945 at Nuremberg, Germany, and continued for many years in various German communities.) English translations of this German testimony are available because the United States armed services employed American translators who issued certificates of translation together with the English versions of such testimony.[11]

The following is a description of mass shootings and gassings as given in an Affidavit on November 25, 1945, by Otto Ohlendorf, Chief of the Security Service of the Main Office of the German Security Police. Ohlendorf relates that he was the commander of one of these "Einsatzgruppen" in Russia. He was told by the overall commander of the German SS that "an important part of our task consisted of the extermination of Jews—women, men and children. . . ."

Ohlendorf continued:

> The unit selected for this task would enter a village or city and order the prominent Jewish citizens to call together all Jews for the purpose of resettlement. They were requested to hand over their valuables to the leaders of the unit, and shortly before the execution to surrender their outer clothing. The men, women and children were led to a place of execution which in most cases was located next to a more deeply excavated anti-tank ditch. Then they were shot, kneeling or standing, and the corpses thrown into the ditch. I never permitted the shooting by individuals in the Group D, but ordered that several of the men should shoot at the same time in order to avoid direct, personal responsibility.

Paul Blobel was also a chief of a "Sonderkommando." His testimony, reprinted from the original English version as given in November 1945, was also published in *The Holocaust* by Fletcher.[12] Said Blobel during his interrogation:

I witnessed several mass executions, and in two cases I was ordered to direct the execution. In August or September of 1941 an execution took place near Korosten. 700 to 1,000 men were shot, and Dr. Rasch was present at the execution. I had divided my unit into a number of execution squads of 30 men each. First, the subordinated police of the Ukrainian militia, the population and the members of the "Sonderkommando" seized the people, and mass graves were prepared. Out of the total number of the persons designated for the execution, 15 men were led in each case to the brink of the mass grave, where they had to kneel down, their faces turned toward the grave. At that time, clothes and valuables were not yet collected. Later on this was changed. The execution squad was composed of men of the "Sonderkommando" 4A, the militia and the police. When the men were ready for the execution one of my leaders who was in charge of this execution squad gave the order to shoot. Since they were kneeling on the brink of the mass grave, the victims fell, as a rule, at once into the mass grave . . . . Each squad shot for about one hour and was then replaced.

Gassings

The gassing of masses of Jews and other persons in the eastern part of Europe was begun on a limited scale in December of 1941. One day after the attack on Pearl Harbor, on December 8, 1941, 80 Jews from the town of Kolo were transferred to a special van. The van set off toward a clearing in the woods . . . by the time the journey was over, the Jews were dead, gassed by exhaust fumes channeled back into the van. Their bodies were thrown out of the back of the van.

The mass murders by gassing were profitable to the murderers. As Gilbert describes, "the corpses would be placed carefully, side by side. Ukrainians and Germans, working in pairs, would pull out gold teeth and take off rings of the murdered Jews." If the rings did not come off easily they would cut off the entire finger. After the gold teeth and the rings had been taken, the corpses were buried.[13]

The slaughter of children was as common to the Nazi killers as the slaughter of adults. For example: "the Gestapo (Geheime Staats Polizei, or Secret State Police) sent German and White Russian policemen to search the ghetto. Reaching a children's nursery, they ordered the woman in charge . . . to take their children to the Jewish Council Building. . . . The order was a trap. On reaching a specially dug pit, . . . the children were seized by Germans and Ukrainians, and thrown alive into the deep sand. At that moment, several SS officers, . . . arrived [and] threw handfuls of sweets to the choking children. All the children perished in the sand."

Another example of the treatment of children by the Nazi killers is this experience reported in a German newspaper: "Moritz saw how SS men tore out the limbs of quaking babies and threw them into the fire." The same interview led to the recollection of a survivor concerning a Nazi who "threw little babies against a wall so often that their brains squirted out. . . ."[14]

Adolf Eichmann, one of the principal organizers of the Holocaust, described his experiences with mass gassings of Jews during his trial in Jerusalem. Here is his testimony as given to the Jerusalem courts:

There was a room . . . perhaps five times as large as this one. Perhaps it was only four times as big as the one in which I am sitting now. And Jews were inside. They were to strip and then a truck arrived where the doors open, and the van pulled up at a hut. The naked Jews were to enter. Then the doors were hermetically sealed and the car started . . . and then I saw the most breathtaking sight I have ever seen in my life.

The van was making for an open pit. The doors were flung open and corpses were cast out as if they were some animals — some beasts. They were hurled into the ditch. I also saw how the teeth were being extracted. . . ."[15]

Kurt Gerstein has perhaps given the most graphic description of the mass killings at the Belzec camp available. His description is quoted in the American edition of *The Trial of the Major War Criminals*.[16] Gerstein was chief of the Waffen SS Technical Disinfection Service and was called upon to advise the camp commander, Christian Wirth, concerning the disinfection of "large piles of clothing coming from Jews, Poles, Czechs, etc."[17] Gerstein came in the company of Professor Wilhelm Pfannenstiel, who was teaching Hygiene at the University of Marburg. Gerstein, watching with Wirth, is quoted as follows:

The following morning, a little before seven, there was an announcement. "The first train will arrive in ten minutes." A few minutes later, a train arrives from Lemberg: forty-five cars arrive with more than six thousand people; two hundred Ukrainians assigned to this work flung open the doors and drove the Jews out of the cars with leather whips.

A loudspeaker gave instructions: "Strip, even artificial limbs and glasses. Hand all money and valuables in at the 'valuables' window. Women and young girls to have their hair cut in the 'barber's hut.'" (A Sergeant told me: "From that they make something special for submarine crews.")

Then the march began. Barbed wire on both sides, in the rear two dozen Ukrainians with rifles. They drew near. Wirth and I found ourselves in front of the death chambers. Stark naked men, women, children and cripples passed by. A tall SS man in the corner called to the unfortunates in a loud minister's voice. "Nothing is going to hurt you! Just breathe deep and it will strenghten your lungs. It's a way to prevent contagious diseases. It's a good disinfectant."

They asked him what was going to happen and he answered: "The men will have to work, build houses and streets. The women won't have to do that. They will be busy with the housework and the kitchen."

This was the last hope for some of these poor people, enough to make them march toward the death-chambers without resistance. The majority knew everything; the smell betrayed it! They climbed a little wooden stair and entered the death-chambers, most of them silently, pushed by those behind them.

A Jewess of about forty with eyes like fire cursed the murderers: she disappeared into the gas chambers after being struck several times by Captain Wirth's whip. Many prayed; others asked: "Who will give us the water before we die?"

SS men pushed the men into the chambers. "Fill it up," Wirth ordered. Seven to eight hundred people in ninety-three square meters. The doors closed. Then I understood the reason for the "Heckenholt" sign. Heckenholt was the driver of the diesel, whose exhaust was to kill these poor unfortunates.

Heckenholt tried to start the motor. It wouldn't start! Captain Wirth came up.

You could see he was afraid because I was there to see the disaster. Yes, I saw everything and waited. My stopwatch clocked it all: fifty minutes. Seventy minutes and the diesel still would not start! The men were waiting in the gas-chambers. You could hear them weeping, "as though in a synagogue," said Professor Pfannenstiel, his eyes glued to the window in the wooden door.

Captain Wirth, furious, struck with his whip the Ukrainian who helped Heckenholt. The diesel engine started up after two hours and forty-nine minutes by my stopwatch. Twenty-five minutes passed. You could see through the window that many were already dead, for an electric light illuminated the interior of the room. All were dead after thirty-two minutes.

Jewish workers on the other side opened the doors. They had been promised their lives in return for doing this horrible work, plus a small percentage of the money and valuables collected. The people were still standing like columns of stone, with no room to fall or lean. Even in death you could tell the families, all holding hands. It was difficult to separate them while emptying the room for the next batch. The bodies were tossed out, blue, wet with sweat and urine, the legs smeared with excrement and menstrual blood. Two dozen workers were busy checking mouths which they opened with iron hooks. . . . Dentists knocked out gold teeth, bridges and crowns with hammers.

Captain Wirth stood in the middle of them. He was in his element and, showing me a big jam box filled with teeth, said "See the weight of the gold! Just from yesterday and the day before! You can't imagine what we find every day, dollars, diamonds, gold! You'll see!". . .

Then the bodies were thrown into big ditches near the gas-chambers, about 100 by 20 by 12 meters. After a few days the bodies swelled. . . .

When the swelling went down again, the bodies matted down again. They told me later they poured diesel oil over the bodies and burned them on railroad ties to make them disappear.

The testimony of Rudolf Hoess, taken at Nurenberg, Germany, on April 1, 1946, is of great importance here. Hoess was the commander of the Auschwitz camp in Poland where the greatest number of gassings had taken place and where mass murder by gassing had been brought to perfection. Hoess testified that he had previously served at the camp in Treblinka, also in Poland, but that he was made commander of the new camp at Oswiesciem, or Auschwitz as the Germans called it, in order to perfect the killing methods begun at Treblinka. Hoess relates in his testimony that he first used two old farm houses for the gassing operations. He attached signs to these houses which said: "To the showers," "To the baths," "To delousing," and "To disinfecting." The two farm houses had been made air proof by cementing the windows and constructing air-proof doors, except for a small hole through which the gas was blown in.

Hoess praised the quality of Cyclone B gas, which he obtained from German manufacturers of insect control materials. His statement about the gassings is as follows:

I saw it happen often enough. Generally it took from three to fifteen minutes. The effect varied. Wherever the gas was thrown into the chamber, the people standing right next to it were immediately anesthetized. It gradually spread to the far corners of the room and generally after five minutes one could no longer discern the human forms in the chamber. Everybody was dead after fifteen minutes and the chambers were opened after half an hour and not once was anybody alive at that time.[18]

Hoess also described the building of crematoria which could hold 2,000 people each. He showed how the trains bringing the victims were unloaded directly in front of these crematoria so that all who were deemed unable to work could be murdered at once upon arrival. Two doctors were used to decide who could work and who was to die. Among those who were sent to the gas chambers were almost all children, since these were not big enough to do the hard labor demanded by the German corporations who had established themselves at Auschwitz in order to use the free slave labor available there. Therefore, only a few children were allowed to live. Thus, only about 15 percent to 30 percent of any trainload of Jews arriving at Auschwitz was not gassed at once. Hoess explained that the bodies of those gassed and the bodies of those who had died on the trains during journeys that lasted as long as ten days, without food or water, were burned in pits dug for that purpose.

He also discussed how the gold from the mouths of the corpses was extracted and melted as was the gold from their rings and other jewelry. Finally he showed that the Christian Polish population never once complained about these murders, or even the smell of human flesh which invaded everything in the area for years.

In the failure to ever complain about these horrible deeds lies a good part of the explanation for this most dreadful of all crimes.

Multiple Murders of Children

The killing of adults did not satisfy the Nazi mania for murder. Relying on the doctrine that all Jews were "ungeziefer," i.e., vermin, they also killed 1,000,000 Jewish children. In that connection, Hoess testified that even small Jewish children were rightly killed because they constituted a future menace to the German people if allowed to grow up.[19] As already noted, 5,000,000 non–Jews were also murdered by the Nazi killing machine. However, there were very few children among them, because the theory of racial inferiority did not apply universally to non–Jews. Jewish children were murdered, however, because no Jew, no matter how young or old, had a right to exist according to the racial doctrines of the Nazi. Hence it seemed legitimate and right to kill small Jewish children who were, after all, the offspring of Jewish mothers and fathers. Examples of massive child murders abound and can be found in the literature. Gilbert quotes the experiences of Ben Edelbaum as follows:

> There was now only one truck waiting. A German soldier got into the truck behind the wheel and drove it closer to the hospital building wall. There was silence for a moment. No one could figure what was going to happen next.
> There were now about six or eight soldiers standing around the truck plus about eighteen people more positioned around the rope. . . . Suddenly, two Ger-

mans appeared in an upper story window and pushed it open. Seconds later, a naked baby was pushed over the ledge and dropped to its death directly into the truck below.

We were in such shock that at first few of us believed it was actually a live, new-born baby. We thought it was an object of some kind until we saw another and another being hurled out the window and into the waiting truck. . . .

The SS seemed to enjoy this bloody escapade. Just then the youngest of the bunch asked his superior if it was all right to catch one of those "little Jews" on his bayonet as it was coming down. His superior gave him permission, and the young SS butcher rolled up his rifle sleeve and caught the very next infant on his bayonet. The blood of the infant flowed down the knife unto the murderer's arm and into his sleeve. He tried his talent once more, and again he was successful in catching the wailing child on his sharp bayonet. He tried a third time but missed and gave up the whole game, complained it was getting too messy.[20]

In a publication entitled *This Is Artukovic* distributed by the government of Yugoslavia, the following is published on page 41 with reference to Miroslav Filipovic, an officer in the Croatian Nazi party (USTASHA):

He entered the classroom of the little village schoolroom wearing the USTASHI cap. He ordered the teacher, Mara Sunjic, to separate the Serbian Orthodox children from the Catholics. When she did that, not suspecting any evil, he slaughtered these Serbian children before the eyes of their little playmates. The children ran around the classroom with their throats slashed, blood spattering all around, their little faces contorted in pain and terror. Most of the remaining children went insane, while Mara Sunjic, once a strong healthy girl today lives and relives in horror that day.

This example serves to show that Serbs in Yugoslavia were also marked for death by the native collaborators of the Nazi invaders.

Mass Murder of the Serbs

On April 17, 1941, the Yugoslav army surrendered to Germany and the latter proceeded to divide Yugoslavia into several provinces according to language and/or religion. Thus, the Italian allies of Germany occupied Montenegro, Slovenia and Dalmatia. Hitler's Hungarian allies seized the Backa Plain in the north of Yugoslavia, the Bulgarians took Macedonia and parts of Serbia and Germany occupied the northern part of Slovenia.

Serbia was given a puppet government obedient to Hitler while Croatia was entirely handed to the Ustase party as a so-called "independent state." Thus, this party, now in control of Croatia by virtue of Nazi backing, let loose a reign of terror in Croatia only equaled by the Germans themselves. The targets of this terror were as usual, the Jews but also Serbs and Gypsies. The new prime minister of this pseudo-state was "Poglavnik" (Führer in German) Pavelic and the Minister of the Interior, Andrija Artukovic.

Directly upon assuming power, several concentration camps were established in Yugoslavia. In the Gradishka camp, children were not only starved to death because of their Serb, Jewish or Gypsy ethnicity but caustic soda was added to their food in order to exterminate them faster.

A survivor of the Ustashi terror, Ljubo Jadnak, relates his experiences of August 21, 1941, as follows:

> They started with one huge husky peasant who began singing an old historical heroic song of the Serbs. They put his head on the table and as he continued to sing they slit his throat and then the next squad moved in to smash his skull. I was paralyzed. "This is what you are getting" an USTASA screamed. USTASE surrounded us. There was absolutely no escape. Then the slaughter began. One group stabbed with knives, the other followed, smashing heads to make certain everyone was dead. Within a matter of minutes we stood in a lake of blood. Screams and wails, bodies dropping right and left. (*This Is Artukovic*, p. 26)

Jadnak escaped because he pretended to be dead and was loaded on a truck together with all the dead bodies murdered in the massacre described above. This took place inside the Church of Glina. The bodies were sent by truck to a huge burial pit, left unattended long enough for the eyewitness Jadnak to get out.

This author is personally acquainted with persons who saw these murders. Professor George Vid Tomashevich, who was born and grew up in Vocin, a small town in Northern Croatia near the Hungarian-Yugoslav border, relates that he and his family were forced to wear a red ribbon around their arm at all times after the so called "Independent State of Croatia" had been proclaimed by the Nazi invaders, so as to identify them as Serbs amidst a larger Croat majority. The purpose of the persecution of the Serbs was to force them to convert to Roman Catholicism, since the only difference between Serbs and Croats is religion. Their language is the same, but Serbs belong to the Serbian Orthodox Church. On pain of death, these conversions were demanded by the Ustasha government.

About one-third of all Serbs so threatened did indeed convert, although some of these converts were murdered anyway. Another third were expelled from their homes in Croatia and forcibly resettled in Serbia, and the rest were murdered. These murders were directed particularly at the Serb clergy for whom conversion was impossible. Therefore, the government of Yugoslavia has published a list of every rabbi and Serbian Orthodox priest slaughtered by the Croatian Ustasha regime.

The Ustashi murders were described in this fashion:

> The Ustashi introduced a totalitarian regime based upon brutal terrorism. Vast pogroms decimated the Jewish population. The treatment of Serbs and Croats who opposed the terrorists was just as harsh. Within the first six months of its rule, the Pavelic regime accounted for 300,000 victims.[21]

Concentration Camp Murders

Only those who survived the Nazi camps can truly appreciate the gratuitous brutality which accompanied the murders there committed. Even during the transportation to the camps the victims were "exposed to constant tortures of various kinds," says the famous psychologist Bruno Bettelheim in his book, *Surviving*.[22] Writes Bettelheim:

During the transportation, they [the prisoners] were exposed to constant tortures of various kinds. Many of these depended on the phantasy of the particular SS soldier in charge of a group of prisoners. Corporal punishment, consisting of whipping, kicking, slapping intermingled with shooting and wounding with the bayonet, alternated with tortures whose obvious goals was extreme exhaustion.[23]

Frida Weiss is one of those who remembered these horrors in 1979, and reported this scene to Saul S. Friedman, a professor at Youngstown State University in Ohio. Friedman interviewed 30 survivors of the Nazi era who happened to have settled in Youngstown and published their stories in a book called *Amcha*.

Said Weiss:

Mauthausen was a men's camp. At Mauthausen they took all our clothes away. They said they were going to disinfect them, boil them. But in the end I wound up with a man's undershirt, a man's shirt, a man's long johns, and a dress. That was in January. It was there I saw a man freeze to death. That was the most awful thing. He did something, probably stole something. So for punishment they left him naked. It was so cold, he got black, frozen. He wasn't tied but he couldn't run either because he was surrounded by SS with guns. He froze to death. Everybody had to see how he was dead. We didn't see him all the time. At "Appel" [a German word meaning roll call, pronounced like bell] we saw him. I just see that man. Somehow, maybe there is a guilty conscience that you help him. But who were we there? Everybody was so sick and so depressed already. . . .

They put us in barracks and there you could see already it was a death camp. You could see that people started to get sick. There was a lot of typhus. It was about a month and we both got typhus. It is something just like I had a machine in my head that was constantly going, grinding. I couldn't hear or see things. We were so sick we couldn't eat. We were full of lice. It was so dirty, I could pick lice from myself like that. We were dirty, sick and we didn't even have mats, only the floor. If you were lucky you had a corner where you could stretch out and nobody would kick you. And when they dealt out the ration of bread, they skipped a few because it was already the end.[24]

Rubin Literman, born in Plock, Poland, described in a taped interview how he lost all his rights, not only as a citizen of Poland, but as a human being, after the Nazi invasion of that land. Forced into a labor batallion he was ordered to wear a yellow badge with the inscription "Jude." His house was confiscated and he was forcibly moved into a "Ghetto," a small, overcrowded enclave. From there he was sent by cattle car, without food or water to the Skojisko camp where numerous of his fellow prisoners were worked to death. No medical care was given them. Yet, anyone who failed to report for work because of a fever was killed at once for shirking work.

This author has viewed numerous tapes in which survivors of these camps were interviewed and described their personal experiences, and has repeatedly spoken to numerous persons who survived these horrors as children and who saw their own family, including mothers and fathers, annihilated before their eyes. These interviews, although often of poor literary quality because of language difficulties, corroborate all those descriptions of these murders already discussed above.

MASS MURDER OF THE ARMENIANS

In 1939, the dictator of Germany, Adolf Hitler, spoke to his top commanders at a meeting in Poland, which the German army had just invaded. He discussed his order to kill all Polish Jews. Thereupon someone asked him what the world might say or do if this dreadful order were carried out. Said Hitler: "Who cares about the Armenians today?"[25]

This was indeed a shrewd and appropriate answer. The Armenians, Christian by religion and Turks by birth and nationality, had been mass murdered by the Turkish government and population only 17 years before Hitler made these remarks. Indeed, hardly anyone remembered them in 1939 and no one helped them in 1922. In an excellent account of that genocide, Abraham H. Hartunian describes these massacres:

> The Turks had begun to set Armenian houses and buildings afire. Even Turkish buildings were being burned if it seemed possible thus to spread the blaze to the Armenian quarters [of the city]. The flames rose everywhere; the city glowed beneath their light. From every side, bullets where incessantly whizzing like hail, and no one knew when he might be hit. The fire horrified us. It was impossible to withstand it. . . . . No horrors can ever parallel the experience of the Armenians in the Armenian quarters and in their houses.[26]

These massacres were witnessed by foreign nationals in Turkey at the time. Most frequently these eyewitnesses were Germans because Turkey was an ally of Germany during the First World War, and therefore many Germans were visiting Turkey for military and economic reasons. Some of the German eyewitness accounts are summarized herewith:[27]

> a. Seven hundred of the Christian inhabitants of the town of Mardin (mostly Armenians) and the Armenian bishop of Mardin were slaughtered like lambs. So said the German Consul Holstein who witnessed these events.
> b. On the 17th and 27th of July, 1915, the German consul of Allepo, Rossler, reported that corpses, all tied together in pairs were being swept along the Euphrates River.
> c. All the Christians in the town of Jerizeh were butchered.
> d. According to the Swedish sisters Alma Johanssen and Bodil Bjorn, the Turkish army captured the town of Mush and then herded hundreds of Armenian women and children into houses and burnt the houses with the people inside.
> e. Herr Greif, a German resident of Aleppo, reported corpses of violated women lying about naked in heaps on the railway embankment at Tell-Abiad. . . .
> f. Herr Spiecker of Aleppo had seen Turks tie Armenian men together, fire several volleys of small shot into the human mass with fowling-pieces and go off laughing while their victims died in frightful convulsions.[28]

Unending examples of additional horrors of this kind could be given here. The literature concerning the Armenian-Christian genocide is not nearly as extensive as the literature concerning the Jewish genocide. The reasons are probably these:

1. There are many more Jewish persons with the education necessary to write and to publish than is true of Armenians competent to write and to publish.

2. The Armenian genocide took place earlier than the Jewish genocide. Therefore there were fewer publishing opportunities at that time than later. Furthermore, movie equipment was far more available to the Nazi killers than to the Turks. Also, the Germans were far more adept and willing to make movies of their own crimes than were the Turks of 1915–1922.

3. Some of the Nazi killers were tried for their crimes at Nuremberg in 1945–1946 and later. This never happened to the Turkish killers. Hence there is no truly good account of the Armenian killings by the Turks as there is of the German atrocities against the Jews and so many others, because there is no court transcript as in the case of the Nazis.

4. There are more persons in the Jewish community in America than there are Armenians. Therefore publications of these murders receives a wider audience in America than do the murders of the Armenians.

While there are, undoubtedly, differences between the Armenian Holocaust and the Jewish Holocaust, and while there are yet other differences between the horrors suffered by both these peoples and others, such as the Cambodians who were massacred by their own government or the native Americans of the Niagara peninsula murdered by the Iroquois Nation in the 16th century, there are nevertheless some general principles of human conduct which underlie *all* genocide.

It is a major mistake to overlook the universal responsibility of all people for genocide by overemphasizing the ethnicity of the victims and the perpetrators. This author believes that everyone is involved and that the problem of genocide, and for that matter the problem of homicide, should concern all those who so far have not been victims. Said Pastor Niemoller, a German Lutheran who was imprisoned by the Nazi government for resisting the persecution of the Jews:

> First they came for the Socialists, but I did not speak out because I was not a socialist. Then they came for the trade unionists and I did not speak out because I was not a trade unionist. Then they came for the Jews and I did not speak out because I was not a Jew. Then they came for me and there was no one left to speak for me.[29]

Richard G. Hovannisian, in his book *The Armenian Genocide in Perspective*,[30] lists six propositions derived from the notion of marginality and from Erikson's psychology, which he thinks determine genocide. These are:

1. Identity crises—these are conditions which cause many people to wonder who they are.

2. Marginality—the new elite, formed from the identity crisis, is unable to escape the feeling that they belong nowhere.

3. New identity—those who are confused about who they are compensate for this by assuming extreme positions, such as belonging to the Nazi party with all its uniforms, songs, violent speeches, actual violence and division of the world into friends and enemies.

4. Projection of patienthood—the belief by the elite that they must solve for

everyone all the problems they really could not solve for themselves and still cannot overcome.

5. Patienthood of the masses — wide segments of the public support the elite and its effort to make patients out of everyone.

6. Medium of salvation — genocide becomes the medium of salvation. By mass murder of the out-group, the elite and its supporters discover who they are. The out-group is painted in horrid terms and therefore the in-group finally has an enemy who makes them feel that they are somebody in comparison to the awful out-group, for example, Jews among the Europeans and Christians among the Turks.

Hovannisian also points out that there are some striking similarities in the manner in which the Turkish government at first, and the German government later, murdered its minority victims. In both cases these governments used organization, planning, bureaucratic efficiency, technology and ideology to achieve their goal of total annihilation. [31]

Helen Fein has explained genocide in somewhat more sociological terms. [32] Her main emphasis is on the isolation suffered by both the Jews of Eastern Europe and Germany as well as the isolation of the Armenians in Turkey. She shows in detail that social isolation preceded genocide in both cases and that social integration prevents this. That is, of course, understandable, since the group or person who is isolated seems strange, nonhuman, foreign and dangerous. Exactly the opposite appears to be true of our friends. It is for this reason that sociologists have discovered that people who live in high crime areas nevertheless believe that low crime areas in which they do not live and where they know no one are more dangerous than their own neighborhood.

Fein further shows that in addition to social isolation, genocide is fostered by the bureaucratic steps taken to achieve it. Thus, each step in the process of attaining genocide becomes the cause of the next step. For example, the Nazi government fired all Jews from government jobs as early as 1933, and prohibited Jews from earning a livelihood in numerous occupations of a private sort. This led next to a boycott of all Jewish-owned stores not only by government officials, but also by many in the population who "didn't want to get involved"; the ensuing poverty of the Jewish population then led to their willingness to do forced labor for very small wages; that in turn led to Jewish undernourishment and starvation; that in turn led to their registration to obtain at least some food; the registration made it possible to round up the weakened victims and ship them to the camps where they were gassed because they were unfit for work.

All of these measures finally led to the two pre-conditions for genocide: the victim is seen as a different species, and the victim does not have the protection of any nation, government or state. [33] Finally, then, the victims are seen as being outside the universe of obligation which binds all men together. Thus, Christians in Europe felt no obligation towards their Jewish fellow-citizens while Moslem Turks had the same attitude toward the Christian Armenians among them.

Everett C. Hughes, writing in *Social Problems* in 1962, came to a similar conclusion. He says:

The greater the social distance from us, the more we leave in the hands of others (agents) a sort of mandate by default to deal with them (i.e., the out-group) on our behalf . . . although we profess to believe that they should not suffer restrictions or disadvantages. And here it is that the whole matter of our professed and possible deeper and unprofessed wishes comes up for consideration. . . .

It is, finally, not unjust to say that the agents were at least working in the direction of the wishes of many people, although they may have gone beyond the wishes of most.[34]

This is one more explanation of genocide. In one word, "segregation" is seen as the catalyst for such murders.

Finally, there are theological explanations for genocide. Writing in *The Christian Century*, the theologian Carl D. Evans[35] recites the sorry history of Christian complicity in what is usually called "Anti-Semitism," the belief that Jews are damned by God and may therefore be persecuted with impunity. This belief is very ancient. It received its current name however, when a German writer, Wilhelm Marr, sought to place anti–Jewish religious hatred on a so-called scientific basis and therefore coined this phrase in the late 19th century on the false grounds that Jews belong to a so-called Semitic race and are not merely adherents of a religion. The word "Semitic" refers to the son of Noah, Sem, who, according to the Bible, travelled north from Mt. Ararat and became the father of all peoples not living in Africa. His brother Ham reputedly moved there. Hence, anthropologists have called African languages Hamitic and Hebrew and other Middle Eastern languages, Semitic. Since Jews use some Hebrew in their religious services, some people came to view all Jews as Semites, although in fact, only the Israeli Jews and the Arabs are Semitic speakers.

Evans continues and shows that numerous Christian writings called for the hatred of Jews, and that others deliberately or unknowingly slandered the Jewish religion, thus making it appear legitimate and divinely sanctioned to commit atrocities against Jews.

In 1961, the World Council of Churches, a Christian organization encompassing all non–Roman Catholic Christians, adopted a statement on the subject of guilt for "anti–Semitism." In 1965, the Vatican also adopted a document forcefully rejecting anti–Jewish hatred as a Christian attitude. Both groups published immense amounts of material since then, documenting the complicity of Christians in the Nazi murders and restructuring their teachings concerning Jews and other non–Christians so as to avoid any possible further interpretations which might seem to some to legitimize such hatred and such conduct.[36]

This then, is a religious explanation of genocide. There are, of course, innumerable other explanations for genocide. None satisfy everyone as they range from abnormal psychiatry to sociology and theology.

Another example of genocide, again with numerous explanations, was the mass killing of several hundred Sioux men, women and children on December 29, 1890, at Wounded Knee Creek, South Dakota. These native Americans were "indiscriminately killed by U.S. Army troops, and their bodies left to the winter snows."[37]

This was, of course, not the only massacre of native Americans during the centuries of American expansion to the West Coast. On the contrary; many such killings occurred all the time in this country until this very century.

Nevertheless, the genocide of the American Indian was not the official policy of the United States, as no deliberate plans for genocide were ever made in this country and total annihilation was never planned by this government. In fact, a detailed review of the battle at Wounded Knee Creek shows that unlike the Jews and Armenians, the Indians at that battle were armed, fought back and were able to inflict some casualties themselves. Furthermore, the U.S. Army did not intend to conduct a mass murder that day but became involved in this massacre as a result of a fire fight and not because of a desire to murder indiscriminately.[38]

Now, murder is part of our history and, as we have already seen in the first three chapters, continues unabated to this day. We may wonder whether there are Americans as brutal as the Nazi guards whom we described in this chapter, or whether cruelty and sadism are confined only to Germans and Turks. Hughes points out that an easy answer to that question would be "[to] . . . attribute to them [the Germans] some special . . . penchant for sadistic cruelty . . . . Pushed to its extreme, this . . . simply makes us, rather than the Germans the superior race. It is the Nazi tune, put to words of our own."[39] Therefore, it is entirely possible that the people about to be described in the next chapter might have been willing to do some of the things contained in this chapter.

I now turn to mass murder and serial murder, two types of multicide known in the United States and, unfortunately, on the increase here over the last fifty years.

5. Serial Killings and Mass Murder

THE "GEOGRAPHICALLY STABLE" SERIAL KILLER

When John Wayne Gacy was arrested for murder on December 21, 1978, he had killed more victims in any one place than any other American before him. There are, however, more mobile killers who kill their victims in various and numerous places and far exceed the record Gacy left behind.

Before his arrest on that December day, Gacy visited a number of his friends and told them that he had informed his lawyer that he had killed about 30 boys. His friends, Ronald Rohde, David Cram and Michael Rossi, testified at his trial that he made this confession. That day, police found the first of 29 bodies buried in the crawl space under his home in Des Plaines, Illinois. Later, the police found yet another four bodies in the Des Plaines River where Gacy had tossed them from a nearby bridge. This brought the total of his victims to 33. On March 13, 1980, Gacy was convicted of all 33 murders and sentenced to death at the conclusion of a death penalty hearing as required by Illinois law.

The reason for Gacy's arrest was that a 15-year-old boy, Robert Piest, was missing and the police investigated all homes and places where Piest was known to have been for any reason. While one of the two officers visiting Gacy's house used the washroom in the house, he smelled the "unmistakable odor" of decaying human flesh.[1] The smell had come through the air blowing from a heating duct. The motive for all of these murders may be the subject of conjecture eternally. As usual, psychiatrists for both the defense and the prosecution argued endlessly whether or not Gacy is "insane." This argument is carried on in every sensational murder trial, but this defense seldom succeeds.[2]

The facts of Gacy's crimes are these: Gacy, although at one time married and divorced, is a bisexual. In order to gain access to young boys and some men for his sexual purposes, Gacy induced youngsters to work for his contractor's business at unusually high wages. In fact, Gacy promised to pay 15-year-old Robert Piest twice as much to work for him than he was making as an employee in a local drug store.

Piest went to Gacy's home to talk about the job but never returned because Gacy had sexually tortured and abused the boy and then placed a rope around his neck tying a series of knots and inserting a stick between the knots. This served as a garrote, so that, "as the victim would convulse, the rope would then tighten around his neck."[3] Gacy did not only attack boys; he also killed adults. Thus, 27-year-old Jeffrey Rignall testified at Gacy's trial that Gacy drove up to him as he was walking on a Chicago street in March of 1978. Gacy offered him a ride and a marijuana cigarette. When Rignall had entered the car, Gacy pushed a chloroformed rag into his face. After Rignall lost consciousness, Gacy drove Rignall to his house, assaulted him sexually, using chloroform repeatedly. Thereafter, Rignall was driven to a park and dumped at the base of a statue. Through his own efforts Rignall discovered that his attacker was Gacy. Thereupon he accepted a $3,000 settlement for expenses in connection with liver damage and facial burns sustained from the exposure to chloroform and injuries to his rectum.

Similarly, 19-year-old Robert Donnelly was abused by Gacy, who posed as a policeman and told Donnelly to get into his car as Donnelly was waiting for a bus. Gacy handcuffed Donnelly, drove him to his house, abused him sexually and not only threatened him repeatedly with a gun, but also tried to drown him in his bathtub. Thereafter, he drove Donnelly to a department store and released him. When Donnelly filed a complaint with the police about this incident, the police refused to believe him and would not process the complaint against Gacy.[4]

Numerous other incidents of homosexual rape and assault were discovered by the police after Gacy was arrested. In all these cases, the victims survived brutal attacks but failed to complain or were not taken seriously by the police when they did complain. It is noteworthy here that the "blame the victim" mentality, which has for so long prevented women from getting adequate action from the criminal justice system in cases of rape, also applies to men and boys.[5]

The testimony of two of Gacy's victims who survived a visit to his house has been described. The evidence shows, however, that Gacy habitually cruised around an area known in Chicago as "bug house square"; that he picked up male prostitutes who agreed to come to his house for money; that he told them he liked to play the clown and would show them his "rope trick"; that he then used the rope to garrote the victim and kill him after using him sexually. Gacy did not go unnoticed throughout all the years of this behavior. In fact, he was indicted by a grand jury for forcing two teen-age boys into committing sexual acts with him, but no trial was ever held and the indictment was dropped.[6]

The story of John Wayne Gacy is unfortunately not unique. Gacy is a "serial killer," in other words, he killed numerous victims over a long period of time. Richard Ramirez is another infamous serial killer, and was convicted of murdering 15 victims in the Los Angeles area between June 1984 and August 1985. Known as "the Night Stalker," Ramirez was 25 years old at the time of his arrest in 1985. His previous convictions included five attempted murders, 17 burglaries, four robberies, six rapes, four acts of oral copulation, six acts of sodomy, three lewd acts on children and two kidnappings.[7] According to sheriff's deputy Jim Ellis, who was guarding Ramirez in his jail cell before his trial, Ramirez told him, "I love to watch people die." According to Ellis, Ramirez also told him that he used a camera and set the timer after he had mortally injured his victims so that he could pose next to the dying person and enjoy the picture later.[8]

Gacy and Ramirez killed all of their victims in the same general area where they lived; consequently they are known as "geographically stable" killers. The same is true of William Bonin who killed 14 boys and young men during the years 1979 and 1980. He abandoned their bodies near the freeways of the Los Angeles area. He was sentenced to death in 1982.

Patrick Wayne Kearney, an engineer, was convicted in 1977 of killing 21 boys and men. He had dismembered the bodies and stuffed them in trash bags which he deposited all over Southern California.

In May 1978, David Berkowitz of New York City was convicted as the ".44 caliber killer," also known as "Son of Sam." He had committed at least six murders in the course of a year.

Juan Corona was convicted in 1982 of murdering at least 25 itinerant farm workers, whose bodies he hacked to pieces. Although his crimes occurred in 1970 and 1971, he was not finally sentenced until 1982 because his first trial was overturned on appeal.

In 1958, Charles Starkweather slaughtered ten people in Nebraska and Wyoming by knife and gun as he traveled about and killed at random. He was electrocuted on June 25, 1959.

These and other serial killings have occupied the attention of the media the last two decades. While all their cases cannot be reviewed, the careers of Mark Essex and Albert DeSalvo, also known as "The Boston Strangler" whose crimes were actually made into a movie, will be presented here.

DeSalvo and Essex are of particular interest because they represent, better than any of the other serial killers so far mentioned, the attitude of class warfare which seems to be a principal motive in so many serial murders.

Multiple murderers differ from ordinary, one-on-one killers in several ways. Principally, the serial killer believes that he has a mission to fulfill and that this mission is the elimination of a certain class of people from the world. Having decided that a class of people is undesirable, the serial killer believes that he is at war with that class and entitled to murder (kill in warfare) all who belong to that class.

Some serial killers have murdered all the prostitutes they could find in order to rid the world of that "despicable" group of persons. Others have killed only Roman Catholics, or only policemen, or only any other category. In this sense, the Nazi murders discussed in the previous chapter follow the pattern of other serial killings, in that Jews were defined as "undesirable," as were Serbs, Gypsies, homosexuals, etc.[9]

DeSalvo began his killing career on June 14, 1962. On that day he drove to Boston, went to a middle class neighborhood, and knocked at several doors at random. When Anna Slesers, a 55-year-old Latvian immigrant, answered, he represented himself as a workman who had been ordered to fix something in her apartment. She led him to the bathroom to show him some work that indeed had to be done. Walking behind her, DeSalvo hit her on the head with a lead weight, placed a belt around the neck of the unconscious woman, and strangled her. Although DeSalvo claimed to have had intercourse with the woman before she died, subsequent investigation showed that this was not the case. However, the cord of the victim's housecoat had been knotted tightly around her neck. Her apartment had been ransacked badly, but according to her son, nothing belonging to the victim had been taken.

On June 28, two days later, DeSalvo killed 85-year-old Mary Mullen, using the same stratagem. This time, after gaining entrance to her apartment, he brought his arm around her neck from behind and squeezed. In an instant she dropped dead. DeSalvo murdered several women in this fashion until he reached his tenth victim, 23-year-old Beverly Samans.

Again he entered her apartment by posing as a maintenance man. This time, however, he brandished a knife almost at once and then forced her into the bedroom. He laid her down on the bed, forced a gag into her mouth and tied her wrists behind her, after first placing a blindfold over her eyes. Here is his description of that murder as reported in the book by Gerold Frank, *The Boston Strangler.*[10]

> Then I was going to have intercourse with her, . . . and she began talking. "You promised, you said you wouldn't do it to me, don't, don't, I'll get pregnant." The words kept coming and coming. . . . I can still hear her saying: "Don't do it—don't do that to me" . . . she made me feel so unclean, the way she talked to me. . . . No matter what I did she didn't like it . . . she started to get loud. . . . She kept yelling . . . and I stabbed her. Once I did it once . . . I couldn't stop. . . . I reached over, got the knife . . . and I stabbed her in the throat. She kept saying something. I grabbed the knife in my left hand and held the tip of the breast and I went down, two times, hard . . . she moved and the next thing you know, blood all over the place. . . . I kept hitting her and hitting her with that damn knife. . . . I stabbed her two times in the breast, too. I hit her and hit her and hit her. Why? That's what I am trying to tell you. . . . It was just like my Irmgard [DeSalvo's wife].

Beverly Samans was found two days later, a stocking tied around her neck, a scarf binding her wrists. She had suffered 22 stab wounds.

DeSalvo continued his horrible career until January 4, 1964, when he murdered his thirteenth victim, 19-year-old Mary Sullivan. That year, DeSalvo was placed into an institution as a "mental patient" because of his conviction on a rape charge. He was not suspected of being the Boston Strangler until he confessed to these murders while at the Bridgewater State Hospital.

How can these murders be explained? Once more, as in so many other cases, psychiatry tried to explain all of this by constant referral to such phrases as "psychopathic tendencies," "polymorphous and perverse inclinations," "fantasies of grandeur and omnipotence," and many other phrases.[11]

It is, however, noteworthy that DeSalvo always killed women of the middle class. Having been raised in the poorest section of Boston by an alcoholic and abusive father who once broke his mother's fingers one by one, he viewed his lower middle class wife and the women he murdered as socially above him. His purpose was to "get even" with that social class, to avenge the manner in which he believed women in that social class were looking down on him.

Elliott Leyton, in his book *Compulsive Killers,* argues that DeSalvo could have used force to enter his victim's apartments, but instead always used a trick or a ruse.

Leyton interprets this manner of gaining entry as DeSalvo's wish "to put one over on high class people." Says Leyton: "his killings were all in bourgeois areas . . . which provided him [DeSalvo] with lower middle class targets. They were middle class enough to provoke his retribution. . . . As with all our multiple murderers, he attacked a very specific social category, a narrow band in a stratified society, the segment that represented all those who oppressed, excluded and annulled him." Thus, to DeSalvo, the middle class represented a totally different kind of human being who had no right to exist.[12]

Anyone who has read the life of Adolf Hitler (see particularly *Hitler* by Joachim Fest and *Adolf Hitler* by John Toland)[13] must be struck with the great similarity in motive between Hitler and American multiple killers, particularly DeSalvo. Like Hitler and some of his most fanatic followers, DeSalvo never took any of the possessions of his victims. This was of course not true of the concentration camp killers who did not necessarily believe in Nazi doctrines, but enjoyed killing and wanted to get rich. His murders, and those of Hitler, were not for pecuniary gain, but for the achievement of a life goal, a cause. The cause was the elimination of a certain class of people. This was also the reason for Hitler's tremendous resentment of the middle class whom he wished to join and who would not let him in. This is in line with the previous observation (page 72) with reference to the motives for genocide on the part of the Nazi and Turkish perpetrators, namely, that the *victim is seen as a different species.*

It was this belief, namely that whites are a different species of mankind who need to be eliminated, that drove Mark Essex to commit the most spectacular public killings in the history of New Orleans. Mark Essex was an unusual killer in every respect. He is one of the few black mass murderers or serial killers in American history. Two others are Wayne Williams of Atlanta, and David Burke, who shot into an airliner in California causing over 40 deaths, including his own.

THE STORY OF MARK ESSEX

Before he was killed himself, Mark Essex had murdered Paul Pernisiaro, Dr. Robert Steagall and his wife, Mrs. Elizabeth Steagall, Louis Sirgo, Phillip Coleman, Frank Schneider, Walter Collins, Alfred Harrell and Paul Persigo. In addition, the police had killed Edwin Hosli because of the actions of Essex. Thus, Mark Essex was responsible for ten deaths. He also wounded ten other people while attempting to kill them and the police wounded nine others, again because of his actions. Mark Essex was born in Emporia, Kansas. Until he enlisted in the Navy in 1969 he lived and went to school there. Throughout all of his life in Emporia, he had never encountered the kind of racism so prevalent in American society generally and particularly vicious in the armed services, at least at that time.

Before August 1970 when he was insulted on the naval base where he was stationed, Essex never encountered racial hatred of this kind. In the Navy, however, he became the object of racial harassment on a daily basis. Consequently he went AWOL (absent without leave). He could no longer endure the mistreatment he received despite his excellent performance as a dental assistant at the base where he was stationed. As a punishment he was not only jailed for a time but expelled from the Navy, as if he were at fault. He believed that the Navy was blaming the victim, himself, and that the entire United States government, and for that matter all whites, were his enemies. He did, of course, have some cause to think so.

While in the Navy, Essex learned how to use guns. When he moved to New York City after his separation from the Navy he joined the Black Panthers, a political party of black activists, particularly violent in the seventies. By the time he left New York and moved to New Orleans, he had read a number of books promising violence against whites as oppressors of the black minority. This was in August of 1972 when he attended a vending machine repair school at government expense, and there met Rodney Frank, a militant black ex–Navy man. Influenced in part by Frank and his Navy experiences, Essex decided to abandon the repair school.

A fatal decision was concurrently announced by the chief of police in New Orleans. The chief promised to "shoot to kill" any rioters who were then plaguing New Orleans, similar to activity in other American cities. Although the chief said nothing about race in his order, the black community believed that the order meant them. And so, when the police killed two black Southern University students within a day after the order was published, and when nothing was done by any authority to punish the police for this killing, Essex decided to kill the police in revenge.

On New Years Eve, 1973, Essex secreted himself near the New Orleans police lockup. When two police recruits became visible to him he fired seven blasts from his .44 magnum carbine at them, killing Al Harrell and wounding the other man. The police then made every effort to find him but were unsuccessful. And so, beginning January 7, 1973, Essex put his plan into effect. He bought an additional rifle and a lot of ammunition, planning to kill police at will. But when he learned that a grocer, Paul Pernisiaro had told the police about a razor he bought from him, he went to Pernisiaro's store and killed him.

He thereupon stole a car and drove downtown where he decided to enter the Howard Johnson Hotel. Once inside he walked into a room occupied by Dr. and Mrs. Robert Steagall. He killed the Steagalls and then set the curtains afire. In addition he set eight more fires on the eighth and ninth floors of the hotel, bringing two hotel employees, Frank Schneider and Walter Collins, the general manager, upstairs to investigate the fires. Essex shot them and killed them both. He then went on the balcony of the hotel room and shot at firemen called to put out the fires he had set. He wounded one of them who subsequently had to have his arm amputated. Four hundred police then surrounded the hotel. When one of them, Charles Arnold, went to the tenth floor of a building across the street from the hotel, Essex shot him in the face as he opened a window. Essex then shot at Robert Beamish who was on the swimming pool deck. Beamish fell into the pool with a serious stomach wound. A panic resulted among the police: they fired at will into the hotel and at the firemen, who consequently could not put out the fires set by Essex.

Meanwhile, a large crowd of citizens accumulated in the streets. Several blacks in the crowd were observed to have cheered Essex with cries of "right on." Essex kept on shooting and hit patrolman Ken Solis who was gravely wounded. When

Sgt. Palmisano tried to help Solis, Essex shot but did not kill him. He did, however, succeed in killing Phil Coleman who also tried to help Solis, and then killed patrolman Paul Persigo as well.

Essex now fired from the roof of the hotel and killed and wounded several others, while the police, to the yelling and screaming of onlookers, fired at will into all the hotel windows. Assistant chief of police Louis Sergo was killed coming up to the eleventh floor in an effort to get at Essex on the roof. Policeman Larry Arthur was shot when the police finally did enter the roof. Many black citizens shouted "kill the pigs" as the police used a helicopter and from there finally shot and killed Essex.

This is another example of mass murder for a "cause," as was the Jonestown massacre, which did not occur in the United States, and the genocides discussed earlier. Essex knew, of course, that he could not survive. But his anger at the injuries he had suffered made his actions worthwhile to him. Some in the black community regard Essex as a hero.[14]

THE GEOGRAPHICALLY TRANSIENT SERIAL KILLER

"Geographically stable" serial killers have been dealt with so far. There are, however, also some killers who travel from place to place and kill within a category of perceived "non-persons" all those who in their judgment deserve death. Such killers are known as "geographically transient," thus gaining the advantage that their murders occur in as many police jurisdictions as they have victims. This makes it very difficult for law enforcement officials to catch up with them, making them even more dangerous than the geographically stable serial killer.

No geographically transient killer has attracted more attention than Theodore "Ted" Bundy. Like DeSalvo, he is the subject of a movie and several books. (See, for example, *Ted Bundy: The Killer Next Door* by Stephen Winn and David Merrill and *Bundy: The Deliberate Stranger* by Richard W. Larsen.)[15] While only 19 of Bundy's murder victims have ever been identified, a number far fewer than those killed by Gacy, this author nevertheless considers Bundy the most prolific killer of them all. This is so because Bundy not only insisted that he killed many more, but because police suspect that he indeed did so, even though they cannot prove any additional murderous activities on his part. This is reasonable not only because Bundy generally left his victims' bodies outdoors where animals mutilated them to a point beyond recognition, but also because he has been executed in Florida and no particular advantage could be gained by proving any additional killings by him, at least from the criminal justice point of view.

While the bodies of most of Bundy's victims were found and forensic examinations determined the cause of death, such as "bludgeoned," seven of Bundy's victims were never found. They had disappeared and became known as Bundy's victims only after he was apprehended in Florida and confessed to having killed these women.

Following is a list of Bundy's victims and the places in which they were killed.

This list illustrates the high mobility of this serial killer, and also serves to show the length of time it took law enforcement to apprehend him, precisely because of the manner in which he moved across the country. It is important to note that a number of Bundy's victims survived, so that this list is short of the number he actually attacked, but did not succeed in killing.

Of the five women who survived, one lived in the Seattle area, one in Bountiful, Utah, and three were students in Tallahassee, Florida. Of these, Mary Adams survived after several months in a coma, having been badly battered in her basement bedroom; Carol DeRonch escaped from Bundy's car as he tried to abduct her, and Kathy Kleiner, Karen Chandler and Cheryl Thomas all survived attacks in Florida.

Theodore "Ted" Bundy's Murder Victims by Date and Place of Death

(Source: *Serial Murder* by Ronald M. Holmes and James DeBurger)

Name of Victim	Age	Place of Murder	Year	Date
Lynda Ann Healy	21	Seattle, Washington	1974	February 1
Donna Gail Manson	19	Olympia, Washington	1974	March 12
Susan Rancourt	18	Ellensburg, Washington	1974	April 17
Roberta Kathy Park	22	Seattle, Washington	1974	May 6
Brenda Ball	22	Burien, Washington	1974	June 1
Georgeann Hawkins	18	Seattle, Washington	1974	June 11
Janice Ott	23	Lake Sammamish, WA	1974	July 14
Denise Naslund	19	Lake Sammamish, WA	1974	July 14
Carol Valenzuela	20	Vancouver, Washington	1974	August 2
Nancy Wilcox	16	Holladay, Utah	1974	October 2
Melissa Smith	17	Midvale, Utah	1974	October 18
Laura Aime	17	Lehi, Utah	1974	October 31
Debra Kent	17	Bountiful, Utah	1974	November 8
Caryn Campbell	23	Snowmass, Colorado	1975	January 12
Julie Cunningham	26	Vail, Colorado	1975	March 15
Denise Oliverson	25	Grand Junction, CO	1975	April 6
Nancy Baird	21	Farmington, Utah	1975	July 1
Lisa Levy	20	Tallahassee, Florida	1978	January 15
Margaret Bowman	21	Tallahassee, Florida	1978	January 15
Kimberly Leach	12	Lake City, Florida	1978	February 9

Ted Bundy was a charming and good looking man. This is a verdict which all who have known him agree upon. A college graduate, Bundy impressed everyone so much that he became involved in the election campaign of the former governor of Washington, Dan Evans, who wrote a recommendation for Bundy asking that Bundy be accepted at the Utah University College of Law. This was a great misfortune for the young women in Salt Lake City, for as soon as Bundy had entered that school, the murder of such women stopped in the Seattle area and began in the Salt Lake City area. Let us now take a look at some of the crimes committed by

Bundy. One way to do this, after so long a time, is to see these crimes from the viewpoint of the investigators who first discovered the victims. Such an account is given by Stephen G. Michaud and Hugh Aynesworth in their book, *The Only Living Witness.*[16]

> On Saturday, March 1, 1975, a call came in to [Detective] Bob Keppel's office. Two forestry students, he was told, had stumbled onto a skull in the wilds ten miles east of Issaquah, four miles to the south of U.S. 90. The discovery had been made on the lower slopes of Taylor Mountain, near the town of North Bend [Washington].
>
> Keppel gathered up his records, the X-rays and dental charts he'd collected and studied since the previous summer, and sped to the scene, a damp, slippery incline covered with brambles, rotting logs and saplings. All along he'd been sure that another dumping ground would be found. This time he hoped "Ted" might have left some trace of himself, some tangible clue. To date, all Keppel had been able to do was to clean up after his quarry.
>
> Earlier, there had been another find near Taylor Mountain. Herb Swindler's [Chief of Homicide, Seattle Police] people had turned up some animal bones in an old house. Still working his occult angle, Swindler wondered if they were goat bones, indicative of black rites. Instead, Dr. Doris Swindler [forensic anthropologist] had identified them as the remains of an immature elk.
>
> But a human skull was something different. Keppel saw to it that the entire mountainside around the skull was sealed off and then sent the bare remains to Seattle for identification. The next morning the report came back: Brenda Carol Ball, 22, last seen alive at the Flame Tavern, had been murdered and dumped on Taylor Mountain. Her skull had been fractured. For the next eight days, Keppel supervised 200 police as they scoured the mountainside inch by inch. Their work was tedious, hideous, heartbreaking.
>
> Keppel himself made the second discovery. The detective was negotiating the steep slope when his feet slipped from beneath him, sending him tumbling down through the tangled underbrush. He landed in a heap, covered in muck and wet leaves. Keppel grunted, stood up and saw before him Death's face, two empty black eye sockets staring frozen in infinity. Death was smiling on him with pretty, expensive teeth; he knew instantly that he had found Susan Rancourt. He looked more closely and saw that Susan's skull was cracked.
>
> Next came Kathy Park's skull. The beauty from Oregon State University had been brought 260 miles north and dumped for the animals to eat.
>
> The last to be identified was the first to have been murdered. Joyce and Jim Healy's eldest child, Lynda, the blue-eyed ski report announcer, was there on Taylor Mountain, too. According to her mother, she was identified on the basis of a single tooth.
>
> The forensic experts who examined the bones could not say with certainty how the girls had died. If the cranial fractures came from human blows, however, some would have required a heavy blunt instrument, such as a tire iron, wielded with incredible fury.
>
> Other factors were more clearly understood. "Ted" had dumped the girls near the roadside after removing all jewelry and clothing. Then the animals had begun their work. Soft, fleshy parts of the bodies were consumed near where they had been left. Then the heads and jaws were torn away and carried back into the

brush. Along the way, a hunk of hair or a lower jaw might drop off. Farthest away from the road were the skulls, which took the scavengers the longest to penetrate and devour.

The horror which this scene evokes in almost anyone is surely enough to make people wonder just who Theodore Bundy might have been. A number of others whose dreadful cruelty equals that of "Ted" Bundy has already been discussed. Surely the Nazi killers in the previous chapter were of the same nature as they calmly worked at their hideous tasks and felt neither remorse nor sorrow for their deeds. It is this total absence of remorse which marks the serial killer. As Levin and Fox point out:

> Though their [serial killers] crimes may be sickening, they are not sick in either a medical or legal sense. Instead, the serial killer is typically a sociopathic personality who lacks internal control—guilt or conscience—to guide his own behavior, but has an excessive need to control and dominate others. He definitely knows right from wrong, definitely realizes he has committed a sinful act, but simply doesn't care about his human prey. The sociopath has never internalized a moral code that prohibits murder. Having fun is all that counts.[17]

On December 30, 1977, Ted Bundy escaped from the Glenwood Springs, Colorado, jail where he had been confined on suspicion of murder. By various means he came to Tallahassee, Florida, where two weeks later he murdered two female students whom he did not know, assaulted three more and killed a 12-year-old child during an interval of yet another three-and-one-half weeks. It is significant that after all these killings, Bundy was picked up by the police for a traffic violation and not because of suspicion of murder.

To achieve all this, Bundy had entered a sorority house on the campus of Florida State University during the night of January 14–15, 1978. There, he crept into the bedrooms of sleeping students and smashed five students with a club so that two died and three were severely mutilated. These killings are briefly described as follows:

> Lisa Levy went to bed early on the eve of Super Bowl Sunday, January 15, 1978. Her roommate was out of town, so she was sleeping alone. Margaret Bowman, living across the hall, was also sleeping without the usual company of her roommate. Karen Chandler and Kathy Kleiner slept in their room separated only by a wall from Margaret's bed. At approximately 3:30 A.M., Ted Bundy went into Levy's bedroom, bludgeoned her to death, sexually assaulted her, and bit her left buttock. These bite marks were later to be the sole physical evidence that proved fatal to Bundy. He left Levy's room and attacked, bludgeoned and strangled Margaret Bowman. He left Room 4, went down the hallway toward Sherrod's [a restaurant] and attacked Kleiner and Chandler. They survived but Levy and Bowman died that night.[18]

There are those who seek psychological explanations for so violent and bizarre an episode on the part of a man who had already killed so often before. This is important, because this author seeks to explain not only the social factors which give rise to so much violence in the United States, but also the motives which compel a particular person to kill at a particular time.

A number of homicide motives have already been listed in Chapter 3 during the discussion of homicide in Erie County, New York. This social explanation for murder and mass murder must be augmented with a psychological explanation which focuses on the individual and answers the question of why Ted Bundy, John Gacy or anyone else commits such horrible crimes while others, also under stress, do not commit any crime.

A PSYCHOLOGICAL EXPLANATION

In a widely quoted book, Danto et al. list some "core characteristics" as present in the behavioral background of serial killers.[19] These core characteristics are: that the serial killer deliberately chooses homicide as his method of coping with important psychological issues, and that the repeated killings are justified, that is, considered right, in the mind of the killer. The serial killer achieves psychological gains by his actions. Thus, Danto et al. cite the case of a serial killer who murdered only small children so as to show the parents how "great their loss could be. The parents are his victims. He kills children to avenge some childhood hurt induced by his own parents toward whom he is now venting angry feelings."

In an interview with Ted Bundy, published in *Serial Murder* by Holmes and De Burger, the psychologist, Dr. Al Carlisle quotes Bundy. Bundy also described the psychological force that drives the serial killer not only from his own experience but also because he had met Otis Toole and Gerald Stano in prison. Toole and Stano both had killed more than 30 times.

Bundy painted a picture of the serial murderer as one who is not sick. According to Bundy, "Such a person is rational and knows what he is doing. He makes plans on a rational and intelligent basis; few serial killers are psychotic, see visions or hear voices." According to Bundy, most serial killers do so for the pleasure of killing. The murder of another human being becomes a psychological "high" for them, so that they have a "need" to kill again and again. The serial killer also learns more and more about killing, that is, he learns how to stalk the victim and how the victim will react. He also learns how to conceal himself and how to get away. Bundy also believed that serial killers eventually become careless because they have succeeded so often, not because they have a wish to be apprehended.

Bundy further explained that serial killers are compelled by a "force" within them to continue these killings and that this "force" goes on and on and will not be satisfied. Bundy saw this "force" as a secret part of the killer's personality which is not visible to others. Thus, many serial killers appear quite normal to their friends and associates so that only their victims know who they really are. Yet, their victims are dead and cannot tell anyone about the killer.

The obvious consequence of this personality structure is that the serial killer cannot be distinguished from other people, a feature already mentioned in connection with the Nazi killers who murdered all day and then went home to wife and children and ate their supper, read their newspaper and played cards with friends just like everyone else. Their many murders did not bother them any more than they worried Ted Bundy. The Nazi murderers, and Gacy, Bundy, Kemper, and

Simmons and a host of others were perfectly willing to continue these murders as long as there was no interference and they were able to live "normal" lives the balance of the time.

CHARACTERISTICS OF SERIAL KILLERS

Compared to the characteristics of persons who commit homicide, serial killers differ somewhat if a composite picture of them is drawn as Holmes and DeBurger have done.[20] According to these authors, the following characteristics may be expected from serial killers:

Age Most known serial killers are 25–35 years old. This differs from the study of homicides in Erie County, New York, and the findings of similar studies in other American cities. Those studies showed that common homicide is mostly committed by persons in the age range of 15 to 30, with a heavy concentration in the mid-twenties group. It is also significant that the victims of serial murderers are not concentrated in any age range. Some murder the young, some the middle aged and others the old. The young are usually victims of homicide.

Gender Unlike other forms of homicide, serial murders kill many more females than males, while homicides kill many more males than females. The reason for this difference lies in the motives of the killers. One-on-one killers murder male opponents who appear to them to deflate their self esteem or impinge on their sense of self worth. Serial killers kill classes of people against whom they feel a general grudge.

Race Serial killings are almost always committed by white males. There are very few blacks involved in this type of murder because class resentment is far more likely to occur to a person with a good education than someone without an appreciation of how society works. It is projected that as the education level of blacks improve, there will be more black serial killers. This is already true in two cases, that of David Burke who killed himself and 42 other people by shooting on a plane in California, and Mark Essex who was undoubtedly a middle class man with middle class expectations.

MASS MURDER

On April 13, 1988, Leslie Lowenfield was executed in Louisiana for the mass murder of five victims. Lowenfield was accused of "barging into the house of his former girl friend" and shooting everyone there. He not only killed his girlfriend, he also killed her four-year-old child, her stepfather, her mother and a visitor whom he viewed as a rival for the affections of his former girlfriend.[21]

On April 15, 1988, James E. Schnick was sentenced to death in Missouri for killing seven members of his family, including a 14-year-old boy.[22]

On March 26, 1988, two men were charged in St. Louis with the murder of five supermarket employees during a robbery. The victims were shot in the back of the head after they obeyed the robbers' orders to lie on the floor.[23]

On January 30, 1988, Carl Isaacs was sentenced to death in Georgia. He was twice convicted of killing six members of a family whom he intended to rob and who had the misfortune of entering their home during his raid on their property. Isaacs was first convicted in 1985. However, the federal appeals court ruled that his trial was not fair by reason of all the publicity it had engendered in Seminole County where the murders had occurred. A second trial was held in Houston County with the same outcome.[24]

On New Year's Day, 1988, a 17-year-old boy killed five people in New York City in a drug related murder spree.[25]

On August 1, 1966, Charles J. Whitman, an honors student in architecture, wounded 31 people and killed 14 as he fired a high powered rifle from the top of a tower on the campus of the University of Texas. After police killed him it was discovered that he had also murdered his mother and his wife the night before.

Howard Unruh murdered 13 people on the streets of Camden, New Jersey, in 1949, and 20 years before that, seven members of the "Bugs" Moran gang were slaughtered in a Chicago garage by the rival Al Capone gang.[26]

These and many other mass murders have occurred with ever increasing frequency in the United States over the past several decades. It will be instructive to note that the number of multicides, both serial killings and mass murders, have become more frequent as the years and decades go by.

There are forces in American society which promote multicide, and a psychiatric explanation of this phenomenon is insufficient. For example, seven multicidial killers were identified in the United States during all of the years 1900 through 1939, a period of 40 years. Between 1940 and 1959, a period of only 20 years, nine multicidal killers were identified. In the 1960s, a period of ten years, there were five multicides committed by five such killers. In the 1970s, however, there were 14 and in the 1980s, there were 15 such nationally known killers.

A SOCIOLOGICAL EXPLANATION

As already seen with respect to serial killers, multicide is related to the belief on the part of such killers that they are fighting a whole class of people in a good cause and, as in the case of DeSalvo, have been excluded by a social class who mean something to them and whom they would like to join. Some may object and ask why then such killers do not murder the richest people, or the most famous or most talented. Some, like Charles Manson and his gang, did this of course. However, those who kill primarily lower middle class people (DeSalvo), or middle class students (Ted Bundy) kill a group who in their judgment has deprived them far more than the rich and the super-rich whom they do not know and to whom they do not compare themselves.

We are dealing here with "relative deprivation," which is the belief that we have been deprived of something that should be ours because those who possess it are like us and have the same expectations, that is, belong to the same reference group.

Few would feel deprived, for instance, because the Rockefellers are millionaires. Many more people would feel deprived if they landed a poor-paying job on graduating from college while their classmates all started at $35,000 per year. Bundy, likewise, who killed college students, had far more reason to feel left out of that group than an upper class group he never met and who meant nothing to him.

Thus, it can be said that multiple killers are usually avenging themselves on a number of representatives of a class whom they envy and whom they believe they cannot ever join. This theme becomes even more evident in respect to the examples of mass murderers that follow. This was also a central theme in the life of Adolf Hitler,[27] whose resentment of the Jews was chiefly rooted in his perceived conviction that all Jews were at least wealthier than he was and were members of the middle class whom he hated as the very epitome of his failure as an artist and an architect.

Mass murder appears to be related more to the belief of the offender that he has been excluded than on any other motive. Mass murder, therefore, differs from one-on-one homicide in that the common homicides discussed in the first three chapters are seen by the perpetrator as a duel between two people defending their "honor," while mass murder is seen by the perpetrators as a war against an enemy who must be eliminated. Not only Hitler and his Nazis, but a number of American mass killers have said as much and acted accordingly.[28]

Mass killers often kill their own families. Thus, David Brom, 16 years old, was arrested and charged with the ax murder of four members of his family in Rochester, New York, on February 20, 1988. He was accused of killing his 42-year-old father, his mother, his 14-year-old sister and his brother, age nine.[29]

Richard Farley returned to the California defense contractor's plant from where he had been fired three years earlier, and murdered seven people while wounding five others in a sudden attack in February of 1988. Farley had walked into the building where he once worked, "wearing two bandoleers criss-crossing his chest. He carried a shotgun in one hand and a 30.06 caliber rifle in the other."[30] According to witnesses, Farley fired about 50 times, making a particular effort to shoot a woman with whom he said he had a special relationship. Farley was fired from that company on the grounds that the woman complained that the "relationship" had turned into harassment.

R. Gene Simmons of Dover, Arkansas, committed a similar deed from December 24 to December 28, 1987. Simmons, 47 years old at that time, killed 16 people in four days. First he murdered 14 members of his family at home and elsewhere and then went to the offices of the trucking company which had once employed him and "went on a methodical shooting spree, killing two and wounding four more."[31] Simmons began his murderous activities by killing his children on Christmas Eve, 1987. The evidence appeared to show that Simmons first shot his wife, Becky, 46, then his sons Gene and Eddie, 26 and 14, and then his daughters, Loretta, Marianne and Rebecca, and finally his granddaughter Barbara. When his son William arrived with his wife and child, Simmons killed them also and then shot his daughter Sheila Simmons McNulty and her husband Dennis as they came in to see the Christmas tree. In addition, he also killed two more grandchildren and two other relatives. Even as the *New York Times* reported this horror, the Associated Press also distributed the story of 38-year-old Rafael Rodriguez who had shot three persons in Nashua, New Hampshire, drove ten miles to Londonderry, New Hampshire, shot two more and died as the police shot him to death shortly thereafter.

In that same story, headed "Eleven Reported Slain" the *Times* mentioned a 17-year-old boy who had killed his mother and stepbrother and wounded his father after setting their house on fire. All that happened in Dayton, Texas, on Thursday, December 31, 1987.[32]

Laurie W. Dann walked into the Hubbard Wood Elementary School in Winnetka, Illinois, on Friday, May 20, 1988, and shot and killed one child and wounded five others before killing herself with the same pistol she had used to shoot the children. Amy Moses, the teacher in the classroom that Dann entered, gave the following account of the shooting: "She [Dann] came in and closed the door. She went up to each child and point blank she shot each child."[33]

In December of 1987, David Burke revenged himself in grand style. His revenge not only cost him his life but also the lives of 42 other passengers on board Pacific Southwest Airlines Flight 1771. Burke had entered the plane in Los Angeles. While the plane was flying to San Francisco at 22,000 feet he shot his former boss who was a passenger on the plane with a .44 magnum pistol and then entered the cockpit where he shot both pilots, sending the plane into an uncontrollable dive into a hill near Paso Robles, California. His motive was revenge, as he plainly spelled out in a note written on the outside of an air-sickness bag. Said Burke to his former boss, Raymond Thompson, who had fired him: "Hi, Ray. I think it is sort of ironical that we end up like this. I plead for some leniency for my family, remember. Well, I got none. And you'll get none."[34]

On July 18, 1984, two days before Walter Mondale was nominated by the Democratic party for the office of President of the United States, an unemployed security guard, James Oliver Huberty, walked into a McDonald's restaurant in San Ysidro, California, and killed 21 people with three guns by firing at the restaurant guests and employees indiscriminately. In addition to those murdered, Huberty also wounded 16 people. Huberty had aimed "a relentless stream of gunfire" at the occupants of the restaurant until bloody corpses lay everywhere. Some were on the counters, others on the floor or across the tables. The dead included several children, some of whom were outside the restaurant and whom he shot from the inside. The rampage continued in this town on the Mexican border until a police sharpshooter killed Huberty, then 41 years old.

According to United Press International, these killings took the largest toll of any mass murder on any one day in United States history.[35] Huberty was armed with an Uzi semiautomatic rifle, a shotgun and a pistol. He carried a bag from which he produced a radio which he put on the counter in the restaurant so that he could listen to reports about his actions. He reloaded his guns several times and kept on firing and killing until he himself died in a hail of police bullets.

It appears that James Huberty fits the very description of a mass murderer that is outlined earlier. A gun lover, Huberty owned numerous weapons even as a boy. He continued to acquire guns of all kinds once he was married and lived with his family in the Massilon-Canton area of Ohio where he worked as a welder in a local plant. In 1984, however, Huberty lost his job and with it the two properties he owned in Massilon. A graduate of Malone College in Canton, Ohio, Huberty had started work as an undertaker's apprentice. In this he was unsuccessful because he was unable to "relate to people" according to his erstwhile boss in the undertaking business, Don Williams.[36] He thereupon went to work as a welder, but could not get along very well with his neighbors and family. His father had remarried after a divorce and seldom saw his son, who was still in grade school at the time of the family breakup.

Thereafter, James Huberty was described as a "loner" who always played with guns. This description continued into adult life when both he and his wife constantly argued with neighbors and threatened neighbors, not only with guns, but with attack dogs he was raising. When he lost his job because his company, Babcock and Wilcox, closed down for lack of orders, Huberty sold his properties to raise cash and declared that he would emigrate to Mexico with his wife and two daughters. This decision was made after he was unable to find any work in the depressed area of northern Ohio.

Those who remembered Huberty in 1984 said that Huberty was "always talking about shooting somebody" and that he blamed "the country" for all his troubles. And so, when he again lost his job, this time as a security guard in his new-found home in California, he became "despondent" and left his home with the remark to his wife: "I am going to hunt humans."

The story of Huberty is so significant because it includes all of the elements which produce mass murderers in the United States. First, James Huberty was the child of divorce. This author consulted a clinical psychotherapist and learned that some children of divorced parents become quite angry, guilty and hostile because they blame themselves for the divorce of their parents. They wonder whether they, the children, did something to cause the family breakup. In addition, children of divorce feel deserted by the parent with whom they are not staying and also feel that the parent in whose custody they are has chased out their other parent. In short, children of divorce have good cause to feel frightened, angry and resentful. James Huberty was one of these.

In addition, it is obvious that Huberty was a failure in the economic world. It is *not* important that his several job losses were not his fault. In the competitive United States, culture men, and now also women, are taught to regard themselves as successful, important and fulfilled on the basis of the occupation they hold. It is no secret that American men, and many women, achieve what sociologists call "existential validation" by means of their job. This phrase refers to the ability to estimate oneself positively in connection with one's occupation and its prestige. While inherited titles or wealth may be the only criteria of prestige in other societies, in United States society and in all of the western industrialized world, occupation is the principal source of prestige. Every study of prestige in 85 different countries has shown this to be true.[37]

This does not mean that wealth is not a source of prestige in the United States. However, most people, including Huberty, have little wealth. Therefore, a steady job, a home, a car and other visible signs of income become tremendously important in validating one's existence, making one's existence real and important. When these symbols of status are removed because of a loss of a job, or retirement, or because of a poor investment, people become very upset because they rightly believe that not only their incomes are threatened, but their esteem in the eyes of others and in their own, also.

In the United States, no excuses for failure are accepted. The man who is not working feels guilty and hostile at those whom he perceives as the originators of his deprivation. This is a universal feeling in industrial societies. In that respect, therefore, Huberty was not alone. On the contrary; his anger at his economic failure is shared by so many that it is to be expected. It is normal. Note also that Huberty had gone to college. Admittedly, Malone College is not a great university. Nevertheless, it is hardly possible that any college graduate would feel good about himself if he can do no better than to be a security guard.

There are, of course, many people who lose jobs and come from a broken home who do not kill and commit no crimes. James Huberty, however, had yet another problem with which he needed to contend. He was a migrant. It is no accident that California has a greater number of mass murders and serial murders than any other state.[38] This is so because California has a large number of migrants, who like Huberty, have no family and no friends in their new home area and therefore cannot share the burden of daily living with those who mean a great deal to them. In such a situation, a good job is even more important than it would be at home.

Huberty faced all of these disconcerting problems and finally concluded that his life was worthless and that suicide was a good way out. Multicide however, seemed even better. Multicide gives the killer both a chance to get even and to die as a consequence. This author contends that a competitive society such as ours must inevitably produce a great deal of aggression at least from those who see themselves as losers. Wherever there is a winner, there must be many losers. This is true in school where competitive grading becomes a source of great anxiety, and surely in the economic world which is based on ruthless and merciless competition, not only for money, but also for all those symbols of success which elude the many and evolve only upon the few.

The vast majority of Americans, nevertheless, live with these daily injuries of class, social debasement and a sense of unfulfilled expectations by establishing alternative status systems. These can be voluntary organizations such as clubs, churches, boards of directors of social agencies and others. The function of these voluntary organizations is to permit numerous persons who are not rich, are not engaged in honorific occupations, and are not talented in the arts to succeed at something. People can be elected to a variety of offices such as president, chairman or treasurer of this or that organization, or serve on the board of something or other. All these activities permit people to feel that they are "somebody" after all, even if otherwise they have to content themselves with a minor position "on the job," or an income smaller than they believe they deserve.

But the Hubertys of this world do not have alternatives. Without the support of a family, separated from their home communities and without any opportunity to ever be "somebody," they feel a deep grievance against a world which has cheated them, a world in which they get no recognition, a world in which they feel exploited and used and unappreciated and unnoticed.

Not only Huberty, but many other mass murderers and, as will be discussed in the next chapter, many assassins of famous persons voice these sentiments. They believe that a spectacular act of violence will finally prove that they made a difference in this world and will at the same time revenge them for all their pain, all their hurts, all the daily insults they have had to suffer at the hands of all those who have treated them with contempt and not given them their due. One-on-one homicide as well as multicide and assassination are principally motivated by status injuries and will continue to plague society and even increase in today's competitive world.

Finally, there is the issue of power. Murder is a power trip. There is good reason to believe that many murders, both of the homicide and the multicide kind, are an effort to compensate the killer for his belief that he has no power. The brutalization of others, the horror and the fear the killers engender in their victims and in the survivors, all this gives the killers a sense of power.

Many people in contemporary mass society feel powerless. Such phrases as "you can't fight city hall" indicate the common belief that the individual is helpless and powerless. There are people, therefore, who will go very far to correct this notion. Some will run for public office. Others will go to extremes to get on television, even if it is for only a minute or a second. Some will even write books . . . and yet others will kill. Killing another human being gives the killer a sense of control. This is also the reason people drive big cars, wear uniforms and collect guns.

In American culture the need for power and control is taught from early youth on and reinforced constantly by word and deed. Sports, movies, politics and the economic, competitive world all militate in favor of the belief that people must have power and must have control over others, at least some of the time, at least on occasion.

Bundy's biographers claim that Bundy risked his own life on several occasions to save others from possible injury or death. The same is true of other eventual mass murderers and serial killers. This is not surprising. The same need to control and to have power will lead an eventual killer to save a life as to take it, for both make him the master over life and death, both make him temporarily important. The wish to be important is as powerful in the United States as it is elsewhere. People want to be noticed; they want to mean something in this world . . . and so, some go so far as to kill important people, to shoot presidents and other political leaders because then, like John Wilkes Booth, they get into the history books. This kind of murder is called assassination and is the subject of the next chapter.

SUMMARY AND CONCLUSION

Status and Role

1. The vast majority of all American mass murderers and serial killers are men. Few women are among the perpetrators, but women are much more often the victims of these crimes. While men are also much more often the perpetrators of one-on-one homicide, they are also the most frequent victims of homicide.

2. Ages 25 to 35 are the most frequent ages of multicidal killers. This differs from homicidal killers in that they are mainly 15 to 30 years old.

3. Almost all multicide is committed by American white males. Black multicide is rare. This is exactly the opposite of the findings concerning homicide.

4. Multicidal killers are generally better educated and come more often from a middle class economic status than is true of homicidal killers.

Socio-psychological Motivation

5. Serial killers believe they are at war with a class who must be eliminated, while homicidal killers see themselves in a duel for their honor.

6. Multicidal killers have an excessive need for control and power over others. This need is taught in United States society.

7. Serial killers see their victims as a different species and therefore have no remorse or conscience concerning them.

8. Serial killers and mass murderers often have no internalized moral code.

9. While serial killers behave in a rational, planned manner, mass murderers do not. Mass murderers "explode" after a long series of failures in their lives for which they blame others.

10. Multicides of both kinds seek to avenge old hurts.

11. Serial killers, but not mass murderers, are often hedonists who must have immediate gratification of their wishes and needs.

12. Mass murderers are often driven by a sense of "relative deprivation."

Social Conditions

13. Serial killers may be geographically stable or transient.

14. Multicide has increased over several decades in the United States.

Part III

Assassination

6. Assassination for Money

In A.D. 874, an "Iraqui peasant named Hamdan ibn al-Ashrath, popularly known as Quarmat, became the leader of the Ismaili sect [of Islam]."[1] Leaving a bloody list of conquests behind, the sect's doctrines and methods of killing indiscriminately inspired the Ismaili of Alamut, or Eagles Nest in Northern Persia, now known as Iran, to wage a campaign of terror and murder against all opponents of their faith. This campaign began about 1092, over 200 years after Quarmat started the sect.

In his spirit however, the Ismaili Moslems organized a sect whose leader was to be absolutely obeyed. Living in a mountain fortress 10,000 feet above sea level, they were impregnable. Alamut became a center for a group of young men who used hashish, a hemp derivative, to give them hallucinations of various kinds, supposedly allowing them the courage to kill at the masters word. These killers were called "hashshasheen" in Arabic, from which the word "assassin" is derived.[2]

Assassins were originally a group of men who sought to further the cause of their religion by terror and murder, and the present use of that word continues to have the same meaning. An assassin is a killer who murders his victim either because the victim represents a public position with which the murderer disagrees, as in political and religious assassinations, or the killer and the victim have different interests in the economic sphere (e.g., they are business rivals). In the latter case, the word assassination is used principally to describe business-motivated killings which involve illegal enterprises, such as drug dealing, prostitution, gambling, loan sharking and a myriad other profitable ways of making money, and which are chiefly in the hands of organized crime, and have many "respectable" customers.

The principal resemblance between economic and political organized assassination is that both are motivated by an effort of the killer or killers to achieve a rational end. In the first instance the end is the protection of income and profit. In the second case, it is the promotion or prevention of a political condition. For example, the murder of Martin Luther King, Jr., was predicated on the assumption that King's death could prevent the further successes of the civil rights movement of the 1960s.

On the other hand, the assassination of William Sciolino in 1980, as already discussed in Chapter 1, was designed to protect the profits of "organized crime" in western New York.

It should be pointed out, however, that the other forms of murder already discussed also appear to have a reasonable end, at least from the viewpoint of the killer. Thus, self-assertion is the principal gain of the one-on-one homicidal killer. Genocidal killers gain or think they can gain the elimination of a group which seems dangerous and corrupting to them. The other multicidal killers, whether serial killers or mass murderers, gain the advantage of not only ridding the world of "undesirables," they also gain revenge upon their actual or symbolic detractors. Murder is profitable, and therefore reasonable, from the killer's point of view. Keeping this in mind, it is now time to explore assassination.

ASSASSINATIONS BY "ORGANIZED CRIMINALS"

"Organized crime" is a business which resembles other business in that it renders services to customers. In that respect, organized crime differs from other criminal activities. Surely, robbers, rapists and muggers do not have customers any more than thieves or burglars have customers. Organized criminals, however, are supported by a huge following of "decent folks" who may well claim to believe in "law and order," but nevertheless supply criminals with money for selling to them numerous goods and services which legitimate business cannot or will not supply.

In 1976, the *Task Force on Organized Crime*[3] listed seven categories of illegal goods and services which they claimed were then, and this author contends still are, the main income source of the organized crime business: *gambling*, including lotteries, numbers, bookmaking and casino gambling; *loan sharking*; *narcotics*, including importation of drugs from sources worldwide; *sex*, including prostitution and pornography; *labor racketeering*, including stealing union funds, robbing pension funds and extortion; *industrial racketeering*, including the protection racket; and *miscellaneous*, including financial burglaries and robberies, counterfeiting money, smuggling untaxed cigarettes, defrauding suppliers and innumerable other crimes.

It has been estimated that the annual gross income from these operations amounts to $50 billion, making organized criminal business more lucrative than all iron, steel, aluminum and copper manufacturing combined.[4] In addition to earning huge profits from these enterprises, the criminal organizations which engage in these seven activities also own legitimate business interests. Consequently criminals earn vast sums of money in the United States and augment their immense income by also evading income taxes and other taxes by dealing in cash, setting up fronts and keeping only minimal records.[5]

These extremely lucrative operations attract a great deal of competition as any very profitable business will. Because of this, organized criminals have always differed in one way from all other corporate enterprises whom they resemble in every other way: they are willing to kill to maintain their profits. To prove this point, a list of assassinations known to have taken place between 1889 and 1986 follows. These are not all or even nearly all the assassinations conducted by organized criminals during that time or later. This list shows that assassination is part of the organized crime business and that it has continued unabated for a long time.

One of the characteristics of organized crime assassinations is that the victims are almost always criminals themselves and that very few customers or law enforcement personnel are murdered in this fashion. This once more underscores that professional assassinations are conducted to protect profits and are good for business.

Selected Assassinations Perpetrated By "Organized" Crime, 1889–1986

Killer	Victim	Place	Date
Unknown	Vincenzo Ottumvo	New Orleans	1/24/1889
Pellegrino Morano	Nicholas Morello	New York	10/ /1916
Johnny Torrio	"Big Jim" Colosimo	Chicago	5/11/1920
Hymie Weiss	Steven Wisniewski	Chicago	7/ /1921
Alfonse Capone	Joe Howard	Chicago	5/ 8/1924
Johnny Torrio	Dion O'Banion	Chicago	11/10/1924
Alfonse Capone	Hymie Weiss	Chicago	10/11/1926
Unknown	Frank Yale	New York	6/ 1/1927
Unknown	Seven victims	Chicago	2/14/1929*
Girolamo Santucci	Steven Ferraro	New York	9/ 5/1930
Nick Capuzzi	Alfred Mineo	New York	9/ 5/1930
"Lucky" Luciano	Joseph Masseria	Coney Island	4/15/1931
"Lucky" Luciano	Salvatore Meranzano	New York	9/10/1931
Joseph Valachi	Michael Peggione	New York	9/25/1932
"Lepke" Buchhalter	"Dutch" Schultz	New Jersey	10/23/1935
John Robiletto	Willie Moretti	New Jersey	10/ 4/1951
Gallo and Genovese	Albert Anastasia	New York	10/25/1957
No convictions	James B. Walsh	New York	1/23/1965
Joe Colombo	Joseph Gallo	New York	4/ 7/1972
Unknown	Thomas Eboli	New York	7/ /1972
Nicodemo Scarfo	Angelo Bruno	Philadelphia	1980
Anthony Accardo	Allen Dorfman	Chicago	1983
Unknown	Paul Castellano	New York	1985
No convictions	Anthony Vendetti	New York	1/21/1986

*St. Valentine's Day Massacre[6]

Inspection of the above table reveals that assassination has been, and continues to be, a part of the organized crime business. While it is undoubtedly true that many of the business methods of organized crime are replicas of American corporate business in general, it is evident that the real difference between legitimate business practices and criminal practices is the willingness to kill competitors or others who may be in the way of gaining profits. There have been exceptions, such as the case in which a judge in Illinois found three officials of the Film Recovery Systems Company guilty of murder in June of 1985. Company officials permitted workers to inhale cyanide poison under totally unsafe working conditions because they failed to spend the money to prevent such a possibility.[7]

The willingness to kill means that organized crime and those engaged in such enterprises will take extreme measures to preserve their monopoly. The role of the boss (capo) in certain organizations is to ensure that no one will compete with an established criminal business in an area, and that a network of contacts is maintained with law enforcement and political powers who can be used in case of "trouble," meaning here the introduction of anyone into an area in which no additional business operations are to be tolerated. Should anyone compete for business with someone protected by organized crime the newcomer will be visited and told to get out; failing to do so, he will be assaulted and killed at once or killed upon a third offense. It is assassination of this kind which keeps the crime bosses in power, year in and year out for they have the "nerve" to kill, and the organization to protect them from the consequences. Other, legitimate business people have neither.[8]

Before 1934, there were numerous killings among criminal gangs on the East Coast as well as in Chicago. However, it appears that prior to that year criminal activities in the United States had not yet been truly organized. It was only in 1934 when Johnny Torrio, Charles "Lucky" Luciano, Meyer Lansky, Joe Adonis, "Bugsy" Siegel and Louis "Lepke" Buchhalter decided to organize a crime syndicate that organized crime was born in this country.

According to the testimony of Abe Reles, a convicted killer who died on November 12, 1941 after falling or being pushed out of a window of the sixth floor of the Half Moon Hotel in Coney Island, New York, the syndicate was a confederation of independent gangs. Reles claimed that a board of directors existed which consisted of the heads of various crime families throughout the country, each with one vote. All were to be equal. This "commission" had the power to settle disputes and among other things, convict offenders against the interests of organized crime and condemn them to death if necessary.[9] The chief "executioner" in this group was Albert Anastasia. Having killed numerous men over many years, Anastasia became the victim of assassination himself on October 25, 1957, while he was sitting in a barber chair at 7th Avenue and 57th Street in New York. Here is a description of that assassination:

> Moving quickly behind the chair in which Anastasia was sitting, the gunmen opened fire. With the first spurt of bullets, Anastasia leaped forward, kicking the barber chair's footrest with such force it was torn away. He was standing unsteadily when a second burst of gunfire propelled him against the glass shelving in front of the mirror. Bottles crashed to the floor. The final shot hit him in the back of the head and he crumpled to the floor. Other bullets had struck Anastasia's left hand, left wrist, right hip and back. . . . Having finished their mission, the killers hurried out the front door and disappeared.[10]

To avoid too many killings and arrests, and too much public exposure, assassinations ordered by this commission were placed into the hands of a so-called "enforcement branch" of the commission. Newsmen later called these enforcers "Murder, Inc.," a name which also became the title of a book by Burton B. Turkus and Sid Feder. Turkus had been the prosecutor of several of these "enforcers."

Assassinations have been seen by organized crime types as practical, rational actions necessary in the course of business operations and best kept at a minimum so as to avoid attracting the attention of the police and other law enforcers. It is, however, a constant companion of the organized crime business. This is so because the fear generated by assassination must be reinforced on occasion, or the power of the boss would be dissipated. To reinforce his command position the boss must occasionally demonstrate that he can and will kill to maintain his and the organization's interests—the primary reason for eliminating any threat and any competitor whenever possible. For example, on June 28, 1988, a federal grand jury in New York City accused 22 people of murdering or conspiring to murder one Irwin Schiff in a Manhattan restaurant in August of 1987. Schiff, like Allen Dorfman in Chicago, was gunned down because he had been an accountant for organized criminals and knew too much about their finances and business operations. In addition to the indictments concerning Schiff, the same grand jury accused members of the so-called "Genovese crime family" of seeking to assassinate John and Gene Gotti, both heads of the so-called Gambino crime family. Genovese and Gambino were crime bosses in the 1950s. At his death from natural causes in 1976, Carlo Gambino was said to have been the last of the "capo di tutti capi," (boss of all bosses).[11]

In Gambino's lifetime the five crime families of New York were the Genovese family, led by Anthony "Fat Tony" Salerno; the Lucchese family, run by Antonio "Ducks" Corallo; the Colombo family, ruled by Gennaro Langella or Jerry Lang; and the Bonnano family, headed by Phillip Rastelli; and the Gambino family.[12] In January of 1987, Federal District Court Judge Richard Owen sentenced Salerno and Corallo to 100 years in prison after they had been convicted as top leaders and "commissioners" of crime in Manhattan.[13] Six other top gangsters were also sentenced to terms ranging from 40 to 100 years for their complicity in Dorfman's murder on January 20, 1983.

Other cities continue to have crime families of their own. It should be understood that these "families" are not necessarily blood related but more probably assocations of friends. It appears to observers that after Gambino, no one has been able to exercise the control he had achieved. Nevertheless, organized crime continues because it is so lucrative. United States prosecutor Michael Chertoff had these words for a jury during a trial of four of New York's five "crime families" in 1986, also known as "the crime commission": "You are going to learn that this commission is dominated by a single principle: greed."[14]

Greed, of course, motivates many men, not only those whose names happen to be reminders of their southern European ancestry. In fact, beginning in about 1978, criminals of South American and Asian ancestry have competed successfully with the so-called "Mafia" (from the Arabic word "Mo 'Hafiat," to defend or remedy an ill) for the money to be made in supplying Americans with illicit goods and services, particularly drugs. Notable among these newer organized criminals are immigrants from Colombia who remain in touch with their home country from where they import large quantities of drugs into the United States. These criminal gangs have organized "death squads" whose purpose it is to assassinate anyone who interferes in their business or their politics. Such death squads are believed to have assassinated as many as 5,000 people in the United States and Colombia since 1982.[15] One such squad is called "Death to Kidnappers" by the leading drug families as they sought to avenge the kidnapping of their children by yet other criminals who hoped to make money by such extortion. So far, few of the members of these squads have been arrested or convicted, as they operate nationwide, are small and unobtrusive and are able to move quickly between Colombia and the United States to escape prosecution in both places.

Criminals of Chinese descent have also become very successful in the heroin trade in recent years. Because they have access to large amounts of Southeast Asian drugs, they have defied the Mafia and won. The reasons for these successes are that recent prosecutions have weakened the Mafia, government agents have done little to prosecute the Chinese as they concentrate on others, and the Chinese have an old and well organized gang structure themselves, thereby gaining all those advantages which are needed to maintain a successful criminal business.[16]

As mentioned earlier, very few victims of organized crime are not themselves criminal competitors of the assassins. Nevertheless, some victims are indeed assassinated not because they are competitors, but because they are in the way of a criminal enterprise. Such was the case with James Walsh and Anthony Vendetti, both of whom were obstacles to profit and therefore assassinated, although neither was a criminal in any manner.

James Walsh, who was assassinated on January 23, 1965, had been the manager of an A&P store in Brooklyn. He was shot to death on a Brooklyn street when he tried to fix a flat tire. The tire was flat because his car had been "fixed" beforehand by the assassins. The manager had been allegedly persuaded by the Catena brothers, Jerry and Gene, to buy an inferior brand of detergent which they wanted to sell to all A&P stores. When that huge chain reversed Walsh's decision because the detergent did not measure up to other brands, the Catena brand was dropped. Thereupon a bomb was tossed into one A&P store in Yonkers, another store was fire bombed and Walsh and John Mossner, another A&P manager, were killed. While one of the Catenas was forced to appear before a grand jury, no indictment was ever handed down and no action was taken in these assassinations. The lesson is clear: Organized crime will do anything for money and usually can get away with it.[17]

Anthony J. Vendetti was a New York City detective. He was assassinated in the borough of Queens in January 1986 "execution style" as he participated in "organized crime surveillance" with his partner, detective Kathleen Burke. Federico Giovanelli, Carmine Gualtiere and Steven Maltese were all tried for this assassination. None were ever found guilty as first one jury and then a second deadlocked on finding anyone responsible, and the judge declared two mistrials in this case. At the first trial, an unemployed cook, Frank Simone, had testified against the three accused. At the second trial, however, Simone changed his story, saying that police coerced him to testify against these defendants, all known to have been involved with the so-called "Genovese" crime family of New York.[18]

Deviant conduct depends on organizational support. This means that any behavior which is labeled "deviant" or "different" or "criminal" by those who have the power to enforce conformity to any rules, will be punished. However, behavior which might be so labeled, but is not discovered, or if discovered is labeled otherwise, usually escapes punishment because the person who deviated has the support of others. Such support is important for two reasons. First, because an organization, as opposed to a lone individual, has many more resources with which to redefine the accused as legitimate or not-so-dangerous after all, or innocent. In addition, the organization can give the deviant person a sense of security and neutrality toward his perceived deviance in that others, associated with the organization, call the actions of the accused right or legitimate. Nothing so alleviates a sense of guilt and promotes deviant conduct, than the approval and support of others. This is no less true in connection with assassinations as is true in connection with all human activities. People want to be supported in all they do and often feel that they cannot do the simplest thing without at least some group support or approval.

It is necessary to explore how assassinations are organized and how the criminal organization makes it possible for assassins to do their work without getting caught and without having any grudge against the victim, whom they usually do not know. The anonymity of assassinations is reminiscent of war, a killing situation in which neither side is personally acquainted with the enemy but kills him just the same.

Assassination differs from homicide and multicide in that it is impersonal and seeks only to enforce the moneymaking schemes of criminals organized for that purpose. Organized criminals normally avoid anger killings, which are so often the motive in one-on-one homicide, and do not kill to eliminate classes of people (multicide). Instead, profit is their only motive.

THE "HIT"

The division of labor is the mark of any advanced civilization. This permits groups of people to engage in all kinds of activities which could not be done by any one alone, or which are too dangerous to be carried on without help. Organized criminals plan their assassinations carefully, not only with respect to the technical ways of carrying out a killing, but also with respect to the personnel involved and the emotional needs of those who kill. The division of labor permits organized criminals to segment the job of killing so that no one person is solely responsible and even more important, no one person knows all there is about the killing.

Once a victim has been designated by the organization, a "finger man" is appointed. "This 'finger man' knows only two things: the face (not necessarily the name) of the victim and the face (not necessarily the name) of the killer."[19] The finger man is responsible for getting the right victim killed, but is not the killer. The killer, on the other hand, kills the person pointed out to him, but is not responsible for the accuracy of the hit. Sometimes the wrong person is killed, a mistake criminal organizations take in stride just as all people must deal with occasional mistakes.

The victim's habits are studied by the finger man and the killer so as to discover a pattern of behavior that can be used to predict the potential victim's presence at a probable killing site. Obviously, it is easier to kill someone with predictable habits, than someone who seldom repeats the same moves.

The weapon used to commit the assassination is almost always stolen, and frequently comes from the military arsenals of the United States government. This insures that no one can be traced by means of the weapon. All serial numbers are removed in advance so that the gun can later be discarded without fear of finding the killer through identifying the weapon. Since a car is almost always used to serve as a vantage point from which to kill, the cars used are generally stolen. Again, all identification numbers are removed and the car is totally scrapped after the murder. The car is driven by a get-away specialist. The killer does not drive himself, not only because he must not be diverted from his murderous intentions, but also because he is usually from another city and does not know the traffic or the terrain. Thus, the division of labor continues.

In addition to the murder car carrying the killer, an "interference" car is used to block visibility in case of pursuit, to provide a possible second chance to get away or, in some cases, to kill the killer if he is in danger of capture, or is deemed unreliable. It is important to remember that "organized crime" assassinations are committed by killers who have no motive. This makes it extremely difficult to ever discover who the killers are.

Even if the criminal justice system should by some means discover the name of a professional assassin and he is arrested, the organization will take care of him again. Police and other criminal justice employees are sometimes on the payroll of organized crime. Those prosecutors, judges and criminal justice employees "connected" to organized crime will be less than zealous in prosecuting someone protected by "the Mob."

Even if a Mob member goes to prison, he is still protected from the harshest realities of prison life. He is given a good cell, allowed extra visiting privileges, etc. Criminal organizations, like all organizations, persist because they take care of their own. Just as the organization will protect its members, so the individual member is expected to show absolute loyalty to the group. That leads to the demand that members kill their friends, even their family, if the organization demands it or if their money is involved. Following is an example from the book *Wise Guy* by Nicholas Pileggi.

> Jimmy once killed his best friend, Remo, because he found out that Remo set up one of his cigarette loads for a pinch. They were so close. They went on vacation together with their wives. But when one of Remo's small loads got busted, he told the cops about a trailer truck load Jimmy was putting together. Jimmy got suspicious when Jimmy invested only five thousand dollars in the two-hundred-thousand dollar load. Remo usually took a third or fifty percent of the shipment. When Jimmy asked him why he wasn't going in on this load, Remo said he didn't need that much. Of course, when the truck got stopped and Jimmy's whole shipment was confiscated, the fact that Remo had somehow not invested in that particular shipment got Jimmy curious enough to ask some of his friends in the Queens DA's office. They confirmed Jimmy's suspicion that Remo had ratted the load out in return for his freedom.
>
> Remo was dead within a week. He didn't have a clue what was coming to him.

Jimmy could look at you and smile and you'd think you were sitting with your best friend in the world. Meanwhile he's got your grave dug. In fact, the very week Jimmy killed him, Remo had given Jimmy and Mickey a round-trip ticket to Florida as an anniversary present.

I remember the night. We were all playing cards in Robert's when Jimmy said to Remo, "Let's take a ride." He motioned to Tommy and another guy to come along. Remo got in the front seat and Tommy and Jimmy got in the rear. When they got to a quiet area, Tommy used a piano wire. Remo put up some fight. He kicked and swung and shit all over himself before he died. They buried him in the backyard at Robert's, under a layer of cement right next to the boccie court. From then on, every time they played, Jimmy and Tommy used to say: "Hi, Remo, how ya doing?"[20]

As the above example illustrates, the motives for assassination in the world of organized crime are almost entirely business related. It is for this reason that the killings, such as the one just described, are widely publicized among those who need to know what happens to anyone who deals "dishonestly." The fact that an assassination has occurred is made known by the crime bosses even though the name of the actual assassin is kept quiet.[21] This method of assassination occurred in Buffalo and Erie County, N.Y., in connection with the killings of the Acquino brothers in 1958, and particularly the assassination of "Billy" Sciolini in 1980 (see pages 5–7).

While assassination is used only when it is deemed necessary to protect the business of the organization or of the individual, organized crime gains control of a good number of legitimate businesses as well. This is done, not by investing money, but by controlling the important officers and/or decision makers in any business or labor union which the organized criminals would like to dominate. To gain control, organized criminals will assassinate rivals, blackmail managers, physically assault union members and use any and all financial devices imaginable. In the end, however, their success rests on two features which insure their continued existence. These are their ability and willingness to supply the public with otherwise "prohibited" goods and services, and their willingness and ability to kill.[22]

7. Assassination for a Cause

Four United States presidents have been assassinated. They are Abraham Lincoln, who was shot to death by John Wilkes Booth on April 14, 1865; James A. Garfield, who died on September 19, 1881, after having been shot on July 2 by Charles Guiteau; William McKinley, who was shot by Leon Czolgosz on September 6, 1901, leading to his death on September 14; and John F. Kennedy, who was assassinated by Lee Harvey Oswald on November 22, 1963.

Because so much has been written and said about these assassinations from both the historical and psychiatric point of view, these will not be repeated in this study. This author contends, however, that assassinations make sense for the assassin. Homicide and all three types of multicide make sense to those who do these things, and there is a continuation of this pattern here.

Examination of the record concerning assassins and would-be assassins shows that even those who suffer from obvious psychiatric disorders and delusions are nevertheless motivated by a strong desire to avenge a perceived wrong, become famous, or achieve notoriety. Furthermore, only a few of the assassins of famous persons have been delusional. Almost all assassins have been normal people who acted out of principle as they understood it. James W. Clarke, in his excellent book *American Assassins*,[1] lists the best known of these women and men. He does not list John Hinckley who attempted to assassinate President Ronald Reagan in 1981, nor did he list David Chapman who did assassinate John Lennon in 1980. His list, however, is shown on the following page.

This list of 18 assassins or would-be assassins establishes the principal motives of those who do not generally murder for money and are rarely psychiatric cases. In fact, even the truly "crazy" Charles Guiteau who assassinated President Garfield hardly did so from delusions or because he was "insane." For despite the fact that Guiteau was an unstable and somewhat erratic individual, he had not shown signs of violent conduct before he killed Garfield. A person who was so deluded and mad that he had to kill would have shown such psychiatric manifestations before he became infamous for his historic murder. Clarke points out the uselessness of imputting "paranoia," "schizophrenia" and other labels *ex post facto* to those who commit these deeds, thus making the entire psychiatric argument tautological.[2]

The author has shown elsewhere that the entire psychiatric argument concerning criminal responsibility avoids the most important issue which it should resolve but does not even address: The potential danger of permitting a person who has

American Assassins

Year	Assassin	Victim	Success or Failure
1835	Richard Lawrence	Andrew Jackson	Failed
1865	John Wilkes Booth	Abraham Lincoln	Succeeded
1881	Charles Guiteau	James Garfield	Succeeded
1901	Leon Czolgosz	William McKinley	Succeeded
1912	John Schrank	Theodore Roosevelt	Failed
1933	Guiseppe Zangara	Franklin Roosevelt	Failed
1935	Carl Weiss	Huey Long	Succeeded
1950	Oscar Collazo & Griselio Torresola	Harry Truman	Failed
1963	Lee Harvey Oswald	John F. Kennedy	Succeeded
1968	James Earl Ray	Martin Luther King, Jr.	Succeeded
1972	Arthur Bremer	George Wallace	Failed
1974	Samuel Byck	Richard Nixon	Failed
1975	Lynette A. Fromme	Gerald Ford	Failed
1980	David Chapman	John Lennon	Succeeded*
1981	John Hinckley	Ronald Reagan	Failed**

*not discussed in Clarke's book
**briefly footnoted in Clarke's book

killed another to be given his freedom and possibly kill again. It is not important to determine whether or not the individual is "sane" or "insane" alone, because these are legal, not psychiatric terms, and cannot be addressed even by a psychiatrist. To this author, the question before any judge and jury ought to be whether the person has indeed murdered someone else or has not done so. In the former event, even if the defendant is found "insane" or suffers from "diminished capacity" he should still be deemed responsible for such an act. In the event that some psychological or mental incapacity is indeed present, then the penalty phase of a trial should take this into consideration so that the penalty can be less or adjusted to the needs of the defendant wherever warranted. It is illogical to allow someone who is known to be dangerous, particularly because of his emotional state, to go free to commit his crimes again, while a person of sound mind is incarcerated or even executed when the chances of repetition in his case are far smaller than in the case of the so-called "insane" person.[3]

According to Clarke, a review of the motives of several of the assassins listed above reveals the following:[4]

Both *John Wilkes Booth* and *Leon Czolgosz* were rational and sane men who believed, in the context of the times and *their* experience that they were assassinating President Lincoln and McKinley, respectively, because the victims were tyrants from whom they, the assassins, were freeing the country. Booth and Czolgosz believed that they were duty bound to kill the president in about the same manner as the German officers who tried to kill Hitler in 1944.

It must be understood that Abraham Lincoln was not seen as a saint or martyr in his own day, but was widely hated, not only by Southerners, but also by numerous Northern citizens. McKinley was seen as an enemy of the working man in 1901 by many laborers, and particularly by immigrants. Booth killed himself, but, according to witnesses, said at the very moment of his death, "Tell mother I die for my country." Many Americans at that time agreed with him. Likewise, one of the last statements made by Czolgosz before his execution was: "McKinley was going around the country shouting prosperity when there was no prosperity for the poor man. I am not afraid to die. We all have to die sometime." Both men and their supporters saw their act as an act of heroism.

Oscar Collazo and Griselio Torresola tried, but failed, to assassinate President Harry S Truman. Sirhan Sirhan did assassinate Robert Kennedy, then a United States senator and a Democratic party candidate for the nomination for the presidency. Since Griselio Torresola was killed in the attempt to assassinate the president, there is no statement of his intentions or views. However, Collazo repeatedly said during and after his trial that he did not expect to free Puerto Rico from United States domination, nor that the death of the president would end in Puerto Rican independence. In a most rational way Collazo believed that his own death would call attention to conditions in Puerto Rico and that his own death would be the beginning, not the end, of a movement in the direction of independence. "The cause was paramount, the ideological theme of the political zealot unmistakable."[5]

When Sirhan Sirhan assassinated Robert Kennedy on June 5, 1968, he also insisted that "I did it for my country." He denied any delusions and answered the suggestion that God told him to kill the senator with the statement: "God didn't tell me to kill Kennedy." In an interview over ten years after the assassination, Sirhan continued to say that he had done a justifiable thing in killing Kennedy, a view he continued to hold years later. Clarke rightly sees him in the same light as any terrorist without being a psychiatric case, who follows the irrational attitudes that produce war and extreme nationalism.

Samuel Byck killed two men he did not know. One was the co-pilot of an airplane he had hijacked in Baltimore on February 22, 1974, and the other was a security guard at that airport whom Byck had killed a little earlier in order to get on that plane to Washington, D.C. It was his aim to crash that plane into the White House and assassinate not only President Nixon, but also anyone else involved in the Nixon administration who might be present when Byck crashed into it. According to Clarke, "it seems reasonable to suggest that if Samuel Byck had had other options in his personal life, he would not have chosen to die as he did."[6]

Byck had failed in his marriage and in the economic world. He was divorced and he had no job. Thus, he had nothing to live for. Rejected by his mother, his wife and children, he hoped to give his life a sense of worth and at the same time place "the burden of guilt" on his uncaring relatives. Here are three victims of a competitive society, one of whom, Samuel Byck, sought to rectify all of his perceived failures by one last act of desperation, an act which he believed would finally gain for him what has been called "existential validation."

This same motive also propelled Mark David Chapman into notoriety when he assassinated John Lennon on December 9, 1980. Lennon was a cultural hero in the sense that his association with rock and roll music, and particularly the British group the Beatles, led many to view him in nearly "super-human" terms, a type of adulation that also devolved upon other popular musicians from time to time. Chapman, who saw himself as a failure, had good reason to think so. He had failed as a student, a musician and as a camp counselor. For a while he had become involved in fundamentalist Christianity and attempted to convert others to that view. This also failed. His girlfriend left him, he dropped out of college after only one semester and attempted suicide. That also failed and he was hospitalized for observation.

Chapman viewed all those who he felt had contributed to his failures as hypocrites. He believed, or enjoyed believing, that only John Lennon was an exception to the world's hypocrisy. He bought all of Lennon's records, read everything he could find about his hero and moved from Honolulu to New York, "hanging around" the apartment house where Lennon lived. He incessantly read *The Catcher in the Rye*, J.D. Salinger's popular novel with overtones of martyrdom. When Chapman shot Lennon in the back in the lobby of Lennon's apartment house, Chapman finally felt that he existed, that he had substance, that he made a difference. He thereby reversed all his disappointments for he truly believed, as he had told a friend, "the world has decided that there is no place for Mark Chapman, that Mark Chapman didn't exist."[7]

All the world knows the name of *Lee Harvey Oswald* who assassinated President John F. Kennedy by shooting him in the back of the head from the sixth floor of the Dallas School Book Depository on November 22, 1963. Oswald was a man who had failed at everything important to him. His wife had rejected him, and his efforts to belong to the revolutionary forces in Cuba had been rejected as well. He was disillusioned by his treatment while in the Soviet Union and he felt unfairly harassed by the FBI who did indeed watch him after his return from Russia. Thus, as Clarke puts it: "Oswald's personal frustrations at a zenith, another plan to resolve the frustrations of life began to emerge. If this one worked, he would be able to even the score with the FBI to prove his mettle and revolutionary credentials to the Cubans who had humiliated him, and to assert his manhood to the wife who had belittled him."[8]

The plan was, of course, to kill the president of the United States. When less than 48 hours after the assassination, Oswald was himself murdered by Jack Ruby, he too fell victim to yet another of life's failures who entered the history books with him.

The fourth person in this quartet of assassins is the unsuccessful would-be killer of President Ronald Reagan, *John Hinckley*. Hinckley's life appeared a failure to him and like Oswald who sought to alleviate his sense of failure and frustration by embracing radical communist politics, Hinckley became a member of the American Nazi party from which he was expelled, just as Oswald was expelled from Cuba.[9]

Prior to this expulsion, Hinckley had failed at college, attending Texas Tech University for seven years without graduating. In his frustration, augmented by the successes of his wealthy family, Hinckley, like Chapman, engaged in a fantasy life concerning a performer, in his case the actress Jodie Foster who had starred in the movie *Taxi Driver*. This movie glorified a mass murderer and turned him into a hero. Hinckley, upon seeing this movie, began to write letters to Foster and fancied himself in love with her, although he had never met her. Hinckley believed that killing the president would give him the "macho" standing that would lead to admiration by Foster and permit him to finally make his life important. Hinckley did not hate President Reagan. His motives had nothing to do with the nature of the president or his policies. They had to do with Hinckley and with a condition in Western civilization far older than the United States.

United States culture is only one branch of the Western tradition which began in ancient Greece and was continued by the Romans. In spite of the so-called Dark Ages, better called the Middle Ages, ranging from the fall of Rome in the fifth century to the fall of Constantinople in the fifteenth, this tradition has been perpetuated to this day through all the wars and all the tribulations that have been a part of Europe. Included in that Western tradition was the belief, instilled in every child from the days of Pericles to this day, that each person must mean something, that each must make a difference in this world, and compete with others for "a place in the sun." Evidence for this belief abounds. The ancients played in the Olympic games for over 1,000 years and sought there to distinguish themselves as people do today. Pitched battles were fought through the centuries to defend the honor of a woman or a man or a family. Achievements were praised and prized in every area of human endeavor from art to science, from sports to warfare. Ambition, the wish to be recognized, and the need for power and influence motivated the ancients as they motivate people today. Such a tradition is not found everywhere. There are billions of people in Asia, Africa and elsewhere who are not acquainted with the Western world view and who do not share its ambitions or failures.

The great and astonishing consequences of the Western tradition cannot be listed here. It is, however, important to recall that the rise of science and industry, of arts and letters, of social reform and political democracy, are all the outcome of that tradition. Founded on the hope of individual rewards for outstanding achievement, the Western tradition is and has been for 3,000 years, marked by an achieving society.

Not everyone can be an achiever. Achievement for some means failure for others — Hinckley and Oswald, Chapman and Byck are only four examples. Assassination of famous persons is not an "insane" act, whatever that word means. Western culture creates failure and disappointment, anger and frustration, because of the emphasis on personal attainment with the concomitant result of personal failure. Western culture invites desperation, aggression, hostility, and in some cases, murder born of envy.[10] Envy is born of a desire to have or to be what another has or is, but it is also the product of impotence. The envious believe that they cannot achieve anything themselves, and therein lies the basis for revolution and for murder.[11]

Envy is related to scarcity. If everyone had everything, then envy could not exist. But such a condition is not conceivable in the Western world. Envy will therefore always plague society, for everyone cannot be beautiful, intelligent, rich, powerful, inventive, etc. Society must always remain on the alert, for the assassin lurks wherever there is achievement and the killer seeks his victims wherever there is success.

One of the beliefs of assassins of famous persons is that they make a difference because they kill someone whose continued life would have altered history. They believe that by killing that person the assassins themselves change the course of history. This belief has been denied by William Shakespeare in his play *Julius Caesar*, and by Leo Tolstoy in the epilogue of his monumental novel *War and Peace*.[12]

Tolstoy denies, as does this author, that history and or social forces are determined by the life or will of one person. Tolstoy, having described the Napoleonic invasion of Russia, concludes that the "wielder of power" cannot alone determine the outcome of history. "The movement of nations," says Tolstoy, "is caused not by power, nor by intellectual activity nor even by a combination of the two as historians have supposed, but by the activity of all the people who participate in the events. . . . Morally the wielder of power appears to cause the event; physically it is those who submit to the power."[13]

Tolstoy contends that assassins wrongly believe that they alter history. It is inconceivable from the sociological viewpoint that United States policy was severely altered by the assassination of President Kennedy and the accession of President Lyndon B. Johnson. The same holds true of the other three presidential assassinations in United States history, and the assassinations of Robert Kennedy and Martin Luther King, Jr. The assassins never had a chance to change the course of events because history is the outcome of the collective will of millions, not the product of one man, however glamorous or famous.

There are certain principles of sociology and history which operate upon the lives of all people. These are collective beliefs developed from the experience of mankind, not the views of any one person. Among these are justice and equity, which abhor murder and violence. "Fiat justitia, ruat caelum" said the Romans. "Let justice be done, though the heavens fall."

Assassination generally results in the opposite of what the assassin wished. The victims are glorified as martyrs. Their policies become enshrined with them and become so sanctified, that contrary to the assassin's wishes, they now have a greater influence than they had before the victim was killed. This is exactly the outcome of the assassination of Abraham Lincoln, and the assassinations of the Kennedy brothers and Martin Luther King, Jr.

Dr. Martin Luther King, Jr., was assassinated by *James Earl Ray* on April 4, 1968. A review of Ray's life indicates a typical "disadvantaged" childhood. The son of poor parents who had too many children to support, Ray became embroiled in "desertion, neglect, despair, alcoholism and crime"[14] at an early age. He was a petty criminal as were his brothers. In and out of jails, the Ray brothers became acquainted with an offer by some racially motivated persons to pay $50,000 for the death of Dr. King. While there is no conclusive evidence that Ray was ever hired to carry out this "contract," it is important to recall that Ray was never tried but pleaded "guilty" and was sentenced to 99 years in prison without revealing the motives for his crime or the conspiracy which may have encouraged him to commit it. Ray believed, and had reason to believe, that he would not be convicted in front of a Southern jury, that the FBI was not interested in bringing the killer of Dr. King to justice, and that he would finally make a lot of money. None of this became true and Ray remains in prison.

Despite his miscalculations, however, Ray is not "crazy" or "insane." Says Clarke: "His decision to kill Dr. King and his conduct to the present has been that of a coldly rational and shrewd . . . hit man. . . . Except for the pre-eminence of his victim, Ray might have still gotten away with his crime, just as had the accused killers of Medgar Evers, James Chaney, Andrew Goodman, Michael Schwerner, Viola Liuzzo, and scores of nameless black persons over the years. Given that record in the southern courts and the fifty thousand dollar bounty, it seemed like a reasonable venture to Ray."[15]

"I wasn't going to shoot him. I just wanted to get some attention for a new trial for Charlie and the girls." So said *Lynette Fromme*, according to the *Sacramento Bee*.[16] She meant to get a new trial for Charles Manson who had become the most notorious mass murderer in America to that time because of the Tate-La Bianca murders. Manson, then and now in a California prison, seemed to Fromme to be another Christ. She followed him slavishly and organized her life around his views and his person. It is tempting to call this "crazy," particularly since Manson appears to be a "crazy" himself. But Clarke argues that Fromme differs from other "true believers" only in the sense that she formed her beliefs around a person and not an abstract ideal such as Christianity, Judaism, Hinduism, fascism or any of the other "isms" in which mankind believes. It is not at all "crazy" to have such an allegiance.[17]

Fromme attempted to shoot, or at least pointed an empty gun at President Gerald Ford on September 5, 1975. This happened in Sacramento. Two and one-half weeks later, on September 22, 1975, *Sara Jane Moore* fired a gun at President Ford during his visit to San Francisco. Moore had been an FBI informant and had betrayed her erstwhile friends in a "radical" movement. When these friends discovered her chicanery, they cut her off from all contacts, a punishment she could not tolerate. Her isolation, loss of credentials among her peers, the unwillingness of the FBI to accommodate her fears, and her desperate hope to belong led her to what Clarke calls "penance." "When she finished, she reasoned, no one . . . could ever again question her loyalty, sincerity, and commitment."[18] Sara Moore has fulfilled her mission. She has been imprisoned for life, but she has lived for a purpose. She is not a nonperson any more. She has a place in history. She is a "certified revolutionary with impeccable credentials."[19] She belongs.

This discussion of assassins ends with a mention of *Dr. Carl Weiss* who allegedly shot Louisiana governor Huey Long to death in 1935. There is no doubt that Dr. Weiss was a sane and adjusted person even on the day he allegedly murdered Huey Long inside the Louisiana State House. Long was a populist governor and senator who had a national following in 1935. He meant to redistribute the wealth in the United States and was so competent an orator that he has been repeatedly compared to William Jennings Bryan. Carl Weiss was a successful doctor. He was married to a woman from a politically active family whom Long attacked, claiming that the Pavy family, Weiss's in-laws, were of partial "Negro" descent. Such a charge was political death at that time in that place. There is the possibility that Weiss was motivated to kill Long because the latter had made such a charge. However, there is an equal chance that Weiss did not kill Long. It is possible that Weiss punched him and that security forces started shooting at the sight of this assault and killed both Long and Weiss in the course of firing indiscriminately. In any case, both died of their wounds and no autopsy was ever performed to settle the question as to who really shot Long.[20]

Additional names of assassins are listed in Clarke's book[21] and more material could be marshalled to bolster the evidence that assassinations are usually performed by persons who are sane, who think reasonably and who perform an act, however abhorrent, which to them seems to make sense. To Brutus, the assassination of Caesar made sense. Shakespeare has him say, "Not that I loved Caesar less, but that I loved Rome more. Had you rather Caesar were living and die all slaves, than that Caesar were dead to live all free men? As Caesar loved me I weep for him; as he was fortunate I rejoice at it; as he was valiant I honor him; but, as he was ambitious, I slew him."[43] So said Shakespeare and so thinks many an assassin.

8. Murder at Random: Terror for a "Cause"

"It's simply murder," wrote Charles Krauthammer in December 1984 with reference to the killing of two passengers and the torture of many more by the hijackers of a Kuwaiti airliner in Tehran that month.[1] This was a reminder many readers needed because, for so many years, a large number of persons have failed to view this type of conduct as murder on the grounds that the so-called root causes of terrorism, that is, oppression, frustration, desperation, etc., were used as unending excuses, even for the most gruesome killings, since the Nazi terror of the 1930s and 1940s.

Terrorism has been defined as: "a tactic or technique by means of which a violent act or the threat thereof is used for the prime purpose of creating overwhelming fear for coercive purposes."[2] The terror-murders begun in the late 1960s came to a climax on December 21, 1988, with the bombing of Pan American flight 103 which blew up over Lockerbie, Scotland, and killed 275 people.[3] This act of mass murder typifies terror-murder in that it was directed, at random, at persons who could not possibly be responsible for the grievances which the terrorists believed gave them the right to kill these victims.

The murderers of the Pan Am passengers were evidently Palestinians who, in the pay of Iran, induced a passenger on that flight to carry a bomb onto the Boeing 747.[4] That bomb, of course, killed the duped passenger as well as all the other occupants of the plane, passengers and crew alike.[5] Concealed in a radio cassette player, the bomb exploded over land, rather than over water as planned, thus permitting British and American investigators to assemble the parts of the wrecked plane on the ground around Lockerbie and thereby reach the conclusion that the plane was deliberately sabotaged.[6]

In addition to the 258 persons aboard the plane who died, 17 residents of Lockerbie were killed as the parts of the plane rained down upon that small Scottish town. "It was like meteors falling from the sky," said Ann McPhail, a resident of Lockerbie. "There were flames in the front and back garden, and I could hear things falling on the roof . . . the house just three doors down went up like a time bomb. We didn't know what hit us."[7] In addition to parts of the plane, the dismembered parts of the passengers also landed on the streets and rooftops of Lockerbie. The passengers of Flight 103 and the citizens of a small town in Scotland

112

and all their friends and relatives became the victims of an attack by persons unknown to them, persons with whom they had no quarrel, and with whose grievances they had nothing to do. That, however, is the nature of terrorism. Terrorism strikes at anyone, particularly persons who have no connection to the perpetrators. Thus, no one feels safe, all are possible victims and nothing anyone may do or fail to do will protect him against murder by terrorists.

It was this method of attacking utterly innocent persons, even supporters of the regime, which made Nazi terror so effective a generation earlier. By suddenly arresting and killing persons who had done absolutely nothing to incur the anger of the Nazi party, by murdering even some loyal followers of Nazi ideology or murdering long standing members of the Nazi party, Hitler and his henchmen announced, in effect, that no one was safe and or could rest secure at any time.[8] This arbitrary use of violence succeeded in promoting utter terror in the population and ended all resistance to Nazi rule. Likewise, it has been the hope of late 20th century terrorists to impose their demands on goverments and nations by striking arbitrarily at targets which happened to be available. Such horrible actions as the bombing of planes, the slaughter of innocent passengers waiting in an Italian airline terminal and the machine-gunning of innocent persons eating in a French restaurant are all excused by terrorists and their supporters by claiming that these murders are all justified by numerous "underlying causes," and that therefore the murderers, and not the innocents who have been wounded, maimed and killed, are the victims.[9]

These "underlying causes" for murder are generally a political statement promoted by various United Nations representatives and other diplomats who seek to label murderers "freedom fighters" even when their victims are schoolchildren utterly unable to defend themselves and in no way connected with the grievances of the killers.[10]

A short and partial list of such mass murders on the part of politically motivated killers shows that the blowing up of Pan Am Flight 103 was surely not the only incident of airplane mass murder. Over the years there have been others, such as:

• The explosion which disintegrated a United Airlines DC-68 on November 1, 1955. This happened on a flight from San Francisco to Portland, Oregon, when a bomb exploded on board about 11 minutes after takeoff. The plane disintegrated and 39 passengers and five crew died. The wreckage revealed that a dynamite bomb had been located in one of the baggage compartments.[11]

• On July 8, 1965, a DC-68 operated by Canadian Pacific Airlines exploded over British Columbia. The tail section of the plane separated from the aircraft and all 52 persons aboard died in the ensuing crash.

• On a scheduled flight to Nicosia, Cyprus, on October 12, 1967, an explosion in the passenger cabin of a British Airways Comet 48 led to the murder of all 66 aboard. This occurred at 28,000 feet. Recovery of some debris and bodies clearly proved that a bomb had been planted on the plane.

• Cathay Pacific Airways CV880 was flying from Thailand to Hong Kong on June 15, 1972, when a bomb exploded in a suitcase under a passenger seat. Eighty-one passengers and crew died.

• A "skyjacker" detonated two hand grenades inside the cockpit of an Air Vietnam B727 on September 15, 1974. The pilot lost control of the plane and all 70 passengers and crew were killed.

• In 1982 a new and yet more deadly device was first used in airplane bombings than had been used heretofore. This new device, a plastic bomb, is impervious to conventional metal detectors. In addition, it is small, hence easily hidden and it has both a barometer and a timer so that it can be set to determine the altitude and the time at which the bomb will go off. This was first used underneath a seat of a Pan Am 747 flying from Tokyo to Honolulu. It killed a 16-year-old Japanese boy when it went off. Two weeks later, a similar device was found, unexploded in another Pan Am plane in Rio de Janeiro.[12]

• One hundred and twelve people were murdered on September 23, 1983, when a bomb exploded in the baggage compartment of a B737 belonging to Gulf Air Bahrain. Again, a plastic device as deadly as the bomb which brought down Pan Am flight 103 in December 1988 was used. The plane was 30 miles from the Kuwait airport.

• Approaching the coast of Ireland at about 30,000 feet, an Air India B747 disintegrated on June 21, 1985, when a bomb exploded aboard, killing 329 people. Plastic explosives had been planted in the baggage compartment and the lavatory of the plane.[13]

Before discussing what has been done or can be done to combat this appalling amount of murder it is well to list some of the principal killers and their various "causes" which lead them to these deeds. Existential validation is heavily involved as a motive for murdering others, and terrorists share this motive with other killers who, despite their lofty protestations, have motives not unlike other murderers discussed in other chapters of this book.

WHERE TERRORISM IS MOST PREVALENT

While the list of countries in which terrorism has occurred is extensive, it is evident by inspecting such a list that some regions of the world are much more likely to suffer a number of terrorist attacks, while other countries are mostly spared that misery. From 1970 to 1973 there was a great deal of terrorism spread all over the world, but particularly in West Germany, Great Britain, the Middle East and South America. This illustrates a pattern which has since continued, so that terrorism even in 1990 is still mostly confined to those three areas. The following list serves to show how terrorism is clustered around some areas of the world. The years studied here are 1970–1974 because they saw an unusual amount of terrorism and are therefore useful in illustrating the global extent of this type of murder. Furthermore, this list serves as a reminder that terrorism is by no means a new form of murder invented in the late 1980s, but has been in its present form for two decades. It also shows that the number of persons who can now be murdered in one attack, such as occurred on Pan Am Flight 103, is far greater than was possible heretofore.

The events listed here were not the only acts of terrorism occurring in each of the countries listed, but they are a complete list of the terrorism-murders which occurred in these countries in those four years. For the purposes of this study, the cases are listed to exhibit the extent and the frequency of terrorism-murder.

• On January 20, 1970, "unknown gunmen entered the British Consulate in Guatemala City, Guatemala, where they shot and killed the consul's bodyguard." When the Guatemalan government refused to negotiate with the rebel armed forces kidnappers of the West German ambassador to that country, the terrorists killed the ambassador on March 31, 1970.[14]

• On February 10, 1970, three Arab terrorists killed one Israeli citizen and wounded 11 other passengers in a grenade attack on a bus at the airport in Munich, Germany.

• On September 5, 1972, also in Munich, eight Palestinian terrorists killed two Israeli athletes taking part in the Olympic Games. Subsequently, nine hostages and five of the terrorists were killed in a gun battle with police.

• The United States Assistant Military Attache to Jordan was shot to death by guerrillas on June 10, 1970.

• A United States public safety adviser in Uruguay was kidnapped by the Tupamaros on July 31, 1970, and murdered when the president of Uruguay refused to negotiate with the terrorists.

• On April 7, 1970, the Yugoslav ambassador to Sweden was murdered by Croatian terrorists in Stockholm.

• Istanbul, Turkey, became the scene for the murder of the Israeli Consul General after the Turkish government rejected the demand of the Turkish People's Liberation Army to release all guerrillas held in Turkish jails on May 17, 1971. Less than a year later, in March of 1972 the TPLA murdered three NATO technicians.

• The Jordanian prime minister was murdered on November 28, 1971 in Egypt by members of "Black September."

• Seven persons were murdered and five wounded when a bomb exploded at Aldershot, England, on January 22, 1972. The Irish Republican Army planted that bomb as well as two more on March 8, 1973, when one victim was killed and 200 wounded in London.

• On February 3, 1974, a 50-pound bomb concealed in a suitcase destroyed a bus in Yorkshire, England, killing 11, and on July 17 of that same year a bomb planted by the Irish Republican Army exploded in the Tower of London, killing one person and wounding 41.

• The manager of the Italian automaker Fiat was kidnapped in Argentina by the "People's Revolutionary Army" on March 21, 1972. He was subsequently murdered as the police were about to discover the hideout of the kidnappers.

• On November 22, 1973, an American executive of the Ford Motor Company, and his three bodyguards were all murdered in Cordoba, Argentina by terrorists calling themselves "The Peronist Armed Forces."

• On May 31, 1972 three Japanese gunmen killed 25 passengers and wounded 76 others at Israel's Lod Airport using machine guns and hand grenades.

• On June 20, 1972 19 Croatian terrorists killed 13 security officers in Bugo-jnok, Yugoslavia.

• The first secretary of the Swedish embassy in Bogota, Colombia, was murdered by shotgun blasts by unidentified killers on July 17, 1972.

• The French honorary consul in Zaragoza, Spain, was murdered when three killers bombed the consulate on November 2, 1972.

• Los Angeles was the scene of murder when the Turkish consul was killed by a man of Armenian origin wishing revenge for the 1915 slaughter of Armenians in Turkey. This happened on January 27, 1973. Later that year, on July 1, an Arab terrorist shot and killed the Israeli military attache in Washington, D.C.

• An airline employee was murdered outside a department store in Rome, Italy, by a Lebanese member of Black September.

• On the 22nd of August, 1973, a United States citizen was murdered when a bomb exploded in his hotel room in Avrainville, France. He had been a member of the anti–Castro "Cuban Revolutionary Directorate."

• Ethiopia was the scene of terrorism-murder on May 26, 1974, when five employees of an American oil company were kidnapped and one murdered by the "Eritrean Liberation Front."

This list of 17 countries in which terrorism-murder occurred from 1970 through 1974 includes eight European countries, four South American nations and three countries in the Middle East. Ethiopia and Egypt are the African countries listed. The United States is also included. While there were 24 incidents of terrorism in those five years, the total number murdered in all of these incidents of terror was 85. This should now be compared to *one* incident of terrorism murder which cost the lives of 275 persons in December of 1988 and seven such incidents as discussed above, leading to the death of 695 persons over four years.

It is obvious that during the 20 years ending in 1990, terror-murder has become far more dangerous than it was when the number of terrorist acts was more frequent than it is now. The evidence indicates that even as more sophisticated devices are used to prevent the sabotage of airplanes and other public conveyances, and even as the actual number of terrorist attacks is reduced by better security arrangements and intelligence work by the international community to defeat the efforts of terrorists, these murderers can kill more victims with one successful attack than numerous such attacks could kill 20 years ago.

As the previous list has indicated, the victims of terrorism-murder in the 1970s were always the political representatives of various nations, serving in one capacity or another in a foreign country. The killings at that time were designed to call attention to the various grievances which the murderers had, not necessarily against the victim, but against the government which he represented. Thus, the mass murder of the Armenians in Turkey, which was discussed in Chapter 4, was the motive for the "revenge" murder of the Turkish consul in Los Angeles in 1973 by a killer of Armenian descent.

By the end of the 1980s, however, the victims had become anyone at all who happened to be flying on an American plane or the plane of some other country whose policies were disliked, or whose government was deemed obnoxious. The murders resulting from these sudden attacks killed victims who were not even nationals of the countries whose planes were bombed, or if they were, such as a group of students from Syracuse University killed on Pan Am Flight 103, they had absolutely no connection with the deeds of the United States Navy in the Persian Gulf the year before. Nor can it be said that the terrorists achieved anything but terror by reason of these murders. No political advantages have yet been gained by these means nor has any government altered its policies to bring an end to terror. This is evident in the Middle East, where the United States has maintained the same policies for years; in Ireland, where British soldiers have been stationed for 300 years; and all over Latin America where despite numerous revolutions, coups and other violence, terrorists have never gained their ends, particularly because the victims of these murders were not Latin Americans, but Americans and Europeans. In view of the singular failure of these tactics of murder and terror against innocent people, it is necessary to explain the motives of killers known as "terrorists."

MESSIANISM

The word "Messiah" comes from the Hebrew and means savior. Hence, messianism refers to the belief on the part of some persons that they have been elected to save the world, or their society or a particular cause by any means whatever, including violence. Messianism has been called "a social illusion" for generating the superhuman efforts revolutions require.[15] Messianism produces an ideal society for the revolutionaries which they believe is imminent. Believing also that their actions will bring the process of a final and perfect society to a quick resolution, they act accordingly.

For example, one tradition in Islam holds that the "Mahdi" (Messia) will come at the beginning of a new century. Thus, in the first hour of the first day of the Islamic year 1400 (1979), a group of Moslems from 12 countries attacked Islam's holiest shrine, the Grand Mosque at Mecca, Saudi Arabia, in the belief that this would produce the instant appearance of the "Mahdi." This was a particularly offensive action to Sunni Muslims not only because of the place, but also because of the time of the attack. It occurred during a holy moment, a time of prayer when the faithful were marking the "Hijira" or migration of Mohammed from Mecca to Medina. The Islamic year begins with this event.[16]

Messianists of whatever stripe also view their opponents as being far more powerful than they really are. Thus, the enemy is seen as "the Sons of Darkness," according to the Dead Sea Scrolls, or "the anti–Christ," a phrase with which the Reverend Ian Paisley, leader of some Protestants in Northern Ireland, designates the Pope. Communists like to label their opponents "counter-revolutionaries" or "running dogs of capitalism," etc. These enemies of "the truth" are viewed by messianists as having no rights. The messianist believes himself to be wholly righteous and his enemies wholly wrong.

In the eyes of Islamic terrorists, for example, a holy war or *jihad* must be fought against apostates in particular. This lies behind the call to kill the author Salman

Rushdie, who, although raised a Muslim, was deemed to have insulted that faith by publishing his book, *Satanic Verses*. Such attitudes are of course by no means limited to the followers of Islam. Such attitudes can be discerned everywhere and in some cases lead to self righteous murder.

Among such messianists have been the German terrorists to whom Jay Becker refers as "Hitler's Children,"[17] the various factions in the endless Northern Irish civil war, and a long list of terrorist murderers of every nationality around the world. Among these, the Germans are here examined first.

DIE ROTE ARMEE FRAKTION

On April 28, 1989, a number of German terrorists, convicted of murder, kidnapping, robbery and other crimes were engaged in a hunger strike inside various German prisons where some had already spent 17 years, while others had been imprisoned only six years. The hunger strikers demanded that the German government place all of them into one prison and that there the 40 or so terrorists be given the privilege of living together in one group apart from other prisoners on the grounds that the terrorists saw themselves as political prisoners engaged in a war against Germany, or at least the German government.

Supported in their demands by some outside sympathizers, the terrorists and their friends called the practice of distributing them to various prisons throughout Germany "Isolations Folter," i.e., isolation torture. They demanded this grouping of terrorists, not because they were kept in isolation, but because they were housed with all other prisoners in their respective prisons and hence were seen by prison officials as common criminals. This, however, is a label they wished to avoid at all cost, even at the cost of starving to death. Such are the views of Irmgard Möller, who has been in prison for 18 years, and other members of the Red Army Command imprisoned since 1977 (Lutz Taufer), since 1982 (Christian Klar) or since 1983 (Gisela Dutzi).[18]

In this attitude (the belief that one is fighting for a cause against the enemy as in war) lies a good deal of the explanation for terrorist activities, however bizarre. The German terrorists serve as a good example of the belief that even the most brutal murder is not a crime as long as the motive for committing the murder is righteous. This belief, by no means new or unique, has now been embraced by two generations of German terrorists, just as it has fired the fuel of hatred and murder in the minds of numerous Palestinian, Irish and other terrorists.

The Red Army Command was founded in the early 1970s by Ulrike Meinhof, Andreas Baader, Astrid Proll and Gudrun Ensslin. Of the four founders, Baader was the only man. Subsequently, a number of men and many women became associated with this terrorist organization which has succeeded in attracting new, younger members in recent years, and promises to continue to attract members even as the Irish Republican Army has done over an even greater time span.[19]

The murders committed by the nearly 40 terrorists now serving in German prisons are best illustrated by the killings of the German chief prosecutor Haas

Buback, the prominent German banker Jurgen Ponto and the murder of Hans Schleyer, president of the German National Association of Manufacturers, all in 1977. Baader and Meinhof were not directly involved in these killings—Meinhof died in the Stammheim prison on May 9, 1976, and Baader, as well as Ensslin and another early terrorist, Jan Carl Raspe, all died in German prisons on September 18, 1977. There are those who believe that Meinhof was murdered by the German prison authorities at the command of the German or Bavarian government. (Stammheim is located in Bavaria.) Buback, Ponto and Schleyer were abducted by various ruses and then murdered while in the captivity of the Red Army Command as revenge for the death of Meinhof who was viewed as a martyr to the cause.

Ulrike Meinhof was important to the cause of terrorism because she gave these activities a *raison d'être*. Not only did she organize terror actions, she explained to all who were willing to listen that terrorism was and is necessary in order to change not only German but world society into an ideal which she had mainly gained from the writings of Karl Marx. When Palestinian terrorists abducted and murdered several Israeli athletes during the Munich Olympic Games in 1972, Meinhof and her friend Horst Mahler justified these murders on the grounds that "a symbiosis exists between Zionism and Imperialism."[20] Meinhof also talked about Germany as "the territory of a power participating in war."[21] She labeled terrorists "combat troops" and made numerous observations which did not then, nor now, correspond to reality.

It is, of course, true that reality is in part subjective. Nevertheless, political surroundings, in addition to physical conditions, lend themselves to some common agreement among people. No one would deny that Cuba is in the hands of a dictatorship and does not have a democratically elected government. To claim otherwise is not real. Similarly, Germany was a parliamentary democracy in the 1970s despite many admitted shortcomings evident in that type of arrangement. The German terrorists. and all terrorists everywhere, use language which seems to contradict the facts of life and experience so that their motives in carrying out murder and other crimes become obscure and even incomprehensible to outsiders.

Ulrike Meinhof understood this well and therefore preached that the only manner in which the German public would become convinced that the "imperialist German government" must be overthrown would be through the "Primacy of Practice."[22] By that she meant large numbers of Germans and others would become willing to support her revolution by the demonstration of terror, such as the murder of prominent persons, because that would show the risks she and her friends were willing to take to bring about that revolution. This belief can be called "conversion by deed" rather than conversion by persuasion.

Another theorist of the German "Rote Armee Fraktion" was Andreas Baader, who was one of the founders of that organization and also one of its martyrs. Baader was a classical Marxist, and dealt with Marx as if nothing had been learned since Marx died in 1883. Baader wrote in 1975 that, "the guerrillas have two feet," meaning that one of these "feet" was the class struggle in the metropolitan areas of Europe and the second "foot" the "proletarian freedom fighters of the third world," (the terrorists originating in the Middle East, India and Latin America).[23]

Marx, unlike Baader, understood and wrote that revolutions occur in societies oppressed by an inherited aristocracy whose oppression makes all other avenues of relief, except revolution, impossible.[24] Such conditions did not exist in Germany in the 1970s, however, negating the Baader-Meinhof analysis. Their analysis was further refuted by the facts: None of their acts of terror and murder led to the general strike they hoped would occur, nor did the public support them. On the contrary, their killings led to general fear of them, not the government, and caused revulsion for their "cause." Both Baader and Meinhof were fortunate to have died before they had to witness the massive changes in China and in the Soviet Union against dictatorships, which indeed have forced millions of people to take to the streets to demand freedom from a tyranny imposed by Marxists.

Baader, Meinhof and their followers also claimed that Germany was and is in the grip of "terror from above," meaning Nazi-style terror forced upon the population by government. While the shortcomings of capitalist democracy with respect to the poor and the homeless deserve no excuse, it is an utter fabrication and an unreal argument to liken such social conditions to the Nazi murders described earlier in this book. Everyone, except the Baader-Meinhof group, knows this. Thus, again, the insistence on unreality makes the "Rote Armee Fraktion" appear to be no more than a gang of criminals with a hidden agenda.

The entire Marxist argument, even from the pen of Marx himself, is based on many assumptions that are contrary to reality. This unrealistic world view was imposed upon the followers of Marx by Marx's insistence on turning the Hegelian dialectic upside down and substituting the material dialectic for Hegel's ideational dialectic. This is not to say that a material view of history cannot be supported by real evidence. The problem lies in the conclusions which Marx and his supporters drew from this observation. These conclusions became dogma in the hands of Marx and "holy writ" in the minds of his followers. Those of Marx's followers, such as the "Rote Armee Fraktion," concluded that in the name of the coming revolution they were entitled to kill the representatives of the current oppressors as they saw fit. They therefore killed prominent German businessmen and politicians even as other terrorists killed representatives of the United States in Latin America and elsewhere.

RELIGIOUS STRIFE IN IRELAND

For 300 years, since William of Orange defeated James the II at the Battle of the Boyne in 1690,[25] Protestants and Catholics have fought one another in Northern Ireland and elsewhere. (Historians will agree that there was a good deal of killing and fighting in Ireland even before that.) Today this fighting continues to take its toll in human lives and suffering. While attacks on British forces by Irish "freedom fighters" are not the province of this discussion, terrorism in Northern Ireland consists of attacks on private citizens carried out at random by both Catholics and Protestants against each other, and can therefore be deemed terrorism-murder.

While the history of Ireland and the motives of the participants in these killings are not the same as in Germany, there is nevertheless a good deal of similarity between "Die Rote Armee Fraktion," and the Irish Republican Army, or the Ulster Defense Asssociation. All believe that murder is justified in the name of their cause and all commit atrocities of the most hideous kind. It is not the purpose of this book to deal with the merits of these "causes," but rather to mention but a very few of the murders in which various of the Irish factions have engaged recently.

In March 1988 three Irish "terrorists" (Maired Farrell, a woman, and two men, Sean Savage and Daniel McCann) were murdered while walking unarmed on a street in Gibraltar. All three were admittedly members of the Irish Republican Army and all three were suspected of terrorist activities. Yet, the British Special Air Service which killed the three in Gibraltar had no evidence at the time that all or any one had breached the law in any way or was in any manner dangerous. They had parked a car in the center of Gibraltar, which was found to be empty of any explosives, but it had been rumored that the car had a bomb. Later it was discovered that the three had rented yet another car which was found on the Spanish side of the frontier and did contain 140 pounds of explosives. No wonder that the *Economist* headlined the story of the killings, "Quis custodiet ipsos custodes?" or, "Who is watching the watchers?"[26]

The round of murders did not end here, however. At the funeral of the three in a West Belfast cemetery in the Catholic area of the city, Michael Stone ran into the crowd of mourners and threw grenades while also shooting at people with an automatic pistol. This attack left three mourners dead, five seriously wounded and 50 injured. The murderer was chased and beaten by the crowd. He was then arrested by the Royal Ulster Constabulary who discovered that he possessed "high quality new weapons," given him by the Protestant Action Force, a terrorist group with a record of murder equal to that of the Irish Republican Army. The leader of the Irish Republican Army's political wing, Gerry McAdam, promptly accused the police of being in collusion with the murderer and vowed revenge on both the Protestants and the police.[27]

An effort to understand the motives for all the murder in Northern Ireland was made in the summer of 1988. An unnamed correspondent for *The Economist* interviewed six killers in Belfast and Londonderry to discover the motives and inducements which led these men to kill people whom they generally did not know and whose only offense was membership in another religion.[28] Both Protestant and Catholic killers claimed in these interviews that they were motivated only by a desire to protect their families, friends and neighbors from the killers on the other side. They regarded themselves as soldiers forced to kill so as to prevent the other side from winning the war. All believed they were doing a legitimate thing and that they need not have difficulties with their conscience because of these killings.

Killers on both sides were unsympathetic to their victims because they did not know them—Catholics did not know Protestants and vice versa—because of total segregation of the two groups. None of the killers had ever gone to school with someone of the other faith, nor had they worked with them or spent any time socializing. In fact, there are 22 points in Belfast "where high metal and concrete fences were erected," called "peace fences." Protestant and Catholic killers viewed their victims in a detached and impersonal manner because of this utter segregation. All killers insisted that they had no religious hatred for their victims; instead, they claim to have had political motives only. The IRA is fighting to unite Northern Ireland with the Irish Republic, while the Protestants are fighting to keep Northern Ireland British. It is remarkable that public opinion polls in Ireland and Great Britain reveal that only two percent of the Irish seek to incorporate Ulster, and very few British want to hang on to it. All agree that the British Army will eventually be removed from Northern Ireland and that then a civil war will decide the fate of that unhappy community.

When five bombs caused damage at a real estate office in London on the morning of November 26, 1988, it was believed that the Irish Republican Army must have been responsible. An anonymous caller revealed, however, that the bombers were Welsh nationalists who had been attacking British installations in England for nine years. The bombers had for years used fire bombs to make their demands known—the wish for Wales to be independent of Great Britain, although it has been united since the 13th century. Their inspiration is the Reverend R.S. Thomas, a minister and poet who responded to the deaths of victims of these fire bombs with the admonition, "What is one death against the death of the whole Welsh nation?"[29] Similar attitudes were recorded in South Africa when a bomb exploded in a Durban supermarket killing a two-year-old child and wounding a 20-year-old woman.[30]

A long list of yet other terrorist acts can be recorded for every year since 1970, including a North Korean woman who placed a bomb on a South Korean jetliner in 1987, for which she was condemned to death after a trial held in 1989.[31]

Meanwhile, bombs exploded during the first five months of 1989 in Belgium, Sri Lanka, San Diego, California, Syria, Bristol, England, West Berlin, Jerusalem, and, of course, Lebanon and Ireland, sometimes with lethal results and sometimes leading to the destruction of property only. Many of these terror attacks are motivated by political considerations having to do with nationalistic grievances whether real or imagined. In a sense no grievance is imagined, since those who feel deeply about Welsh independence or the need to remain a British citizen in Northern Ireland are no doubt sincere in their beliefs and have real cause for feeling deprived and misunderstood.

Added to these political motives and interpretations of history, however, is the issue of existential validation, (the issue of self worth, of being "somebody," when people are convinced they are "nobody"). Encouraged by media attention, those who kill or threaten to do so suddenly become important in a world which they feel never knew that they existed. Just as the assassins of famous persons seek to enter the history books by killing their famous victims, so the terrorist seeks to state his case on television and in the newspapers. It is now time to examine the role of the media in the drama of terrorism-murder.

"ALL THE WORLD'S A STAGE"

Political motivation has to do with achieving power or at least depriving someone else of power. Although some terrorists do indeed wish to attain power, the strategy of violence known as terrorism is not always linked to that idea alone, but also to the idea that the media can provide almost anyone with at least temporary fame, if they can be employed to promote a cause, opinion or deed. The powerful always have access to the media whether in the United States, in Germany or elsewhere. It has been the tactic of terrorists in all the world, therefore, to focus the attention of the media and hence the public upon their cause or opinions by doing something that would insure media coverage. The media, and particularly television, make it possible for a small group of terrorists to intimidate millions and to broadcast their demands to everyone. Violence and murder are more easily achieved because of technology, as in the case of plastic bombs, and are also easily diffused throughout the world by means of television.[32]

A definition of terrorism, including the use of the mass media to further the ends of the terrorists, is given by Cherif Bassiouni, who calls terrorism "a strategy of violence designed to inspire terror within a particular segment of a given society."[33] By strategy is meant the dramatic nature of so many terrorist acts which focuses world attention on individuals who perpetrate such acts by involving the media. This worked well in West Germany in the early 1970s and has worked again and again in numerous countries and in an infinite number of situations since then.

Not all terrorists are motivated by political ideologies. There are terrorists who are psychotic or who seek financial gain for themselves alone. However, all three categories have an affinity for the use of the media because the media can broadcast their demands for political change, for personal attention or for gain in a manner which they themselves could never do alone. The relationship between terror killings and the media is symbiotic. While the murderers rely on the media to give them the publicity they seek, either to advance their "cause" or to gain personal attention, the media use the terrorists to sell their wares, that is, news.[34] Two kinds of terrorism have been given wide attention by the media, particularly television. Terrorism "from below" (sponsored by private persons or terrorist organizations), or terrorism "from above" (sponsored by a government, such as the Iranian seizure of the United States embassy in 1979).

In all cases, the media further the objectives of terrorist killers because the wide publicity given these acts demonstrates the vulnerability and impotence of the government, attracts public sympathy by choosing a target whose death may be rationalized (a very rich man viewed as an exploiter), creates dissension within the public as to the merits of the terrorists' "cause," discredits the government because it is goaded into repressive actions, and makes violence and murder seem heroic.

Bassiouni, a major student of terrorist activities, makes this comment regarding the influence of television upon terrorism-murder:

> So close is the interaction between the media and terror-violence that terrorist groups conform to certain media stereotypes in their internal organizational

structure, chain of command and even in the attitudes of their members. Likewise, the choice of targets and the time, manner and place of action frequently correspond to media created perceptions of what is expected in such spectacles. . . . Three consequences of the cinematogenic effect are critical in shaping terrorist events. First, the perpetrators' patterns of behavior seek to meet media expectations. . . . Second, responding to stereotyped portrayals provides a framework facilitating communications . . . third, conforming to stereotype provides a sound basis for predictability of behavior and responses on the part of perpetrators, the media and the general public.[35]

There is yet another consequence of media coverage for sensational terrorism murders: the strong possibility that individuals who believe they cannot redress a grievance any other way will resort to terrorism although they are "normal" from the psychiatric point of view. This is the opinion of Dr. Robert Lifton, a Yale University professor of psychiatry. Said Lifton:

> [When the press] makes the person of the terrorist something close to the total news of the week, the imagery of terrorism becomes much more active psychologically for the average person. Therefore it must contribute to stimulating similar acts among people who feel frustrated and for whom other avenues are closed.[36]

THE GODFATHERS

Traditionally, the first duty of governments has been the protection of its citizens by the maintenance of peace. In the extreme, governments have gone to war in the belief that they had no other choice, or that they could aggrandize themselves at the expense of a weaker neighbor.

Now, however, governments have also entered the terrorism-murder business, or have excused the most atrocious crimes for political expedience. Some governments have become the sponsors of indiscriminate murder of foreign nationals and even their own citizens by means of terror-murder, alternately defined as "a tactic or technique by means of which a violent act or the threat thereof is used for the prime purpose of creating overwhelming fear for coercive purposes."[37]

Some governments have aided terrorist-murderers because it appeared advantageous to them to protect such killers. Notable among the governments sponsoring terrorism are Iran, Lybia and Syria, although others, such as North Korea, are also involved. Collaboration by Italy, Egypt and Yugoslavia with terrorist murderers in connection with one of the most cruel and dramatic murders by terrorists occurred on October 8, 1985, when the Italian cruise ship *Achille Lauro* was "hijacked" by four armed men off the coast of Egypt in the Mediterranean. Calling themselves the "Palestine Liberation Front," the terrorists held the captain and crew at gunpoint and threatened to kill the American passengers, one by one.[38] They seized the passports of the passengers from the offices of the ship and composed a "death list" beginning with Leon Klinghoffer heading the list. Klinghoffer was confined to a wheel-chair. They then numbered the others "like cattle," according to the United States ambassador to Egypt, Nicholas A. Veliotes. Unable to move, Leon Klinghoffer was shot in the forehead, and his body thrown into the sea. Instead of continuing the killings, the murderers surrendered to Egyptian authorities near Port Said, and were unmolested until they flew out of Egypt on Friday, October 11, 1985, heading northwest toward Tunisia. At that point, four F-14 fighter planes from the U.S.S. *Saratoga* intercepted the Egyptian plane and forced it to land at a joint Italian-American air base at Sigonella, Sicily. All four hijackers were on board the Egyptian plane.

It had been the intent of the United States government to bring the killers of Klinghoffer to the United States for trial. However, the Italian government refused to extradite them, including Abdul Abbas, called "one of the most notorious terrorists" by the White House on the grounds that "he has been involved in savage attacks on civilians." From Italy, Abbas and the other killers flew to Yugoslavia, which also would not extradite them to the United States. Instead, they left Yugoslavia with Iraqi passports and literally "got away with murder" through the collaboration of three governments.

On November 29, 1987, a bomb exploded on board a South Korean airliner, a Boeing 707, as it approached the coast of Burma. The bomb had been planted aboard by Kim Hyan Hui, an agent of North Korea. At her trial she testified that the bombing had been ordered by Kim Il Sung, the dictator of North Korea, with the intent of frightening away potential visitors to the Olympic Games held later in Seoul.[39]

The Lybian government was accused by President Reagan of organizing and paying for the murder of two American soldiers and a Turkish woman when a bomb exploded at the La Belle discotheque in West Berlin on April 5, 1986. Two hundred people were wounded in that attack. Ten days later the United States Navy bombed Tripoli and Benghazi in Lybia, hitting the Lybian dictator Col. Khadaffi's home and killing one of his children.[40]

An international uproar ensued in February 1989 when the government of Iran ordered the murder of novelist Salman Rushdie upon the publication of his book, *Satanic Verses*. Claiming that this book blasphemes the Muslim religion, the Iranian ayatollah, Ruallah Khomeini, and his followers demanded the death of the author.[41] These are only a few examples of government sponsored or government excused terrorist murders. Others are:

• The seizure of the United States embassy in Tehran in November 1979.

• The murder of 63 persons in a car bomb attack at the American embassy in Beirut, Lebanon, April 18, 1983, attributed to the Syrian government.

• The suicide bombings of American and French installations in Lebanon on October 23, 1983. Two hundred forty-one Americans and 58 French soldiers died. Attributed to the Iranian government.

• The murder of 60 persons in a car bomb attack in Lebanon on November 4, 1983. Attributed to the Iranian government.

• The murder of seven when a car bomb exploded in Kuwait on December 12, 1983. Attributed to the Iranian government.

• The murder of Malcolm Kerr, president of the American University in Beirut, Lebanon, on January 18, 1984. Attributed to the Syrian government.

- The murder of 14 on September 14, 1984, at the American embassy in Beirut. Attributed to the Iranian government.
- The murder of U.S. Navy diver Robert Stetham during the hijacking of TWA Flight 847 on June 14, 1985. Attributed to the Iranian government.

These killings and many more were government sponsored or at least sanctioned and thereby present those who seek a defense against this type of murder with yet additional difficulties. One way to make such a defense is to use force. The United States government not only intercepted the airliner carrying the *Achille Lauro* killers, but the U.S. Navy bombed and strafed the headquarters of the Lybian dictator. Three additional examples are the Israeli nighttime raid on the Entebbe airport in Uganda on July 4, 1976; the storming of the Iranian embassy in London by the British Army in April 1980 and the storming of a Lufthansa airliner by German commandos at Mogadishu, Somalia, in October of 1977. In the Israeli raid 103 hostages were saved after a French airliner was held for a week at the Entebbe airport and the hijackers threatened to kill their hostages.

After two hostages of Iranian terrorists were murdered inside the Iranian embassy in London, the British Special Air Service raided the building and killed five of the murderers in the ensuing gun battle. German commandos similarly approached the rear of the plane in which hostages were held and fired at four hijackers as they rushed inside to free hostages whose lives were in imminent danger.[42] Such strong-arm methods do, of course, have some salutary results. However, these methods are very dangerous to those undertaking them, succeed only in some cases and are not effective in sudden bombings such as the disaster on Pan Am Flight 103 in December 1988.

CHALLENGE AND RESPONSE

In view of the challenge to civilization which terrorism poses, the question of how to combat these killings became the subject of a speech by the late director of the Central Intelligence Agency, William J. Casey, on April 17, 1985. Said Casey: "International terrorism has become a pitiless war without borders."[43] Casey recognized that state supported terrorism as an instrument of foreign policy constituted a new departure at that time. He also accused drug traders of collusion with terrorists, the former making huge profits and the latter deriving arms from that trade. To combat all this Casey hoped to rely on intelligence analysis; forewarning through American embassies in foreign countries; the development of a worldwide counter-terrorist network; pressure on governments who condone terrorism or sponsor it; the use of an armed strike against terrorist bases and other sanctions such as refusal of landing rights to aircraft of a nation supporting terrorism. While all of these measures have indeed been used on a few occasions, no one measure has ever alone succeeded in preventing terrorism. Improvements in security procedures have reduced the *number* of terrorism incidents, even if the toll for just one such bombing has recently been very high.

Politics, however, stand in the way of truly effective antiterror measures around the world, as has been seen in connection with the capture of the *Achille Lauro* murderers. In addition to difficulties arising from international political problems, United States antiterrorism efforts are further hindered by internal politics, logistic and bureaucratic obstacles. During the *Achille Lauro* disaster, members of the United States Army's Delta Force, an antiterrorist commando unit, planned an assault upon the hijackers of that ship. However, they were delayed 18 hours in carrying out their mission because a transport plane had broken down and no replacement was available at once.[44] These problems are so severe that some believe that these elite units will never be used because the endless difficulties confronting them cannot be solved, or will not be solved to serve various "special interests." Nevertheless, "Delta" has been used on a few occasions and with success.

Because one of the principal obstacles to the successful use of American special forces is distance from Europe and the Middle East where most terror attacks occur, Transportation Secretary Samuel Skinner has asked friendly governments in Europe and the Middle East for permission to station U.S. antiterrorist agents in their countries. Countries whose permission has been asked are Britain, Israel, Italy and West Germany.[45]

Terror-murder is likely to continue, as some messianists will always find means to circumvent the ever more sophisticated methods used to prevent these killings.

9. Murder by Death

The number of people who say that they favor deliberate death for those who have murdered someone else and advocate, the so-called "death penalty," has increased to such an extent in the United States that one presidential candidate in 1988 used his appeal to the death penalty as an issue in his campaign. If readers consider what they have read about murder in the preceding chapters, then surely they may favor the death penalty as well. Does it not seem reasonable that Ted Bundy was put to death? Surely, the Nazi who spiked little children thrown from the window of a hospital on his bayonet has forfeited his life. Is John Gacy fit to be in this world among other human beings? Consider the attitude of Ron Wikberg, editor of a prison magazine at the Louisiana State Prison where he has been imprisoned for 19 years for a murder he committed in the course of a robbery. Said he: "If someone were to kill my mother or my sister or commit some heinous crime in which I lost a family member, I think any man in those circumstances would have to say he believes in the death penalty."[1]

Before discussing the opinions on both sides of this issue, the meaning of the "death penalty" must be examined. One of the real difficulties in favoring or opposing this punishment is that very few have any idea of what is really meant by those two words. There is good reason for this, namely that death is hidden in the United States. This is not only true of deliberate death inflicted by means of the rope, gas, electricity or injections. It is even true of normal death which occurs in hospitals and nursing homes and seldom in the home of the dying person. Americans are generally ignorant of death, except for the four percent who live on farms. By taking a closer look at what is meant by the death penalty, it will be possible to discuss potential merits and disadvantages.

THE NATURE OF CAPITAL PUNISHMENT

The deliberate infliction of death on a human being mutilates his body in three of the five methods of execution now in use in the United States. When a person is hanged, death is not usually caused by breaking the neck, but by strangulation. It takes about eight to ten minutes to bring about death by hanging and, as Clinton Duffy, for many years warden at California's San Quentin prison, reveals, "when a body is cut down and the mask removed the side of the face has been torn open, more often than not." The reason for the use of a mask is that by law, witnesses must be present to see the execution. These witnesses often become sick or pass out if no mask is used, because the sight of what happens to the face of the victim is too much to bear. If the prosecutors, judge and jury who condemn the victim to death were witnesses as well, and no mask used, perhaps this form of execution would be drastically curtailed.[2] Great Britain used hanging as the only method of inflicting the death penalty until it was abolished in 1965. Two principal reasons for its abolition were the repeated execution of innocent persons, and that hanging often caused the victim's head to be torn off, depending on the weight of the body.[3]

Electrocution has been used as a method of execution in the United States since William Kemmler was subjected to it on August 6, 1890. "The first jolt failed to kill him, and he had to be strapped back into the chair for more shocks."[4]

An eyewitness to 189 executions, Don Reid, has described what happens to the human body during that experience:

> The man is pale. His arms are lashed to arm rests, his legs to the chair legs, his body to the chair with a broad strap so taut that it straightens his spine to the chair back.
>
> He smiles—but he tries to cringe away as a guard stuffs cotton in his nostrils to trap blood that might gush from ruptured veins in his brain.
>
> A mask is placed across his face. The guard steps back quickly. The warden glances around once more; every man is in his place. He turns and nods in the direction of the one-way mirror behind which the executioner is waiting.
>
> The *crunch*. The mounting whine and snarl of the generator. The man's lips peel back, the throat strains for a last desperate cry, the body arches against the restraining straps as the generator whines and snarls again, the features purple, steam and smoke rise from the bald spots on head and legs while the sick sweet smell of burned flesh permeates the little room.[5]

Lewis E. Lawes, for years warden of New York's Sing Sing prison, described an electrocution in his autobiography as follows:

> The condemned prisoner undergoing electrocution at Sing Sing Prison is given one shock of . . . alternating current at an average starting potential of approximately 2,000 volts. This voltage is immediately reduced at the end of three seconds to the neighborhood of 500 volts where it is held for an additional period of 57 seconds. . . .
>
> This initial force sends a starting current of 8 to 10 amperes through the human body, which causes instantaneous death and unconsciousness by its paralysis and destruction of the brain. The current is then cut down under the lower voltages to from 3 to 4 amperes in order to avoid burning the body and at the same time to hold paralysis of the heart, respiratory organs, and brain at a standstill for the remaining period of execution. This insures complete destruction of all life.
>
> As the switch is thrown into its socket there is a sputtering drone, and the body leaps as if to break the strong leather straps that hold it. Sometimes a thin gray wisp of smoke pushes itself out from under the helmet that holds the head electrode, followed by the faint odor of burning flesh. The hands turn red, then white, and the cords of the neck stand out like steel bands. . . .

If temperatures are taken during and immediately after an application of electricity it will be found that the electrodes making the contact may reach a temperature high enough to melt copper . . . that the average body temperature will be in the neighborhood of 140 degrees . . . and that the temperature of the brain itself approaches the boiling point of water. . . .

Although it would be absolutely impossible to revive any person after electrocution in Sing Sing's death chair, an autopsy is immediately performed as provided by law. Thus justice grinds out its grist; the hand of the law drops a living man or woman into the death house hopper, where the chair and the surgeon's knives and saws convert it into the finished product—a grisly corpse.[6]

This from an American prison warden, not a Nazi killer. Is there a difference?

On December 7, 1982, Charles Brooks, Jr., became the first American to be executed by lethal injection. He was killed in Huntsville, Texas.[7] This method of execution is achieved by first placing the victim on a lorry to which he is tied by straps. Unable to move, he is placed in front of a window-like opening where the executioner waits with a needle that is then injected into his arm. The catheter is placed into a vein in the arm and a saline solution is injected. This is sterile salt water used as a medium for drug injections in hospitals. Then, a dose of barbiturates and potassium chloride is added. This paralyzes the victim, stops his breathing and guarantees his death.[8] It does not mutilate the body.

Killing by gas is yet another method used in seven states. Here is an eyewitness account of death by gassing, a method already mentioned in connection with the Nazi mass murders discussed in Chapter 4:

He is dressed in blue jeans and a white shirt. He is accompanied the ten or twelve steps by two officers, quickly strapped in the metal chair, the stethoscope applied, and the door sealed. The Warden gives the executioner the signal, and out of sight of the witnesses, the executioner presses the lever that allows the cyanide eggs to mix with the distilled water and sulfuric acid. In a matter of seconds the prisoner is unconscious. At first there is extreme evidence of horror, pain, strangling. The eyes pop, they turn purple, they drool. It is a horrible sight; witnesses faint. It is finally as though he has gone to sleep. The body, however, is not disfigured or mutilated in any way.[9]

Only Idaho and Utah use the firing squad as a means of execution. This, of course, mutilates the body of the victim. Following is a table of all the states who use the death penalty, along with the method of execution. States which do not have the death penalty are: Alaska, Hawaii, Iowa, Kansas, Maine, Massachusetts, Michigan, Minnesota, New York, North Dakota, Rhode Island, West Virginia and Wisconsin. Washington, D.C., also does not have the death penalty.

States and Methods of Execution, 1988*

State	Method	State	Method
Alabama	Electrocution	Nevada	Injection
Arizona	Gas	New Hampshire	Injection
Arkansas	Injection	New Jersey	Injection
California	Gas	New Mexico	Injection
Colorado	Injection	North Carolina	Gas &
Connecticut	Electrocution		Injection
Delaware	Injection	Ohio	Electrocution
Florida	Electrocution	Oklahoma	Injection
Georgia	Electrocution	Oregon	Injection
Idaho	Injection &	Pennsylvania	Electrocution
	Shooting	S. Carolina	Electrocution
Illinois	Injection	S. Dakota	Injection
Indiana	Electrocution	Tennessee	Electrocution
Kentucky	Electrocution	Texas	Injection
Louisiana	Electrocution	Utah	Shooting &
Maryland	Gas		Injection
Mississippi	Gas &	Vermont	Electrocution
	Injection	Virginia	Electrocution
Missouri	Injection	Washington	Injection &
Montana	Injection &		Hanging
	Hanging	Wyoming	Injection
Nebraska	Electrocution		

Bureau of Justice Statistics, October 1989

THE DEBATE ABOUT CAPITAL PUNISHMENT

It is not possible to describe the actual horrors of waiting for death for months, years and even decades as the various appeals, always taken in capital cases, slowly grind through the courts. Nor is it possible to ever feel the monstrous misery in which the condemned live out their days in the small cells on "death row." But keeping in mind the killing methods just discussed, it will be helpful to review some of the most frequently used arguments in favor of the death penalty and some of the arguments opposing it. Some views not usually included in this endless debate will also be presented.

Popularity

This argument simply states that most people want this penalty, and that in a democracy the majority rules. For centuries, arguments in favor of the death penalty were hardly formalized and published, simply because there was so little debate concerning this matter. It was simply taken for granted that the death penalty should exist. It is true, however that the death penalty was not used in ancient Rome after 384 B.C. for Roman citizens.[10] Outside of Rome, however, it was in constant use until the abolition movement began to make serious inroads in the attitude generally deemed to have begun with the 18th-century publication of the Marquis of Beccaria, Cesare Bonesana's book, *Essay on Crimes and Punishments*.[11]

Since then, proponents of the death penalty have also come forward with their arguments and have succeeded in convincing the majority of the American public of their position. Every poll taken on this matter since 1981 has shown that at least 61 percent of Americans favor the death penalty, even in states such as New York, in which the legislature has abolished it. In fact, New York does not have the death penalty because two governors, Hugh Cary and Mario Cuomo, have repeatedly vetoed it after the legislature passed bills in its favor. However, the legislature has so far not been able to muster the two-thirds majority to override the governors' veto. If only a majority were necessary to make this into law, or a governor were ever elected who would sign such a bill, New York would install the death penalty.

It is necessary that a bill vetoed by a New York governor must receive at least 100 votes in the New York State Assembly to override such a veto. On September 26, 1988, the Associated Press predicted that voters would send at least 98 death penalty advocates to the Assembly in 1989, thus making the return of that penalty to New York much more likely than has been true in the past 25 years. However, as of November 1, 1989, the effort to reinstitute the death penalty in New York has not succeeded.[12]

The argument from popularity is, of course, a good one. Legislators generally vote for those measures which most voters want, since they would not otherwise be in office for long. Nevertheless, there are a number of constitutionally guaranteed rights which even the smallest minority enjoys, such as freedom of religion or freedom of speech. Majorities cannot abolish minority religions by voting them illegal, nor curtail free speech by the same means. It can therefore be argued that the majority has no right to make the minority who opposes the death penalty into accomplices in the killing of other citizens. Since executions are at least in theory imposed by "the people" and not the individual judge or executioner, all citizens become responsible for these deaths. Therefore, those who do not want to kill, ought not to be made killers against their will even in the name of the law. A minority, admittedly must in many instances succumb to the will of the majority since otherwise the rule of law could not succeed. But should that majority rule extend to the taking of life, or is that tyranny rather than democratic procedure? This author makes this point in particular because the taking of a human life involves a religious issue. Therefore, it would seem that citizens who belong to a religion opposing the death penalty are forced to violate their religion by becoming unwilling participants in the death of the victims of capital punishment.

A judge who condemns another human being to death plays God. This is also true of the prosecutors and juries who participate in this macabre state-sanctioned killing. It is even more true of the executioners who carry out such sentences. American religious groups have taken specific positions death concerning the penalty which usually differ from the views of the American majority. For example, the American Baptist Convention passed a resolution concerning capital punishment in June 1977 which states in part: "THEREFORE, we as American Baptists, condemn the current reinstatement of capital punishment and oppose its use . . . and call for an immediate end to planned executions throughout this country."

The American Jewish Committee adopted the following resolution on May 6, 1972:

> WHEREAS capital punishment degrades and brutalizes the society which practices it; and . . . WHEREAS we agree that the death penalty is cruel, unjust and incompatible with the dignity and self respect of man; NOW THEREFORE BE IT RESOLVED that the American Jewish Committee be recorded as favoring the abolition of the death penalty.

While that Committee may not speak for all Jewish denominations any more than Baptists can speak for all Protestants, it is nevertheless important to note that the Jewish scriptures reject the death penalty in Ezekiel 18:23: "Have I any pleasure at all that the wicked should die? saith the Lord God: and not that he should return from his ways and live." Assuming that all Jews, whatever their denomination, view the Bible as the very essence of their belief, it can reasonably be proposed that Judaism rejects the death penalty on theological grounds despite the numerous references to it in the Five Books of Moses. Rabbinic opinion has held that "A Sanhedrin which executes a person once in seventy years can be called 'destructive.'" A Sanhedrin (from the Greek word *synedrion*, or assembly) was the Israeli Supreme Court of 70 members which sat in Jerusalem before its abolition by the Roman occupiers in 57 B.C. This council was first mentioned in Numbers 11:16.[13]

The Church of the Brethren Convention equally rejected the death penalty by resolution at their annual conference in 1957. At a meeting of the General Convention of the Episcopal Bishops in 1979, the Episcopal leadership passed this resolution: "RESOLVED, the House of Bishops concurring, that this 66th General Convention of the Episcopal Church reaffirms its opposition to Capital Punishment. . . ."

The Lutheran Church in America passed a similar resolution in 1972, as did the Presbyterians, the Mennonites, the Reformed Church in America and the United Church of Christ. The United Methodist Church "declares its opposition to the retention and use of capital punishment in any form or carried out by any means. . ." in the text of a resolution passed by that group in 1980.

Finally, it is worthwhile to present in full the text of a "Statement on Capital Punishment" accepted by the U.S. [Roman] Catholic Conference in 1978. This statement deals with the whole issue at once and encompasses almost all of the objections to the death penalty presented by religious leaders throughout the country:

> The use of the death penalty involved deep moral and religious questions as well as political and legal issues. In 1974, out of commitment to the value and dignity of human life, the Catholic bishops of the United States declared their opposition to capital punishment. We continue to support this position in the belief that a return to the use of the death penalty can only lead to the further erosion of respect for life in our society. Violent crime in our society is a serious

matter which should not be ignored. We do not challenge society's right to punish the serious and violent offender, nor do we wish to debate the merits of the arguments concerning this right. Past history, however, shows that the death penalty in its application has been discriminatory with respect to the disadvantaged, the indigent and the socially impoverished. Furthermore, recent data from corrections resources definitely question the effectiveness of the death penalty as a deterrent to crime.

We are deeply troubled by the legislative efforts being undertaken under the guise of humanitarian concern to permit execution by lethal injection. Such practice merely seeks to conceal the reality of cruel and unusual punishment. We find this practice unacceptable.

The critical question for the Christian is how we can best foster respect for life, preserve the dignity of the human person and manifest the redemptive message of Christ. We do not believe that more deaths are the response to the question. We therefore have to seek methods of dealing with violent crime which are more consistent with the Gospel's vision of respect for life, and Christ's message of God's healing love. In the sight of God, correction of the offender has taken preference over punishment, for the Lord came to save and not to condemn.[14]

There are a number of church groups who do not reject the death penalty. Most of these groups are known as "fundamentalists," and are not members of the National Council of Churches of Christ in the United States, as is true of almost all the Christian groups quoted above. The same attitude also holds true of orthodox Jews who do not necessarily share the views of the American Jewish Committee. Thus, religious views on the death penalty differ in the main from the opinion of the majority of Americans.

Deterrence

It is commonly believed that fear of execution prevents murder or any other crime for which death is the penalty. Even proponents of the death penalty, however, admit that there is no proof that this is true. Every effort to find such proof has come to naught. Professor Isaac Ehrlich of the University of Chicago published a well-known article in 1975 which sought to demonstrate by statistical means that every execution results in seven to eight fewer murders each year. However, numerous statisticians have since then shown Ehrlich's methods to be flawed and have discredited his findings.[15]

As noted in chapters 1, 2 and 3, there has been a decline in the number of murders per 100,000 inhabitants of Erie County, and for all of the United States, since 1980. The reason for this is that the birth rate fell from more than three per woman aged 15 to 45 right after World War II, to only 1.8 in the mid–1960s. This led to a decline in the number of men who reached age 15 in 1980 and beyond (murder is chiefly committed by men in the age group 15–30). As that age group declined, murder also declined. This happened all over the United States and had nothing to do with the death penalty. If the birth rate should increase in the United States, then the murder rate should also increase 15 years later. It is worth remembering that the murder rate fell in New York beginning with 1980, even though that state abolished the death penalty in 1965.

It seems both reasonable and a matter of common sense that there must be some people, somewhere, who have indeed been deterred by the death penalty from murdering someone else. Nevertheless, this is so small a number, that it statistically does not have any impact on murder. It cannot be proved that murder declines because of the death penalty any more than it can be proved that the rate increases because of the death penalty, as some contend.

The debate concerning protection of society by means of the death penalty is an ancient one. In 63 b.c., the Roman politician Cateline conspired to overthrow the Roman Republic by force and violence.[16] This rebellion led to a debate between the consul and writer Cicero and Julius Caesar concerning the punishment the conspirators were to suffer. Cicero favored the death penalty on the grounds that otherwise the state would appear weak, and on the further grounds that the Senate's patience was exhausted.[17] Julius Caesar, however, opposed it. Caesar instead proposed life imprisonment, a view expressed in 1988 by one of the candidates for the presidency of the United States. Said Caesar:

> But imprisonment and that too for life certainly was devised as a notable punishment for foul crimes. . . . Caesar will surround them with grim guards such as the crime of these disgraceful men deserves. He ordains that it may be impossible for anyone, by vote of either the senate or the people, to lighten the penalty of those whom he condemns. He takes away every hope, which alone can console men in their miseries.[18]

Caesar went on to say that he did not believe the death penalty to be a deterrent to any crime because the offenders never consider it until it is upon them. The same arguments are heard in 1988. Psychoanalyst Ernest van den Haag is probably the most vociferous advocate of the death penalty in America.[19] A summary of his principal argument follows: 1) If the death penalty does not add deterrence and we carry out death sentences, we lose the life of the executed convict without adding deterrence. 2) If the death penalty does add deterrence, and we fail to pronounce and carry out death sentences for murder, we fail to deter murderers who could have been deterred had the death sentence been pronounced and carried out. This argument sums up the feeling of most Americans who would rather gamble with the life of a convicted murderer than the lives of unsuspecting citizens.

One of the most interesting efforts to discover whether or not the death penalty deters murder was undertaken by Dane Archer and Rosemary Gartner.[20] Archer and Gartner investigated 12 countries which abolished the death penalty and compared the homicide rate one year before and one year after abolition. They found that the homicide rate went up after abolition in five of these countries—Canada, Denmark, Netherland Antilles, New Zealand and Norway. However, the murder rate went down after abolition in Austria, England, Finland, Israel, Italy, Sweden and Switzerland. Their conclusion is "There is no evidence for the deterrence hypothesis."

Protection

This argument favors the death penalty on the grounds that someone who has killed once may very well do so again. Therefore, killing him will prevent the victim of the execution to ever murder anyone else. This is undoubtedly true, but it is mere speculation whether those who have killed once will kill again. The evidence is that few of those who ever killed anyone do so a second time, except serial killers and mass murderers. One of the most interesting means of testing the theory that people need protection from murderers lest the latter continue to do so comes from an event in California legal history which is not likely to be repeated.

When California executed a prisoner on April 12, 1967, that became the last execution for some time as the California Supreme Court ruled on February 18, 1972, that the death penalty constituted "cruel and unusual punishment" and was therefore unconstitutional. This ruling was made in connection with the appeal of Robert Anderson, convicted of killing a San Diego storeowner during a robbery. Anderson also engaged in a shootout with police, leading to the wounding of several officers. Nevertheless, once death row had been shut down, Anderson became eligible for parole which was granted him in 1976. Forty of the 107 death row inmates who escaped death were subsequently paroled. Of these, two had died a natural death by 1988, six were back in prison, and 32 had adjusted well to their freedom, had founded families and had fathered 22 children between them. These examples are typical:

David Magris, who had been convicted of killing a gas station attendant, was paroled after serving 16 years in prison, of which he spent two years and eight months on death row. In 1988, he became 40 years old, and secured a $30,000-a-year job as a systems manager. Robert Hill, married and the owner of a successful video store, has moved from California to another state to escape harassment because of his past. He too adjusted well. Clay Hines, also paroled after being sentenced to death in 1962, lives in the Idaho community of Spirit Lake. He is married, works as a cook and is well accepted by his community. Milton Earl, now known as Ali Amin, has become a Muslim minister and is also the owner of a bakery. He is married and has four children, and learned the skill of baking while in prison. He too had been on death row.

There are examples of failures. Robert Hye, released from death row, now lives alone in an abandoned milk truck because he is too alcoholic to work as a computer operator. Worse off than he is are James Meeks, who committed several violent crimes since his release and is back in prison, and Bob Massie, who is again on death row for yet another murder. Massie insists that he die. He may well get his wish for the murder of a San Francisco liquor-store owner. Robert Kemp was paroled in 1978, having been on death row for rape and murder. In 1983, he entered a woman's apartment and in a rage, beat, raped and choked her, although he did not kill her after a 42-hour ordeal. He too is back in prison. The vast majority of the 40 former death row inmates have led successful lives since their release, but the voters in California reinstituted the death penalty nine months after the court abolished it.[21]

Retribution

This is a simple argument. It was used by the great philosopher Immanuel Kant in the 18th century, and it is used today. Kant held that anyone who has committed murder must die. According to Kant, nothing else would satisfy legal justice. This, he believed, must be so because even the most miserable life is not the same as death which the killer inflicted on the victim. Kant believed that retribution alone requires the death of the killer; nothing else. That is why he opposed all torture or cruelty in putting the offender to death. He was so convinced of this argument that he proposed that even if a community were to leave an island so as to dissolve the community, then the last act they must perform would be the execution of the last murderer remaining in prison, since otherwise the individuals who made up the community would be guilty of the crime the murderer committed: "If they fail to do so, they may be regarded as accomplices in this public violation of legal justice."[22]

At present the most vociferous proponent of the retribution point of view is Ernest van den Haag.[23] He believes that punishment must be certain and greater than any advantage that may come to the criminal from his crime. Punishment, says van den Haag, must be predictable. Therefore he would abandon all rehabilitative efforts and, in the hope of demonstrating the importance of the law, execute all murderers, not because this may deter others, but because it is just retribution.[24]

Retributionists believe that punishment should fit the crime, no more, no less. Their point of view is that retribution is just regardless of its deterrent effect. Therefore, they would execute the murderer even if it cannot be shown that the death penalty deters anyone. To the retributionist is suffices that murder is "paid for" by death. There are even some retributionists who claim that if the state does not execute the murderer, then lynching will result from this failure by the state, as the victims' relatives will want to get even themselves. Moreover, it is claimed that blood feuds would develop to avenge murder not only on the killer but also on his relatives.

At present there is no evidence that persons living in no-death-penalty states have resorted to either lynching or blood feuds. There have been some "revenge" killings, and it is possible that there are many more than are recorded as such.

The argument from retribution raises yet another issue, however, which is undoubtedly the best argument against the death penalty: the execution of the innocent. That innocent persons are convicted of numerous crimes each year in the United States and elsewhere is a certainty. It is also known that 343 people have been wrongfully convicted of offenses punishable by death in this century. In 32 cases, the so-called murder "victim" was later found alive; no crime had been committed in the first place. Twenty-five innocent persons were executed for these non-crimes. Even in face of this evidence, however, proponents of the death penalty continue to support it. The author has heard a New York state legislator say that the death of innocent persons executed by the state is not a valid reason not to reinstate the death penalty because it occurs infrequently, and because "you have to take the bad with the good." By "good" he meant the death penalty.[25]

Van den Haag argues that society doesn't give up football, automobiles and other activities just because some innocent people die in the course of doing these things. This conveniently overlooks that people drive, play games and ride in airplanes voluntarily. Their deaths in those situations are accidents. The wrongful conviction of an innocent person for a capital crime is, however, no accident. Consider the following:

- On June 5, 1937 Isadore Zimmerman, then 19, was arrested in New York City for the crime of murder in the first degree. New York still had the death penalty then, and Zimmerman was convicted and sentenced to death ten months after his arrest. He was placed into Sing Sing's death row and stayed there until January 1939. During that time, he witnessed the electrocution of 13 others also on death row, including a codefendant in his own case. Two hours before his own execution, then Governor Lehman commuted his sentence to life imprisonment. For 23 years more, Zimmerman lived as one of the many prisoners in New York's prisons. During a three-year stay at Attica he spent eight months in solitary confinement. In February 1962, 25 years too late, a judge of the state appeals court granted a writ of "Coram nobis" ("Before us") ordering the release of Zimmerman, setting aside his conviction and ordering a new trial. This new trial order led to the dismissal of the indictment on March 13, 1967, inasmuch as the original conviction was obtained by perjured testimony and suppressed evidence.[26]

- In November of 1987 the CBS program *Sixty Minutes* broadcast the story of Kelly Joe Coke and others, wrongfully convicted. Pressured by a so-called "lie detector" examiner, she confessed to two murders. She did so not only because of the pressure placed on her by the examiner, but also because the sheriff beat her and two detectives and a state trooper tortured her for several hours. She was kept in police custody for two nights and days. Unaware that she was entitled to see a lawyer, and not allowed to contact her family, she collapsed emotionally. The police predicted that "the jury will hang your ass," and used other epithets and language leading to her self-delusion that she did indeed commit murders with which she had nothing to do. Finally she was forced to sign a "confession" after being kept in solitary confinement for three hours. She was also pressured into accusing two men who were as innocent as she was. Only investigative reporting saved her from further police brutality so that she eventually regained her freedom.

- Worse yet is the case of Elmer "Geronimo" Pratt. Pratt was convicted of the murder of Carolyn Olsen of Santa Monica, California, on December 18, 1968. Olsen was 27 years old at the time. She was white. Although the evidence indicated that two men murdered her, the police "framed" Pratt when they could not find the killers. They did so by asking Olsen's husband, Kenneth, to accuse Pratt, but it was not easy for him to do so. In fact, as Congressman McCloskey uncovered, Pratt had been "neutralized" by the FBI because he was a Black Panther member when Kenneth Olsen was asked to identify him. Olsen identified Eugene Perkins as one of the killers, a situation the police "rectified" by holding another lineup, resulting in the identification of Pratt. Meanwhile, the file concerning the lineup resulting in the identification of Perkins was removed from all files so that the jury never heard about this. Since then several jury members have said that they would have voted "not guilty" if they had known about the identification of Perkins. Upon hearing all of this the parole board nevertheless refused to release Pratt although he continued to insist on his innocence.

• Frank Fiel spent four years on death row in Philadelphia, although the district attorney, Ed Randall, knew for three of those four years that Fiel had not committed the murder for which he was convicted in 1981. Fiel was identified by a supposed eyewitness who was given a three-second view of a "mug shot" which he identified as Fiel. When a second eyewitness was unable to identify Fiel, she was not allowed to testify lest the jury heard her views. To make sure of a conviction, the police also made a deal for a lighter sentence with Fiel's cellmate, Frank Ferber, who then falsely testified that Fiel had confessed the alleged murder to him. Ferber told this lie in order to get out of jail himself.

• In August 1978, Floyd Fay, then 26 years old, was convicted by a Wood County, Ohio, jury of shooting to death storeowner Fred Ery. This conviction was based on a reputed "dying declaration" of the storeowner that Fay was guilty and testimony from a state polygraph expert that Fay had done this. Normally, no one takes an interest in a person already convicted. But Floyd Fay's lawyer, Adrian Cimerman, continued to search for the real killer of Ery. By diligent work, far more than anyone else would usually do, Cimerman discovered that the real killer was a soldier with the United States Army in Germany. In addition, another man from Perrysburg, in Wood County, Ohio, was also arrested in the case as an accomplice. It so happened that at that time the moratorium on the death penalty caused by the Supreme Court decision in the *Furman* case was still in effect. Otherwise, Fay quite possibly would have been executed.

• Eugene Jerome Klein spent 13 years in a New York prison on the charge that he had murdered Diana Goodman in 1967. This, despite the fact that another man had admitted the murder, an admission which the judge would not let the jury hear. After 13 years of appeals, another judge finally reviewed the case and discovered that Klein did not receive a fair trial because that admission was not permitted in the court. Klein was released. New York does not now have the death penalty.[27]

• In 1972, Aaron Owens was convicted of a double murder in Alameda County, California. Owens was convicted together with his codefendant Glenn Bailey who finally admitted, eight years later, that his partner in the killings was someone other than Owens, whereupon Owens was released.[28] Owens was convicted on the worst and most unreliable form of evidence, eyewitness testimony.[29] This conviction also occurred during the "Furman" moratorium on the death penalty.

• In 1985, Pedro Torres was convicted of murder and sentenced to 75 years in a Texas prison. Three months later, the original trial judge ordered the defense attorney to file a motion for a new trial because he had seen records showing that Torres was at work 250 miles from the scene of the crime at the time of the murder. The defense attorney had not presented these records at the time of the trial.

• In 1982, Nathaniel Carter was convicted of murder in New York, and sentenced to 25 years to life. Carter's friends, however, persisted in reexamining the evidence and finally succeeded in getting his former wife to confess to the killing. She had been the state's chief witness against Carter and had been given immunity from prosecution in return for that testimony. Said Carter's lawyer, "If New

York State had the death penalty, God knows what would have happened to this poor man."[30]

• Neil Ferber was convicted of murder in Pennsylvania and sentenced to death in 1982. In 1986, the trial judge ordered a new trial because it had been discovered that a former cellmate of Ferber had falsely claimed that Ferber confessed the killing to him. All this had been known to detectives and prosecutors even before Ferber's trial; he was released.[31]

• Anibal Jaramillo was sentenced to death in Florida in 1981 despite the recommendation of the jury that he be sentenced to life in prison. On appeal the convictions were reversed, and Jaramillo was released because the prosecution witnesses told conflicting stories and were unable to identify him. Strong evidence suggested someone else had committed the murder. Nevertheless, the trial judge hastily sent Jaramillo to his death.

• Christian Adamo was convicted in 1980 of a murder committed by someone else. He was released in 1982 after having been sent to prison in Massachusetts, which does not have the death penalty. Eyewitness accounts, no doubt the worst possible form of evidence, convicted him. Yet, on appeal it became evident that eyewitnesses contradicted themselves and that some first claimed to have seen him and then were positive they had not seen him at the scene of the crime.

• Two weeks before his scheduled execution in Indiana, Larry Hicks received the benefit of a volunteer attorney financed by the Playboy Foundation. This investigation proved that eyewitness testimony against him was perjured. A new trial was ordered and Hicks found innocent of all charges and released. No doubt Hicks represented "the case of a young man with no family, no friends or funds who avoided the electric chair mainly by a stroke of extraordinary good luck."[32]

• An Ohio judge sentenced Gary Beeman to death in 1976. Beeman had been convicted of aggravated murder. The Court of Appeals ordered a retrial for technical reasons, which led to the discovery that the chief prosecution witness had in fact committed the crime. Five witnesses testified that the prosecution's witness had actually murdered the victim; Beeman was released.[33]

There are innumerable additional such examples all of whom are now known to have been innocently convicted, and whose cases were rectified later. In a sense the word "rectified" is not correct, for how can anyone ever recompense those who have been unjustly arrested or dragged through the criminal justice procedure without cause? The pain and suffering of an innocent person who has been imprisoned for years can hardly be compensated. Yet, most states have no laws compensating a person innocently mistreated by the criminal justice system. Instead, each such person must sue the state on his own, if permission to sue is given by the legislature. In some states the legislature can compensate such a victim of injustice to any amount the legislature is willing to vote. There must undoubtedly be thousands of others who are now or have been in the past imprisoned innocently and without hope of ever gaining justice.

The following two tables list the names of those, although innocent, who were almost executed and those who were in fact innocently killed by the "death penalty."

Close Calls   Executed in Error

Defendant	Proximity to Execution	Defendant	State
J.B. Brown	at gallows	Garner	Alabama
Zajicek	three days	Sanders	Alabama
Sherman	a few days	Collins	Alabama
Stielow	in chair	Anderson	Florida
Larkman	ten hours	Dawson	Florida
Reno	seven hours	Adams	Florida
Vargas	head shaved	Tucker	Massachusetts
Cero	four hours	Sacco and	
Weaver	a few days	Vanzetti	Massachusetts
Hollins	thirty hours	McGee	Mississippi
Langley	25 minutes	Shumway	Nebraska
Bundy, Harry	three days	Lamble	North Jersey
Bernstein	minutes	Becker and	
Jones	five hours	Cirofici	New York
Zimmerman	two hours	Bambrick	New York
Wellman	in chair	Grzehowiak and	
Irvin	two days	Rybarczyk	New York
Bailey	two days	Applegate	New York
Morris	three days	Wing	New York
Labat and Poret	three hours	Sberna	New York
Miller	seven hours	Mays	Tennessee
		Hill	Utah

From: Bedau and Radelet, "Miscarriages of Justice" in *Stanford Law Review*, November 1987.

• The most notorious injustice committed by the courts in this country had to be the executions of Nicola Sacco and Bartolomeo Vanzetti on August 23, 1927. Accused of the murder of Frederick Parmenter and Allesandro Berardelli at a Massachusetts shoe factory, Sacco and Vanzetti's deaths aroused worldwide protests because it was painfully obvious that they were convicted, sentenced and executed not because they had committed any crime, but because they were immigrants and held unpopular, left-leaning political beliefs.

At present, political prejudice and prejudice against immigrants are not as likely to influence a jury as racial bias does. People who murder whites are put to death at 11 times the rate as those who kill blacks in the United States. A study concerning the effect of race on murder convictions and the allocation of the death penalty was carried out by the *Dallas Times-Herald* in 1975 and reported widely by the Associated Press.[34] According to that study, the killer of a white person in Maryland is eight times more likely to get the death penalty as the killer of a black person. In Arkansas the chances are six times greater, and in Texas the chances are five times greater.

In the states that have the death penalty, the killer of a white has one chance in nine of reaching death row, while the killer of a black has only one chance in 20 of suffering the same fate. According to FBI records, 2.5 percent of killings solved by the police and carrying a death sentence involved a white killer and a black victim, but such cases represent only 1.6 percent of all cases on death row. Black killers of white victims constitute 25.8 percent of all murders solved; such cases are 29.4 percent of all on death row. Accordingly, racial bias is clearly involved in the process of sending a defendant to his death. The same study showed that in an eight-year period, 30 percent of murder victims were black, but that only 14.4 percent of death row inmates were killers of blacks. The study also found that in Texas a white is 12 times more likely to be sentenced to death for killing a white than a black. The study found this to be true in 25 states.

M. Dwayne Smith has studied the pattern of discrimination in assessment of the death penalty in Louisiana.[35] He found that "patterns of discrimination and capriciousness in assessing capital punishment in Louisiana have continued to persist in the post–*Furman* era." First, Smith found that those charged with murdering whites were twice as likely to receive a death sentence as those who killed blacks, and that those who murdered females are more likely to receive the death sentence than those who murdered males. In short, risk of the death penalty in Louisiana depends on who is murdered, thus placing more value on the lives of some citizens than others.

All of this is particularly important because the Supreme Court of the United States had declared a four-year ban on executions in 1972 (the court did not prohibit the death penalty, but forced the states to alter their laws so as to preclude racial bias in their administration). It should be noted that from 1968 until January 1977 there were no executions in the United States. The *Dallas Times-Herald* study and the study by Smith plainly show that racial bias continues in this area and that the moratorium did not achieve its purpose. There are many who believe that a permanent end to the death penalty is the only solution to this problem.

Governor Michael Dukakis of Massachusetts declared August 23, 1987, as "Sacco and Vanzetti Memorial Day." It would be fitting to have a memorial day to all those innocently executed every year. The number of persons innocently executed is, of course, unknown. So is the number of persons innocently convicted of non-capital crimes. It is known, however, that the criminal justice system is not infallible, that errors and even malicious prosecution exist. Can we risk the death penalty knowing this?

In 1791, Robespierre participated in the debate in the French National Assembly on the abolition of the death penalty. Said he,

> Listen to the voice of justice and reason. It tells us and tells us that human judgments are never so certain as to permit society to kill a human being judged by other human beings. . . . Why deprive yourselves of any chance to redeem such errors? Why condemn yourselves to helplessness when faced with persecuted innocence?[36]

Cost

Uninformed people often believe that it is far cheaper to execute a prisoner than to keep him behind bars for many years. The fact is, however, that the innumerable appeals, together with salaries of prosecutors, the time of other court personnel and the maintenance of the prisoner for years before his execution can cost up to $500,000. Since it costs about $18,000 per year to keep a prisoner in a state or federal institution, this means that a 30-year stay in prison costs about as much as one execution. This also does not take into account whether a financial value can ever be placed on human life. If appeals become more difficult then juries will be less likely to convict because few are willing to be responsible for death.

Brutalization

Is the death penalty "deterrence or brutalization"?[37] William Bowers and Glenn Pierce claim that two additional murders a month are committed following an execution, and therefore believe that violence-prone potential killers become more likely to follow the state's example and kill because executions teach killing. Bowers and Pierce also claim that states without the death penalty have lower murder rates than states with the death penalty. This can be tested by comparing the murder rates with and without the death penalty, particularly if they are in adjoining states, with social conditions. Such a comparison has been made a number of times in an effort to argue either against or for the death penalty. Following is a table comparing murder rates of states without the death penalty to adjoining states with that penalty relative to the number of killings per 100,000 population.

	Northeast Murder Rate		
States with No Death Penalty	*per 100,000*		*States with Death Penalty*
Maine	2.0	4.6	Connecticut
Massachusetts	3.6	2.2	New Hampshire
Rhode Island	3.5	2.0	Vermont
Middle Atlantic			
New York	10.7	5.2	New Jersey
		5.5	Pennsylvania
Midwest			
Michigan	11.3	8.9	Illinois
Minnesota	2.5	3.1	Nebraska
Wisconsin	3.1	5.5	Ohio
South			
District of Columbia	31.0	9.0	Maryland
West Virginia	5.9	7.1	Virginia
West			
Alaska	8.6	11.3	California
Hawaii	4.8	6.6	Oregon
United States average	8.5		

From: *Vital Statistics* 1988, pp. 820–821 and 823.

This table shows that three states (New York, Michigan and Alaska) and the District of Columbia, all non–death penalty states, have a murder rate in excess of the United States average of 8.5 per 100,000 population. In addition, Illinois, Maryland and California, which have the death penalty, also exceed the United States average, but not by nearly as much as the District of Columbia. In the Northeast, Connecticut, which has the death penalty, exceeds three adjoining states in murder. In the Middle Atlantic it is New York, without the death penalty, which has a truly phenomenal murder rate. In the Midwest, Michigan, without the death penalty, and Illinois, with the death penalty, both have large murder rates. In the south, the District of Columbia exceeds all adjoining states by far in the number of murders sustained, but Maryland and Virginia both have more murder than the non–death penalty state, West Virginia. Note that the District of Columbia and West Virginia are the only southern states without the death penalty. Finally, in the west, only Alaska and Hawaii do not have the death penalty. Compared to California and Oregon, their murder rates are lower. Obviously, the comparison shows that there is no relationship between the death penalty and murder. Adjoining states will exhibit murder rates that reflect social conditions in those states and not the presence or absence of any penalty. The District of Columbia has a very large black population. As already discussed in chapters 1–3, black homicide exceeds white homicide, suggesting that the distribution of the population, and not the absence of the death penalty, determines that outcome. New York, including New York City, has an annual homicide rate in excess of 20 per 100,000. The same thing holds true of Detroit and Los Angeles. Note that Michigan, without the death penalty, has the same murder rate as California, with that penalty. The presence or absence of the death penalty makes no difference – opponents of the death penalty who claim that it brutalizes the population are just as wrong as are proponents who claim that it reduces murder. The fact is that it does neither.

Brutalization can have yet another dimension, besides the effect that the death penalty has on the population as a whole, and that is of those who actually conduct executions and the judges, prosecutors and even jurors who send citizens to their death. Sing Sing's warden, Duffy, as well as prison guards who have been interviewed concerning the task of killing a prisoner condemned to death, universally complain that they view the job of killing as emotionally draining and revolting.

When the death penalty is mandatory for some crimes, juries are often reluctant to convict a person whom they believe to be guilty because they are reluctant to assume the responsibility of deciding that someone should lose his life. It is for this reason that the courts have been given some discretion in capital cases.[38] There is also a good deal of evidence that a large number of people who support capital punishment in principle do so only as long as they are not confronted with it. Sixty-one percent of Americans have said they support the penalty, but when faced with the prospect of actually voting for death as jury members, 29 percent say that they would not vote for the death penalty in the first place, and 63 percent express neutral attitudes, meaning that they are not ready to vote for the death penalty, either. Thus, fully 92 percent of persons who have been confronted with using the death penalty do not favor it.

Guards have seldom been interviewed in this regard. However, the few who have come forward have generally agreed with this statement, made by a 35-year veteran at Kilby Prison in Alabama:

> We begin to dread electrocutions weeks before they take place. We're almost glad when someone is commuted regardless of what crime he committed.
>
> The guards are always nervous before and during an electrocution. In my opinion it is something you never become accustomed to. It's the most gruesome job I've come in contact with during my 35 years with the department. . . . The more you see, the more you hate it. Even when things are routine, it's a horrible thing to watch.[39]

There are, however, guards who enjoy describing the death agony to those on death row, who tell the condemned how much they will enjoy seeing them die, and who make a fetish of this kind of verbal harassment. The issue is not so much what any guard may or may not say about this work, but rather why it is that anyone would do this gruesome task. It must be asked from the interactionist perspective whether there is really any difference between a judge, who pronounces the death sentence, a warden, who organizes death, and a prison guard, who drags a helpless human being to his death, and those who are executed. One can argue from the principle of legitimacy and show that executions are legal and murder is not. However, the impact of actually killing a fellow human with deliberation has to reduce those who do this to a level of insensitivity to the sufferings of others, which a decent society can hardly tolerate. This is widely known, and for this reason executioners are generally held in contempt. They are frequently avoided and sometimes assaulted, and their families have often been insulted and avoided. Executioners have had their houses bombed and their lives threatened. Because participation in executions is contrary to the Hippocratic Oath, the American Medical Association has recommended that its members not participate in executions in any manner. In the past, physicians repeatedly had been asked to bring about the recovery of persons condemned to die who were in danger of dying a natural death. In addition, physicians are usually asked to certify that the death penalty has been effective, once the execution has been carried out.

The essential issue with which physicians must deal is whether they want to concur in the view that anyone condemned to death is essentially so evil that he should be regarded as worthless and unredeemable. Such a view is particularly questionable because it must of necessity include those who are condemned but innocent. In any event, this is hardly the medical point of view, nor is it this author's. It is, however, the opinion of those favoring the death penalty, as expressed by the former chief justice of the Georgia Supreme Court, Hugh Nichols:

> You know, you don't put up a mad dog and feed him and take him home—you get rid of him. What good are they to society? They are incorrigible. Scientists prove now beyond any question that they are just born that way. You can't correct them. It's genetic. They're animals. There's no way you can do anything about them.[40]

It is worth speculating here whether those who hold similar views would find it appropriate to return to the days when even animals were executed in public. An example of this is given in E.P. Evan's book, *The Criminal Prosecution and Capital Punishment of Animals:*[41]

> The sow, dressed in human clothes, legs pinioned, is held down on the scaffold by the executioner, who is fixing the noose around its throat. Facing the sow is the town clerk, reading the sentence from a scroll; at the foot of the scaffold is a jostling crowd, much of the same kind as the crowds which used to assemble around the Tyburn Tree. Mothers are lifting up their children to give them a better view; and a stern worthy is pointing his finger at the screaming sow, obviously explaining: "She is only getting what she deserves."

Animals guilty of killing a human being were, in the Middle Ages, and in isolated cases up to the 19th century, tried by lawful procedure, defended by counsel, sometimes acquitted, more often sentenced to be hanged, burned or buried alive. A horse which had killed a man was hanged in Dijon, France, in 1389; another sow, with a litter of six, was sentenced for the murder of a child at Savigny in 1457, but the baby pigs were reprieved "in lack of positive proof of complicity." It appears that this is carrying too far the ancient proverb: "Bonis exemplis, magis impetramus, quam bonis verbis" (good examples achieve more than good words) as the following examples show.

THE LEGAL ISSUES — SOME DECISIONS

The principal Supreme Court decisions concerning the death penalty have been made over a period of many years. All cannot be presented here, but the legal issue has been before the court so often in recent years that the role of the Supreme Court in this matter can hardly be ignored. One of the principal errors made by many superficial observers of the Supreme Court is the unjustified belief that justices who uphold the death penalty are somehow in favor of that penalty while those who reject it, as does Justice Thurgood Marshall, are against it. The latter may be true with reference to the Eighth Amendment, which Marshall believes prohibits the states from imposing such a penalty. However, justices such as William Rehnquist and others before him, who would not interfere with the states' right to impose such a law, were not necessarily in favor of the death penalty. They were in favor of states' rights, an entirely different matter. (As an example, it is possible that a legislator in one of the several states may have voted against the death penalty becoming law in his state, and that the same legislator later became a Supreme Court Justice and that in that capacity he voted in favor of the right of one of the states to impose the death penalty, which he opposes privately.)

It is significant that the Court ruled positively in the matter of the death penalty in 1878 in *Wilkerson vs. Utah* (99 U.S. 130), then waited 12 years to rule again *in re Kemmler* in 1890 (136 U.S. 436), then dealt with the death penalty 58 years later in *Trop vs. Dulles* (356 U.S. 86), and then only peripherally, since Trop is really not a death penalty case. It wasn't until *Witherspoon vs. Illinois* in 1968 (391 U.S. 510) that a decision limiting the death penalty was made, thus letting 78 years pass since Kemmler. This once more illustrates that previous generations took the death penalty for granted and did not question its legality before the courts. It seems that only the civil rights movement of the 1960s truly called the death penalty into question until it became, and continues to be, one of the foremost civil rights issues in the United States.

Wilkerson vs. Utah dealt only with the question of whether the then territory of Utah had the right to shoot a man condemned to death for murder, or whether another method of execution must be found. The issue of the death penalty itself was not raised. The facts were that Wilkerson was found guilty of murder in the first degree by a jury, having been charged with the "willful, malicious and premeditated murder of William Baxter, with malice aforethought."[42] Murder, as defined at that time by the territory of Utah, was the "unlawful killing of a human being with malice aforethought, . . . express or implied. Express malice is when there is manifested a deliberate intention unlawfully to take away the life of a fellow creature, and it may be implied when there is no considerable provocation, or when the circumstances attending the killing show an abandoned or malignant heart."

Such language seems quite old-fashioned today, but serves to make the point that the death penalty was not itself seen as violating the Constitution in respect to the prohibition against "cruel and unusual punishment." That, said the court, would be only torture or unnecessary cruelty. The Supreme Court held that since shooting is neither cruel nor unusual it is also constitutional, since the courts have the right to decide the mode of execution.

In re Kemmler was decided in 1890.[43] That decision dealt with electrocution in New York, which the court held to be constitutional on the grounds that electrocution had been introduced by the New York legislature on the assumption that it was in fact more humane than hanging and other methods used previously. The court said the following:

> Punishments are cruel when they involved torture or a lingering death; but the punishment of death is not cruel, within the meaning of that word as used in the Constitution. It implies there is something inhuman and barbarous, something more than the mere extinguishment of life.[44]

In the Kemmler case and in all cases involving the death penalty, reference is made by the Supreme Court to the Constitution of the United States, including the Eighth Amendment and the first section of the Fourteenth Amendment, which reads as follows:

> Article VIII. Excessive bail shall not be required, nor excessive fines imposed, nor cruel and unusual punishment inflicted.

> Article XIV. Sec. 1. All persons born or naturalized in the United States, and subject to the jurisdiction thereof, are citizens of the United States and of the State wherein they reside. No State shall make or enforce any law which shall abridge the privileges or immunities of citizens of the United States; nor shall any State deprive any person of life, liberty or property, without due process of law; nor deny to any person within its jurisdiction the equal protection of the law.[45]

It is important to keep these two amendments in mind when dealing with the interesting decision of *Trop vs. Dulles* (356 U.S. 86). This decision does not deal directly with the death penalty. Instead it concerned an American soldier of foreign birth who had deserted, and from whom the government proposed to take his naturalized citizenship. The court prohibited the government from doing that and based its decision in part on the "death penalty as an index of the constitutional limit on punishment."[46]

The court, in the words of Chief Justice Earl Warren, said that the death penalty cannot be said to violate the constitutional concept of cruelty. This was in 1957. It is important that Chief Justice Warren traced the history of the Eighth Amendment to the English Declaration of Rights of 1688 and the subsequent English Bill of Rights, enacted December 16, 1689. That bill states, "excessive bail ought not to be required, nor excessive fines imposed, nor cruel and unusual punishment inflicted." These words then found their way into the United States Constitution in the Eighth Amendment.

That declaration and the many subsequent decisions based on it were made, according to Warren, in the interest of the dignity of man. Further, the Chief Justice declared in *Trop vs. Dulles* that the power of the state to punish must be made within "the limits of civilized standards." All of these considerations led the court to reject the idea of expatriation, but not the death penalty. In other words, the court held, in effect, that deprivation of American citizenship is worse than death.

Witherspoon vs. Illinois, decided in 1967, dealt with the issue of a "death qualified" jury. In that case, the state had refused jury participation in the trial of Witherspoon of those persons unwilling to impose the death penalty, choosing only jurors who had no such scruples. The court held that, "in its quest for a jury capable of imposing the death penalty, the State produced a jury uncommonly willing to condemn a man to die." The phrase "uncommonly willing" should be understood in the context of public opinion at that time. In 1966, approximately 42 percent of the American public favored capital punishment for convicted murderers, while 47 percent opposed it and 11 percent were undecided.[47]

The court held that the state may not entrust determination of whether a person is innocent or guilty to a tribunal organized to convict. The decision as to whether a defendant deserves to live was also to be made "on scales that are not deliberately tipped toward death."[48] Consequently the court ruled that a "death qualified jury" stacks the deck against the defendant, and reversed the death sentence under that circumstance.

On May 5, 1986, however, the Supreme Court sharply limited the application of that earlier ruling. In *Lockhart vs. McCree* (not a capital case), the court majority held that

> 1) the Constitution does not prohibit removal for cause, prior to the guilt phase of a bifurcated trial, of prospective jurors whose opposition to the death penalty is so strong that it would prevent or substantially impair performance of their duties as jurors at sentencing phase of trial; 2) "death qualification" does not violate fair cross section requirement of Sixth Amendment [which guarantees an impartial jury and a fair trial]; and 3) "death qualification" does not violate constitutional right to an impartial jury.[49]

In another case, *McGautha vs. California,* which also dealt with the role of the jury in capital punishment decisions, the Court held in 1971 that a jury could decide whether punishment should be life imprisonment or death.

Most famous of all Supreme Court decisions concerning the death penalty was the decision called *Furman vs. Georgia;* the length of the written decision alone is remarkable as it ran 235 pages in *United States Reports.* This decision has sometimes been misunderstood as to render the death penalty unconstitutional. This was never the opinion of the majority. However, the Court did rule in *Furman* that racial discrimination in regard to the death penalty is unconstitutional because it violates the Eighth Amendment prohibition against "unusual" punishment. It is worth portraying the words of Justice William O. Douglas who wrote the majority opinion as follows:

> It would seem to be incontestable that the death penalty inflicted on one defendant is "unusual" if it discriminates against him by reason of his race, religion, wealth, social position, or class, or if it is imposed under a procedure that gives room for the play of such prejudices.[50]

Within the pages of this decision is an interesting table included in the concurring opinion of Thurgood Marshall. This concerns the abolition of the death penalty in 21 American states since 1846. It should be pointed out that of the 18 states which had abolished that penalty by 1972, five had reimposed it by 1988. Several states have abolished and reimposed the death penalty repeatedly, and it appears that the presence or absence of that penalty is political. Current public opinion as reflected in voting patterns will remove and then bring back the death penalty in the several states, and unless the Supreme Court rules out this penalty on constitutional grounds, it will always be a part of United States law in at least some of the states. As of 1990, states with the penalty are by far the majority.

In his concurring opinion, Marshall also held that the death penalty will never be free from racial bias, and therefore the order by the Supreme Court to demand that States write a death penalty statute preventing bias from entering into the decision to use it is doomed to failure. It is quite likely that those who seek the end of that penalty will argue that regardless of its deterrent value, bigotry and the death penalty go hand-in-glove, and the abolition of the death penalty is the only guarantee that it will not be unfairly applied on the basis of race. Just such an argument was made in the case of Warren McCloskey, who was sent to death in the murder of an Atlanta police officer in 1986.

On April 22, 1987, the Court rejected in a 5–4 decision a study which showed that blacks who kill whites are the most likely defendants to receive the death penalty. That study, made by Professor David Baldus of the University of Iowa, examined all Georgia murder convictions from 1973 to 1978. Baldus found that 22 percent of blacks who killed whites received the death penalty. Only one percent of blacks who killed blacks were so treated, the same being true for the three percent of whites who killed blacks and the eight percent of whites who killed other whites. The court rejected that study for fear that it "would throw the entire criminal justice system into question."[51] Indeed it would do so; in fact, it should.

In view of the composition of the present Supreme Court, it is highly unlikely that it will soon return to the 1972 view holding that racial discrimination is cause for halting the death penalty. The conclusion is, at least for the present, that *Furman* is obsolete, despite subsequent rulings which have been based on it. One of these decisions was *Gregg vs. Georgia,* in which the court dealt with the issue of a bifurcated jury and other matters relative to the death penalty as instituted by the state of Georgia after *Furman.* (A "bifurcated" jury is one which decides guilt or innocence only, while the punishment is decided either by another jury or by a judge or a court of appeals.)

Since it was the purpose of the *Furman* decision to insure fairness in capital cases, Georgia altered its procedures, as did 35 other states and the United States Congress, to meet any possible objections to the death penalty on fairness grounds. The court recognized this and made the following affirmation:

> 1) The punishment of death for the crime of murder does not, under all circumstances, violate the Eighth and Fourteenth Amendments.
>
> 2) The Eighth Amendment . . . forbids the use of punishment that is "excessive" either because it involves the unnecessary and wanton infliction of pain or because it is grossly disproportionate to the severity of the crime.
>
> 3) Though the legislature may not impose excessive punishment, it is not required to select the least severe penalty possible. . . .
>
> 4) The existence of capital punishment was accepted by the framers of the Constitution, and for . . . two centuries the Court has recognized that capital punishment for the crime of murder is not invalid *per se.*
>
> 5) Legislative measures adopted by the people's chosen representatives weigh heavily in ascertaining contemporary standards of decency; and the argument that such standards require that the Eighth Amendment be construed as prohibiting the death penalty has been undercut by the fact that in the . . . years since *Furman* . . . was decided, Congress and at least 35 States have enacted new statutes providing for the death penalty.
>
> 6) Retribution and the possibility of deterrence of capital crimes by prospective offenders are not impermissible considerations for a legislature to weigh in determining whether the death penalty should be imposed. . . .
>
> 7) Capital punishment for the crime of murder cannot be viewed as invariably disproportionate for the severity of that crime.
>
> 8) The concerns expressed in *Furman* that the death penalty not be imposed arbitrarily or capriciously [are] . . . best met by a system that provides for a *bifurcated proceeding.* . . . Before the death penalty can be imposed, there must be specific jury findings as to the circumstances of the crime or the character of the defendant and the *State Supreme Court thereafter reviews the comparability of each death sentence with the sentences imposed on similarly situated defendants to ensure that the sentence of death in a particular case is not disproportionate.*[52]

This was the substance of the attitude of the Supreme Court relative to the death penalty in 1975 when the case of *Gregg vs. Georgia* was decided.

In 1977 and 1980, the Court put these views to the test in *Coker vs. Georgia* and in *Godfrey vs. Georgia,* respectively. In these cases the Supreme Court held that death cannot be imposed for rape (Coker), nor even for murder unless the murder involves aggravating circumstances under the Georgia statute. According to the Georgia Code, the death penalty was possible for murder, rape, robbery, or kidnapping, providing that these crimes were committed "by a person with a prior record of conviction for a capital felony."[53]

In the case of rape, the Supreme Court reasoned as follows:

Rape is without doubt deserving of serious punishment; but in terms of moral depravity and of the injury to the person and to the public, it does not *compare* with murder, which does involve the unjustified taking of human life. Although it may be accompanied by another crime, rape by definition does not include the death of or even the serious injury to another person. The murderer kills. The rapist, if no more than that, does not. . . . We have the abiding conviction that the death penalty . . . is an excessive penalty for the rapist who, as such, does not take human life.[54]

Even in Godfrey, the Court rejected the death penalty as excessive punishment because the killer did not include in his crimes an "aggravating circumstance." It must be understood that the Supreme Court used the test of "aggravating circumstances" only because it is required under Georgia law, and not because it is to be applied universally. In any event, the facts in the Godfrey case are this. In September 1977, Godfrey and his 28-year-old wife had an argument in their home. Godfrey not only threatened his wife with a knife but also cut up some of her clothing. Mrs. Godfrey thereupon moved out, stayed with relatives and secured a warrant charging her husband with aggravated assault. In addition she filed for divorce. Before a court hearing on these matters could be held Godfrey asked his wife to return home, which she refused to do, and for which Godfrey blamed his mother-in-law, with whom his wife was then living.

On September 20, 1977, Mrs. Godfrey telephoned her husband twice to say that no reconciliation was possible and that she wanted him to turn over to her the proceeds from the sale of their house. She said repeatedly that her mother supported her position. Thereupon Godfrey took his shotgun and walked to the trailer where his mother-in-law lived. Arriving outside, he pointed his gun at his wife through a window. Mrs. Godfrey was there playing cards with her mother and the Godfrey's 11-year-old daughter. Godfrey shot his wife in the forehead and instantly killed her, in front of the child and her mother. He then ran into the house, beat his fleeing daughter with the butt of the gun and murdered his mother-in-law by shooting her in the head as well. Despite the horror of this double killing the court held that these crimes "cannot be said to have reflected a consciousness materially more 'depraved' than that of any other person guilty of murder. . . . There is no principled way to distinguish this case, in which the death penalty was imposed, from the many cases in which it was not."[55] The court reversed the death sentence.

On July 2, 1976, the Court once more ruled in the area of the death penalty. The case of *Woodson vs. North Carolina* dealt with the issue of whether the state of North Carolina could make the death penalty mandatory for all murders, regardless of the circumstances. The majority held that North Carolina's mandatory death-sentence statute violated the Eighth and the Fourteenth Amendment because "It treats all persons convicted of a designated offense not as uniquely individual human beings, but as members of a faceless, undifferentiated mass to be subjected to the blind infliction of the penalty of death."[56]

It is significant that the dissenting opinion of Justice Rehnquist held that since the penalty of death is not invariably a cruel and unusual punishment for the crime of murder, then it must be a proportionate and appropriate punishment for any and every murder regardless of the circumstances of the crime and record of the offender.[57]

On April 21, 1987, the Supreme Court even ruled that a person may be sentenced to die for a murder he did not commit. This ruling came about in the cases of Ricky and Raymond Tison who, in 1978, together with their brother Donnie, smuggled guns into Arizona State Prison during a visit with their father, Gary Tison. Subsequently Gary Tison and Randy Greenawalt, another inmate, escaped. This escape triggered a manhunt which led to the killing of Donnie Tison at a police roadblock after Gary Tison and Greenawalt had kidnapped and murdered Marine Sgt. John Lyons, his wife, Donnelda, their two-year-old son, Christopher, and a 15-year-old niece, Teresa Tyson. Gary Tison died in the desert. However, the younger Tisons and Greenawalt were caught, convicted and sent to death row. Six persons had died because of this escape and indirectly, because the brothers had furnished their father with guns, the Tison brothers were held responsible. While evidence developed in their sentencing hearing indicated that the Tisons were off looking for water when the Lyons family was killed, the majority agreed with Justice Sandra Day O'Connor who wrote that:

> A narrow focus on the question of whether or not a given defendant "intended to kill" . . . is a highly unsatisfactory means of definitively distinguishing the most culpable and dangerous of murderers. . . . This reckless indifference to the value of human life may be every bit as shocking to the moral sense as the "intent to kill."

Commenting on this ruling, Henry Schwartzschild of the American Civil Liberties Union called it "extraordinarily barbaric."[58]

In view of this decision and the belief in the legal community that poor defendants on death row need to be represented better than is now the case, many of the country's most prestigious corporate law firms are volunteering to help such defendants. This is done also because there is an acute shortage of criminal lawyers willing to take on a capital case which may take years to defend and pay very little.

In 1988, there were over 2,000 people on death row in the United States. Of these, one-third had no legal representation as of July of that year. However, 1,200 members of the American Bar Association responded to a mailing by that group indicating a willingness to serve as counsel to the condemned. The consequences of this involvement are already visible. Since large law firms have the resources to deal with such cases, prosecutors have begun to complain about the numerous delays and lengthy legal briefs such firms can produce. For example, the Wall Street law firm of Cahill, Gordon and Reindel represented Samuel Johnson, convicted of the murder of a Mississippi State Police officer. The firm spent over $1,000,000 in legal time to finally get Johnson's death sentence overturned. Evidently, no private practitioner could spend that much time without giving up his entire practice.

Another example is the defense of Andrew Legare in Georgia. He was sentenced to death three times in nine years. However, each time the firm of

Sutherland, Asbill & Brennan of Atlanta won reversals on the basis of Legare's youth, jury charging and consideration of background in sentencing. The entrance of these large firms into the area of indigent defense in capital cases lends at least some balance to the proceedings in such cases in which heretofore the state had overwhelming resources and the defendant hardly any.[59]

In June of 1988, the Supreme Court ruled 5 to 3 that States may not execute people for crimes committed when they were less than 16 years old. This decision is not final. The justices announced that they would consider banning the execution of juvenile murderers during the term beginning in October 1988 and that they would use two cases, one from Georgia and one from Missouri to consider the fate of young killers.

Meanwhile, William Wayne Thompson, who was 15 years old when he participated in the murder of his sister's former husband in 1982, was spared the death penalty in Oklahoma. Justice John Paul Stevens, speaking for a plurality of four justices said that "evolving standards of decency" led to the conclusion that it would be unconstitutional to execute a person for a crime he committed when he was only 15 years old. Justice Sandra Day O'Connor held that a State may not execute someone younger than 16 unless that State's legislature specifies no minimum age. Since four justices dissented from this majority of five, it is entirely possible that the Court will yet permit the executions of children on reconsideration.[60]

THE CURRENT STATE OF THE DEATH PENALTY

On March 1, 1989, there were 2,186 persons in American prisons who were sentenced to death. During the year 1987, 25 persons were executed. Since murder is the only reason for meting out the death penalty which the Supreme Court will allow, this means that the penalty is extremely rare in this country. In 1987 there were 17,859 known murders in the United States, constituting a murder rate of 8.3 per 100,000. In 1986, there were 20,613 killings, constituting a murder rate of 8.6 per 100,000 persons in a population of 243 million people, a decline of .03 per 100,000, or three percent. This decline was due mainly to the earlier decline in the birthrate, in that fewer young men reached the ages of 15 to 30, which are the ages during which most murders occur.

At the end of 1987, there were 556,748 prisoners in state and federal prisons in the United States with 1,984 prisoners sentenced to death, slightly more than three-tenths of one percent of the prison population. Since then, the number of persons sent to death row and the rate of executions has increased, but the number executed still remains very small compared to the over 20,000 murders committed every year.[61] The evidence is, that the American people are not willing or interested in punishing every murder with death. This is, of course, known to the courts whose attitudes reflect the views of the American majority.

It is striking that the opinions of Supreme Court justices are replete with references to public opinion, "standards of decency" and other phrases, plainly indicating that they know and want to know what Americans think about various issues before them, including the death penalty. Since justices are appointed by an elected president and confirmed by an elected Senate, it is reasonable to assume that at least initially, they reflect the will of those who elected the president and the Senate. Of course, justices of the Supreme Court and other federal judges are appointed for life in order to guarantee their independence, meaning that public opinion may change faster than the Supreme Court. It is, however, a wise provision of the Constitution that judges remain tenured lest otherwise they become the tools of public passion, a situation far worse than the possibility of becoming antiquated, a fate that after all, awaits all men and women.

The death penalty will not be universally abolished in the United States in the foreseeable future. This is so because the American people do not want to do this in every state, feeling that the option of death as punishment should be available to them. Restrictions upon the use of that penalty will in all likelihood increase, as for example in the case of convicted murderers less than 18 years old. The continued use of the death penalty will, of course, not halt murder, nor does it increase murder. Indeed, it is unrelated to the murder rate, unless one wishes to regard the death penalty itself as murder.

In 1970, Great Britain abolished the death penalty. During the long debate preceding this change in the law, Arthur Koestler lent his famous name to the opposition by writing *Reflections on Hanging*. Said Koestler:

> The division is not between rich and poor, highbrow and low brow, Christians and atheists: it is between those who have charity and those who have not. . . . The test of one's humanity is whether one is able to accept this fact—not as lip service, but with the shuddering recognition of a kinship: here but for the Grace of God, drop I.[62]

There are many social reasons why murder is not subject to punishment in most cases. The principal social reasons for murder have not yet been explored in this book, although the surface motives were listed in the first three chapters and in other situations. It is now time to turn to an in-depth analysis which will seek to demonstrate why the United States has eight times more murder than European countries.

Part IV

The State of Murder

10. Murder Now and Then

Murder has a long history and for the foreseeable future, mankind will not desist from it. This being the case, can anything at all be done about the horrors so far described, or must people forever suffer these self-inflicted wounds upon humanity? Is society condemned to eternal crime, or is there any chance that kindness and patience, forebearance and response, can yet capture the hearts of all people?

To answer these questions, one needs first to understand why people kill one another, a question only partially answered in Chapter 3, where some of the principal motives for homicide were discovered. These motives included sudden anger, jealousy, business dealings, the commission of other crimes such as robbery and rape, and even "insanity," revenge and gang wars. (See Table 21, Chapter 3.) This does not truly explain why people get so angry at one another as to assault fellow citizens. Motives such as jealousy do not fully explain what it is in United States society that leads people to believe that they should deal violently with one another in the first place; there are other responses people could have despite the emotions that have just been listed. There *are* jealous persons who do not assault or kill anyone, people who seek revenge but use no violence, and gang members who have never beat, assaulted or killed anyone. Violence is not a necessary condition of life, it is only a far too frequent one. It is not inevitable, however; people can control it, and this book can help. To do so, people need to understand why they are so violent, and then comprehend how they might better deal with one another without so much anger and hostility. There are other outcomes of violence such as assault, rape, robbery and arson, but this book deals exclusively with murder in all its forms.

THE CURRENT STATE OF MURDER IN THE UNITED STATES

In all of 1988, the United States Department of Justice reported 20,675 murders, or a murder rate of 8.4 per 100,000 inhabitants of the United States.[1] A breakdown of the murder rate by region and by states reveals a very important aspect of murder: Different regions have sharply different murder rates. If murder were merely the outcome of psychiatric conditions such as frustration or "sudden anger" or jealousy, then all regions of the country should be expected to have the

157

same number of murders per 100,000 inhabitants, because people get angry everywhere, and jealousy, frustration and disappointment exist in all places. Murder, however is related to culture as well as emotions, and it is in these cultural differences that the answer is found to the question, Why do people murder, and why do some folks murder more than others?

The following table of murder by region and states has an "index number" indicating whether a particular area is more or less dangerous to live in compared to the United States as a whole. For example, Connecticut has a rating of 64, meaning that the murder rate there of 5.4 per 100,000 is only 64 percent of the national average of 8.4 per 100,000. Connecticut is a fairly safe state but not as safe as Vermont, for example, but a good deal better than New York, which has an index of 149, making it 49 percent more dangerous than the average state.

There is every reason to believe that different cultures take different attitudes toward human life; that different cultures value or devalue human life, and produce different kinds of personalities willing to be aggressive or not depending on the interpretations people have been taught and firmly believe are "only natural." In fact, each society's belief that its own, learned, arbitrary interpretations of life are "only natural" and must be shared by everyone is a universal belief. Anthropologists never tire of showing how the "strangest" customs appear quite natural to those who practice them, and how customs most familiar to them appear utterly "unnatural" to those who do not know them. The culture concept, then, explains human behavior. People are enculturated, meaning they act according to the manner in which their culture interprets life and death. People get angry and become violent at some situations and conditions because they were taught to do so.[2]

Crime in the United States, 1988

Murder Rate by Region

Region	Population	Rate	Index
United States	245,810,000	8.4	100
South	84,880,000	10.3	123
West	50,425,000	8.5	101
Northeast	50,611,000	7.5	89
Midwest	59,894,000	6.4	76

According to this table, the South is far more violent than the Northeast and the Midwest, and that the West rates in the middle. This can be further broken down for various areas within these regions, and then further by states and even by cities, showing that the inclination to murder is by no means the same everywhere. The information also shows that the United States resembles other countries in its murder rate in some parts of the country, but not others. The United States cannot be compared with West Germany, France, England or other countries because those countries are much smaller than the United States is. For example, all of Germany is smaller than Montana, and Alaska is a good deal bigger than France and Germany. Europe as a whole, outside the Soviet Union, does have a population as large as the United States, does have many large cities and other features similar to America, but has an overall murder rate of only about 1.1 per 100,000 persons. The rate in the United States is eight times greater. Before this is explained, regional rates need to be looked at more closely.

Murder Rate by Region and Area, 1988

Region	Area	Population	Rate	Index
South	W.S. Central	26,885,000	11.1	132
	South Atlantic	42,601,000	10.4	124
	E.S. Central	15,394,000	8.6	101
Total South		84,880,000	10.3	123
West	Pacific	37,134,000	9.2	110
	Mountain	13,291,000	6.6	74
Total West		50,425,000	8.5	101
Northeast	Middle Atlantic	37,645,000	8.8	105
	New England	12,966,000	3.8	45
Total N.E.		50,611,000	6.9	82
Midwest	E.N. Central	42,149,000	7.3	87
	W.N. Central	17,745,000	4.3	51
Total Midwest		59,894,000	6.4	76

This table shows that the chances of being murdered are 32 percent greater than average for people living in the West South Central states such as Louisiana or Texas, and that citizens who live in the West North Central states, such as Iowa and North Dakota, are almost twice as safe from murder as the average American, because the murder rate in that area of the country is only 51 percent of the average murder rate of 8.4 per 100,000 for the whole country. Now, it is time to examine murder rates by state within each area.

Murder by Region, Area and State, 1988

Region	Area	Population	Rate	Index
South	W.S. Central			
	Arkansas	2,422,000	8.7	104
	Louisiana	4,420,000	11.6	138
	Oklahoma	3,263,000	7.4	88
	Texas	16,780,000	12.1	144
	E.S. Central			
	Alabama	4,127,000	9.9	118
	Kentucky	3,721,000	6.2	74
	Mississippi	2,627,000	8.6	102
	Tennessee	4,919,000	9.4	112

Region	Area	Population	Rate	Index
	South Atlantic			
	Delaware	660,000	5.2	62
	District of			
	Columbia	620,000	59.6	710*
	Florida	12,377,000	11.4	136
	Georgia	6,401,000	11.7	139
	Maryland	4,644,000	9.7	115
	North Carolina	6,526,000	7.8	93
	South Carolina	3,493,000	9.3	111
	Virginia	5,996,000	7.8	93
	West Virginia	1,884,000	4.9	58*
Total South		84,880,000	10.3	123

No death penalty

Region	Area	Population	Rate	Index
West	Pacific			
	Alaska	513,000	5.7	71*
	California	28,168,000	10.4	124
	Hawaii	1,093,000	4.0	48*
	Oregon	2,741,000	5.1	61
	Washington	4,619,000	5.7	68
	Mountain			
	Arizona	3,466,000	8.5	101
	Colorado	3,290,000	5.7	68
	Idaho	999,000	3.6	43
	Montana	804,000	2.6	31
	Nevada	1,060,000	10.5	125
	New Mexico	1,510,000	11.5	137
	Utah	1,691,000	2.8	33
	Wyoming	471,000	2.5	30
Total West		50,425,000	8.5	101

No death penalty

This table again indicates that murder follows certain regional, area and state patterns, and that these patterns are bound to the culture in those regions, areas and states.

Murder by Region, Area and State, 1988

Region	Area	Population	Rate	Index
Northeast	Middle Atlantic			
	New Jersey	7,720,000	5.3	63
	New York	17,898,000	12.5	149*
	Pennsylvania	12,027,000	5.5	65

Region	Area	Population	Rate	Index
	New England			
	Connecticut	3,241,000	5.4	64
	Maine	1,206,000	3.1	37*
	Massachusetts	5,871,000	3.5	42*
	New Hampshire	1,097,000	2.3	27
	Rhode Island	995,000	4.1	49*
	Vermont	556,000	2.0	24
Total Northeast		50,611,000	7.5	89

*No death penalty

Again, there is a relationship between the region of the country and the area or state in which murders occurred. Obviously, these are not the same everywhere. In fact, if the largest cities were removed from these statistics, there would be yet sharper differences in murder rates, displaying great regional variations.

Murder by Region, Area and State, 1988

Region	Area	Population	Rate	Index
Midwest	E.N. Central			
	Illinois	11,544,000	8.6	98
	Indiana	5,575,000	6.4	76
	Michigan	9,300,000	10.8	129*
	Ohio	10,872,000	5.4	83
	Wisconsin	4,858,000	3.0	45
	W.N. Central			
	Iowa	2,834,000	1.7	20*
	Kansas	2,487,000	3.4	40*
	Minnesota	4,306,000	2.9	35*
	Missouri	5,139,000	8.0	95
	Nebraska	1,601,000	3.6	43
	North Dakota	663,000	1.8	21*
	South Dakota	715,000	3.1	37
Total Midwest		59,894,000	6.4	96

*No death penalty

Total United States		245,810,000	8.4	100[3]

Please note that all rates are compared to the total for the United States, so that 8.4 murders per 100,000 is considered as 100 and each "Index" is either less, more or the same as the U.S. average.

MURDER AND THE CULTURE OF VIOLENCE

Inspection of the preceding tables reveals a number of facts concerning murder. It is therefore in the interest of establishing scientific evidence that this material is presented. It has been alleged that there are in the United States and elsewhere values and attitudes which approve of violence, including murder, and that the high overall rate, as well as the high rates in the South and West as compared to other regions, are the product of such cultural legitimacy.[4] Murder rates differ considerably over long periods of time between regions and areas of the United States, and between states and cities within such regions. On an index basis, the South has 45 percent more murder than the Northeast, and all parts of the country have more murder than New England.

The District of Columbia has nearly six times times the number of murders as other parts of the South, with the truly phenomenal rate of 59.5 per 100,000. It must be understood, however, that this large murder rate is the outcome of the geopolitical condition of the District of Columbia, and does not reflect an excessive proclivity to kill in that location. The fact is, the city of Washington has a very large number of black inhabitants, whose murder rate everywhere in the United States is six times greater than is true of whites. Since almost the entire white population of the Washington metropolitan area (over 3,000,000 people) does not live in the District, the statistics for that district are in effect confined to murder rates typical for all inner cities in America. If the state of Illinois consisted only of the inner city of Chicago, or the state of New York consisted only of Harlem, then these states would have as great a rate of murder as the District of Columbia. In the West, New Mexico, Nevada and California exceed the average murder index by 22 to 29 percent, and in the Northeast, New York, with a murder rate of 12.5 and an index of 149, has 40 percent more murder than the Northeast normally exhibits. The same holds true for Michigan in the Midwest. The index for that region is only 96, but for Michigan it is 149, fully 55 percent more.

Several contributing factors are responsible for so much murder. Among these are the conflict between the "Puritan" and the "Western" tradition in America; the rise of cities and overcrowding in urban areas; the Black experience in America; the frustration-aggression syndrome; relative deprivation; drugs; and family violence.

The Puritan and Western Traditions

Those familiar with Nathaniel Hawthorne's *Scarlet Letter* have some insight into the life of those people of English birth and ancestry who settled in the New World in the 17th century and left an indelible mark—Puritanism—upon the culture of the United States which is visible to this day. "The Puritan settlement is an event in history that has . . . marked the American nation forever."[5] This is one of the many themes Nathaniel Hawthorne conveys in this tale of adultery in early New England, although it is surely not the only one. It is important to remember that despite Henry Ford's oft-repeated comment that "history is bunk," the contrary is the case. The

United States is in effect a Puritan society, not because any substantial number of Americans know of John Calvin or his doctrines, but because the influence of Calvinism and Puritanism is an ingrained, though largely unrecognized, part of society. That is, of course, true of all philosophical orientations. Few ever really understand why they believe what they believe. They only know that some things are true, right, just and "only natural." This author has traveled a good deal and has never met a group anywhere who do not know what is "only natural." This belief, which sociologists call ethnocentrism, gives people the assurance that they and their group are right, and that the out-group is at best wrong, if not dangerous, and that people's own worldview *(Weltanschauung)* is the purest expression of morality and justice anywhere. When people are raised from childhood to believe that their surroundings, myths, legends and laws are eternal, they teach them to their children, who in turn teach their own children. This is how systems of belief continue for generations, though often their origins are lost in the mist of history. So it is with Calvinism. Altered no doubt by the years and by innumerable interpretations, Calvinism nevertheless survives, particularly in New England where it was once at home. But it also survives in the Constitution and laws of the United States.

It is for this reason that vice is viewed as crime. Gambling, prostitution, drinking and addictions of all sorts are seen as police matters in this country, but this is hardly the case anywhere else. Wherever Calvinism governs the affairs of people, a strict code of rather narrow morality also prevails. In such communities, sex is suspect and pornography a crime. Even leisure is viewed as antithetical to the good life, and work is raised to an ideal. In fact, "From the Calvinistic point of view laziness is the most dangerous vice; it is hurtful to the soul from the standpoint of ... discipline and harmful to the community from the standpoint of utilitarianism."[6]

Calvinist utilitarianism (usefulness) refers to the peculiar Calvinist view that the individual is to cultivate his own personality and be independent while at the same time have a strong sense of community "for common, positive ends and values. . . . This explains the fact that all the Calvinistic peoples are characterized by individualism and democracy, combined with a strong bias toward authority . . . ."[7]

This description of the Calvinist viewpoint, which was brought to New England in the 17th century, is prevalent even to this day. The strong sense of community has protected New Englanders of previous and current generations from high crime rates, including murder, experienced elsewhere in the country. The Midwest has benefited equally. Calvinism reigns in the small towns and countryside of the region, even among those who believe in other religions and systems. The Calvinist view is not only widespread geographically, it is also class-bound, particularly among the American middle class.[8]

This is not a matter of choice in the United States. There are undoubtedly millions of Americans who would not identify with Calvinism if they were ever asked, who neither know nor wish to know of Calvin's great work, *The Institutes of the Christian Religion*, but they live by it. The Calvinistic notions of working for the sake of working, saving for the sake of saving, self-control for the sake of self-control and the sense that "there is a right and wrong way to do everything" are the so-called "middle class values" that have for nearly four centuries captured the minds of Americans. This attitude, with its many limitations, somewhat narrow interpretation of the world and fairly rigid life style, has dominated American law for centuries. Authoritarian in its origins, the attitude continues to this day in such expressions as, "there ought to be a law" against almost everything. This attitude also supports the death penalty.

Even while Puritanism and Calvinism taught these middle class values, the same doctrine also taught individualism. The cornerstone of Calvin's doctrine is that the individual must gain his own salvation, independent of churches, doctrines or systems. This sense of independence suited all those who could or would not tolerate the rigidity of Puritan New England and who moved West. The United States' Western tradition, which rests on the rights of the individual to make his own fate, and its Puritan tradition, are the outgrowth of the same source. This conflict has had fatal consequences, a paradox not yet resolved.[9]

In early New England, this conflict led to the expulsion of persons who would not conform, or to the migration of people who took the teachings of individualism seriously and left on their own accord because they could not tolerate repression. Among these were "Roger Williams, who founded Rhode Island, Thomas Hooker and John Haynes who founded Hartford, Connecticut; Theophilus Eaton and John Davenport who settled New Haven and William Pynchon who founded Springfield, Massachusetts."[10]

As the United States expanded and more colonies were founded on the Puritan model, more and more individualists moved out of these communities, either voluntarily or forcibly. Faced with the difficulties of the environment, the hostilities of native Americans and other Europeans, far removed from any government and convinced by their Puritan heritage of their right to bear and use arms, millions of migrants from the East Coast expressed their independence in the West by tough action and a willingness to kill to stay alive. There was, however, also a willingness to kill for lesser reasons, because in a lawless land each person makes his own decision as to what is necessary and when to use force. The movement west continued until at least 1880, when the frontier on the western edge of the United States was finally settled.[11] Those who moved into new territory needed courage. An example of what faced Americans who settled Texas is found in Robert A. Caro's book on the life of President Lyndon Johnson.[12] Lack of water, great difficulty in farming, abject poverty and primitive living conditions even into the 20th century insured that only the most determined could survive. Writes Caro:

> This was the very edge of the frontier. These families had left civilization as far behind as safety. Their homes were log cabins—generally small and shabby cabins, too. Shocked travelers found conditions in Texas rougher and more primitive than in other states. . . . The home of the ordinary Hill Country family often set in a fire blackened clearing still dotted with tree stumps was a "dog run," two separate rooms or cabins connected under a continuous roof, with an open corridor left between for ventilation.
>
> The only thing plentiful was terror; . . . Remington paintings—lines of

mounted men charging on horseback—came to life on that frontier. The first battle in which Texas rangers were armed with the new Colt revolver which was to equalize warfare with the Comanches—previously one of these savage Cossacks of the Plains could charge 300 yards and shoot twenty arrows in the time it took a frontiersman to reload his single shot rifle—took place in 1842 . . . as late as 1849 at least 149 white men, women and children were killed on the Texas frontier.[13]

Such dangers and such hardships were known all over the South and the West and laid the foundations for those traditions which make for an insistence on the literal interpretation of the Second Amendment to the United States Constitution.

In sum, the old Eastern states faced the dangers of the new frontier as communities. Those who went West and South, however, faced these dangers alone. Independent, but deprived of the support which Puritanism lent its followers, they experienced the need for self reliance more than anyone. Their descendants believe it still—often at the end of a gun. Violence is part of the culture of the Southwest because it was first a necessity, but a violent culture cannot choose its violence. Those raised to view violence as a normal and necessary way of life are much more likely to kill than those who have other values. This is one reason for the high murder rate in southern and western states; it is also the reason for the extensive use of the death penalty. It is used not because it deters, but because history dictates that people view the world as violent.

Added to this frontier experience was the Civil War. That horror affected all Americans in both the North and South. Fifteen percent of all Union men volunteered for that war and an even greater proportion defended the Confederacy, with over five million men serving on both sides: "Not even World War II . . . has found a deeper place in the American heart and memory."[14] Much untold violence has come from that war, making history the primary contributor to the high murder rate in the United States.

Murder in the Big City

That cities are violent is part of American legend, but is this really true? Are cities disproportionately violent? To test this, the murder rates in some cities should be compared to the murder rates in states without those cities. For example, in 1988, New York state had a murder rate of 12.5 per 100,000 inhabitants. Of the 2,244 murders which occurred there, 1,946 were committed in New York City, which had a 1988 population of 8,563,248 in the metropolitan area. New York City constitutes 48 percent of the state's population and 87 percent of its murders, exceeding the expected percentage of murders within the state of New York by 39 percent. In fact, the murder rate for New York without the city was only 3.13 per 100,000 in 1988, which resembles the murder rates of Maine and Idaho. Obviously, it is far more dangerous to live in New York City than to live in any other part of that state, as also evidenced by the murder rate in Rochester (5.5), Syracuse (2.9), Buffalo (5.0), and Binghamton (only 2.2).[15]

Detroit, Michigan, reveals the same situation. Detroit has a murder rate of 17.4 per 100,000 inhabitants, while Michigan has a rate of 10.8. The population of metropolitan Detroit is 4,411,000 and constitutes 47 percent of the state total. However, of the 1,009 murders in Michigan in 1988, 764, or 76 percent took place in Detroit. Thus, Detroit murders exceed the expected percentage of Michigan murders based on population by 29 percent. Without Detroit, Michigan would have a murder rate of only 6.6 per 100,000, resembling Indiana or Kentucky.

In California, Los Angeles has the highest murder rate—15.5 per 100,000 inhabitants. The population of the Los Angeles metropolitan area is 8,659,880, and of the 2,936 murders reported in California in 1988, 1,346 were committed in the Los Angeles area. Consequently, the remaining murders (1,590) result in a murder rate of 10.4 per 100,000 for the rest of California, including San Francisco, thus exceeding the average for the United States as a whole (8.4 per 100,000). It is obvious that the state's biggest city skews the murder rate upwards.

The last city examined is Atlanta, Georgia. Atlanta has 14.3 murders per 100,000 inhabitants, while the state has a murder rate of 11.7. With a metropolitan population of 2,732,939, Atlanta constitutes 44 percent of all Georgia residents, and there were 392 killings in 1988. This exceeds the expected amount of murder, based on the remaining population for Georgia, by 2.6 percent.[16]

The murder rate of 20 additional cities is examined in the following table.

Murder in Selected Metropolitan Statistical Areas, 1988

M.S.A.	Population	# of Murders M.S.A.	City	Rate per 100,000 M.S.A.	State
Baltimore, Maryland	2,358,510	293	234	12.4	9.7
Boston, Massachusetts	2,864,197	128	93	4.5	3.5
Buffalo, New York	963,921	48	43	5.0	12.5
Chicago, Illinois	6,116,667	743	660	12.1	8.6
Cleveland, Ohio	1,866,471	173	137	9.5	5.4
Denver, Colorado	1,641,505	118	69	7.2	5.7
Houston, Texas	3,227,118	564	440	17.5	12.1
Indianapolis, Indiana	1,238,929	108	79	8.7	6.4
Kansas Cities, Mo. & Kan.	1,555,581	194	171	12.5	3.4
Miami, Florida	1,822,255	367	140	20.1	11.4
Milwaukee, Wisconsin	1,404,042	88	81	6.3	3.0
Minneapolis, Minnesota	2,367,942	89	82	3.8	2.9
Newark, New Jersey	1,902,505	188	115	9.9	5.3
New Orleans, Louisiana	1,308,848	251	228	20.0	11.6
Philadelphia, Penn.	4,901,859	502	371	10.2	5.5
Phoenix, Arizona	2,006,966	174	106	8.7	8.5
Portland, Oregon	1,175,118	72	45	6.1	5.1
St. Louis, Missouri	2,480,742	280	140	11.3	8.0
Salt Lake City, Utah	1,061,151	36	23	3.4	2.8
Washington, D.C.	3,704,981	547	369	14.8	59.5

From: Uniform Crime Report, 1989

Inspection of this table clearly reveals that, except for Buffalo, N.Y. and Washington, D.C., these urban areas always have a higher rate of murder than the state in which they are located. Washington, D.C., is an exception because it is in effect the inner city of a much larger metropolitan area. Buffalo is the exception because the state includes New York City with its large murder rate of 22.7. As shown above, the state of New York, without the city, has only 63 percent of the murders Buffalo has. Even here the conclusion is correct: Cities are more murderous than other areas in this country.

Aggression, including murder, caused by several factors, including a people's history. There is no doubt, however, that human aggression also has a biological root derived from our evolutionary past. This becomes particularly pertinent in overcrowded situations in which humans attack one another. Psychobiologists have restricted the use of the word "aggression" to conflicts between members of the same species. Konrad Lorenz makes this distinction in his famous work *On Aggression*, because he found that predatory attacks of one species upon another are the result of hunger, not anger. Lorenz points out that vicious fights between different species are very rare, and are usually brought about only when an animal has its escape route cut off or is half-starved.[17] Studies concerning human behavior have shown that people reserve their aggression mostly for other humans. Particularly, people tend to fight over territory or "personal space."[18]

Ordinarily, people become upset or fidgety if their personal space is invaded beyond the boundaries determined by culture. In North America and in Northern Europe, acquaintances stand about two or three feet apart during conversations. In Latin speaking countries, such as Spain, Italy or South America, less space is kept between conversants. This leads to northerners believing that Latins are too intimate, and southerners' feelings that northerners are too cold. There are also differences in spatial arrangements between the genders during a conversation. All of this is affected by the culture and influenced by learning.[19] Cultural factors play a major role in territoriality and humans are affected by this, as are animals. Therefore, "there is some biological foundation for strife and conflict."[20]

The Urbanization of the United States

In 1732, when George Washington was born, over 90 percent of Americans lived on farms; in 1988, only 2.2 percent did so.[21] Meanwhile, the rise in the number and size of cities became one of the most outstanding features of American life. Since urban life produces more murder than other life styles, it is significant that in 1790 there were only six American cities with a total population of 131,472, constituting 3.35 percent of all Americans. In 1890, this had risen to 18,285,697, or 29.2 percent of the total population of 62,622,250 people. In 1988 almost the reverse is the case, since even Americans living in smaller towns are involved in urban life by means of superb communication and transportation systems. In short, America has become an urban country.[22]

For example, New York County (Manhattan) had a population of 1,428,285 in 1980 in a land area of only 22 square miles—meaning that nearly 6,500 people were living in each square mile, not counting the visitors who worked there each day, creating far greater crowding during working hours. The District of Columbia, the capital of the United States, currently is the murder capital of the world.

There the population density is 6,880 per square mile. Such crowding exists in other cities also, although a calculation of the average number of persons living in the land area of each city would not reveal the impact of overcrowding on the murder rate. The reason for this is that the citizens of American cities are not evenly distributed throughout the land area available. On the contrary. While some have a good deal of space, others have very little. This affects particularly the black population, which has a murder rate six to seven times greater than whites. Thus, of the 1,788,000 black Americans living in New York, 290,000 live in Manhattan, a situation by no means unique to that city.

Immigrants from countries outside the United States, speaking a variety of languages other than English, also crowd into the most densely populated areas of large U.S. cities. The following table depicts this situation with particular reference to those cities having the greatest amount of murder.

Population Per Square Mile of Selected American Cities

City	Number	City	Number
New York	11,458	Miami	6,971
Los Angeles	8,682	Washington, D.C.	6,880
Philadelphia	8,546	Houston	6,787
Chicago	8,544	Detroit	6,694

These cities, and many others, have high population densities because the very definition of "city" is an area of at least 5,000 persons per square mile. There is, therefore, no evidence that there is a direct correlation between population density and murder. In fact, Washington, D.C., with its immense murder rate, has somewhat fewer people per square mile than Boston, which has a population density of 8,152 and a far smaller murder rate than either Washington or Houston.

The relationship between population density and murder is therefore only partial, as is the relationship between historical traditions and murder. Thus, urbanization and crowding are the second contributors to murder in the United States, because the number of citizens who must live in crowded conditions increases as the number of cities also increase and vice versa.

Race, Ethnicity and Poverty

Only about 10 percent of all residents of Erie County, N.Y., are black, but this group has a murder rate about six times greater than expected on the basis of population (see Chapter 3). Other urban homicide studies reveal the same disproportionate murder rate for inner-city blacks in other American locations (see Table 7, page 34). Keeping in mind the Southern residence and/or origin of so many American blacks, together with the residence of blacks and other minorities in the overcrowded inner cities of America and the high rate or urbanization of the black population, it is evident that this population exhibits all three of the characteristics shown to be associated with aggression, hence homicide. It is not within the scope of this book to discuss the history and current state of race relations in America. Suffice it to point out that murder has always been the province of those who suffer the greatest frustration in American life—inner-city minorities, mostly black or Hispanic, and in both cases, poor.

While it has been repeatedly shown how the black population in Erie County and elsewhere has a homicide rate a good deal greater than is true of whites, no figures are available with respect to the Hispanic lingual minority because Erie County does not have a large number of Hispanic-Americans, and because the Hispanic group does not present as great an excess of homicide cases as do blacks compared to the overall homicide rate, or the rate for whites alone. It should also be kept in mind that a Spanish speaking American may be either black or white or both, since the word Hispanic refers to a culture or language and not to a race. "Race" is defined as a *biological* subdivision of the human species.

Be that as it may, the rate of homicide for Hispanics in Manhattan is very large and deserves exposition. A table of Manhattan murder statistics for 1981 reveals this excess. Please note also that in Manhattan, the age of murder victims is quite young, as evidenced by the fact that even in the age group 10–24, the rate of homicide per 100,000 was 52.077.[23]

Manhattan Murder Statistics, 1981

	# of Victims	Population	Rate per 100,000
All groups	578	1,428,285	40.468
Sex: Male	500	669,704	74.656
Female	78	758,581	10.282
Race: Black	293	290,218	100.959
Hispanic	180	336,247	53.532
White	105	801,820	13.095

While the murder rate for all ethnic or racial groups in Manhattan is greater than is true for the country as a whole, it is far greater for both blacks and Hispanics. The Hispanic murder rate exceeds the white rate four times, the black rate exceeds the Hispanic rate twice, and is eight times greater than the white rate. Being a minority, whether by race or by language, causes excessive amounts of murder. This demonstrates that it is not race per se, but the frustrations associated with minority standing that lead to so much aggression in both the black and Hispanic groups. In the study of Erie County, murder was found not only to attach itself to racial minorities, but also that the poor committed a good deal more murder than other economic groups. This was revealed by the fact that 71 percent of the murderers and 64 percent of their victims in Erie County lived in the poorest part of that county (see Tables 11 and 12, pp. 37–38), and that both murderers and their victims were disproportionately employed in the lowest paying occupations (see tables 13 and 14, pp. 39–40).

Obviously, then, frustration is added upon frustration for those who for any reason suffer not only the impact of poor housing and overcrowding, but also the consequences of poor employment. One of the most frustrating and anger-producing events in life is the belief that a person is an occupational failure. Occupation is the most important criterion of social standing in America, and is heavily related to educational attainment. It would take a whole library to list all the studies available to show that this is true. Suffice it to say here that these distinctions are well known and felt strongly by those who do not have them, and that this leads to great resentment, frustration and aggression.[24] Thus, race, ethnicity and minority-majority relations, as well as poverty, are a third reason for the high murder rate in the United States.

Frustration and Aggression

The author has made a detailed study of the relationship of frustration to aggression and particularly murder.[25] To do this, nine categories of sociological significance were used and tested to see whether in each category the group suffering more frustration also exhibited a greater rate of homicide than the category of persons suffering less frustration. The nine categories so tested were: (1) life insurance; (2) geographic region; (3) urban zones; (4) race; (5) occupation; (6) sex; (7) age; (8) relationship and (9) religion.

A dichotomy was established in each of these categories, comparing those who had a dominant position to those with a subordinate position relative to the amount of murder suffered by them. In all of these categories the subordinate group *always* committed more homicide and was the victim more often than the dominant group. Beginning with ordinary life insurance holders as compared to (group) industrial life insurance holders over five different years, the following was the case:

Homicide Death Rates per 100,000 Lives Exposed

	Year 1	Year 2	Year 3	Year 4	Year 5
Type of insurance					
Ordinary life	1.5	1.2	1.7	1.7	1.5
Industrial	4.7	3.7	5.5	5.7	5.4

From: Gerhard Falk, "Status Differences and the Frustration-Aggression Hypothesis." *The International Journal of Social Psychiatry* 5, No. 3, Winter 1954, p. 214

Since ordinary life insurance is more expensive and usually must be paid by the insured, while group industrial insurance is normally paid by the employer, we can assume that ordinary life insurance holders are wealthier than industrial life insurance holders, and are generally employed in positions requiring a higher level of education. Industrial life insurance holders usually work in hourly paid jobs. The preceding table clearly shows that murder is far more frequent among those who suffer the frustrations of lower level employment. This supports the frustration-aggression hypothesis. When tested by region, the same conclusion is reached. The South has exhibited, as of 1988, a far greater rate of murder. For example, the East South Atlantic states showed a murder rate of 20.9 per 100,000 in 1958, while the New England States had only a rate of 1.4 per 100,000.

Relative to urban zones such as Chicago and Cincinnati, past and present findings indicate, "the largest number of homicides took place in the central business district of each city and that the number decreased as the distance from the center of the city increased."[26] The test for race had the same results. Then, as now, blacks had a homicide rate out of proportion to their numbers, in that they killed ten times as often as whites. Others at that time reported a black homicide rate seven times greater than was to be expected by numbers alone.[27]

Occupation revealed once more that those most frustrated by "external restraint over behavior" had the greatest murder rate. Thus, of all killings in Washington, D.C., in the years 1953–1956, owners, managers and professionals were least involved while unskilled workers were most involved. This again corroborates this study and proves the frustration-aggression hypothesis.

Following is a table taken from annual police reports of Washington, D.C., and compared to the occupational structure of the United States at that time. The evidence is that murder was and continues to be the province of those most frustrated in their occupational life.

Occupational Groups and Homicides in the U.S. in Washington, D.C., 1955

Occupation	% of Homicide	% of Labor Force
Not occupied	12.2	2.4
Unskilled	38.2	11.0
Domestics	9.2	10.1
Semi-skilled	5.9	19.0
Skilled	15.5	14.0
White Collar	10.1	19.0
Owners	1.8	16.0
Professionals	7.1	8.5

From: Falk, *op. cit.*, p. 217.

Note in particular that these findings showed more murder in comparison to their share of the labor force among the "not occupied" than those occupied. This supports the view that aggression follows frustration. Being unemployed is evidently more frustrating than being employed in menial work, even though that involves considerable "kow-towing" to bosses and much more regimentation than enters the lives of those not working.

It is equally significant that owners of businesses have the lowest proportionate homicide rate. This fits directly into the status position of men in United States culture. Since men derive their status almost entirely from their occupation, and since independence is highly prized as indicated earlier, and since business ownership relieves men of the need to deal with "superiors," their frustration is evidently far less in the occupational world, than is true even of professionals.

Andrew Henry and James Short have dealt with this matter at some length,[28] and although this author does not subscribe to a number of assertions made by them, it is of interest to present here their conclusion that "[there is] a positive relation between homicide and the strength of external restraint."[29] This means, according to Henry and Short, "Low status persons are required to conform to the demands and expectations of others by virtue of their low status . . . [and] homicide varies positively with the strength of vertical external restraint."[30]

This and a great deal of similar research suggests that frustration does indeed promote murder. Since those who are most affected by the history of conflict between Puritanism and the Western tradition in the United States are also most enmeshed in the consequences of overcrowding and urbanization and suffer a good deal of frustration from numerous sources, the reasons for the high murder rate linking together in the most affected population are readily seen.

At first glance it would seem that the hypothesis concerning the influence of low status on homicide does not hold for gender because women commit murder so much less than do men. Recall that the study in Erie County showed that only 12.2 percent of all killings were committed by women (see Table 10, p. 36). Since women earn less than men because they are less often employed in prestigious and well paying occupations, it should be expected that they have a higher homicide rate than men if the frustration-aggression theory holds for gender. At first glance this seems not to be the case, since as of 1986, women constituted only 18 percent of lawyers, 15 percent of physicians, 36 percent of professors and six percent of engineers.[31]

During World War II, when most American men were in the armed forces, the proportion of women arrested and incarcerated for murder declined a good deal in proportion to all female arrests and incarcerations. After the war, however, female rates of murder as a proportion of all female crime increased to the same level as before. Thus, the source of frustration (men) for females having been removed during the war, their murder rate declined.[32]

The test of the frustration-aggression hypothesis for age holds true. Fifty-nine and four-tenths percent of the Erie County sample of murderers were 15 to 30 years old, and 35 percent of victims were in that age category. It is reasonable to assume that the age group 18 to 29 in particular suffers greatly from failure to gain useful employment (Black unemployment has been as high as 40 percent in that age category). Evidently, then, frustration invites aggression under such circumstances. In addition, younger people, notably men, suffer from many other status-role problems during the late adolescent years, which adds to their frustration. These problems include sex roles and peer pressure. With reference to the killing of relatives and friends, 26 percent of all the killers in the Erie County study murdered relatives, lovers or spouses, and another 16 percent murdered friends (see Table 18, page 45).

This also supports the frustration-aggression hypothesis as a reason for murder, since it is rare that anyone would find strangers so frustrating that he might wish to kill them. Exactly the opposite is the case with respect to relatives and friends. This was found to be true not only in this study, but also in the author's previous study of homicide.[33]

An attempt was made to discover whether adherence to a religion is in any manner correlated to the commission of homicide. This could not be ascertained in the earlier study, and was not attempted here because religious affiliation of persons arrested or convicted is not available. Nevertheless, in Chapter 11, the author will present a hypothesis concerning this. Aggression, subsequent to frustration, is the fourth reason for murder in the United States and no doubt elsewhere. Next is the concept of "relative deprivation," which allows the reader to understand the motivation of Americans relative to many kinds of conduct in addition to murder.

Relative Deprivation

Let us assume that we have just heard that our neighbor, with whom we have been on friendly terms for years, is moving to another neighborhood and has spent a very large sum of money on his new house. We know we cannot afford to follow him there. We also know the neighborhood. Until now we never thought about those who live in that "hoy paloy" suburb. But now we do. Because now we compare ourselves to the neighbor who can afford what we cannot afford. We ask ourselves why he should be able to pay such a price when we cannot, even though we are "as good as he is any day." We compare ourselves unfavorably and are jealous. We feel deprived of having what ought to be our due. That is relative deprivation. Relative deprivation is a far more powerful motive than deprivation. A deprived person, someone who has no shoes and lives with millions of others in the slums of a South American city where no one has shoes, may feel deprived. But if he never believed that anyone in his circle of acquaintances, friends and family, ought to have shoes, he will not feel relative deprivation. Conversely, the country-club member who cannot afford a cruise around the world in a luxury liner may feel keenly deprived relative to other members who are doing just that.

Despite the fact that relative deprivation can involve almost anyone of any social class, and is responsible for numerous economic crimes, it motivates the truly deprived the most, because it "combines economic inequality with feelings of resentment and injustice among those who have the least in the society."[34] The relationship of murder to economic inequality and particularly relative deprivation has been studied extensively. Six studies, all independently produced, have concluded that countries with the most economic inequality also have the highest homicide rates, while those having the least economic inequality have the lowest. Note that the emphasis here is not on poverty or wealth but on inequality.[35]

No studies have reached the opposite conclusions. In addition to the six studies just mentioned and involving some foreign countries, additional studies of this matter were made only in the United States with the same results. In fact, one of these studies was replicated and found once more that inequality, relative deprivation and homicide are strongly correlated. Thus, the conclusion is that poverty amidst plenty is related to homicide. Therefore, when one speaks of frustration leading to aggression, it is meant that the frustration comes from relative deprivation. Relative deprivation is the fifth reason for the high murder rates in the United States.

Drugs

Conclusions reached in a study of homicide in Manhattan[36] differ from all other urban homicide studies in one respect. Unlike any other area investigated for homicide, Manhattan, *not* all of New York City, had a homicide rate of 40.5 per

100,000. That, however, is not the only difference between Manhattan and the entire United States with reference to homicide. The most startling difference Tardiff and Gross found was that: "More than one third of men killed in Manhattan were killed during drug-related homicides."[37] The authors report that a Chi square analysis demonstrates that drug-related homicides were more likely to involve "friends" in Manhattan; robbery-related murders, as anywhere, involved mostly strangers and, again as in any other city, dispute-related homicides involved family members. The phrase "drug related" should not be interpreted to mean that drug addicts commit a great number of homicides. On the contrary; it means that the victims of Manhattan homicides are often persons who "were more likely to have narcotics in their blood streams than was true of people dying from non-violent causes."[38] This Manhattan study agrees with the author's Erie County study concerning the relative infrequence of alcohol as a contributing factor to murder.

Killings which are drug related are mostly accomplished by the use of firearms. Drugs, therefore, constitute a sixth, albeit minor reason for the high murder rate in this country.

Family Violence

The seventh reason for murder in the United States is finally getting well deserved attention although it had been "swept under the rug" for years: family violence. Beginning with the work of Stuart Palmer in 1960, this problem has received increasing attention in the media over the past 30 years. Nevertheless, family violence leads to other crimes of violence, and particularly murder.[39] Palmer and numerous other students of family violence have concluded that the effects of physical abuse in the home are directly related to violence by the victim outside and inside the home. Says Palmer: "The more violent the experiences of the child at the hands of his parents, the more violent he is likely to be to others as an adult."[40]

To reach this conclusion, Palmer interviewed 51 men convicted of murder. In addition he also interviewed their relatives, friends and correctional officers. A control group was also interviewed so as to make comparison with nonmurderers possible. The findings were these:

1. Among the mothers whose sons had been convicted of murder, mothers generally admitted having beaten their sons severely. For example, a mother said: "I remember one time I got so upset with him I took this poker we had for the stove and I hit him with that. I kind of lost control of myself and I couldn't stop."

2. The control group, consisting of brothers of the murderers, were also beaten by the mothers as often as the murderers were, about once every six months.

3. More severe beatings were conducted by the fathers of the murderers. Fathers beat their sons about every three months and then with great vehemence. The murderers were beaten at a younger age than their nonmurdering brothers, but the frequency was the same. Palmer mentions the case of a murderer who had beaten to death a man 30 years older than himself. According to the murderer's

mother, his father had beat him so terribly when he was six that he nearly died, and his blood was all over the walls of their apartment.

4. About three times as many murderers were beaten severely once or more by people other than their parents. These other people were either relatives, teachers or neighbors.[41]

Using an "Index of Physical Frustration," Palmer then determined that there was a "tremendous" difference between the amount of physical frustration suffered by murderers and their nonmurdering brothers. The index included these factors: a difficult birth; serious effects of forceps at birth; each serious operation; each serious illness; each serious accident; each serious beating by someone other than a parent or stepparent; one or more serious beatings by the mother; and one or more serious beatings by the father or stepfather.

Attaching a value to each event, Palmer found that 40 of the 51 murderers he had interviewed had a higher score than their brothers. The 11 whose physical frustration was no greater than their brothers' were found to have been psychologically more abused than their brothers, thus having suffered a great deal more also. Palmer discusses these psychological frustrations at length in his book, *The Psychology of Murder.*[42]

In the study of murder in Erie County, ten percent of all killings in that sample were between spouses, and other relatives were killed in five percent of those cases (see Table 18, p. 45). Numerous other victim-killer relationships were in the category of friends or acquaintances. This indicates that a spiral of violence often affects these relationships, meaning that people who deal with each other violently often cannot escape the progress of the violence they have engendered because they live together. It is easier to withdraw from strangers, or even coworkers or neighbors, but how does one withdraw from husbands or wives? Thus, family violence tends to increase once that road has been entered and is therefore far more dangerous than violence towards outsiders.

Murray Straus has studied domestic violence for years. In a recent publication he points out that physicians and hospitals tend to ignore family violence, treating such violence as a private matter.[43] In addition, it is evident that a large number of Americans approve of family violence. Thus, Richard Gelles found that 56 percent of American couples use physical force against each other; that one in four men and one in six women approve of slapping the spouse, and that 62 percent of high school seniors used physical force on their brothers and sisters.[44]

As a result of the attitude that private violence should not be reported, the extent of it is unknown. Estimates range from 650,000 cases of child abuse to over 6,000,000 such occurrences every year. The same holds for the abuse of women by men and vice versa. The reasons for this silence is shame. Our culture has taught us not to complain about abuse in the family, thereby throwing a screen around this crime. It is commonly believed that people must not pry into the private affairs of others and that family violence is a private affair. Yet, most rapists have been sexually abused as children in their own homes, most violent criminals have been raised in violent homes, and, most of all, murderers have the same background. Studies of prison populations show that upward of 90 percent of all persons convicted of a violent crime claim to have been abused as children and that the abusive parent was an abused child.[45]

It is also important to note that women are more often child abusers than are men. This is the consequence of the obvious fact that women spend more time with children and are therefore more provoked than men, and that women have more opportunity to beat children for the same reason.

Consider the fate of Shawn Nicely. Beaten to death at age three by his mother, Renee Nicely, with the help of his father, Allen Bass, his short life was a nightmare of torture from the day of his birth. At once, on being born, his mother denied that he was her child. Renee Nicely claimed that she had been given the wrong child in the hospital. This is a common claim by abusing parents and is frequently used as a rationale for finding fault with beaten children. Renee Nicely had three children, Shawn being her youngest. She knew nothing about child rearing and had no patience. Innocent childish conduct threw her into a rage and led her to beat the child on the head even when he was only a baby. Her husband, Allen Bass, beat all three children regularly. (Bass supported himself by selling drugs. He had also been arrested, although not convicted, on robbery and possession of stolen goods charges.) Renee Nicely continued the cruelties she had initiated at birth, even in public. Neighbors reported that they had seen her drop the child on his head in the street, had called him obscene names, punched him and whipped him with a belt.

All of this was not unknown to various authorities. The State Division of Youth and Family Services knew about the abuse, so did a judge and a doctor, but no one put a stop to it because no one had the power to stop it. The family service agency offered to help with foster care, paying a homemaker to come and help, day care and psychiatric help. They were even willing to give Renee Nicely a blood test to prove that Shawn was hers and, they offered counseling for her. She turned down all of this. Then, on September 26, 1982, Shawn dirtied his pants and died for it. Angered by this behavior, his mother hit Shawn on the head with a broom and his father stomped on his back as he fell on the floor. "At the time of his death Shawn Nicely stood 36 inches tall and weighed 31 pounds," according to the *New York Times*.[46]

It must be asked, if Shawn had lived to reach age 15 as most abused children do, what kind of adult would he have become? Would not he have been a monster of anger and violence? What else could be expected? The murderers in society are very often the Shawns of this world. Their parents were victims before them and so were their grandparents and so will be all the generations of the abused, like mirrors locked in an infinite corridor of despair and anger.

Men, of course, also beat children. In addition, they are more often sexually abusive to children than women are, thus creating even more difficulty.

All of this can hardly be controlled by law enforcement because so many people, including law enforcement personnel, believe that it is legitimate to "spank" children. Consequently the difference between permissible beatings and impermissible cruelty cannot be determined. Obviously, the best policy would be to refrain from all beatings, no matter how labeled. Such a policy is important, not only because the line between justified and unjustified beatings can hardly be maintained, but also because anyone who enters upon the road of violence cannot know how far his own emotions will carry him. The great difficulty for children caught up in violence by adults is that they cannot report their own misfortune, and nothing can be done to help them as long as their victimization is not reported. It must be insured that teachers, physicians, nurses and all who come in contact with such abuse, report such cruelties to an agency equipped to deal with it. Murder is better prevented by preventing child abuse than using the electric chair. It also saves more lives.

There was more awareness of child abuse in 1988 than in the past, but it is doubtful that very many understand its true consequences. As Magnuson says:

> At stake is America's most precious asset, its human capital. At stake, too, is simple human dignity. If wolves and bears and birds take meticulous care of their young, why are human beings subjecting theirs to whippings and punches and sexual perversion? Children with their unrestrained love and unquestioning trust, deserve better....[47]

This author adds to that admonition, that all the potential murder victims who are later killed by today's abused children also deserve better. What can be done about child abuse, and some suggestions as to how to prevent murder, is the topic of the next and final chapter.

11. "Logos"

The Greek word *logos* implies meaning. What, then, in conclusion of this study of murder, does murder mean? All human interactions carry with them a message; they mean something in the sense that they communicate something about the persons interacting. Human conduct, however, also means something in connection with those who witness behavior, even if they themselves do not participate. Thus, murder has a meaning for those who kill, for those who are killed and for the vast majority who are not involved in murder, but who have no choice except to recognize that it is pervasive. Murder means that not only those who are directly involved as killers and victims, but all people, place little value on human life. Murder is a signal. It tells us that some people suffer despair and anguish beyond endurance. It tells us that many are desperate in a world they believe does not care. Murder is a cry for help both by the murderer and his victim. Yet, little has been done to help each other reduce the murder rate and stay alive. This is true because people don't believe anything can be done about murder. As a result, desperate measures are resorted to, like the death penalty, which will not work and only makes things worse.

In short, society so far has not been able or willing to do anything about murder. Instead, public policy continues to ignore what might be done and keeps doing what will not work: imprisonment does not prevent murder, and "insanity" is a rare and useless defense. It has also been demonstrated that murder follows certain patterns of behavior, and is the outcome of social organization rather than psychiatric disorders.

People need not despair and assume that they must suffer 20,000 murders per year, and are helpless in the face of this destruction. The truth is that people are not helpless at all and that they can, if they have the will, reduce the murder rate and prevent a good deal of murder in the future.

Assume that a disease were killing 20,000 Americans a year. Most would agree that society would insist that something be done about it, as has been the case in other situations. An example is the amount of effort being put forth to finding a cure for AIDS. Similar efforts were made to reduce the death rate from various childhood diseases that at one time killed so many. Other examples abound: in 1900, the death rate for influenza and pneumonia was 202 per 100,000, but in 1980 it was only 24. Tuberculosis killed 194 Americans per 100,000 and typhoid fever killed 34 in the same proportions in 1900. Only one person died of tuberculosis in the United States per 100,000 in 1980, and none died of diphtheria, smallpox, measles or scarlet fever because of mass immunization of children.[1]

Yet, the deaths of 20,000 from murder are permitted every year. The reason for this difference is that murder has a different meaning for people than death from disease. People believe that they can deal with disease, that disease can be conquered by scientific means. It is not believed that this can be done concerning human behavior; the widespread belief is that human behavior is unpredictable, that nothing can be done about it and that "you can never know what people will do." This book has demonstrated that the exact opposite is the case. We do know what people will do. We even know who will murder whom, at what temperature, indoor or outdoor, in what room of the house and with what weapon. We are the masters of our own conduct. We are not helpless pawns who must subject ourselves to senseless murder. There are some things that can be done to reduce murder among us:

1. *Reduce family violence. Children and adults must be educated not to behave violently toward one another in their homes, and admit that violence exists when it does.* This goes hand in glove with admitting to drinking large amounts of alcohol, or suffering from alcoholism. First and foremost, affected people must admit that there is violence in the home and stop the denial of violence, which is almost universal.

The author has interviewed numerous attorneys and has been told that women who seek a divorce will almost always deny violence when first complaining of infidelity, the most common reason for divorce in America. Women will say usually that there is no or very little violence in their home, and that violence occurs only "when he drinks." Asked how often their husbands get drunk, they will say that it is most uncommon for them to do so. Then they volunteer that their husbands drink "only a six pack after dinner each day." Since six bottles of beer have the same alcohol content as 12 shots of whiskey, it is truly astonishing that so many people will deny the obvious alcoholism from which they and their family suffer. The author has dealt with the problems of alcohol consumption in another study.[2]

Suffice it to say that while there is no direct evidence that the use of alcohol is the cause of murder, there is evidence that excessive use of alcohol is rooted in the same beliefs as excessive use of force.

In the study of murder in Erie County only 15 percent of all murder cases reported in the *Courier-Express* were said to have involved alcohol at the murder scene. This does not necessarily mean that only 15 percent of offenders, victims or both were drunk at the time of the murder; it *can* mean that it was only reported in 15 percent of all cases. Other urban homicide studies have shown that alcohol is present more frequently than 15 percent of the time, and some studies have claimed that alcohol was present in one-half of all murders. But even if that is so, it cannot be said that it is the cause of murder, since the absence of alcohol in the other 50 percent of murders could be equally blamed for killing. In addition, it would have to be held that if the presence of alcohol were the cause of murder, then murder would be far more common than it already is, since drinking is so widespread.

2. *People must also admit that violence occurs at home.* Denial of violence is very common, and the reason for this lies in contemporary culture. People are taught that both drinking and violence are shameful and should not occur. While this book is not concerned with the alcohol problem, it is recommended that battered family members take action to protect themselves by changing their *beliefs* about themselves and their situation.

Ferraro and Johnson have shown that battered women all too often rationalize the violence against them, using all those "techniques of neutralization" with which so many other victims and offenders are so familiar.[3] Thus, an abusing husband is excused as "sick." He is said to suffer from a disease. Even the injuries suffered at the hands of the offender are denied and "normal" life resumes after serious attacks. Victims even blame themselves for the ill-tempered conduct of their spouses, while some resort to Christian beliefs concerning the role of women as servants to their husbands.

Compliance with one's own victimization, and even cooperation with one's own murder, is not confined to Americans; it is quite common elsewhere. The slaughter of the European Jews by the Nazi killers, which was helped by the compliance of the victims, was discussed in Chapter 4. There is a great deal of evidence that the Jewish leadership actually helped organize the transports that brought millions to the gas chambers, because they were so imbued with bureaucratic compliance that they could not envision defying orders given by a higher authority, even orders that meant to kill them.[4]

These killings have given rise to a tremendous literature, attempting to explain how such massive murders were possible in face of a civilized European population which knew about these killings but did little or nothing to halt them. One very pertinent answer to that question came from the German-Jewish historian Hannah Arendt, who came to the United States before the Second World War. She became a prolific author in the United States, reaching a large, academic audience with her voluminous writings. She became the target of considerable criticism however, when she published *Eichmann in Jerusalem* in 1963.[5] The criticism came about because Arendt claimed that the European Jews had cooperated with their own killers and that the whole democratic world also cooperated. The historical fact is, that Arendt is right. They did cooperate just as the American community cooperates with its own murderers.

In a review essay of Arendt's book, the renowned author and psychologist Bruno Bettelheim defends her work.[6] Bettelheim shows that this cooperation begins with society's inability to

> grasp tragedy every day. If one individual suffers, or a few—as in an airplane crash, a mine explosion or, typically when a neighbor's child has a serious accident—immediately our sympathy is roused to the quick. We feel for the victims and their relatives. We anxiously wait for future news. We all hope and some pray. We feel compelled to do something to help.
>
> But let thirty thousand be killed by a volcano emptying, where we are not on the scene to see it—then we are not deeply moved. We may collect money, we may talk and read about it, but we are not really shaken up inside. . . .
>
> We have not yet learned to deal with the experience of the total mass state

[United States as of 1990]. We simply cannot think in terms of millions, (or thousands) – or at least most of us cannot – but only in terms of the individual. A few screams invoke in us deep anxiety and a desire to help. Hours of screaming without end lead us only to wish that the screamer would shut up.[7]

The problem raised by Arendt and discussed by Bettelheim is of concern, because both authors show that in any mass state, including the American democracy, there is a serious tendency to place the reputed needs of the state ahead of the individual. Unable to assert ourselves in the enormity of bureaucracy, we suffer unending injustices and do nothing to defend ourselves, not only because we do not comprehend the sufferings of others as already shown, but because we do not fight back against injustices committed against us.

Arendt shows that the Jews of Europe were so imbued with taking orders from bureaucrats that they assembled peaceably at railroad stations so as to be shipped in cattle cars to their deaths. She argues that the sight of these peaceable victims gave the non–Jewish population the feeling that there really was nothing wrong. She argues that if every one of the 6,000,000 Jews had fought publicly and had to be dragged personally through the streets to those cattle cars, that alone would have roused the population against the Nazi killers. But they did not. They were taught by their leaders not to fight, but to cooperate – not because they were Jews, but because they were citizens of a totalitarian state.

The United States is not a totalitarian state, but it is a mass society, making it possible for people "to put it all out of [their] minds fairly soon."[8] People do not take the individual suffering of one beaten child, one abused woman to heart, because they read about this every day, because so many scream and there are so many problems. Thus, people are seldom confronted in a personal way with murder or violence unless they live in a violent family themselves. The loss of community contributes greatly to the perpetuation of murder. Many victims of violence feel that their families do not care about them either, and that they have no alternative but to suffer violence, together with their children. Since violent conduct in the home is a public issue because it can turn into murder, it is obvious that violent men and women must continue to be treated as criminals who are guilty of assault. There are, of course, those who say that one cannot legislate morality. This is not true: the entire civil rights movement and the legislation that has come from it changed people's behavior first and their beliefs thereafter. This is also true of the women's suffrage movement. It was at one time believed that women could not learn, and that therefore they should not go to school, etc. Since the introduction of voting rights for women in 1920, all that has changed. The law forced behavior to change, ergo, beliefs changed. This can be done in the case of family violence as well. If assault is a criminal offense, then a husband and father who assaults his family is a criminal and his family must act accordingly. This will take a great deal of education. The public must understand this and support, not condemn, those who seek to defend themselves against aggression in the home. All too often, the police make light of family violence. Jokes are made at the expense of the victims who are often labeled derogatorily in such sentences as, "He is only beating *the old lady* around a little bit."

Children must also be taught that family violence is a crime. This is not to say that teachers should become indirect spies who question children concerning private conduct. Children should have the opportunity to tell school counselors about violence at home, however, so that intervention becomes possible. This author contends that few would risk the kind of brutality now visited on so many children and adults *at home* if they believed that this cruelty would have unpleasant consequences for them. It is often said that such and such person committed violence because he was too drunk to know better. I disagree; people who are already sado-masochistic because they were raised in such circumstances use alcohol as an ex post facto excuse for behavior which has other roots.[9] Whatever the reasons, abuse must be recognized to be prevented the next time. This can only be done if the community supports such recognition and supports those who are in a position to call attention to such abuse. Nothing is a social problem until it is recognized as such. This was true of child abuse for years because pediatric radiologists, for instance, were unaware of what they were looking at, or were unwilling to report it if they were aware of it. Thus, in a study of the social reaction to the "battered child syndrome," Stephen J. Pfohl found that abuse was reported more and more as physicians became convinced by persons outside the medical profession to report these matters.[10]

For years, physicians did not "see" abuse despite evidence of bone fracture in children. This was due to a number of factors, including the origin of the physicians' income, (the parent); the "norm of confidentiality" which denies physicians the right to disclose medical records; unwillingness to believe that a parent would do so much violence to his or her own child; and fear of becoming involved with the criminal justice system.[11] The change in "discovering" child abuse came when radiologists who had always witnessed these tell-tale signs of abuse but never "saw" them found that reporting the signs of abuse began to have advantages for them. Thus, *The Journal of the American Medical Association* published two reports on the use of radiology in finding such abusive behavior in 1955 and 1961. These were the first articles on a radiological topic to be published in that prestigious journal in years. Next, pediatricians and psychiatrists asked the help of radiologists in discovering abuse. This enhanced the erstwhile "marginal" position of radiologists in the medical community. Third, the new alliance between radiologists, psychiatrists and pediatricians succeeded in labeling child abuse with a medical slogan – "the battered child syndrome." This meant that medicine had now discovered a whole group of conditions which together were a new medical entity and could be "treated." Hence the syndrome was now "seen," particularly since it was endorsed by the American Medical Association. Finally, this labeling by the AMA led to the reporting of these abuse symptoms, and thereby the "syndrome" also received the blessings of law enforcement, the social work community and the media. In addition, various medical "shows" on television have shown episodes dealing with child abuse while magazines abound with articles on that subject.[12]

Since the abusers were labeled "sick" in conjunction with the "discovery" of child abuse, there has been very little prosecution of such persons. Nevertheless, numerous states have now developed child protective agencies to deal with this problem. In New York, Governor Mario Cuomo declared the eighties the "Decade of the Child" and in 1988 accepted a report by a commission which was appointed by the previous governor, Hugh Carey, 12 years before. This report dealt with the "State of the Child" and among other things recommended that a Task Force for the Child be established in every county consisting of the County Executive, the mayors of towns and cities in each county and the chief of police. The idea of such a "task force" is to elevate the importance of child welfare to an executive level.

In any case, there is more said and known about child abuse today, in 1990, than at any time in United States history. This is primarily due to the falling birth rate since anything that is rare is also dear in both senses of that word. This author recommends that a "Council of the Child and the Family" be established in each county so as to exchange information about child abuse between the police, medical observers, social work agencies and churches so as to coordinate efforts on behalf of those who suffer abuse and those who suffer its infliction. The beater needs help also. In short, the pain of each person must be taken seriously. This author is firmly convinced that a reduction in child abuse will lead to a reduction in murder and many other forms of social misery in the next generation. We must do this *before* we execute. Thereby each murder not committed saves two lives.

3. *The reduction of stress.* Family violence does not occur in a social vacuum. Those who lash out at others are under stress, defined in this case by a high score on the "Stress Index" developed by Linsky and Straus. They identified 15 conditions as being highly correlated with violent crimes, including murder.[13] These conditions are: *economic stressors* (business failures, unemployment, being on strike, personal bankruptcies and mortgage foreclosures); *family stressors* (divorce, abortion, illegitimate births, infant deaths and fetal deaths); and *other stressors* (disaster assistance, state resident less than five years, new houses authorized, new welfare cases and high school dropouts). Using these 15 stressors, Linsky and Straus show that for each increase of one point on their stressor scale there is an increase of .2 murders per 100,000 population. This means that an increase of ten stress points on their scale results in an increase of 27 percent in the average state murder rate. They also show that for every one percent increase in the black population there is an increase of .14 murders per 100,000 in that state.[14]

From a regional point of view, the Linsky/Straus stress index is very important as it confirms this analysis of murder in various sections of the country. Thus, a table concerning regional differences in crime presented by Linsky and Straus looks like this:[15]

Regional Differences in Crime

State Characteristics 1976	North-east	North Central	South	West
Murder, Manslaughter per 100,000	4.7	5.3	10.6	7.2
Forcible Rape per 100,000	15.4	19.8	23.7	31.9
Robbery per 100,000	149.1	119.8	118.3	126.9
Aggravated Assault per 100,000	159.1	145.1	237.9	237.9

This table reveals that Linsky and Straus found the same pattern concerning the commission of crime in their 1976 study which this author found in the 1980s, and that three violent offenses other than murder are also high in the South and West and low in the Northeast and North Central states. When Linsky and Straus applied their stress variables to all of the 50 states they again found a high correlation between stress and murder and other forms of violence.

There is, then, no doubt that murder is associated with stress just as it is associated with family violence. The 15 stress factors already listed come from the same root as murder and are associated with it, and have the same cause. This means that it cannot be said that divorce, mobility or dropping out of school cause murder. Where these conditions are frequent and exist over a long period of time, however, murder is more frequent. Thus, those people who suffer all of the other ills of mankind also suffer the most murder. This leads to the conclusion that political action is needed to prevent and alleviate the 15 conditions here called "stressors." It may be a matter of public debate between the two major political parties as to how this is best accomplished. There is, however, no doubt in the minds of current leadership in either national political party that the alleviation of stress as defined by Linsky and Straus is a principal responsibility of government on all levels.

It is seldom recognized that an attack on any of the problems listed, such as unemployment or divorce, will also reduce the rates of other social ills, such as murder. Many more lives will be saved by reducing the murder rate through the alleviation of poverty and business failures than will ever be saved by executing murderers. All of these problems go together; there is no need to make a priority list here. If the rate of mortgage foreclosures can be lowered other problems are also alleviated. The same is true of high school dropouts or abortions. Any effort is worthwhile; all programs help.

4. *Gun control.* The evidence indicates that people whose lives mean something to them do not need to aggress against others. It is lack of existential validation not poverty, which leads to violence. It is excessive competition and self depreciation, not the possession of a gun, which leads to murder. This raises the issue of whether "gun control" can be achieved in the United States, and whether the murder rate would decline if it were instituted.

This author's opinion is that "gun control" is doomed to failure in the United States as a whole because public opinion will not support it. It will be a matter for speculation for some time to come as to whether or not murder would truly decline if all the guns, including handguns, were taken away in America. In Erie County, N.Y., 45 percent of all murders were committed by the use of firearms, and 27 percent of all murders were committed by the use of a handgun (see Table 20, p. 47). Although the findings concerning murder in Erie County over a 40-year period apply generally to all of the United States, there are differences between local findings anywhere and conditions in the whole of the United States. It is not surprising, therefore, that a reputable study of the use of guns in homicides has shown that on a nationwide basis the use is higher than the findings concerning Erie County would indicate. This is particularly true because Erie County is in the North where citizens are less often armed than in the South or the West.[16]

There are about 75 million American households. About half of these have a gun. This ownership is, however, not evenly distributed. In the East, only 15 percent of residents have a gun. In the West, 29 percent have a handgun and 49 percent of all Westerners have some weapon. Thirty-three percent of all residents in the Northeast have some type of weapon, 40 percent of all Midwesterners have a weapon, 49 percent of all Westerners have a weapon, and among Southerners, the rate is 59 percent.[17] Since the South and the West also have more murder than the Northeast, it is tempting to rush in and claim that the higher murder rates in those regions are "caused" by gun ownership. That, however, is far from certain. Marvin Wolfgang, writing in 1958, makes these comments:

> More than the availability of a shooting weapon is involved in homicide. Pistols and revolvers are not difficult to purchase. . . . The type of weapon used appears to be, in part, the culmination of assault intentions or events and is only *superficially* related to causality.
>
> To measure quantatively the effect of the presence of firearms on the homicide rate that would not have occurred had not the offender—or in some cases the victim—possessed a gun . . . [it] is the contention of this observer that few homicides due to shootings could be avoided merely if a firearm were not immediately present, and that the offender would select some other weapon to achieve the same destructive goal. . . .[18]

A more recent statement of this position is found in the work by Wright, Rossi and Daly:[19]

> Even if we were somehow able to remove all firearms from civilian possession, it is not at all clear that a substantial reduction in interpersonal violence would follow. . . . Even the most ardent proponents of stricter gun laws no longer expect such laws to solve the hard core crime problem, or even to make much of a dent in it. . . . [C]rimes occur because some people have come to hate others, and they will continue to occur in one form or another as long as hatred persists. . . . [I]f we could solve the problem of interpersonal hatred, it may not matter very much what we did about guns, and unless we solve the problem of interpersonal hatred, it may not matter very much what we do about guns. . . . [I]t definitely does not follow that, in the complete absence of handguns, crimes now committed with handguns would not be committed! The more plausible explanation is that they would be committed with other weaponry.

Viennese psychiatrist, Viktor Frankl, has captured the essence of this issue in his famous volume, *Man's Search for Meaning.*[20] Frankl argues that "responsibleness" is the very essence of human existence. He paraphrases Immanuel Kant and casts Kant's categorical imperative into this mold: "So live as if you were living already for the second time and if you had acted the first time as wrongly as you are about to act now."[21] In short, responsible people with guns are far less dangerous than irresponsible people without guns.

Frankl has a number of additional recommendations. His point is, however, that all things are not to be gained only by the introduction or elimination of material objects, such as money or guns. Frankl shows that through a process he calls "Logotherapy," people can move away from their fears and deal with others without hostility. Any social movement, idea, or group aim can be used to give its members a sense of dignity and worth, a sense of achievement and meaning. Most of all, this dignity comes from work. The work ethic, which has always been so strong in America, is a great cure for so many ills and so many disappointments. Whatever people's shortcomings or disadvantages, work is still a great healer and in the end the only reasonable way to spend one's life.

5. *The development of a "moral community"* is the fifth recommendation designed to reduce not only murder, but many other conditions which are associated with so much human misery and suffering in the United States. The very word "moral" is a signal for the rejection of anything traveling under this rubric, since so many insist of pretending that anything so labeled is "unscientific." A "moral community" is, however, one which gives its members a sense of meaning, of being worthwhile, of having a purpose and a future.

Raoul Naroll has devised a model for a moral order in which he uses the phrase "Moralnet" to indicate strength of relationships and the concomitant reduction of social ills.[22] He proposes that the more a society has of his "twelve causes of 'moralnet strength'" the less it will have of murder, theft and fraud, hard drinking and alcoholism, drug abuse, suicide, brawling, wife beating, child battering and mental illness. Without listing all of Naroll's 12 causes as set forth in his massive volume *The Moral Order*, at least a few of them can be mentioned: 1) emotional warmth from parents; 2) protection from outside enemies; 3) a plausible ideology (an explanation supporting and justifying a moral code); 4) promptness and certainty of punishment for crime (it is promptness and certainty, not severity of punishment, that discourages crime, says Naroll); 5) intensive schooling through stern discipline. Naroll points to the military academies as examples and holds that these create moralnets of unusual strength.

In sum, there are suggestions based on research and good methodology which support this author's contention that murder can be reduced by an effort to establish a "moral community." The evidence now available indicates that it will take a very long time to alleviate all the social ills associated with murder. Furthermore, the concept of "relative deprivation" guarantees that no matter what is done to alleviate anything, there will always be losers, disappointed people, ill people, emotionally upset and frightened people. Workable answers to these difficulties must be sought before the legendary "millenium" relieves us of all our burdens. To do this, it must be asked whether there is now or has ever been a community which did indeed have numerous problems and difficulties but which did not succumb to family disruption, alcoholism and drug addiction, violence and murder.

Chapter 4 of this book describes the mass murder of the European Jews. That community, which has not existed since 1945, was a "moral community" in the sense that the 11,000,000 European Jews survived under great pressure from the outside without becoming enmeshed in the problems that have by now been repeatedly discussed. They were able to give their lives a meaning beyond that which the world about them allowed. Their strength, then, lay in their ability to find meaning in their lives by turning inward, away from the world which rejected them, and finding meaning in the Jewish culture which defined them and gave them everything from hope for the future to social stratification. They were, of course, only one example of people who were able to give their lives a meaning in spite of, and in the face of, great danger and suffering. The Irish are another such group as are the Serbs, the Dhukobors and others.

However, the Jews of Eastern Europe were an excellent example for the purposes of this study, because their position of inferiority, especially in Poland, resembles so very much the position of the black community in the United States, a community which suffers from so much murder. It has been said that the Jewish communities of Europe *before* the Nazi episode were treated "like the blacks in Mississippi before the Civil Rights movement."[23]

Nevertheless, drunkenness, crime, illegitimacy and illiteracy were almost unknown in that community. Heller has described this in her analysis of the Polish Jews who constituted ten percent of that country's population in 1939. Of the 3,000,000 Jews then living there, four out of ten lived in a city, the others in segregated Jewish communities. Their daily income was about 20 cents, converting the Polish zloty to American coinage, and the stock in their numerous "businesses" was worth about $4.00 in U.S. money. Thus, they were the poorest of the poor, living a "hand-to-mouth" existence at best.[24] More important is that the Jews of Poland were an inferior caste, i.e., "a closed status group."[25]

This is, of course, the same problem which faced the black population of the United States until recently. Thus, Jews, like American blacks, were totally excluded from the majority society. Although no laws prescribed this, Jews were at all times reminded of their inferiority: They were expected to take off their hats when speaking to a Pole; Jews assumed an attitude in bodily posture and speech resembling that of blacks in the United States before 1960; and most of all, Jews could not under any circumstances rid themselves of the stigma of being Jewish. Even Jewish converts to Christianity were treated as Jews, a word which in itself was considered an opprobrium. This stigma was so strong that Poles who had any Jewish ancestry, however remote, hid this at all cost. In fact, the very word "Zid," meaning Jew, was an insult. Well meaning Poles always substituted the word "Israelite" or "Hebrew" for the word "Jew," because "it brought forth a feeling of distaste."[26] Added to all this poverty and mistreatment was the overcrowding of the ghetto into which Jews were forced by medieval law, perpetuated by custom until the Nazi invasion of Poland.

The preceding is an example of a community under severe stress. Yet, despite oppression, terror and abuse, that community did not disintegrate from within. The reason for this was the ability of the Polish and other European Jews to maintain a "moral community." Thus, by means of religious proscription, "temperance and sobriety were obligatory."[27]

Getting drunk was severely criticized, as was excessive eating. All behavior or experiences which cost a person self-control were avoided, and self-awareness and self-control were highly prized. Learning was stressed and intellectual achievement became a means of social mobility. Learning, however, was not used to gain better employment since in Polish society none was available to Jews. Learning became important for its own sake and the most learned man, however employed, ranked the highest in the Jewish system of stratification. A sense of community was taught to young and old alike and charity received high acclaim. All this was to be done for its own sake. This description is, of course, a model, not a living reality. Thus, all European Jews were not learned; all were not charitable; all were not self-controlled. However, these ideals, whatever their influence on each person, led to Jewish survival under great stress. Centering their daily existence upon religious law and practice, the Jews of Europe *gave meaning to their lives.*[28]

This is not to say that all Americans become orthodox Jews, although some citizens do live in that cultural milieu in Brooklyn, N.Y., and elsewhere. Nor is it implied that the Eastern European Jewish community was the only "moral community," or that there are no others. It must be pointed out, however, that American failure to develop a sense of meaning for so many of its people is a principal cause of despair, not only for the poor and the disadvantaged but also for people of means and affluence.

This is the reason for widespread drug addiction in the United States and elsewhere. A sense of meaninglessness is also responsible for suicide and illegitimacy. Worst of all, people who do not believe that their lives have any meaning can hardly believe that the life of another person has any meaning. Thus, the real communication behind the act of murder is that life has no meaning. *Neither the life of the killer nor the life of the victim has meaning for those who kill.* The reason for the belief in the meaninglessness of life is the experience of so many Americans and others that they have no power to determine their own fate. Therefore, murder becomes a means by which the murderer can temporarily gain more power than he would otherwise never have. The person who kills another human being is compensating himself for being otherwise impotent in a world which admires power at any price and tramples on all who have no power.

Some will object and point out that the vast majority of mankind has even less power than the average American and European. Therefore it would appear that there ought to be more murder everywhere else than here. That, however, is a spurious argument because other cultures do not teach their citizens that power is important for everyone. That is only taught in industrialized democracies, particularly the United States. People in the United States feel far worse about the impotence of everyday life than do Europeans, even those living in parliamentary democracies. The reason for that difference is that parliamentary democracies are, by their very nature, elitist societies. In all of the parliamentary democracies, the citizen does not even vote for the head of state. That is done for him by the parliament. A small upper crust of bosses dominates almost all the "democracies" on this earth so that few ever see themselves as candidates for power, be that political or economic.

In the United States, however, the myth abounds that every boy (and girl) can grow up to be president of the United States or of General Motors, and it has happened. Richard Nixon and Lee Iaccoca were poor boys. So was Elvis Presley and so are scores of folk heroes and other achievers. In so open a society, then, a member has cause to sometimes ask himself whether or not "he made it." There are many who answer that question negatively because their experience confirms this estimate they have of themselves. Most important is that in a culture which insists that all have at least some power and success, many have none. Among these are a few who want to correct that imbalance once and for all by murder. They take a life. This places them into control over another human being at a level that normally not even the most powerful business tycoon can ever achieve.

This phenomenon has been seen again and again in this book. The one-on-one killer who commits homicide will kill another person for reasons that seem ridiculous and utterly unimportant. But the recorded reasons for killing are not truly the issue. When a man kills another over 40 cents lying on a bar, he does so because he wants to assert himself. He wants to be somebody, even if it is only once. When one man kills another over the attentions of a woman his message is clear. He is for once letting it be known that he has power, the power to decide that someone else shall not live. This is also true of the judge, the prosecutor and the prison officials who "execute" a helpless prisoner. It is true of the assassin who works for organized criminals and the assassin who kills a famous person. The judge plays God. So does the prosecutor and so does the mass murderer and the serial killer. The wish to show power over life and death motivates the gang who murdered a polio victim in a park, and it motivated the Nazi killers as they murdered millions.

6. *Alienation.* The father of American criminology, Edwin H. Sutherland, published his important work, *White Collar Crime*, just 40 years ago.[29] This book pointed criminology into a new direction because Sutherland recognized the need for students of deviant behavior to study the whole society, not only its parts, in order to comprehend any one aspect.

Murder in all its forms has been described in this book: one-on-one killing (homicide); multicide, the killing of numerous persons by government bureaucracies and by individuals; assassinations both by organized criminal enterprises and by lone assassins; and executions in the name of "the people." Some of the "causes" of all of this killing have been reviewed. But following Sutherland, the whole of society, indeed Western civilization, must be examined, and it must be recognized that murder is only one manifestation of the malaise that troubles industralized people. Numerous writers have called this malaise "alienation." The essence of alienation is the inability to deal with any event or person unless that event or person satisfies a person's immediate need at that moment. Otherwise people are not interested. Alienation is a condition which arises from competition for goods, social honor, and above all, private satisfaction. Alienation leads people to see others as objects, not subjects. Alienation is a condition which leads people to believe that others are commodities to be exploited and then discarded.

Innumerable writers have commented on this phenomenon. But it was the sociologist Ferdinand Tonnies who first introduced consideration of this condition to the sociological literature, by showing the important distinction between "Gemeinschaft" and "Gesellschaft."[30] This distinction revolves around the growth of the urban industrialized community, which Tonnies calls "Gesellschaft," at the expense of the folk community, which Tonnies calls "Gemeinschaft." This is an important distinction which cannot be translated into English without depriving the terms of their intended meaning. "Gemeinschaft" is derived from the German word "gemein" (as in guest), and "mein" (as in coal*mine*). The word can be translated as "common" in the sense of holding something in common. Thus, "Gemeinschaft" is a primary community in which all hold the same values and principles in common. "Sich gesellen" is a German phrase which means to associate with one another. From that root comes the word "Gesellschaft" meaning an association or a corporation. Thus, German business firms often follow their names with the letters G.m.b.H., meaning, "Gesellschaft mit beschrankter Haftung," or company with limited liability.

The point of all this is that "Gesellschaft" refers to the impersonal, the cold, the formal, the financial world. In 1935, shortly before his death, Tonnies published his last work, entitled *Geist der Neuzeit*.[31] In this, his last work, Tonnies returns to the theme of community and makes this observation which really summarizes what he had first said in *Gemeinschaft und Gesellschaft* in 1887:

> In the Middle Ages there was unity, now there is atomization; then the hierarchy of authority was solicitous paternalism, now it is compulsory exploitation; then there was relative peace, now wars are wholesale slaughter; then there were sympathetic relationships among kinfolk and old acquaintances, now *there are strangers and aliens everywhere;* the society was chiefly made up of home and land-loving peasants, now the attitude of the businessman prevails; then the man's simple needs were met by home production and barter, now we have world trade and capitalist production; then there was permanency of abode, now great mobility; then there were folk art, music and handicrafts, now there is science — and the scientific method applied, as in the case of the cool calculations of the businessman, leads to the point of view which deprives one's fellow men and one's society on their personality, leaving only a framework of dead symbols and generalizations.

Creating strangers is, then, the first step in the alienation of man. The sociologist Simmel wrote in a similar vein in 1908 in his essay "Der Streit," best rendered into English as "conflict," although in its strictest sense the word means quarrel.[32] Simmel shows that

> . . . where direct personal forces wrestle with one another, we are more easily subject to consideration and restraint and find it more difficult to resist appeals to charity. In fact, within direct antagonisms, we are sometimes prevented by a kind of shame from unfolding our energies unreservedly, from playing all our cards, from investing our whole personality in a fight in which one personality stands against another.
>
> In struggles which are carried out in terms of objective accomplishments, these ethical, aesthetic delays do not interfere. For this reason we can compete with individuals with whom we would at all costs avoid any personal controversy. By turning toward objects, competition attains the *cruelty* of all objectivity, a cruelty which does not consist in the enjoyment of the other's suffering, but, on the contrary, in the elimination of all subjective factors from the whole action.

This, then, is the second step in alienation. People make an object out of other human beings, an object to be used and to be discarded. The stranger becomes an object.

Lest it is assumed that only 19th-century Germans saw the alienation to come, mention should be made of the work of Alvin Toffler, who wrote *Future Shock* in 1970.[33] Inspection of his "Table of Contents" reveals at once the nature of his message. There is a discussion of "The Death of Permanence," "Transience," the "throw away society," and most distressing, as Toffler puts it, "the average interpersonal relationship in our life is shorter and shorter."[34]

The evidence is that all this destabilizes people. Impermanence, a sense of being left out and unwanted on top of all the competition from everything from grades in school to money in the bank, makes people suspicious of the motives of others, frightened of being unfavorably compared, fearful of "getting involved" and willing to live in a society which seems not to care for anyone. No better example of alienation exists than the events at Kent State University, Ohio, on Monday, May 4, 1970. On that day, the Ohio National Guard killed four students and wounded nine on the campus of that university in an effort to disperse a crowd of students who had collected to protest the Vietnam War.[35]

Whatever the reasons for this tragedy, the concern here is with alienation, the inability to see another human being in those who appear different, and the willingness to kill or support killing in the name of conformity. James Michener, in his book *Kent State*, reprints a number of letters to the editor of the Kent newspaper concerning the killing of Jeffrey Glenn Miller, Allison Krause, William K. Schroeder and Sandra Lee Scheuer. Following are some significant examples and Michener's comments: "Congratulations to the Guardsmen for their performance of duty on the Kent University Campus.... The governors of our states cannot waste the taxpayers' money playing games..." or "Authority, law and order are the backbone of our society, for its protection. Would you want authorities to stand by if your home was threatened?" or "I extend appreciation and whole hearted support of the Guard of every state for their fine efforts in protecting citizens like me and my property."

Numerous letters favored vigilante movements to control students, while others were outraged by peculiar dress or long hair. Michener wrote of these letters: "Several intimated that the penalty for nonconformity should be death."[36] Michener goes on to say, "The most deplorable aspect of these letters was not the explosive outpouring of hatred ... nor the obvious obsession with property values as opposed to human life [which is often observed in American life] but rather the willingness to condemn all students perceiving them as a mass to be castigated." Numerous people, according to Michener, said to him that "they should have shot most of the professors, too." A prominent Kent lawyer said in an interview with a newspaper that, "if I had a sub-machine gun there would not have been 14 shot, there probably would have been 140 of them dead, and that's what they need."[37]

There was constant reference to violence in the wake of these shootings, as citizens of Kent and students contemplated arming themselves to kill the others. Michener points out, however, that "an undue proportion of the demands for more killing came from women; the most intransigent opposition to students came from them, and the harshest dismissal of the young." Michener recites how women marched in front of a Toledo, Ohio, church where a memorial service for the dead students was being held and produced signs that read: "The Kent State Four Should Have Studied More."

Yet more astonishing to Michener and this author were the number of students whose own parents told them that it would have been a good thing if they, their children, had been shot. Michener interviewed 400 students and found "a depressing number" who were confronted with such parental hostility. This is the best example of such an attitude on the part of one mother:

> MOTHER: Anyone who appears on the streets of a city like Kent with long hair, dirty clothes or barefoot deserves to be shot.
> RESEARCHER: Have I your permission to quote that?
> MOTHER: You sure do. It would have been better if the guard had shot the whole lot of them that morning.
> PROFESSOR OF PSYCHOLOGY (listening in): Is long hair a justification for shooting someone?
> MOTHER: Yes. We have got to clean up this nation. And we'll start with the long hairs.
> PROFESSOR: Would you permit one of your sons to be shot simply because he went barefooted?
> MOTHER: Yes.
> PROFESSOR: Where do you get such ideas?
> MOTHER: I teach at the local High School.
> PROFESSOR: You mean you teach your students such things?
> MOTHER: Yes. I teach them the truth. That the lazy, the dirty, the ones you see walking the streets and doing nothing ought all to be shot.[38]

Michener reports yet another case of parental aggression and alienation as follows:

> . . . that night when she returned to her home in a small town in western Ohio, her nerves wracked by the tragedy she had just seen, her parents said, "It would have been better for America if every student on that hill had been shot."
> "Mother," she cried in profound protest, "I was there. Only a miracle of some kind saved me. What about that?"
> "You would have deserved it," said her mother.[39]

The outcome of such remarks by parents was the alienation of their grown children who could hardly believe what they heard their parents say. Similar language was of course used by the student generation in the 1970s as they assailed all police as "pigs" and promised to shoot them.

Another example of utter alienation of some Americans from others is the fate of the homeless. There were, in 1988, about 735,000 homeless Americans who slept on sidewalks, in doorways and in parks. It is estimated that in 1990 there are 2,000,000 homeless Americans.[40] These examples show that alienation exists not only in the slums of Manhattan but also on Main Street, U.S.A. For alienation is the inability to see others as human beings like ourselves. To the alienated there are only "they," who are different, dangerous and unworthy of life itself. Such an attitude leads to murder.

The philosopher Martin Buber showed that there can be no "I" unless there is also a "you."[41] This is also the thrust of the work of the sociologist George Herbert

Mead, whose students published his thoughts in *Mind, Self and Society* after his death.[42] Mead said, "The process out of which the self arises is a *social process* which implies interaction of individuals in the group, implies the pre-existence of the group. . . . Thus, there is a social process out of which selves arise and exist."[43] That includes the murderer and his victim. Each represents all of us, even if we don't want to know it.

However, humans have the capacity to objectify, not only other people, but also themselves. "Man's behavior," says Mead, "is such in his social group that he is able to become an object to himself; . . . fundamentally, it is this social fact . . . that differentiates him from them [the animals]."[44]

Because people can become an object to themselves, they certainly can see others as an object and not as living, vital and important persons, and that is why people murder and animals only kill for food. The outsider can be seen as an object, a nonperson, a thing. Thus, murder comes about because so many people have learned that other people and objects, can have more power over their lives than each individual. Some have also learned to liberate themselves from such domination; but others have learned that physical violence is an acceptable means of achieving such liberation, and that there are no other means of communicating to others what they feel and need. The killer and his victim live in a loveless world, a world where anger, hate and aggression rule, and where each man knows only himself.

Genesis IV reads in part, "And the Lord said unto Cain: 'Where is Abel thy brother?' And he said: 'I know not; am I my brother's keeper?' And He said: 'What hast thou done? The voice of thy brother's blood crieth unto Me from the ground. And now cursed art thou from the ground, which hath opened her mouth to receive thy brother's blood from thy hand. . . .' And Cain went out from the presence of the Lord and dwelt in the land of Nod." "Nod" is the Hebrew word for "wandering" in the land of alienation.

Murder has a meaning—that human life is cheap and means very little. Murder, however, is also a cry for help by those who are desperate, because they have lost in competitive society. Since murder is human conduct, it is not inevitable but can be alleviated. To do so we must first admit that we have a great deal of violence in the family; that family violence is a public issue, not only a private one; and that people must not cooperate with violent people by excusing their conduct. Stress must also be reduced by giving life a meaning beyond the material and developing a moral community which will serve to alleviate alienation (the view that others and even people themselves are only an object).

This book has demonstrated that those who kill others in a variety of circumstances share at least one belief or attitude: They view their victims as objects, not people. This is the reason for calling murder "the final alienation." An alien is, of course, a stranger. But the Greco-Latin origin of this word refers to a stranger whom we once knew. A stranger now, but someone with whom we had a close relationship in the past. Alienation is not merely the accident of not knowing someone else; people are alienated from erstwhile spouses after divorce, or from former friends or even parents and children.

However, we do know, or we ought to know, that each of us shares his humanity with us; that despite all differences of gender, age, race, ethnicity and religion, no person ought to be an alien, even if he is a stranger or a foreigner. For at the very minimum, all people share the wish to live. If people have nothing else in common, surely they know that all hold life dear. It is, as stated in the Introduction, "the only possession any of us truly have," for obviously, without life people have nothing. Those who kill others no longer feel that their victim is indeed a subject, a person, a living, feeling human like themselves. Those who kill, and many others, have objectified, made "nonpersons," out of their fellow human beings. It is so much easier to kill an object, distant and different from us, than to kill someone like ourselves.

The horror is, that people kill relatives and friends more often than strangers. This is true because people even objectify, feel alienated, from their own families and friends and associates. Alienation is not only visible in the high murder rate; it is also visible with respect to society's treatment of the elderly, prisoners, and each other in so many situations which occur in everyday life.

Therefore, this book serves two purposes: to explain the phenomenon of murder in a succinct and understandable manner, and fulfill the author's intention to contribute to love in this world, although the book's topic would hardly seem to qualify for such high hopes.

Appendix. Statistical Analysis
(by Clifford Falk and Gerhard Falk)

METHOD AND PRESENTATION

The following are statistics derived from murders in Erie County, New York, as reported in the now defunct *Courier-Express*. There are 912 of these in the *Courier-Express* archives, involving at least 970 victims. Nine hundred and two of them bear dates beginning in 1943 and ending in 1983; ten stragglers are from earlier years, including, oddly, one from 1916.

A form (Murder Study Data Sheet) listing 105 categories of information that might be obtained from any given newspaper story was filled out for each reported murder. A copy of this form is on pages 249–251. The resultant pool of information was used to derive statistics that give a good picture of what makes for murder.

A number of statistics derived from this study have been used elsewhere in this book. Those used elsewhere are primarily "summary" statistics, i.e., overall averages or frequencies for one particular category. This chapter is devoted primarily to the relationship of one category of data to another (and frequently the relationship between three or more categories of data). The outcomes are illustrative of many facts about the causes of murder, the justice system, press coverage, and other matters, which may in some instances confirm common beliefs and in other cases surprise the reader.

A "population" is all the cases there are to study. This is as opposed to a "sample," which is, hopefully, a representative selection of cases from a population, which is then used to draw conclusions about the population. Because the data upon which this study is based is a population, it would be perfectly proper to list the results of all relationships tested, without any further testing as to what is known as "strength" of a relationship. That is so, because the primary use of finding the strength of a relationship is to determine the odds that a relationship found in a sample will hold true in the population from which the sample is derived.[1] Since this study is based on data from a population, *any* relationship between categories might be termed "significant."

The drawback to taking the attitude that any relationship between categories of data is significant is that with 105 categories, there are over 5,000 relationships between pairs of categories alone, and many more when one holds constant for the effects of a third or fourth category. Therefore, one must pick which statistics to highlight.

The criteria used to select which statistics to highlight were based upon the following goals, which are consistent with the purposes of this book: (A) To provide a snapshot of murder in one American metropolitan area; and (B) to showcase facts about murder which are likely to be facts in most metropolitan areas in America. Accordingly, the selection criteria are:

1. Sufficient data to draw a conclusion.

2. Direct causal relationship between the change in one category and the change in another.

3. High likelihood of repetition in other American metropolitan areas.

4. Value of conclusions.

5. Chances that the conclusions drawn would be substantially the same if one had knowledge of every murder that happened in Erie County between 1943 and 1983.

These criteria will be briefly explained one at a time.

1. *Sufficient data to draw a conclusion.* This can be best illustrated by an example. Two of the categories for which data was originally sought were "Weight of Murderer" and "Weight of Victim." If it is found that, in all three cases where both weight of murderer and weight of victim is reported, the weight of the victim is less than the weight of the murderer, it can be said with absolute certainty that, of all the murders reported in the archives of the *Buffalo Courier-Express*, those which report both weight of murderer and weight of victim indicate that the weight of the victim is less than the weight of the murderer. What else does this indicate? Nothing. Therefore it would not be included in the statistics selected.

2. *Direct causal relationship between the change in one category and the change in another.* It is frequently the case that two categories of information have a strong statistical relationship[2] which is not due to any cause and effect relationship between them but is rather due to the effect of one or more intervening variables which affect both. (This holds true in reverse, as well. Often an intervening variable disguises a cause and effect relationship between two categories.) For example, at first glance, it would appear that there is an inverse cause and effect relationship between the number of winter coats worn in Canada and the number of birds present in that country on any given day. That is, the more winter coats, the fewer birds. One could of course stop at that and either conclude that birds dislike the Canadian winter fashions or that Canadians go out of their way to expose themselves to birds. The more reasonable thing to do, however, is hold constant for the effects of both temperature and season. It will surely be found that these two variables control the other two, and that when the effects of temperature and season are taken into account, the relationship between coats and birds will be exposed as spurious.

A less obvious, but real, example from this study is the relationship between press coverage and ethnicity of murderer. It was initially found that the average number of column inches in the *Courier-Express* devoted to a murder involving a white murderer was more than twice as much as the average involving a black murderer. One could, of course, conclude that the editors of the *Courier* paid attention to the race of the murderer when deciding the importance of a murder to their readers. When the effect of the ethnicity of the *victim* on the number of column inches of coverage was controlled, however, this relationship between the ethnicity of murderer and column inches disappeared. It was simply the case that blacks were usually murdered by blacks, and whites by whites. Where a black murdered a white, the press coverage was greater than where a white murdered a white.

It should be pointed out here, incidentally, that even if one is unable to *quantitatively* show that the cause of a relationship between two categories is both those categories' relationships to a third (or more) category, it is still decidedly possible that that third category is indeed the reason for the strong relationship between the two categories being examined. It is frequently the case that the data is simply insufficient or inconclusive. Where this is believed to be the case, it is included in the explanation accompanying each statistic.

3. *High likelihood of repetition in other American metropolitan areas.* A somewhat unorthodox technique was used to determine likelihood of repetition in other metropolitan areas. Measures normally used to determine whether a population is likely to have the same relationship characteristics as a sample were applied to the pool of data from the *Courier-Express* archives.[3] The accuracy of this measure of repeatability is dependent upon how "typical" Buffalo is as an American metropolitan area. That is, the conclusions drawn herein, while they are probably by and large accurate for most American metropolitan areas,[4] should be most accurate for Great Lakes industrial cities, and somewhat less so for cities which are less similar to Buffalo.

4. *Value of conclusion.* Example of valueless conclusion: Married murderers kill their spouses more often than single murderers kill theirs.

5. *Chances that the conclusion drawn would be substantially the same if one had knowledge of every murder that happened in Erie County from 1943 to 1983.* Some murders that occurred in Erie County during the time period 1943 to 1983 are certainly missing from the *Courier-Express* archives. Police reports for that time period would lead one to believe that the murders reported in the *Courier* archives reported on roughly 85 percent of the victims killed. The reader can easily determine, by examining the "Column Inches" category, which murders would be likely left out. Where an unemployed East Side black is killed in self-defense with a kitchen knife by his girlfriend, there is a decent chance that his ultimate tragedy is going to be crowded out of the newspaper by a Little League box score. Those statistics which would be greatly affected by the underreporting of certain classes of murders, or by the unreliability of a *Courier-Express* archivist, were left out. For example, the number of murders per year by population for that year would be worth reporting if one could trust that a consistent percentage of murders occurring in Erie County was archived each year from 1943 to 1983. There was no means of determining this, however; therefore this statistic is not featured herein.

The examples accompanying each statistic are, in most instances, listed only for extreme values. Categories not listed are either between the extremes or are not listed because data is not sufficient to warrant listing them. There were, for example, 23 distinct categories of murder weapons found in the pages of the *Courier-Express* archives. The listing of the statistic for "Sex of Murderer vs. Weapon Used," however, contains only two weapons, clubs and kitchen knives. The former is listed to show that users of clubs or bludgeons are disproportionately male; the latter to show that users of kitchen knives are disproportionately female. Users of other weapons either tend to have a more "typical" male-female mix, or are esoteric means of killing (e.g. scalding, defenestration) which were used in too few cases to draw any conclusion about them. For nonlinear relationships, expected values at or near the "peaks and valleys" of the relationship are listed. For example, there is a strong relationship between age of murderer and age of victim. It is not the sort of relationship, however, where one can correctly say that "the older the murderer, the older the victim," or "the younger the murderer, the younger the victim." If one knows the age of the victim, the "best guess"[5] for age of the murderer rises until the age of the victim is about seven years old, declines until the age of the victim is approximately 20 years old, rises again until the victim is roughly 50 years old, and declines thereafter. Therefore all these values are listed under the statistic "Age of Murderer vs. Age of Victim."

COLUMN INCHES

Column inches vs. number of murderers. Murders by more than one murderer tend to yield more column inches than murders where the murderer acts alone. Examples of expected values: 53″ mean for murders where there was but one murderer; 158″ mean for murders where three murderers took part.

The production of more space or column inches of newspaper coverage in cases of homicide involving more than one murderer is simply the consequence of the number of killers who needed to be described. In short, we can assume with confidence that the extra amount of space used by the *Courier* in such cases comes about because there is more to write about when there are several killers instead of only one. In fact, the difference between 53 inches of space used to describe a killing involving one killer is approximately one-third of the amount of space used to deal with three killers, and is therefore to be anticipated without having any particular meaning as to race, class or ethnicity of either the killer or the victim.

Column inches vs. zone of murderer's residence by year of murder. The press coverage accorded a murder differs based upon the area of the county from which the murderer comes. Examples: For the years 1955–59, 19″ mean for murderers living downtown (18 cases), 91″ mean for murderers living in the residential area surrounding downtown (23 cases); for the years 1970–74, 39″ mean for murderers living in the residential area surrounding downtown (138 cases), 80″ mean for murderers living in the outlying residential area of the city (28 cases); for the years 1975–79, 53″ mean for murderers living downtown (18 cases), 62″ mean for murderers living in the residential area surrounding downtown

(97 cases), 83" mean for murderers living in the outlying residential area of the city (19 cases), 133" mean for murderers living in near suburbs (14 cases), 129" mean for murderers living in far suburbs or rural area (14 cases).

During the 20 years between 1955 and 1975, the mean inches of space devoted to murderers living in the downtown Buffalo area increased almost 36 percent. This increased interest in such killers was the result of the revitalization of Buffalo during those 20 years. Between 1955 and 1959 the downtown area of Buffalo had declined severely. Residence downtown was limited at that time to a transient and almost entirely poor population. The killings they committed usually victimized other poor people, mostly blacks. Hence newspaper coverage was short and scarce. After 1975, as the city began to rebuild the downtown area, business returned. This led to robbery-murders of white businessmen in greater numbers than was true 20 years earlier and hence more news coverage. Undoubtedly it was the judgment of the *Courier* staff that the public is more interested in the murders of storeowners, particularly white storeowners, than in the murder of poor blacks. This, then, is one piece of evidence indicating that the lives of all citizens are not given equal value by newspapers or their readers.

The same social class bias is visible in the reporting concerning murder in the next zone of the city of Buffalo. During the period of 1975 to 1979 the amount of space devoted to murderers living in Zone 2, i.e., the zone surrounding downtown Buffalo, dropped to two-thirds of what it had been during the years 1955–1959. The reason for this drop was that the mid-1970s saw a decline in the social standing of citizens living and working in Zone 2. This became particularly the case after the riots motivated by the bombing of Cambodia during the Vietnam War in 1972. These riots led to the closing of numerous Zone 2 business establishments whose windows and property were severely damaged and thereafter not reopened. The consequences were robberies, hence robbery-murders, declined, while homicides involving poor blacks increased as that population moved into the areas abandoned by wealthier blacks and whites after the riots. Our hypothesis, namely that the number of column inches in the *Courier-Express* concerning murderers were dictated largely by the social class of the murderer and his victim, is additionally born out by the number of inches used to describe the killers living in the outlying residential areas of the city of Buffalo and in the surrounding suburbs. Thus, the amount of space devoted to these murderers remained the same during the years 1970–1974 and 1975–1979. In addition, murderers living in the near suburbs and those living in rural areas near the city received considerably more coverage than any other murderers. These killers were almost all white, well-to-do and ranked in the middle to upper class of citizens. We hold therefore, *that social class as defined by residence confirms the hypothesis that the life of an American citizen is valued according to his membership in one or another social class.*

Column inches vs. minimum prison term. There is more press coverage of a murder where the perpetrator gets a longer sentence. Examples of expected values: 60" mean for five-year minimum terms; 95" mean for 20-year minimum terms.

The amount of newspaper space devoted to a prison sentence which is longer than usual is also extraordinarily high. This is no doubt the consequence of the probability that longer sentences are given to murderers whose crimes seem particularly obnoxious to the judge or the community. It ought to be understood, however, that the degree of revulsion which a murder will produce in both the judiciary and the public is not always related to the method of killing the victim or the conduct of the murderer. Thus, Erie County saw some rather gruesome murders involving blacks, even including the murder of children by their mothers, without provoking a very long prison sentence. This is true because some of the worst murder cases, including even the mutilation of the dead body of the victim, were committed by blacks and or adjudicated as the product of "insanity." Other cases led to much harsher punishments, including the death penalty, because of the social standing of the killer and the victim. For example, a young man of native American descent who killed a prominent lady socialite wife of a wealthy corporate executive was given the death penalty at a time when it was still available in New York State. Yet, innumerable killings of a similar sort, involving victims of lesser prominence, never resulted in a long prison sentence, and sometimes even led to probation for the black perpetrators whose victims were black as well. Clearly, ethnic considerations were involved in the uneven application of punishments over the 40 years and 912 murder cases investigated for use in this study.

Column inches vs. place of occurrence. Large numbers of column inches of newspaper coverage are devoted to murder which occur in residential areas. Examples: 52″ mean for murders occurring downtown (118 cases); 98″ mean for murders occurring in near suburbs (84 cases).

Almost the entire black population of Buffalo and Erie County lives in the Downtown or Zone 1 area or in the Zone 2 area surrounding downtown. There are very few blacks in the suburbs of Buffalo, and murder is very rare there. Therefore, the considerable discrepancy between the amount of space given suburban murders as compared to downtown murders once more underscores the significance of social class when murder is reported. In addition, that which is rare is always more interesting than that which is common. Since murder decreases as the distance from the center of the city increases, newspaper space devoted to murder is affected in the reverse. It increases as distance from the center of the city also increases.

Column inches vs. occupation of murderer. Unemployed or student murderers garner more press coverage than murderers of other occupations. Laborers and murderers employed in service occupations get the least. Examples: 207″ mean for unemployed murderers (21 cases); 200″ mean for student murderers (23 cases); 91″ mean for murderers in service occupation (25 cases); 90″ mean for laborer murderers (47 cases).

The phenomenon of giving more than twice the amount of coverage to murderers who are either unemployed or students than to murderers who are working in service occupation or as laborers clearly indicates the marginality of both students and the unemployed in our work-oriented culture. In fact, students are seen as unemployed by many whose views are reflected by newspaper coverage. Students are also believed to be radical politically and deviant in conduct. Thus, both deviants, that is the unemployed and students, arouse more anger and publicity as murderers because their crimes seem less excusable than the crimes of working, employed people.

Students and the unemployed earn the hostility of their peers and are seen as pariahs whose murderous behavior confirms the common view that they are on the outside of "society." The comments, descriptions and discussions of these murderers in newspapers reflect these attitudes and dwell on these beliefs.

Column inches vs. relationship between murderer and victim. Where there is a close relationship between murderer and victim, there is little press coverage. Examples: 239″ mean for police murderers (9 cases); 109″ mean for coworker murderers (17 cases); 97″ mean for stranger murderers (137 cases); 34″ mean for neighbor murderers (41 cases); 34″ mean for spouse murderers (67 cases); 26″ mean for lover murderers (34 cases). Occupation and other relationships between the murderer and the victim decidedly influence the amount of space a newspaper is willing to devote to an account of murder and particularly the murderer. Our findings plainly show that nothing excites the public interest more than killings undertaken by the police. Thus, the average number of inches of news coverage given a police-committed murder is twice that of a stranger murderer.

This discrepancy is so great that police employees who commit murder receive more than nine times the coverage available for so-called "lover" murder, that is, triangles. It is, of course, possible for police to murder someone engaged in a rivalry with them. In a sense, the label "lover" is not comparable to the label "police" because the former status is not an occupation. It is, however, significant that newspapers will make an issue of occupation when police are involved as murderers no matter what their motive in carrying out the crime, while the occupation of murderers labeled "lover" or "spouse" is not given the coverage that police and coworkers receive.

Since everyone, including the retired and the unemployed, has an occupational status but may also be labeled according to his relationship to others, it is evident that newspaper coverage of a murderer depends on his *master status*. The *master status* is that status among many, which is considered most important to each person and the life audience which each of us collect. The master status can be occupation for some, family for others and a skill or special ability, such as sports or art for yet others. In the case of murderers, the master status is usually the label "murderer" with particular reference, however, to the occupation of police who, if they turn out to kill the innocent, have gathered a master status related both to the disappointment of many citizens with conduct contrary to the police motto ("To serve and protect"), and also contrary to the expectations of their peers.

Column inches vs. ethnicity of victim. There is much more press coverage when the victim of a murder is white than when he or she is black or

Hispanic. Examples: 102″ mean for white victims (344 cases); 37″ mean for black victims (367 cases); 40″ mean for Hispanic victims (25 cases).

While the number of Hispanic victims is fairly small because Erie County had only 20,000 citizens of Hispanic origins as of 1988, it is significant that the number of white victims is almost as great as the number of black victims. Obviously, the excess of newspaper coverage in cases of murder involving white victims rather than black victims is almost three to one. Nothing illustrates racial bias in newspaper reporting better than this difference. Added to the difference in race is, of course, the difference in income. Thus, blacks also suffer the disadvantage of poverty, thus making their murder distinctly less interesting than the murder of someone in better financial condition.

Column inches vs. ethnicity of murderer by ethnicity of victim. Where black killers kill white victims, murders receive the greatest newspaper attention. Examples: 101″ mean for white murderers and white victims (196 cases); 37″ mean for Hispanic murderers and Hispanic victims (16 cases); 36″ mean for black murderers and black victims (313 cases); 132″ mean for black murderers and white victims (57 cases). This underscores the racial bias in reporting even more. White victims not only get more coverage concerning their death by murder, but were featured in more column inches in the *Courier-Express* when their murderer was black than when he was white. This too has a financial meaning, inasmuch as almost all whites, killed by blacks, were members of the business community. Thus, blacks and whites generally kill each other, not members of the other race. There were, however, 57 cases involving black killers and white victims because the killers were almost always engaged in the robbery of a white storeowner or other whites deemed to have money. White killers almost always murdered other whites, and black killers almost always murdered blacks, but again, the amount of newspaper space allotted white killers exceeded the amount of space allotted black killers by a ratio of 3 to 1.

Column inches vs. sex of victim by year of murder. Previously, male victims received greater press coverage. More recently, female victims were more extensively covered. Examples: for the years 1955–59, 90″ mean for male victims (46 cases), 75″ mean for female victims (30 cases); for the years 1965–69, 88″ mean for male victims (71 cases), 63″ mean for female victims (29 cases); for the years 1975–79, 67″ mean for male victims (169 cases), 83″ mean for female victims (52 cases). There is a clear reversal in the amount of newspaper space allotted to men and women victims of murder when we compare the years 1955–1959 with the years 1975 to 1979. The difference is not small but it is significant. Thus, in the earlier years, men received twenty percent more coverage than women. In the latter five-year period the exact reverse occurred. Now women received twenty percent more coverage than men. Evidently, the status of women rose dramatically between 1955 and 1979 by reason of the women's liberation movement subsequent to the publication of *The Feminine Mystique* by Betty Friedan.[6]

Column inches vs. sex of victim by relationship between murder and victim.[7] Where there is a close relationship between murderer and victim, female victims receive more column inches. Examples: for a murderer who is a relative, 56″ mean for male victims (38 cases), 102″ mean for female victims (24 cases); for a murderer who is a friend, 35″ mean for male victims (75 cases), 76″ mean for female victims (29 cases).

Murder committed by a relative of the victim was obviously more interesting to the newspaper than murder committed by a friend. This was true for both male and female victims. Newspaper space devoted to the killing of the victim by a relative is almost one and a half times greater than murders committed by "friends" in the case of both sexes. However, it is remarkable that female victims received much more attention than male victims whether the killer was a friend or a relative. This is so because women are seen as far more defenseless than men, and because the killing of women is rare compared to the killing of men.

Column inches vs. zone of victim's residence. Victims who live in outlying areas garner more press coverage than victims who live in inner cities. Examples: 105″ mean for victims who live in outlying residential area of city; 47″ mean for victims who live in residential area surrounding downtown.

Here again, race and social class dictated the amount of coverage of a murder as reported by the *Courier-Express*. Three factors explain the excess of coverage of persons living in "outlying" residential areas as compared to victims living in the near downtown area. These three factors are race, income and political influence.

Column inches vs. occupation of victim. White collar victims attract more press attention than blue collar victims. Examples: 158″ mean for professional victims (20 cases); 144″ mean for managerial victims (49 cases); 59″ mean for laborer victims (54 cases); 53″ mean for unemployed victims (17 cases).

Clearly, the occupation of the victim is closely related to the amount of newspaper space devoted to his murder. Occupation is, of course, the most important criterion of social class in the United States. It is also well known that professional occupations enjoy a higher prestige in the United States than other occupations, managerial occupations following close behind. The difference in the amount of space devoted to victims in different occupation categories reflects the fact that professionals and managerial workers always receive more news coverage concerning their activities than is true of laborers or the unemployed.

Column inches vs. weapon used. Murder with bare hands is covered extensively. Murder with a kitchen knife is covered sparsely. Examples: 99″ mean for hands (109 cases); 69″ mean for handguns (190 cases); 33″ mean for kitchen knives (89 cases).

The use of hands in killing the victims is almost entirely restricted to suburban males. The reason for this is that suburban males are frequently willing to beat their wives and children, but are not likely to seek their murder. However, some beatings become killings, albeit unintentionally. Consequently, almost all murder by hands is committed by whites living in the suburbs of the city. This led the old *Courier* to report hand killings with three times the coverage devoted to killings by knife, almost always committed by poor blacks. Murder committed by handgun was committed by both whites and blacks.

Column inches vs. apparent motive. Organized crime murders and murders by insane murderers get many column inches. Examples: 198″ mean for organized crime murders (17 cases); 171″ mean for insane murderers (21 cases); 47″ mean for murders caused by jealousy (67 cases); 39″ mean for murders caused by business dealings (42 cases); 38″ mean for murders caused by sudden anger (156 cases); 21″ mean for murders for victim-precipitated murder (69 cases).

"Organized" crime has been entertainment for years. Hence it is not surprising that this type of murder received far more attention than any other kind of murder, followed closely by the rare "insanity" plea. That, too, is of great interest to the public, although the "insanity" defense is very rare and constituted only 21 cases in a total of 912 cases collected for this study.

Column inches vs. sentence. Where a murderer is sentenced to a psychiatric hospital, there is a great deal of press coverage. Examples: 155″ mean for sentences to psychiatric hospital (22 cases); 82″ mean for sentences to prison term (328 cases); 32″ mean for sentences to probation (33 cases).

This excessive interest in those cases of murder leading to a sentence to a psychiatric hospital is illustrated once more by the huge amount of excess coverage given such cases as compared to those sent to prison. This is in part due to the fact that such cases generally involve bizarre behavior including bizarre types of murder, and that they are uncommon.

DATE

Most popular murder weeks. February 8–14 (26 cases); February 11–17 (26 cases); April 7–13 (27 cases); May 29–June 4 (26 cases); June 28–July 4 (27 cases); June 30–July 6 (26 cases); September 1–7 (26 cases); September 2–8 (26 cases); September 10–16 (26 cases); September 19–25 (26 cases); September 20–26 (26 cases); November 19–25 (26 cases).

Least popular murder weeks. January 13–19 (9 cases); March 24–30 (9 cases); July 21–27 (8 cases); July 22–28 (9 cases); July 23–29 (9 cases); July 24–30 (9 cases); July 25–31 (8 cases); October 10–16 (9 cases); October 11–17 (8 cases); October 12–18 (8 cases); October 13–19 (8 cases); October 14–20 (8 cases).

It is consistent with other observations concerning murder that the most popular weeks for killing in Erie County during the years 1943–1983 almost always included a holiday. Since murder predominates between relatives and friends and is seldom directed at strangers, it is reasonable to expect an increase in killings on days when work is not required and people otherwise occupied are in the presence of their family and leisure-time associates.

Thus, the weeks between February 8 and February 17 included Lincoln's birthday, Washington's birthday and St. Valentine's Day. While the latter is not a legal holiday, the former two were both legal holidays during the years here analyzed.

Although Good Friday and Easter are celebrated on different dates each year, these days did frequently coincide with the week of April 7–13, and therefore confirms the view that holidays increase the amount of murder each month. The same holds true for the week of May 29 to June 4, including Memorial Day which was observed on May 30 each year before the U.S. Congress moved all legal holidays to Monday.

The week of June 28 to July 6 includes Independence Day and the week of September 1 to September 8 includes Labor Day. Thanksgiving Day always occurs during the last week in November when murder is high. Thus, while high murder rates during some weeks of the year almost always coincide with a holiday, this does not explain the large number of killings during the week of September 19–26, nor the absence of the Christmas to New Year's week from the weeks with high rates of murder.

Previous studies have shown that Christmas Day in particular was a day of considerable murder activity, especially directed against family and friends who were of course available for murder on that day. It is possible that the reason for the failure of Christmas Day to show a higher than normal murder rate in Buffalo and Erie County is the religious composition of the population. Over 60 percent of all residents of Erie County are Roman Catholics. The finding that Christmas has an unusual amount of murder across the whole United States is of course based on murder occurring in a predominantly Protestant country. Since religion has a definite effect on life style, philosophy and attitude towards a host of events and people, it is entirely conceivable that attitudinal differences between Catholics and Protestants also shape the differential murder rates visible at Christmas.[8]

Season. Winter is the slowest season for murder. More murders occur during the summer than any other season. *Winter:* From December 21 to March 19 (89¼ dates, including February 29), there were 213 cases reported, or 2.39 murders per winter date. *Spring:* From March 20 to June 20 (93 dates), there were 231 cases reported, or 2.48 murders per spring date. *Summer:* From June 21 to September 22 (94 dates), there were 245 cases reported, or 2.61 murders per summer date. *Fall:* From September 23 to December 20 (89 dates), there were 216 cases reported, or 2.43 murders per fall date.[9]

As with earlier research which found a consistently high rate of murder in the summer months and a lower rate of murder in the winter months, such a pattern is also evident in the present study.[10] As indicated above, murder follows the seasons because murder victims are more available in warmer temperatures than in colder temperatures. This is true despite the fact that so much murder occurs at home. This means, therefore, that it is the outdoor murder rate and the murder rate of victims found in public places which are affected by temperature and availability of potential victims.

Year of murder vs. average temperature for day. The average temperature of the dates on which murders occur have tended to decline over the years. Examples of expected values: 51.0 degrees F. for murder occurring in 1943; 47.0 degrees F. for murder occurring in 1983.

Two explanations come to mind with reference to the change by four degrees in the average temperature when murder occurred in Erie County in the course of 40 years. Either there was a decline in the average temperature in Erie County with which the murder rate had nothing to do, or murder occurs less often in hot temperature than was once the case.

We hold that there has been a decrease in murder on hot days as compared to cooler days. This is the result of an increased use of air conditioners during the 40 years from 1943 to 1983. Thus, the lack of air conditioners in 1943 drove more people outdoors during the hot months, making them more available for murder. The increased use of air conditioners decreased the number of people outdoors on hot days and thereby also decreased the number of killings in the summer months generally. The use of air conditioners, therefore, has evened the number of killings performed over the year.

Year of murder vs. zone of occurrence. It is proportionately more common for murder to occur in the suburbs than used to be the case. Examples: 1973 mean for murders in near suburbs (91 cases); 1967 mean for murders downtown (132 cases).

As the business community expanded and residential movement spilled into the near suburbs of Buffalo the average (mean) number of murders also moved from downtown into the suburbs. Murder follows residential patterns because it is a family affair. Thus, fewer people lived downtown in 1973 than lived there in 1967. The reverse was true of the suburbs with the result that murder decreased downtown and increased uptown, relatively, between 1967 and 1973.

Year of murder vs. ethnicity of murderer. A larger proportion of murderers are black and Hispanic than used to be the case. Examples: 1974 mean for Hispanic murderers (24 cases); 1972 mean for black murderers (424 cases); 1968 mean for white murderers (256 cases).

The average number of murders committed by whites occurred in 1968 with 256 cases that year. For blacks, the average number of murders occurred in 1968 because blacks moved into Erie County in large numbers during the years 1941 to 1950 to take advantage of the expanding labor market created by the consequences of World War II.

The children of these migrants reached ages 15 to 30 in the decade of the 1960s and thereby contributed more to the murder rate in those years than their parents had done in years before the 1960s. Thus, these later arrivals reached their average murder year later than whites, a condition which is repeated among Hispanic Americans in 1968 when children of migrants from Puerto Rico and immigrants from other Spanish speaking areas matured in Erie County.

The significance of arriving at the average murder rate in different years among three different ethnic groups is that all three groups exhibit the same proclivity to murder when the ages 15–30 are most prominent.

Year of murder vs. sex of suspect by disposition. In the past, female suspects were much more likely than male suspects to have their cases dismissed before trial. More recently, a larger proportion of female suspects have been tried, rather than had their cases dismissed before trial. Examples: 1973 mean for male suspects whose case was dismissed before trial (34 cases); 1970 mean for female suspects whose case was dismissed before trial (70 cases); 1968 mean for male suspects tried by jury (230 cases); 1972 mean for female suspects tried by jury (20 cases). This observation corresponds well with the change of status achieved by all American women after the mid-1960s. As female status increased by reason of greater occupational mobility for women and subsequent higher earnings, women were also held more responsible for their actions, both noncriminal and criminal, than was true before the 1960s. Consequently, dismissals became less common after a higher status had been attained.

Year of murder vs. zone of murderer's residence. Murderers are proportionately more likely to live in outlying areas than used to be the case. A smaller proportion of murderers live downtown than used to be the case. Examples: The mean for murderers whose residence are the far suburbs or rural areas (37 cases) occurred in 1973; the mean for murderers who lived downtown (79 cases) occurred in 1966.

Between 1966 and 1973 a large number of businesses moved out of downtown Buffalo and relocated in the near and far suburbs. Therefore, robbers and robbery-murders also moved to these suburbs. In addition, the number of firearms owned by suburban citizens increased, as did the number of black citizens who moved to the suburbs. All of these factors increased the rate of murder there.

Year of murder vs. marital status of murderer. A larger proportion of murderers are single than used to be the case. Examples: 1970 mean for single murderers (195 cases); 1967 mean for married murderers (140 cases).

This phenomenon is not peculiar to murderers. The fact is, that there were many more single young men in America in 1970 than in 1967, a trend which has continued to 1989 and is likely to continue past that year. Since murder is principally committed by men aged 15 to 30, and in particular by men 20 to 28 years of age, it is not surprising that the numbers of single murderers are higher in later years than in earlier years.

Year of murder vs. occupation of murderer. The proportion of murderers who are students has increased over time. The proportion of murderers who are laborers or operatives has decreased. Examples: 1974 mean for student murderers (24 cases); 1965 mean for operative murderers (11 cases); 1965 mean for laborer murderers (54 cases).

This observation confirms the observation concerning single murderers. Students are much more likely to be single than married because their income is generally low. As the college student population increased, the student murderer population therefore also increased.

Year of murder vs. relationship between murderer and victim. It is proportionately more common than it used to be for murderers to be the lover or friend of the victim. It is proportionately less common than it used to be for the murderer to be police, a relative, or a spouse. Examples: 1973 mean for lover murderers (36 cases); 1972 mean for friend murderers (113 cases); 1968 mean for spouse murderers (74 cases); 1968 mean for relative murderers (77 cases); 1965 mean for police murderers (12 cases).

As the number of single persons of both sexes who live together increased, the number of "lovers" who killed each other also increased. Therefore, the proportion of killers who were otherwise related to the victim decreased.

Year of murder vs. sex of victim. The murder rate for male victims is increasing faster than the murder rate for female victims. Examples: 1971 mean for male victims (643 cases); 1969 mean for female victims (261 cases).

The increase in male victims is the consequence of the drug trade. Drugs and the drug business have become responsible for a great deal of murder. Since men are much more often involved in the drug business than are women, the rate for male victims has increased much more as well.

Year of murder vs. zone of victim's residence. A higher percentage of victims live in residential areas than lived in such areas previously. A smaller percentage of victims live out of town or downtown than used to live in those areas. Examples: 1973 mean for victims from near suburbs (103 cases); 1972 mean for victims from outlying city residential areas (124 cases); 1972 mean for victims from residential area surrounding downtown (446 cases); 1967 mean for victims from downtown (106 cases); 1967 mean for victims from out of town (36 cases).

As businesses have moved uptown, so has murder. Increased business construction in uptown and suburban areas not only caused more robbery murders to occur uptown, but it also necessitated the movement of a good number of employees of such business to uptown locations, that is, closer to their place of employment. Therefore, more victims of murder lived uptown than downtown after 1970. The out-of-town victims remained the same in number, but fewer in percent as the number of victims increased.

Year of murder vs. weapon. Rifles and shotguns are more popular murder weapons than they used to be; hands and blunt instruments are less so. Examples: 1973 mean for rifle or shotgun (157 cases); 1969 mean for club, bludgeon, or hammer (45 cases); 1969 mean for hands (122 cases).

In 1973, there were more people in the suburbs and in outlying areas of cities than was true before 1970. People who live in areas which are closer to hunting opportunities are more likely to own a shotgun or rifle. The number of murders committed by persons with hunting equipment became greater, therefore, as the population moved out of the city.

Hands and blunt instruments are used a good deal more as murder instruments by white, affluent persons than are knives or handguns which are used a good deal more by poor and black killers. Therefore, those who used their hands also had the money to buy hunting equipment and to live in the suburbs. Consequently, the same population which participated in the increase of hunting equipment as a murder weapon also had a history of using their hands or blunt instruments as a means of beating their victims to death. Therefore, it is altogether reasonable to expect a decrease of hands and blunt instruments as a murder weapon where there is an increase in the use of rifles and shotguns.

Year of murder vs. apparent motive. Drug dealing has become a more common motive recently. Jealousy and business dealings were relatively more common in the past than in the present. Examples: 1977 mean for drug dealing (15 cases); 1969 mean for business dealings (49 cases); 1969 mean for jealousy (75 cases).

While jealousy was at one time the principal cause of murder in the United States, and while it is still one of the main reasons for murder, the proportion of killings by reason of drug dealing has ever increased during the decade ending in 1983. The present study included the first nine months of that year. Thus, as the proportion of killings related to drugs increased, the proportion, not the number, of jealousy-related killings decreased.

Year of murder vs. disposition of case. Trial by judge has increased in popularity with time. Examples: 1971 mean for trial by judge (223 cases); 1968 mean for trial by jury (250 cases).

We have evidence that defendants tried by a judge generally receive a lesser prison term than defendants tried by a jury, and in the few cases in which probation is given to a defendant convicted of murder, the case was most often tried by a judge and not a jury. Therefore it is understandable that these results would influence a defense attorney to try murder cases before a judge, although we also have evidence that juries are less likely to convict a defendant than a judge would. Hence it is reasonable to assume that judges hand lighter sentences to defendants they themselves tried than to those tried by a jury, because the judge flatters himself into viewing his choice as the sole instrument of justice in the absence of a jury to mean that he is trusted personally. Judges reward such trust and flattery with a lighter sentence.

Year of murder vs. sentence. The proportion of murderers sentenced to psychiatric hospitals has dropped immensely. Previously, it was a far more typical sentence than it has been lately. Examples: 1971 mean for probation (36 cases); 1971 mean for prison term (359 cases); 1963 mean for psychiatric hospital (27 cases).

Trust in psychiatric treatment has declined considerably in the United States, and in particular with reference to the criminal justice system. Psychiatrists have demonstrated that they are for hire by both sides in any criminal litigation and that their testimony is bought. There have been innumerable cases in many courts in which psychiatrists on either side of an issue have confused everyone from the judge to the newspaper reader as to the efficacy of psychiatry. There is a great disillusionment with psychiatric testimony in face of more and more violent street crime, despite a 100-year-old record of psychiatric advice and treatment.

DAY OF WEEK

Number of murders reported vs. day of week. Weekends were the most popular murder days among the 908 cases where the day is known. The distribution is as follows: Sunday—139 cases (15.3%); Monday—113 cases (12.4%); Tuesday—106 cases (11.7%); Wednesday—101 cases (11.1%); Thursday—114 cases (12.6%); Friday—137 cases (15.1%); Saturday—198 cases (21.8%).

If we rearrange the week and begin with Friday, thereby including the first weekend evening in our weekend calculations, then the following distribution results: Friday—137 cases or 15.1%; Saturday—198 cases or 21.8%; Sunday—139 cases or 15.3%.

The weekend murder totals are 474 cases or 52.2 percent, clearly showing that over half of all murders during the years 1943 to 1983 in Buffalo and Erie County took place on the weekend. This is, of course, by no means surprising if we keep in mind that murder is most often a family affair or occurs between friends and acquaintances. Thus, the present study revealed that 10 percent of all killers murdered their spouse, 11 percent murdered other relatives, five percent murdered "lovers," 16 percent murdered friends and nine percent murdered neighbors and coworkers. Thus, fully 70 percent of killers murdered someone they knew. Strangers were murdered in only 30 percent of all cases.

It is also significant that murder decreases to an all-week low on Wednesday and increases to an all-week high on Saturday. Undoubtedly this pattern of behavior is related to the use of leisure time, the cycle of work and drinking behavior and the availability of potential victims on the weekend. Thus, Saturday exhibits twice as much murder as Wednesday, the day furthest removed from Saturday, a day on which few Americans work and a day when families get together both for shopping and leisure time activities during the day and for partying at night.

Day of week vs. hour of day. Murders occurring on weekends are more likely to occur between 9:30 P.M. and 5:30 A.M. than murders occurring on weekdays. Examples: 53.4 percent of murders occurring on Friday through Sunday occurred between 9:30 P.M. and 5:30 A.M.; and 42.9 percent of murders occurring on Monday through Thursday occurred between 9:30 P.M. & 5:30 A.M.

This phenomenon is related to a number of assumptions and beliefs current in American culture. The first of these is the belief that the cycle of activities should be based on a seven-day week. This is an ancient belief, mainly derived from numerous Middle Eastern cultures and perpetuated in the Jewish religion through the story of creation as told in *Genesis*. When, in the third century, *Genesis* also became a part of the Christian scriptures, the custom of basing the cycle of human activities upon the seven-day week became the common inheritance of Western civilization, a custom later adopted by peoples such as the Japanese who do not share in the Judeo-Christian tradition.

While there is no physical or natural law demanding the existence of a seven-day week, belief has anchored this custom so firmly in the psyche of mankind that so far no effort to "reform" the calendar or alter this custom has ever succeeded — nor is it likely to succeed. Hence, Saturday and Sunday have been designated the "weekend" not only in the chronological sense of that word, but more so in the sense that the "weekend" implies a round of activities which are designated as expected or normative by those who adhere to the seven-day calendar.

In the Western industrialized world, a world certainly including the United States, the weekend was at one time shorter than it is now. That is, Jews observed on the weekend their traditional Sabbath, from sundown Friday night until sundown on Saturday night. Christians observed "the Lord's Day," being Sunday. After the rise of labor unions had become effective in the 1930s and the work week was reduced to 40 hours or less, the weekend become longer.

In the United States, the weekend came to include Saturday as fewer and fewer people worked on that day. Saturday became a day devoted to sports events, shopping tours, family activities, etc. It came to augment Sunday in that it permitted families to do all those things which were either viewed as morally or legally impermissible on Sunday, such as drinking liquor, spending money or engaging in recreational activities. As puritanical views diminished in America and in Europe, these activities were also instituted on Sunday. These two days, and Friday evening, became long periods involving intense interaction within the circle of family and friends. From Friday night until Sunday evening, millions of Americans participate in various functions from drinking bouts to shopping sprees that involve those people most likely to become murder victims, that is relatives, friends and neighbors.

Numerous studies of murder in the United States have shown that up to 70 percent of all killings occur between persons who know one another, that 10 percent of these are the spouses of the killer and that the other 50 percent are other relatives, coworkers, neighbors and friends. It can therefore be accurately predicted that weekend murder will continue to be related to weekend activities because murder will continue to be related to weekend activities because murder is a cultural phenomenon imbedded in the American life style and supported by our norms (expectations) and mores. The relationship between murder, the hour of the day and the day of the week is also visible in connection with the frequency of evening murders on weekends.

Day of week vs. number of murderers by ethnicity of victim. White victims are more likely to be killed by groups of murderers on Tuesday through Saturday than on Sunday or Monday. Examples: 1.1 mean murderers for white victims on Sunday (42 cases) and Monday (43 cases); 1.3 mean murderers for white victims on Wednesday (36 cases) and Thursday (29 cases); 1.4 mean murderers for white victims for Tuesday (39 cases), Friday (48 cases) and Saturday (68 cases).

No adequate explanation for this phenomenon exists. While it is of course understandable in light of the foregoing that Friday and Saturday would involve groups of murderers more often than is true of the middle of the week, there is no real explanation for the relatively low rate of involvement by groups of murderers on Sunday. The use of means such as 1.1 on Sunday refers to the fact that two or more persons committed some killings and that the average number of killers, when there was more than one, came to 1.1, 1.3 or 1.4.

Day of week vs. ethnicity of murderer by ethnicity of victim. Interracial murders are less common on Sunday than other days. Examples: 4 of 69 (5.8%) murders involving either a black murderer and white victim or white murderer and black victim occurred on Sunday; 102 of 577 (17.7%) murders involving a black murderer and black victim or white murderer and white victim occurred on Sunday.

The reason for the low rate of interracial murders on Sunday as compared to intraracial murders on Sunday is the amount of business activity on that day. Almost all interracial killings involve robberies in which black robbers hold up white-owned stores and kill the owners. Since stores are almost always closed on Sunday, it is not surprising that interracial killings are so infrequent on that day.

Day of week vs. sex of murderer by ethnicity of victim. Black victims killed by women are more likely to be killed on a weekend than black victims killed by men. Examples: 135 of 296 (45.6%) black victims who were killed by men were killed on Monday through Thursday; 21 of 62 (33.9%) black victims who were killed by women were killed on Monday through Thursday.

The reason for this difference is relationship and location. Since men are much more often available for killing on the weekends when they are home, it is not surprising that women can kill men more often between Friday and Sunday than between Monday and Thursday.

Day of week vs. sex of murderer by age of victim. Women who kill victims aged 40–49 are more likely than men who kill victims in the same age range to kill their victims on Saturday. Nineteen of 91 (20.9%) victims aged 40–49 of male killers were killed on Saturday; 10 of 21 (47.6%) victims aged 40–49 of female killers were killed on Saturday.

This discrepancy once more affirms the relationship between the killer and the victim and the availability of the victim to the killer. Older men are more likely to stay home than younger men. Older men are also more likely to be married than younger men. Thus, more husbands are available for killing on Saturday than is true of unmarried men who are more often younger than married men.

Day of week vs. sex of victim by age of victim. Male victims aged 40–49 are more likely to die on Saturday than female victims in the same age range: 28 of 100 (28.0%) male victims age 40–49 are killed on Saturday; and 5 of 34 (14.7%) female victims age 40–49 are killed on Saturday.

Exposure to a situation which has a high murder potential is much more likely on Saturday for males than females. This is the case because fewer men work on Saturday than on other days, a situation also true of females. However, men are more likely to commit robberies on Saturday, to enter bars and other public places and to be available for murder at home.

We hold that the excessive number of murders of men on Saturday are related to higher male mobility than female mobility. This means that men are more likely found in situations which produce murder than is true of women, particularly during leisure time.

Day of week vs. ethnicity of victim. White victims are more likely to be murdered on Monday than black victims. Black victims are disproportionately more likely to be murdered on Sunday than white victims. Examples: 70 of 401 black victims were murdered on Sunday; 51 of 389 white victims were murdered on Sunday; 41 of 401 black victims were murdered on Monday; 58 of 389 white victims were murdered on Monday.

The poor spend a great deal more time in public places than do people with more affluence. Therefore, blacks are more likely to spend their time in bars and taverns on Sunday than is true of whites. Hence, the kinds of altercations that occur in public places and result in murder will involve blacks more often on Sunday than it will involve whites on Sunday.

Obviously, those who were murdered on Sunday cannot be murdered over again on Monday. Therefore, the animosities that lead to murder have been "taken care of" in the black community by perpetrating Sunday murders. Hence, the murder of a black is somewhat less frequent on Monday than is true of the murder of a white.

Day of week vs. age of victim. Victims murdered on weekends are younger, on the average, than victims murdered on weekdays. The mean age of victims on Friday is 35 (133 cases); Saturday, 35 (195 cases); Sunday, 34 (134 cases). The mean age on Monday is 36 (109 cases); Tuesday, 36 (103 cases); Wednesday, 41 (100 cases); Thursday, 38 (112 cases).

This undoubtedly reflects the greater mobility of young victims over older victims. Since older persons are more likely to be married than is true of younger persons, the younger visitors to bars and other places of recreation increase their risk of murder over the older persons who are more likely to stay home or go out in the company of their spouse.

HOUR OF DAY

Hour of day vs. day of week *see* Day of week, page 210.

PLACE

Zone of occurrence of murder vs. column inches of newspaper coverage *see* Column inches, page 200.

Zone of occurrence of murder vs. year *see* Year, page 206.

Zone of occurrence vs. temperature. Murders which occur in far suburbs and rural areas tend to occur on days with a higher average temperature than murders which occur in other areas of the county. Examples: 53.6° mean average temperature for far suburb and rural murders (50 cases); 46.9° mean average temperature for downtown murders (130 cases).

The reason for this phenomenon is that people who live in semirural and rural areas are far less likely to remain indoors in hot weather than people who live in cities where air-conditioning is more common than in rural areas. Even with air conditioning, rural persons are more likely to go outdoors on hot days than are city people because the outdoors are more accessible and enjoyable in rural areas than in cities. Since people who go outdoors are more available for murder than people who remain indoors, hot weather causes more murder in rural areas.

Zone of murder vs. relationship between murderer and victim. It is highly likely that a downtown murder is committed by someone unknown to the victim. It is highly likely that a murder committed in the suburbs near the city are committed by a relative of the victim. Examples: 29 of 94 (30.9%) of murders downtown involved strangers; 5 of 40 (12.5%) of murders committed in far suburbs or rural areas involved strangers; 16 of 66 (24.2%) of murders in near suburbs involved relatives; 4 of 94 (4.3%) of murders downtown involved relatives.

About 28 percent of all murders in Buffalo and Erie County recorded in the *Courier-Express* during the years 1943–1983 involved strangers. This finding coincides with the additional finding that 31 percent of downtown murders also involved strangers, since strangers are met most often in downtown areas, particularly in bars, hotels, bowling alleys and other commercial recreational facilities. The most common cause of murder in such encounters is "sudden anger" usually revolving around perceived insults. This has been well documented in a variety of homicide studies in numerous American cities over a number of years.

The involvement of relatives and strangers in the homicide situation in the proportions listed above reflects the same conditions and prerequistes for murder as does the proportion of strangers murdered, and just discussed. Thus, fewer strangers are encountered in suburban or rural situations than is true of downtown areas, while relatives are far more accessible to be murdered in a suburban or rural home than in a recreational facility. In short, each observation in the above sequence fits the other observations and for the same reasons.

Zone of murder vs. age of victim by relationship between murderer and victim. Where murder is committed by a stranger, the victim of a downtown murder tends to be older than the victim of an uptown murder. Examples: 47 years is the mean age of victims of downtown murders committed by strangers (28 cases); 34 years is the mean age of victims of outlying residential murders committed by strangers (21 cases).

Since strangers are most often murdered in recreational facilities, we can safely conclude that recreational facilities that are located downtown are more often visited by older persons than is true of suburban recreational facilities. Men are also more likely to visit such facilities than are women. Since men are the most common victim, older men are more often murdered by strangers downtown, and younger men are more often murdered by strangers uptown.

One reason for this age differential is that older men are more likely to live downtown than younger men. This comes about because the suburbs have been built more recently than the downtown areas, and therefore the suburbs contain more young persons who were born there and never lived downtown. Many of those who live downtown have been there since birth when there were no suburbs, or very few. In addition, older men who are single or divorced are less likely to have a parental home in which to live at the average age of 47 than are younger men whose average at becoming murder victims is 34.

TEMPERATURE

Average temperature of day vs. year of murder *see* Year, page 206.

Average temperature of day vs. ethnicity of victim. On the average, black victims are murdered at higher temperatures than white victims. Examples: 50.4° average temperature of days on which a black was murdered (392 cases); 46.0° average temperature of days on which a white was murdered (382 cases).

The reason for this discrepancy between the races is poverty, that is, the lower income of blacks. Evidently, blacks are more likely to live in overcrowded conditions than whites and are less likely to have air-conditioning available to them. Therefore, blacks are more easily annoyed by overcrowding intensified by heat. In addition, blacks are more likely than whites to be outdoors in great heat, and are therefore more likely to be available for murder than whites.

Average temperature of day vs. age of victim. Younger victims tend to be murdered on hotter days. Examples: 49° expected average temperature for 20-year-old victims; 46° expected average temperature for 70-year-old victims.

Younger people are more mobile than older people. Therefore, younger people are more exposed to the possibility of becoming the victim of strangers in violent situations in bars, taverns and other places of public entertainment. Since younger people are poorer than older persons who are more likely to own their homes, have cars and air conditioners, younger people are more exposed to the possibility of becoming the victims of murder than is true of older people because they are more often in the company of potential murderers who are also younger people.

Average temperature of day vs. age of murderer by age of victim. As seen from the discussion immediately preceding this paragraph, older victims tend to be murdered on relatively cool days. When one controls for this negative correlation between the temperature and the victim's age, however, it turns out that, if two victims of the same age are murdered by two different murderers, chances are that the older murderer will murder his victim on the hotter day.

Examples of expected values: 49° for 40-year-old murderer; 47° for 20-year-old murderer.

There is a higher proportion of murder in the course of another crime on cooler days than on warmer days. Where an older person is murdered by a younger person, another crime is a common motive. On warmer days, jealousy murder becomes more common. Where an older person is murdered by another older person, jealousy is a common motive.

Average temperature of day vs. apparent motive. On hot days, more people are motivated by jealousy to murder than on cooler days. On cool days, murderers are disproportionately motivated by victim precipitation and murder in the course of other crimes. Examples: 53.6° mean for jealousy (74 cases); 45.0° mean for murder in the course of other crimes (189 cases); 44.9° mean for victim precipitation (76 cases).

Jealousy murders occur between relatives and friends. Therefore it is reasonable to view such murders as occurring within the family and among lovers. Such murders occur more often in the summer because the potential victims are more available than in the winter. Murder occurs mostly during leisure hours and in circumstances relating to leisure activities. In the summer, such activities involve the family more than in the winter when there is a greater attendance at bars, bowling alleys and other recreational facilities. It is in such facilities that potential killers and their victims meet each other. Thus, victim precipitation occurs more often in a bar than elsewhere as the victim starts a fight which the other participant finishes by murder. The same is true of rape, the "other crime" which precedes murder so often. The victim meets the potential killer in a bar and then allows him to take her home or drive her in his car. This is less likely in hot temperatures in Erie County because fewer women are in bars and, therefore, fewer are exposed to the possibility of rape and murder.

NUMBER OF MURDERERS

Number of murderers vs. column inches *see* Column inches, page 198.

Number of murderers vs. marital status of murderer by sex of murderer. A single male murderer is more likely to kill as part of a group than a married male murderer. Examples: 1.24 murderers per murder for male single murderers (170 cases); 1.09 murderers per murder for male married murderers (99 cases).

Single men are more likely to have single friends, particularly a group of male friends. Therefore, they and their friends are more likely to undertake any activity as a group than are married men whose membership in friendship groups is far more likely to include married couples, but not a whole lot of single men. The line from an old song, "those wedding bells are breaking up that old gang of mine," is literally true in the instance of gang or group murder.

Number of murderers vs. age of victim. Older victims are more likely to be murdered by groups of murderers than younger victims. Younger victims are more likely to be murdered by individual murderers. Examples of expected values: 1.34 murderers per murder for 70-year-old victim; 1.15 murderers per murder for 20-year-old victim.

If it is true that younger men are more likely to be associated with groups of other young men, then it follows that younger men cannot be easily entrapped into a murder situation alone. They "hang" with their friends, particularly in situations in which gangs are congregating.

Older men seldom have gangs of friends. Hence they can be more easily victimized alone. The reverse is also true. Younger men are more available for murder on a one-on-one basis and can be more easily murdered alone than in their group. Older men are more often alone, not only because they have fewer male gang members with them than do younger men, but also because the old are much more often alone than are the young in our "gerontophobic" society. People who are murdered by gangs are generally alone because gangs will succeed in murdering a lone person.

Number of murderers vs. marital status of murderer by sex of victim. A single murderer who kills a male victim is more likely to murder as part of a group than a married murderer who kills a male victim. Examples: 1.30 murderers per murder of male victims where murderer is single (132 cases); 1.15 murderers per murder of male victims where murderer is married (67 cases). As explained above, single men have more single friends who travel in groups.

Number of murderers vs. relationship between victim and murderer. Groups of murderers are more often unknown to their victims than individual murderers. Examples:

1.63 mean murderers when murderer is stranger (137 cases)

1.45 mean murderers when murderer is police (11 cases)

1.30 mean murderers when murderer is coworker (20 cases)

1.27 mean murderers when murderer is casual acquaintance (116 cases)

1.08 mean murderers when murderer is relative (77 cases)

1.05 mean murderers when murderer is neighbor (44 cases)

1.00 mean murderers when murderer is lover (37 cases)

1.00 mean murderers when murderer is spouse (74 cases)

This is true because one-on-one murders take place between friends and family, motivated by jealousy, sudden anger and drinking together. All these motives occur in "close-knit" situations. Drug related murders, however, are connected with business situations and therefore groups of persons all interested in drug profits. Robberies are committed by groups of robbers who gain courage by association and who like to rob individuals who travel alone, i.e., single persons.

Number of murderers vs. ethnicity of victim. White victims are more often killed by groups of murderers than black victims. Examples: 1.31 mean murderers when victim is white (306 cases); 1.14 mean murderers when victim is black (358 cases).

The chances that a white person has money or other valuables worth stealing or robbing are much better than the chances that this would be true of a black man. Therefore, groups of robbers are more likely to kill whites than blacks.

Number of murderers vs. sex of victim. Male victims are more often killed by groups of murderers than are female victims. Examples: 1.25 mean murderers when victim is male (540 cases); 1.10 mean murderers when victim is female (222 cases).

Males have more money and are more often in control of valuables than are women. Furthermore, men are more often charged with guarding valuables, whether as police, private guards or otherwise. Therefore, males are more often murdered by groups of robbers than are females.

Number of murderers vs. marital status of victim by sex of victim. A married male victim is more likely to be murdered by a group than a single male victim. Examples: 1.40 murderers per murder of male married victims (97 cases); 1.22 murderers per murder of male single victims (166 cases).

This is true because married males are more likely to own stores and other businesses and are therefore more often victims of robbery murders. This should be viewed as a proportionate issue. That means that single men are murdered more often than married men and that the murders of single men occur more often in a one-on-one conflict situation. Hence the proportion of single men killed by groups is less because the number killed is greater.

Number of murderers vs. zone of victim's residence. Victims who live in outlying residential areas and near suburbs are more likely to be murdered by groups than victims who live in other areas. Victims who live in far suburbs or rural areas, or who live in the residential area surrounding downtown, are more likely to be murdered by individuals.

Examples: 1.35 mean murderers when victim lives in outlying city residential area (105 cases); 1.31 mean murderers when victim lives in near suburbs (80 cases); 1.18 mean murderers when victim lives in far suburbs or rural areas (38 cases); 1.15 mean murderers when victim lives in residential area surrounding downtown (382 cases).

This phenomenon is once more the outcome of robbery murders which occur much more often in residential areas where there is something worth robbing.

Number of murderers vs. weapon. Hands and blunt instruments are more often used by groups of murderers than by individuals. Knives are almost the sole province of individual killers. Examples: 1.37 mean murderers when hands used (94 cases); 1.31 mean murderers when club, bludgeon, or hammer used (36 cases); 1.11 mean murderers when switchblade or stiletto used (125 cases); 1.03 mean murderers when kitchen knife used (88 cases).

Groups of killers are often gangs who sought to give someone a beating. These beatings then resulted in the death of the victim, hence murder. Individual killers are much more likely to have used a knife because beatings by only one person do not result in death as frequently as beatings by several persons. A knifing by one person, however, can easily result in death.

Number of murderers vs. apparent motive. Drug dealing and other crimes are most commonly the motive of group murderers. Jealousy and victim-precipitated murders are almost always carried out by individuals. Examples: 2.27 mean murderers when motive is drug dealing (11 cases); 1.60 mean murderers when murder committed in course of another crime (146 cases); 1.03 mean murderers when victim precipitated (77 cases); 1.00 mean murderers when motivation is jealousy (75 cases).

It would be peculiar for a group to feel jealous towards one victim, and equally bizarre for any one person to precipitate a fight with a whole group. Therefore, these motives are absent from group killings and present in individual killings. Drug dealing, however, almost always involves groups of persons as the drug business, like any business, is dependent on the division of labor.

Number of murderers vs. disposition of case. Groups of murderers are tried by jury more often than solo murderers. Examples: 1.35 mean murderers for cases tried by a jury (250 cases); 1.12 mean murderers for cases tried by a judge (223 cases).

If it is true that all members of a group of murderers must accept a jury trial if any one of them demands a jury trial, then the outcome must be that groups of murderers will more often be tried by a jury than a judge.

220   Appendix

ETHNICITY OF MURDERER

Ethnicity of murderer by ethnicity of victim vs. column inches
see Column inches, page 202.
Ethnicity of murderer by ethnicity of victim vs. day of week *see*
Day of week, page 212.
Ethnicity of murderer vs. year *see* Year, page 206.

Ethnicity of murderer vs. sex of murderer. Female murderers are
more likely to be black women than white women. Examples: 66 of 424 (15.6%)
black murderers are female; 19 of 256 (7.4%) white murderers are female; 1 of
24 (4.2%) Hispanic murderers are female.

This is the consequence of status differences for women within the black community and the white community as well as the dangers with which each community
presents to its women. Thus, there are many more black women who are heads of
households than there are white women whom must rear children alone. Black
women have more reason to be violent than white women, because black women
must defend themselves more often than do white women. This need for self
defense is further enhanced in the black community because blacks are more
violent than are whites, so that black women see more violence at any time and are
more likely than whites to have been raised in a violent family. In sum, differences
in experience concerning violence create this differential.

Ethnicity of murderer vs. marital status of murderer. Black
murderers are more likely to be single than white murderers. Examples: 112 of 175
(64.0%) of black murderers are single; 68 of 152 (44.7%) of white murderers are
single.

There are more single men among blacks than is true among whites. Therefore,
black murderers are also more often single than are white murderers.

**Ethnicity of murderer vs. relationship between murderer and
victim.** White murderers are disproportionately likely to be a relative or spouse
of the victim. Black murderers are disproportionately likely to be a lover or
neighbor of the victim. Examples:

45 of 236 (19.1%) of white murderers are relatives of victim
24 of 332 (7.2%) of black murderers are relatives of victim
34 of 236 (14.4%) of white murderers are spouses of victim
30 of 332 (9.0%) of black murderers are spouses of victim
10 of 236 (4.2%) of white murderers are neighbors of victim
30 of 332 (9.0%) of black murderers are neighbors of victim
5 of 236 (2.1%) of white murderers are lovers of victim
26 of 332 (7.8%) of black murderers are lovers of victim

Marriage costs money, resulting in a larger number of black singles who live
with a person of the opposite sex without marriage than is true among whites.

Therefore, whites are more likely to murder a spouse than are blacks. Because the white family is more stable than the black family, whites also have more relatives and are visited more often by relatives than are blacks, whose relatives are more often out-of-town or moving about. The rate of mobility for blacks is a good deal greater than is true for whites, hence relatives are not as accessible for murder as are white relatives.

Ethnicity of murderer vs. ethnicity of victim. Murder victims usually are of the same ethnic background as their killers. Examples: 234 of 244 (95.9%) of white murderers killed white victims; 344 of 408 (84.3%) of black murderers killed black victims; 16 of 20 (80.0%) Hispanic murderers killed Hispanic victims.

There is no doubt about this. Obviously this is true because persons of the same ethnicity live in the same neighborhoods are more often available for murder than is true of nonrelated persons.

Ethnicity of murderer vs. age of victim by relationship between murderer and victim. When a white murderer kills a relative or a spouse, it is likely that his victim will be older than the victim of a black murderer who kills a relative or a spouse. When a white murderer kills a stranger or a friend, it is probable that his victim will be younger than the victim of a black murderer who kills a stranger or a friend. Examples:

34 is the mean age of people murdered by white relatives (44 cases)
19 is the mean age of people murdered by black relatives (24 cases)
38 is the mean age of people murdered by their white spouses (34 cases)
34 is the mean age of people murdered by their black spouses (29 cases)
29 is the mean age of people murdered by their white friends (41 cases)
34 is the mean age of people murdered by their black friends (57 cases)
39 is the mean age of people murdered by white strangers (43 cases)
46 is the mean age of people murdered by black strangers (80 cases)

Whites get married at an older age than is true of blacks. This is so because whites are more often interested in finishing their education or attaining economic advancement before marrying than is true of blacks. Therefore, the spouses of white killers are older than the spouses of black killers. Since whites who are younger are not married, the killers of younger whites, as well as their victims, are not married. Older victims among whites are married more often than unmarried.

Ethnicity of murderer vs. sex of victim. White murderers are more likely to kill female victims than black murderers: 87 of 256 (34.0%) victims of white murderers are female; 105 of 423 (24.8%) victims of black murderers are female.

White murder is proportionately less frequent than black murder. When it does occur, it is more often the outcome of jealousy and family disputes than altercations in bars and other places of public recreation. Therefore, whites kill their wives more often than is true of blacks if we consider the killing of spouses as a proportion of all killings by either race.

Ethnicity of murderer vs. survivors of victims. When a murderer is white, the chances of the victim leaving a spouse and child behind are greater than when a murderer is black. Examples: 48 of 130 (36.9%) white murderers left a spouse and child surviving the victim; 23 of 105 (21.9%) black murderers left a spouse and child surviving the victim.

Since whites are more often married than is true of blacks, they of course are more likely to leave a spouse behind at death.

Ethnicity of murderer vs. apparent motive. A higher proportion of white murderers than black murderers are considered insane. Motives substantially more common for blacks than for whites are business dealings, sudden anger, and victim precipitation. Examples:

16 of 212 (7.5%) of white murderers were insane

5 of 343 (1.5%) of black murderers were insane

9 of 212 (4.2%) of white murderers were motivated by business dealings

37 of 343 (10.8%) of black murderers were motivated by business dealings

46 of 212 (21.7%) of whites were murdered due to sudden anger

96 of 343 (28.0%) of blacks were murdered due to sudden anger

20 of 212 (9.4%) of murders by whites were victim precipitated

46 of 343 (13.4%) of murders by blacks were victim precipitated

The insanity defense depends on the availability of a skilled lawyer. Such services cost money, meaning that whites are more likely to use the insanity defense than blacks.

Ethnicity of murderer vs. sentence. Whites are more likely than blacks to be sentenced to a psychiatric hospital. Blacks are more likely than whites to be given probation. Examples: 20 of 142 white murderers were sentenced to a psychiatric hospital; 3 of 242 black murderers were sentenced to a psychiatric hospital; 8 of 142 white murderers were sentenced to probation; 22 of 242 black murderers were sentenced to probation.

Because the insanity defense is costly and is more often used by whites than blacks, whites are more frequently sent to psychiatric hospitals. Blacks are more often given probation for murder than is possible for whites because the lives of black victims are not held in the same esteem as the lives of white victims. The amount of publicity given to blacks is far less than that given to whites. That alone prevents probation for white killers.

SIMILARITIES BETWEEN MULTIPLE MURDERERS

Where there is more than one murderer involved in a murder, all murderers tend to be of the same age. Where the first murderer listed is 20 years old, the expected age of the second murderer in the group is 21.0 years old, and the expected age of the third murderer is 21.5 years old. Where the first murderer is 40 years old, the expected age of the second murderer is 37.5 years old, and the expected age of the third murderer is 36.3 years old.

Other similarities are: 131 of 135 second and third murderers in a group were of the same ethnicity as the first reported murderer; 110 of 120 second and third murderers in a group lived in the same residential zone as the first reported murderer; 44 of 44 second and third murderers in a group had the same marital status as the first reported murderer; 24 of 28 second and third murderers in a group were in the same occupational category as the first reported murderer; and 116 of 119 second and third murderers in a group had the same relationship to the victim as the first reported murderer.

It is evident that murder is an in-group activity. There are several reasons for this, the most important being the affinity which people of the same age have for each other, particularly in our agist society. Not only murder, but almost all activities in the United States are conducted within the same cohort (age group). This is also true for people of the same ethnicity and hence the same residential area, since people tend to live in areas having a population of similar ethnicity.

Occupational segregation is also not foreign to us. Many people interact a great deal with those of the same occupation, simply because they meet each other at work.

SIMILARITIES BETWEEN MULTIPLE VICTIMS

Where there is more than one victim of a murder, all victims tend to be of the same age. Where the first reported victim is 20 years old, the expected age of the second victim is 19.1 years old. Where the first reported victim is 70 years old, the expected age of the second reported victim is 60.1 years old.

Other similarities: 49 of 52 second and third victims are of the same ethnicity as the first reported victim; and 36 of 47 second and third victims lived in the same residential zone as the first reported victim.

The same comments apply to victims as to perpetrators.

AGE OF MURDERER

Age of murderer by age of victim vs. temperature *see* Temperature, page 216.

Age of murderer vs. age of victim. Younger murderers murder very young children, young adults, and older adults. Older murderers murder older children and middle-aged adults. Examples:

26 is the expected age of a murderer of a two-year-old child

32 is the expected age of a murderer of a seven-year-old child

26 is the expected age of a murderer of a 20-year-old victim

37 is the expected age of a murderer of a 50-year-old victim
26 is the expected age of a murderer of a 70-year-old victim
Very young children and the old are generally in the care of younger adults and therefore targets for possible murder. Young adults associate with others of their age group and hence murder them as well. Older murderers are more often in the company of persons of their age groups and therefore are more likely to murder older victims. This is also true of children. Older murderers have children who are older than is true of younger adult murderers. Children are most often killed by their own parents. Hence the age differential remains the same and thus, the older killer kills older children.

Age of murderer vs. relationship between murderer and victim. Murderers of spouses and neighbors tend to be older. Murderers of strangers tend to be younger. Examples: 39.0 mean age of spouse murderer (72 cases); 37.6 mean age of neighbor murderer (42 cases); 25.1 mean age of stranger murderer (137 cases).

Younger people are more mobile than older people. Younger murderers are mostly young single men who are involved in an altercation in a bar, restaurant or other place of public entertainment. Older men are more often married than is true of young men, meaning older men are more likely to have a spouse whom they can murder. Furthermore, because they are at home more, older men meet the neighbors more often than is true of younger men, and hence are more likely to have an opportunity to murder neighbors. Moreover, younger single men are more likely to live in large, impersonal apartment houses, while older married men are more often living in residential neighborhoods where neighbors visit, talk and become acquainted. Since murder occurs much more often among people who know each other than among strangers, younger people are more likely to murder strangers than is true of older people.

Age of murderer vs. sex of victim. More female victims are murdered by older murderers than are male victims: 30.4 is the mean age of murderers of males (528 cases); 32.7 the mean age of murderers of females (216 cases).

Older men are more jealous than are younger men because older men are less certain that they can attract another female if they are abandoned by their "significant other" woman. Furthermore, older men are much more likely to have a younger female "significant other," but have male friends of the same age group.

Age of murderer vs. residence of victim. Victims who live downtown or out of town are murdered by older murderers more often than victims who live in other neighborhoods. Examples: 35 is the mean age of murderers of victims who live downtown (87 cases); 35 the mean age of murderers of victims who live out of town (30 cases); 29 the mean age of murderers of victims who live in suburbs near city (79 cases); 29 the mean age of murderers of victims who live in far suburbs or rural areas (36 cases).

Age of murderer vs. occupation of victim. White collar victims are typically killed by younger murderers than are blue collar or unemployed victims. Examples:

21.8 mean age of murderer who kills a professional (13 cases)
23.4 mean age of murderer who kills a student (32 cases)
26.4 mean age of murderer who kills a managerial victim (39 cases)
32.0 mean age of murderer who kills a laborer (42 cases)
33.1 mean age of murderer who kills an unemployed victim (13 cases)

Age of murderer vs. apparent motive. The oldest murderers kill disproportionately often due to victim precipitation or jealousy. The youngest murderers murder disproportionately often due to gang war, accident, other crime, or drug dealing. Examples:

36.7 mean age of murderer for victim precipitation (74 cases)
34.9 mean age of murderer for jealousy (75 cases)
25.4 mean age of murderer for drug dealing (11 cases)
24.0 mean age of murderer for other crime (142 cases)
23.6 mean age of murderer for accident (11 cases)
19.6 mean age of murderer for gang war (18 cases)

This is due to the greater frequency with which younger people get involved in gang warfare, reckless driving and robbery than older people. Jealousy and victim precipitation occur more among older persons than younger persons because younger people are more confident of being sexually attractive than are older persons. Victim precipitation means that the defendant was adjudicated "not guilty." Therefore it is possible that older defendants have more money to hire better lawyers thus increasing the number of "not guilty" verdicts concerning them and hence creating the impression of victim precipitation to a larger extent than is true of younger, poorer defendants.

Age of murderer vs. conviction of suspect. Younger suspects are more likely to be convicted than older suspects. Examples: 29.9 mean age of suspects convicted (439 cases); 35.3 mean age of suspects acquitted (63 cases).

This supports the above contention of lawyers and the outcome of a criminal procedure.

Age of murderer vs. sentence. If convicted, younger murderers are more likely to be sent to prison than older murderers. Examples: 35.4 mean age of murderers sentenced to probation (36 cases); 32.8 mean age of murderers sentenced to psychiatric hospital (27 cases); 23.3 mean age of murderers sentenced to prison (356 cases).

Younger convicts have cheaper lawyers, older convicts have more expensive lawyers. Therefore, younger convicts go to prison more often.

SEX OF MURDERER

Sex of murderer by ethnicity of victim vs. day of week *see* Day of week, page 212.

Sex of murderer by age of victim vs. day of week *see* Day of week, page 212.

Sex of murderer by disposition vs. year *see* Year, page 207.

Sex of murderer vs. ethnicity of murderer *see* Ethnicity of murderer, page 220.

Sex of murderer by relationship between murderer and victim vs. age of victim. Females murder younger relatives than do males. Females murder older spouses than do males. Examples: 32 the mean age of relative killed by male murderer (57 cases); 14 the mean age of relative killed by female murderer (18 cases); 34 the mean age of wife killed by her husband (51 cases); 42 the mean age of husband killed by his wife (22 cases).

Women are more often in charge of children than are men. Therefore the proportion of children murdered by women is greater than the proportion of children murdered by men. Consequently, the mean age of relatives killed by women is lower than the mean age of relatives killed by men. Since women are generally married to men older than themselves and, ipso facto, men are married to women younger than themselves, females murder spouses older than themselves.

Sex of murderer by ethnicity of victim vs. age of victim. White victims of female murderers are typically younger than white victims of male murderers: 38 is the mean age of white victims of male murderers (282 cases), and 29 is the mean age of white victims of female murderers (25 cases).

This is true because females have greater opportunity to murder children than is true of men.

Sex of murderer vs. marital status of murderer. Female murderers are more often married than male murderers. Examples: 99 of 289 (34.3%) male murderers were married; 41 of 70 (58.6%) female murderers were married.

Women are much more inclined to murder their spouse rather than a stranger. Female murderers are often provoked to commit murder by abusive spouses, and such murders frequently take place with a weapon belonging to the abusing husband.

Sex of murderer vs. relationship between murderer and victim. Female murderers more commonly kill spouses and lovers than do males. Males more often kill strangers than do females. Examples: 14 of 86 (16.3%) females killed lovers; 23 of 546 (4.2%) of males killed lovers; 23 of 86 (26.7%) females killed their husbands; 51 of 546 (9.3%) males killed their wives; 3 of 86 (3.5%) females killed strangers; 138 of 546 (25.3%) males killed strangers.

The killing of strangers and coworkers is related to male "machismo," that is, pride and sudden anger. Furthermore, men are more likely to visit places of public recreation such as bars, pool halls, etc., where altercations between them are common. This is very unlikely among women. Therefore, the opportunity and occasion to murder strangers is far less common among females than males.

Sex of murderer vs. ethnicity of victim. Female murderers kill blacks more often than male murderers kill blacks: 62 of 89 (69.7%) female murderers killed black victims; 296 of 606 (48.9%) male murderers killed black victims.

Females seldom participate in robbery killings and do not participate in rape killings. Therefore, their murders are nearly entirely of the domestic variety. Hence, females kill almost only within the circle of family and friends, meaning they kill within their own ethnic group. Thus, black female killers kill blacks more often than do black male murderers who do sometimes kill whites in the course of robberies and sexual assaults.

Sex of murderer vs. sex of victim. While both sexes of murderers kill males more often, a higher proportion of female murderers kill males than do male murderers: 85 of 99 (85.9%) female murderers killed males; 462 of 668 (69.2%) male murderers killed males.

Female killers kill males more often because males also kill females in greater number than do females. Females kill their spouses and lovers in self defense much more frequently than is true in reverse.

Sex of murderer vs. weapon used. Murders with a club or bludgeon are almost always performed by males. Kitchen knives are disproportionately used by females. Examples: 36 of 38 (94.7%) users of club or bludgeon were male; 58 of 89 (65.2%) users of kitchen knife were male.

The use of a club or bludgeon demands are muscle strength than many females possess. Kitchen knives are more available to women than other weapons because women are more often involved in doing kitchen work.

Sex of murderer vs. apparent motive. Almost all murders committed in the course of another crime, or attributable to business dealings, are committed by males. Females commit a disproportionate share of victim-precipitated murders. Examples: 146 of 150 (97.3%) murders committed in the course of another crime were committed by males; 46 of 48 (95.8%) murders attributable to business dealings were committed by males; 46 of 77 (59.7%) victim-precipitated murders were committed by males.

Robbery and rape are almost solely male crimes. The phrase "victim precipitated" means here that the killer was adjudicated innocent by reason of self defense. This happens to women much more often than to men, because so many female killers murder men who have abused them.

Sex of suspect vs. disposition of case. Female suspects more commonly have their cases dismissed before trial than do male suspects. Examples: 230 of 460 (50%) male suspects are tried by jury; 20 of 66 (30.3%) female suspects are tried by jury; 34 of 460 (7.4%) male suspects have case dismissed before trial; 16 of 66 (24.2%) female suspects have case dismissed before trial. This is again a function of the abuse factor. Females can often prove that they killed because their victim mistreated and brutalized them.

Sex of murderer vs. sentence. Males more commonly are sent to prison than are females. Females are more commonly sentenced to probation than are males. Examples: 333 of 387 (86.0%) male murderers were sentenced to prison; 26 of 45 (57.8%) female murderers were sentenced to prison; 22 of 387 (5.7%) male murderers were sentenced to probation; 14 of 45 (31.1%) female murderers were sentenced to probation.

In part, this may be the result of "chivalry" as it existed at least during the early years of this study, between 1943–1973. In addition, the large number of female murders committed in self defense influences judges in sentencing even when a female killer is convicted.

RESIDENCE OF MURDERER

Residence of murderer by year vs. column inches *see* Column inches, page 198.

Zone of murderer's residence vs. year of murder *see* Year of murder, page 207.

Zone of murderer's residence vs. relationship between murderer and victim. Murderers living in the inner city are proportionately less likely to kill victims who are well known to them than are murderers living in the suburbs or rural areas. Examples:

16 of 64 (25.0%) murderers living downtown killed casual acquaintances
5 of 44 (11.4%) murderers living in near suburbs killed casual acquaintances
74 of 331 (22.4%) murderers living in residential area surrounding downtown killed strangers
5 of 36 (13.9%) murderers living in far suburbs or rural areas killed strangers
11 of 44 (25.0%) murderers living in near suburbs killed spouse
5 of 64 (7.8%) murderers living downtown killed spouse

People who live in the inner city are less likely to know very many people intimately than people living in the suburbs. Research has shown that the inner city poor do not have many friends outside their family and do not invite the few they have into their home because it is too expensive. Thus, inner city murderers are much more likely to meet people in places of public recreation and it is there that their murders take place.

Zone of murderer's residence vs. zone of victim's residence. Murderers and victims tend to live in the same area of the county, and 502 of 675 (74.4%) murderers lived in the same zone as their victims (6 categories). This is evidently explained by the far larger in-group murder rate than out-group murder rate.

Zone of murderer's residence vs. weapon used. The choice of weapon is largely determined by where a murderer lives. Downtown murderers disproportionately prefer handguns. Residents of the older suburbs near the city are more likely to use their hands than residents of other areas. People who live in far suburbs or rural areas are more likely, proportionately, to use rifles and shotguns than are killers in other areas. Examples:

20 of 77 (26.0%) murderers who live downtown used handguns

4 of 45 (8.9%) murderers who live in near suburbs used handguns

13 of 45 (28.9%) murderers who live in near suburbs used hands

3 of 38 (7.9%) murderers who live out of town used hands

11 of 37 (29.7%) murderers who live in far suburbs or rural areas used rifles or shotguns

14 of 77 (18.2%) murderers who live downtown used rifles or shotguns

Handguns are cheap and are therefore used more in poor areas than wealthy areas. Moreover, many people in the downtown areas believe that they need a handgun to protect themselves against the high crime rate in their area. This turns into an excess of murder because there are so many opportunities available to kill. Those who commit murder with their fists are mostly white men who beat their wives and female associates. Sometimes this becomes murder since any beating can kill the victim, even if not intended. Rifles and shotguns are hunting equipment and are used much more in the far suburbs because hunting opportunities are available.

Zone of murderer's residence vs. apparent motive. Murderers who live downtown are more likely to be motivated by business dealings than are murderers who live elsewhere. Murderers who live in near suburbs are commonly motivated by jealousy. Examples: 13 of 65 (20%) murderers living downtown were motivated by business dealings; 0 of 38 murderers living in near suburbs were motivated by business dealings; 10 of 38 (26.3%) of murderers living in near suburbs were motivated by jealousy; 1 of 30 (3.3%) of murderers living in far suburbs or rural areas were motivated by jealousy.

Downtown areas house many more single men than uptown areas. Therefore, jealousy killings are less common in downtown areas where triangles, involving females, are also less common than in areas where there are many more married couples: uptown, suburbs, etc. Consequently, other motives become proportionately greater as jealousy declines in importance.

Furthermore, business dealings are conducted more often downtown than elsewhere in any city. By "business dealings" is meant any interaction involving money. Thus, a poor, single murderer who kills a victim of the same background for a small sum is regarded as having been motivated by "business dealings." In addition, downtown is the business district and hence has more killings motivated by business dealings because such business as bowling alleys, bars, used clothing stores, etc., are available to the poor, even if they are not likely to enter expensive department stores.

Zone of suspect's residence vs. disposition of case. Inner city suspects are more likely to have their cases dismissed before trial than are suspects who live elsewhere. Non-city residents are unlikely to have their cases dismissed before trial. Examples: 37 of 356 (10.4%) residents of downtown and residential areas surrounding downtown had cases dismissed before trial; 2 of 58 (3.4%) residents of near and far suburbs or rural areas had cases dismissed before trial.

The dismissal rate for downtown residents is three times greater than it is for uptown residents. This is true because murder is so much more common among the poor who live in downtown areas that judges are hardened to murder cases, few attract much attention in the press and most are seen as "routine" by the police. Large proportions of the downtown cases occur among minority group members whose lives are not considered as important as the lives of majority group members. Killings in suburbs come before judges who have seldom seen murder and frequently attract a great deal of attention making dismissal impossible.

Zone of murderer's residence vs. sentence. Suburban murderers are more likely to be sentenced to a psychiatric hospital than are others. Downtown murderers are rarely sentenced to a psychiatric hospital. Examples: 1 of 42 (2.4%) residents of downtown were sentenced to psychiatric hospital; 7 of 44 (15.9%) residents of near and far suburbs or rural areas were sentenced to psychiatric hospital.

The introduction of psychiatric testimony and the entire idea of a psychiatric defense for murder is a middle- and upper middle-class phenomenon. This is true not only because it costs a good deal to hire a psychiatrist, but also because some education is needed to be acquainted with this type of defense and the uses of psychiatry.

MARITAL STATUS OF MURDERER

Marital status of murderer vs. year see Year, page 207.

Marital status of murderer by sex of murderer vs. number of murderers see Number of murderers, page 217.

Marital status of murderer vs. ethnicity of murderer see Ethnicity of murderer, page 220.

Marital status of murderer vs. sex of murderer see Sex of murderer, page 226.

Marital status of murderer vs. sex of victim by marital status of victim. A single murderer is more likely to murder a married male victim than a married female victim. A married murderer is more likely to murder a married female victim than a married male victim. Examples: 17 of 28 (60.7%) single murderers who murdered married victims murdered males; 30 of 85 (35.3%) married murderers who murdered married victims murdered males.

Married men are far more likely to murder females than is possible for single men who do not have a female readily available to murder.

Marital status of murderer vs. age of victim by relationship between murderer and victim. Single killers murder older relatives more than do married killers. Examples: 38 is the mean age of victims murdered by a single relative (17 cases); 20 is the mean age of victims murdered by a married relative (32 cases).

The lower average age of victims murdered by married relatives is the result of including children of the murderers.

Marital status of murderer vs. marital status of victim. Killers and victims tend to have the same marital status: 207 of 303 (68.3%) murderers are of the same marital status as victims (5 categories).

Once more it is evident that murder is an intra-family affair.

Marital status of murderer vs. relationship between murderer and victim. Single murderers are disproportionately likely to kill strangers or friends. Married murderers are disproportionately likely to kill mates or relatives. Examples:

52 of 179 (29.1%) single murderers killed strangers
4 of 133 (3.0%) married murderers killed strangers
42 of 179 (23.5%) single murderers killed friends
7 of 133 (5.3%) married murderers killed friends
17 of 179 (9.5%) single murderers killed relatives
33 of 133 (24.8%) married murderers killed relatives
18 of 179 (10.1%) single murderers killed lovers
70 of 133 (52.6%) married murderers killed spouses or lovers (67 spouses, 3 lovers)

Single murderers associate with strangers and friends because they have no mates. Married murderers murder mates and relatives (including children) because of availability of victims.

Marital status of murderer vs. apparent motive. Single murderers disproportionately kill in the course of another crime, as well as due to gang war and accident. Married murderers disproportionately kill due to sudden anger, jealousy and insanity. Examples:

49 of 154 (31.8%) single murderers' motive was another crime
3 of 119 (2.5%) married murderers' motive was another crime
12 of 154 (7.8%) single murderers' motive was gang war
0 of 119 married murderers' motive was gang war
8 of 154 (5.2%) single murderers' motive was accident
1 of 119 (0.8%) married murderers' motive was accident
6 of 154 (3.9%) single murderers' motive was insanity
9 of 119 (7.6%) married murderers' motive was insanity

17 of 154 (11.0%) single murderers' motive was jealousy
22 of 119 (18.5%) married murderers' motive was jealousy
31 of 154 (20.1%) single murders' motive was sudden anger
40 of 119 (33.6%) married murderers' motive was sudden anger

Murder within the family is obviously motivated by jealousy, promoted by sudden anger and labeled "insanity" among at least those who can afford a psychiatrist. All of this is hardly possible for the single, who are much more likely to be associated with violent crimes than are the married, solely because persons wishing to be so engaged are less likely to seek marriage and because the single are more exposed to the possibility of becoming involved in such crimes.

Marital status of murderer vs. sentence. Single murderers are more likely to receive a prison term than are married murderers. Examples: 10 of 125 (8.0%) single murderers sentenced to probation; 12 of 80 (15.0%) married murderers sentenced to probation; 7 of 125 (5.6%) single murderers sentenced to psychiatric hospital; 8 of 80 (10.0%) married murderers sentenced to psychiatric hospital; 103 of 125 (82.4%) single murderers sentenced to prison; 59 of 80 (73.8%) married murderers sentenced to prison.

Single men are seen as more dangerous, more unstable and more likely to engage in further crimes than the married. Judges, and the general public, view married persons as more reliable.

OCCUPATION OF MURDERER

Occupation of murderer vs. column inches *see* Column inches, page 200.

Occupation of murderer vs. year of murder *see* Year, page 208.

Occupation of murderer vs. occupation of victim. Murderers tend to kill victims who have the same occupation as the murderer: 33 of 94 (35.1%) murderers killed victims with the same occupation (14 occupational categories were found in this study).

Evidently, murder is an intra-group affair. People murder those whom they know and who are available to be murdered. These are often people who work together and engage in altercations in work situations. Moreover, jealousy and rivalry is very common "on the job" and leads to interpersonal difficulties everywhere. In short, "office politics" can become murder.

RELATIONSHIP BETWEEN MURDERER AND VICTIM

Relationship between murderer and victim vs. column inches *see* Column inches, page 201.

Relationship between murderer and victim vs. year *see* Year, page 208.

Relationship between murderer and victim vs. zone of murder
see Place, page 214.

Relationship between murderer and victim vs. number of murderers *see* Number of murderers, page 217.

Relationship between murderer and victim vs. ethnicity of murderer *see* Ethnicity of murderer, page 220.

Relationship between murderer and victim vs. age of murderer *see* Age of murderer, page 224.

Relationship between murderer and victim vs. sex of murderer *see* Sex of murderer, page 226.

Relationship between murderer and victim vs. zone of murderer's residence *see* Residence of murderer, page 228.

Relationship between murderer and victim vs. marital status of murderer *see* Marital status of murderer, page 231.

Relationship between murderer and victim vs. number of victims. When the victims of a murder are relatives of the murderer, there is a good chance that there will be more than one victim. Examples: 1.21 mean victims where murderer and victim are relatives (77 cases); 1.00 mean victims where murderer and victim are neighbors (44 cases).

This is true because the "relatives" are often the children of the murderer who kills all children available to him. Moreover, relatives are much more likely to live together or visit with one another than is true of non-relatives. This makes relatives more accessible for murder in groups.

Relationship between murderer and victim vs. ethnicity of victim. White victims are more often killed by relatives and strangers than are black victims. Black victims are more often killed by lovers and neighbors than are white victims. Examples:

49 of 294 (16.7%) white victims killed by relative
23 of 278 (8.3%) black victims killed by relative
87 of 294 (29.6%) white victims killed by stranger
50 of 278 (18.0%) black victims killed by stranger
9 of 294 (3.1%) white victims killed by neighbor
31 of 278 (11.2%) black victims killed by neighbor
7 of 294 (2.4%) white victims killed by lover
23 of 278 (8.3%) black victims killed by lover

The phrase "lovers" refers to persons of the opposite sex who live with their eventual killers. Possibly because of the high cost weddings can reach, blacks are more likely to live with someone to whom they are not married than is true of more affluent whites, meaning that blacks are more likely to kill unrelated persons than are whites. Neighbors are killed more often by blacks than by whites. One possible explanation is that whites have greater mobility, giving them more opportunity to leave their neighborhood than is true of blacks.

Relationship between murderer and victim vs. sex of victim.

Female victims are much more commonly killed by spouses and lovers than are males. Male victims are much more commonly killed by casual acquaintances than are females. Examples: 102 of 448 (22.3%) male victims were killed by casual acquaintance; 14 of 197 (7.1%) female victims were killed by casual acquaintance; 24 of 448 (5.4%) male victims were killed by spouse; 50 of 197 (25.4%) female victims were killed by spouse; 15 of 448 (3.3%) male victims were killed by lover; 22 of 197 (11.2%) female victims were killed by lover.

Females are victimized by men much more often than the reverse. Hence, females are much more often the victims of murder by spouses and lovers than can be true in the reverse. Women do not kill as much as do men, not because wielding a knife or beating the victim to death is hardly possible for the "weaker" sex, but because women traditionally have not taken the agressive role in male-female relationships. Men have more "casual" acquaintances than do females. It is too dangerous for big-city women to have casual acquaintances, while men will often develop such relationships on entering bars, bowling alleys and other places of public amusement.

Relationship between murderer and victim vs. marital status of victim.

Widowed victims are very commonly killed by relatives. Single victims are killed by neighbors more often than are people with another marital status. Married victims tend to avoid murder by either relatives or neighbors. Examples: 15 of 217 (6.9%) single victims killed by neighbor; 1 of 169 (0.6%) married victims killed by neighbor; 22 of 169 (13.0%) married victims killed by relatives; 9 of 19 (47.4%) widowed victims killed by relatives.

Widowed persons are likely to seek the company of relatives and are therefore killed by relatives since the presence of the victim is of course an essential feature of the murderer-victim relationship. Single persons are more commonly in the presence of neighbors on whom they depend for companionship more often than is true of the widowed or married, as these two categories of victims have relatives with whom to associate. Many single people are living far from their families of origin and therefore are much more dependent on neighbors than are the married. The married are less likely to deal with relatives or neighbors than those not married. Even when they do, they are likely to be accompanied by their spouse, making victimization more difficult.

Relationship between murderer and victim vs. weapon used.

The weapon used to kill a victim varies by the relationship the killer has with the victim. Examples of weapons disproportionately used by relationship (20 categories of weapons were found in this study): 21 of 74 (28.4%) relatives used hands; 10 of 37 (27.0%) lovers used kitchen knives; 13 of 44 (29.5%) neighbors used rifles or shotguns; 36 of 114 (31.6%) casual acquaintances used stilettoes or switchblades; 49 of 147 (33.3%) strangers used handguns.

Relatives are more likely to use hands than the other categories because killings by hands or fists occur most often when murder or severe wounding is not intended. These killings are the outcome of an attempt to administer a beating which then resulted in an unintended murder. "Lovers," that is adults living together in an unmarried state, are more likely to use knives than other weapons because the proportion of black persons who live together as "lovers" is a good deal higher than the proportion of whites who do so. In addition, the number of blacks who use knives is greater than the proportion of whites who do so. Neighbors are more likely to kill with rifles and shotguns because they live at a fair distance and therefore must use a weapon that can kill over distance.

Relationship between murderer and victim vs. apparent motive.
The reason a murder is committed varies by the relationship the killer has with the victim. Motives found in this study were divided into 15 categories. Examples of most common reasons for murder by relationship are:

26 of 63 (41.3%) relatives of murderers were killed due to sudden anger

8 of 18 (44.4%) coworkers of murderers were killed due to business dealings

13 of 36 (36.1%) neighbors of murderers were killed due to sudden anger

22 of 77 (28.6%) friends of murderers were killed due to sudden anger

28 of 104 (26.9%) casual acquaintances of murderers were killed due to sudden anger

91 of 136 (66.9%) strangers were killed due to murder committed in the course of another crime

20 of 61 (32.8%) spouses of murderers were killed due to sudden anger

10 of 29 (34.5%) lovers of murderers were killed due to jealousy

Sudden anger is so frequent a motive for murder among people who know each other because it is the outcome of intense, emotion-laden situations. It is rare to feel anger or any emotion toward strangers. However, the victims of rape and robbery can easily be strangers, and therefore strangers are murdered frequently in the course of such commissions.

Relationship between murderer and victim vs. sentence.
Murderers convicted of murdering relatives disproportionately tend to be sentenced to probation or a psychiatric hospital. Murderers of strangers rarely are so sentenced: 16 of 41 (39.0%) murderers of relatives were sentenced to probation or psychiatric hospital; 7 of 94 (7.4%) murderers of strangers were sentenced to probation or psychiatric hospital.

The relatives of the victim can also be related to the killer when the latter kills a relative. These relatives are less likely to demand that the courts impose harsh punishment on the offender than is true when a stranger kills a loved one. In addition, it seems more plausible to the court that a killer who murdered his own wife or children is "insane" compared to a robber or rapist who killed a stranger.

NUMBER OF VICTIMS

Number of victims vs. relationship between murderer and victims *see* Relationship between murderer and victim, page 233.

Number of victims vs. minimum prison term. When someone convicted of a multiple murder is sent to prison, it is commonly for a longer time than when a murderer of a single victim is sent to prison. Examples: 14 years mean minimum prison term when murderer of one victim is sentenced to prison (340 cases); 44 years mean minimum prison term when murderer of two victims is sentenced to prison (12 cases).

It is evident that almost any judge will inflict a longer sentence on a multiple murderer than a murderer of only one person. This would also be demanded by the public because of the publicity such multiple killings generate.

Number of victims vs. apparent motive. Murders of multiple victims commonly occur when the motive for murder is drug dealing and insanity. Solo murders most commonly occur when the motive is business dealings, organized crime–related killing, gang war, and accident. Examples:

1.47 mean victims when motive is drug dealing (15 cases)

1.30 mean victims when motive is insanity (23 cases)

1.00 mean victims when motive is business dealings (50 cases)

1.00 mean victims when motive is organized crime (17 cases)

1.00 mean victims when motive is gang war (19 cases)

1.00 mean victims when motive is accident (11 cases)

The phrase "insanity" is an afterthought. It is used to label some multiple murderers, either because the deed is *ipso facto* taken as evidence that mass murder must be caused by insanity, or because the mass murderer is truly a psychotic person. It is of course more likely that defense attorneys will use the insanity defense in cases involving the grotesque act of mass murder.

Drug dealing is more often related to the killing of several victims because the effort in committing such killings is often the erasure of all witnesses to the drug crime. In addition, some drug killings become multiple killings because the drug business involves gangs or groups of drug merchants, all of whom are held responsible for failure to gain money, or for police involvement, or revenge.

ETHNICITY OF VICTIM

Ethnicity of victim vs. column inches *see* Column inches, page 201.

Ethnicity of victim vs. day of week *see* Day of week, page 213.

Ethnicity of victim vs. average temperature of day *see* Temperature, page 215.

Ethnicity of victim vs. number of murderers *see* Number of murderers, page 218.

Ethnicity of victim vs. ethnicity of murderer *see* Ethnicity of murderer, page 221.
Ethnicity of victim vs. sex of murderer *see* Sex of murderer, page 227.
Ethnicity of victim vs. relationship between murderer and victim *see* Relationship between murderer and victim, page 233.

Ethnicity of victim vs. minimum prison term. Murderers of black victims are sentenced to less prison time than are murderers of white victims. Examples: 19.1 mean years for killers of white victims (146 cases); 12.3 mean years for killers of black victims (174 cases).

Nothing illustrates the racism of the courts better than this difference. While there is no evidence to support the frequent accusations that police will arrest and prosecutors prosecute black killers more vigorously than white killers, there is a good deal of evidence that black citizens are not as well protected as white citizens because murderers of black victims are given lesser prison sentences.

Ethnicity of victim vs. sex of victim by sex of murderer and marital status of victim. There is a relationship between ethnicity of victim and sex of victim among those victims who are both married and are killed by a male. In other words, a black married victim who is killed by a male is more likely to be a female than a white married victim who is killed by a male: 48 of 103 (46.6%) married white victims of male murderers were female; 25 of 37 (67.6%) married black victims of male murderers were female.

This means that blacks are more likely to kill their wives than is true of whites.

Ethnicity of victim vs. marital status of victim. Black victims are more likely to be single than are white victims. Examples: 18 of 296 (6.1%) white victims were widowed; 5 of 200 (2.5%) black victims were widowed; 131 of 296 (44.3%) white victims were married; 59 of 200 (29.5%) black victims were married; 132 of 296 (44.6%) white victims were single; 128 of 200 (64.0%) black victims were single.

Blacks generally have less income than whites and tend to marry less often, therefore black victims are more likely to be single than are white victims.

Ethnicity of victim vs. weapon used. White victims are more likely to be killed by hands than black victims. Black victims are more likely to be killed by knives than white victims. Examples: 70 of 374 (18.7%) white victims killed with hands; 38 of 388 (9.8%) black victims killed with hands; 49 of 374 (13.1%) white victims killed with switchblade or stiletto; 79 of 388 (20.4%) black victims killed with switchblade or stiletto; 27 of 374 (7.2%) white victims killed with kitchen knife; 51 of 388 (13.1%) black victims killed with kitchen knife.

Blacks own knives in greater proportion than do whites because they have reason to believe that they may need to defend themselves. Consequently, killings by knife are more frequent as well. Many white women are killed by the hands of husbands and lovers who meant to administer a beating which resulted in the death of the victim.

Ethnicity of victim vs. apparent motive. Whites are disproportionately killed due to an organized crime motive, insanity, and in the course of another crime. Blacks are disproportionately killed due to business dealings, sudden anger, and victim precipitation. Examples:

15 of 305 (4.9%) whites died due to organized crime motive
2 of 299 (0.7%) blacks died due to organized crime motive
16 of 305 (5.2%) whites killed by insane murderer
4 of 299 (1.3%) blacks killed by insane murderer
115 of 305 (37.7%) whites died in course of another crime
58 of 299 (19.4%) blacks died in course of another crime
23 of 305 (7.5%) whites precipitated their own murders
41 of 299 (13.7%) blacks precipitated their own murders
47 of 305 (15.4%) whites died due to sudden anger
93 of 299 (31.1%) blacks died due to sudden anger
14 of 305 (4.6%) whites died due to business dealings
32 of 299 (10.7%) blacks died due to business dealings

See also ethnicity of murderer.

AGE OF VICTIM

Age of victim vs. day of week *see* Day of week, page 213.

Age of victim vs. average temperature of day *see* Temperature, page 216.

Age of victim by relationship between murderer and victim vs. zone of occurrence *see* Place, page 215.

Age of victim vs. number of murderers *see* Number of murderers, page 217.

Age of victim by relationship between murderer and victim vs. ethnicity of murderer *see* Ethnicity of murderer, page 221.

Age of victim vs. age of murderer *see* Age of murderer, page 223.

Age of victim vs. sex of murderer by relationship between murderer and victim *see* Sex of murderer, page 226.

Age of victim vs. sex of murderer by ethnicity of victim *see* Sex of murderer, page 226.

Age of victim vs. marital status of murderer by relationship between murderer and victim *see* Marital status of murderer, page 231.

Age of victim vs. weapon used. Victims killed with a club or bludgeon are typically older than victims killed with other weapons. Victims strangled with a weapon, killed with both hands and knife, or killed with a rifle or shotgun are commonly younger than other victims. Examples: 45.5 the mean age of victims killed with club or bludgeon (45 cases); 32.3 the mean age of victims killed with rifle or shotgun (155 cases); 31.8 the mean age of victims killed with both hands and knife (11 cases); 28.0 the mean age of victims strangled with weapon (12 cases).

Older victims are less likely to survive an attack by club or bludgeon than are younger victims. In addition, clubs and bludgeons are used more often on white, married persons than on black or single persons. Married persons are generally older than single persons. Black victims are younger than white victims because they begin heterosexual association earlier and are often killed by a spouse or "live-in."

Age of victim vs. apparent motive. Victims killed in the course of another crime are older, on the average, than other victims. Victims killed due to gang war or drug dealing average a younger age than other victims. Examples: 48.6 the mean age of victims killed in course of other crime (191 cases); 25.3 the mean age of victims killed due to drug dealing (15 cases); 19.9 the mean age of victims killed in gang war (19 cases).

Robbery and rape are the most common "other crimes" leading to murder. Store owners are generally older than persons otherwise killed because it takes some years to gain possession of a store. The victims of rape-murder are generally grown women, while other murders include the child victims often murdered by their own parents.

SEX OF VICTIM

Sex of victim by sex of murderer and marital status of victim vs. ethnicity of victim *see* Ethnicity of victim, page 237.

Sex of victim vs. residence of victim by residence of murderer. A victim who lives in the same zone of the county as the murderer is more likely to be female than a victim who lives in a different zone from the murderer: 342 of 502 (68.1%) victims who lived in the same zone of the county as their killer were male; 140 of 173 (80.9%) victims who lived in a different zone of the county than their killer were male.

Men are more likely to kill women they know very well or who are living with them than women not well known to them. Since most killers are men, this indicates how much more mobile men are than women.

Sex of victim vs. marital status of victim. Male victims are more likely to be single than female victims. Examples: 195 of 331 (58.9%) male victims are single; 87 of 211 (41.2%) female victims were single. This is because men kill their wives much more often than the reverse.

Sex of victim vs. weapon used. Males are disproportionately killed with handguns, switchblades or stilettoes. Murderers of females disproportionately use their bare hands. Examples: 174 of 218 (79.8%) victims of murderers using a handgun were male; 113 of 143 (79.0%) victims of murderers using a switchblade or stiletto were male; 64 of 123 (52.0%) victims of murderers using hands were male.

Men often kill women whom they wanted to beat but not kill. However, many beatings become murder when the victim dies of the violence. Trying to kill a man with bare hands is far more difficult than doing this to a woman.

Sex of victim vs. apparent motive. Males are disproportionately likely to be killed due to organized crime, gang war, and victim precipitation. Females are disproportionately likely to be murdered due to a divorce situation, insanity, and jealousy. Examples:

17 of 514 (3.3%) males died due to organized crime motive
0 of 179 females died due to organized crime motive
18 of 514 (3.5%) males died due to gang war
1 of 179 (0.6%) females died due to gang war
71 of 514 (13.8%) males precipitated their own murder
7 of 179 (3.9%) females precipitated their own murder
42 of 514 (8.2%) males died due to jealousy
33 of 179 (18.4%) females died due to jealousy
12 of 514 (2.3%) males died at the hands of insane murderer
11 of 179 (6.1%) females died at the hands of insane murderer
1 of 514 (0.2%) males were murdered in connection with divorce
9 of 179 (5.0%) females were murdered in connection with divorce

Men engage in crime and gang warfare a great deal more than do women. Anger resulting from divorce and jealousy is far more often directed at female victims by both male and female killers than it is directed at possible male victims.

Sex of victim vs. disposition of case. When a male victim is killed, it is more likely that the case against the suspect will be dismissed before trial than when a female victim is killed. Examples: 42 of 373 (11.3%) cases with male victims dismissed before trial; 10 of 155 (6.5%) cases with female victims dismissed before trial.

Male victims appear more likely to have precipitated their own murder by threatening conduct than is believed true of women. Therefore the suspect, male or female, has a better chance pleading self defense than is true of someone who killed a woman.

ZONE OF VICTIM'S RESIDENCE

Zone of victim's residence vs. column inches *see* Column inches, page 203.

Zone of victim's residence vs. year of murder *see* Year, page 208.

Zone of victim's residence vs. number of murderers *see* Number of murderers, page 218.

Zone of victim's' residence vs. age of murderer *see* Age of murderer, page 224.

Zone of victim's residence vs. zone of murderer's residence *see* Zone of murderer's residence, page 228.

Zone of victim's residence by zone of murderer's residence vs. sex of victim *see* Sex of victim, page 240.

Zone of victim's residence vs. marital status of victim. Victims living in the inner city are more likely to be single than those living in outlying areas. Examples: 35 of 51 (68.6%) victims living downtown were single; 13 of 37 (35.1%) victims living in far suburbs or rural areas were single.

People who live in the inner city are more often single than is true in the outlying areas which house many families and married couples. People who live in the inner city are more often single because the accommodations available there are not generally suited to the housing of families. Even married couples without children are more interested in owning a house in the suburbs than living in an inner city apartment.

Zone of victim's residence vs. survivors of victims. Victims living in outlying areas are more likely to be survived by a spouse and one or more children than are victims living in the inner city. Examples: 2 of 20 (10.0%) victims living downtown were survived by spouse and child; 26 of 123 (21.1%) victims living in residential areas surrounding downtown were survived by spouse and child;

13 of 24 (54.2%) victims living in far suburbs and rural areas were survived by spouse and child. This is true because victims living in the inner city are more likely to be single and victims living in the far reaches of the city are more likely to be married and have children.

Zone of victim's residence vs. weapon used. Victims living downtown are disproportionately likely to be killed with a switchblade or stiletto, and are disproportionately unlikely to be killed with a handgun. Victims living in residential areas surrounding downtown are more likely to be killed with a handgun than residents of other areas, and are relatively unlikely to be killed with the killer's hands. Victims living in the outlying residential areas of the city are disproportionately likely to be killed with their murderers' bare hands. Examples:

22 of 104 (21.2%) victims living downtown were killed with switchblade or stiletto

5 of 48 (10.4%) victims living in far suburbs or rural areas killed with switchblade or stiletto

125 of 429 (29.1%) victims living in residential area surrounding downtown killed with handgun

19 of 104 (18.3%) victims living downtown were killed with handgun

24 of 120 (20.0%) victims living in outlying residential area of city were killed with hands

52 of 429 (12.1%) victims living in residential areas surrounding downtown killed with hands

See also residence of murderers.

Zone of victim's residence vs. apparent motive. Victims living downtown are disproportionately likely to be killed due to business dealings. Victims living in a residential area surrounding downtown are more likely than others to be killed due to sudden anger. Victims living in the country or in the suburbs are unusually prone to murder in the course of another crime. Examples:

12 of 76 (15.8%) victims living downtown were killed due to business dealings

2 of 74 (2.7%) victims living in near suburbs were killed due to business dealings

101 of 346 (29.2%) victims living in residential area surrounding downtown were killed due to sudden anger

5 of 35 (14.3%) victims living in far suburbs or rural areas were killed due to sudden anger

10 of 74 (13.5%) victims living in near suburbs were killed due to sudden anger

26 of 74 (35.1%) victims living in near suburbs were killed in course of other crime

14 of 35 (40.0%) victims living in far suburbs or rural areas were killed in course of other crime

15 of 76 (19.7%) victims living downtown were killed in course of other crime

See also residence of murderers.

MARITAL STATUS OF VICTIM

Marital status of victim by sex of victim vs. number of murderers *see* Number of murderers, page 218.

Marital status of victim vs. marital status of murderer *see* Marital status of murderer, page 231.

Marital status of victim vs. relationship between murderer and victim *see* Relationship between murderer and victim, page 234.

Marital status of victim vs. Ethnicity of victim *see* Ethnicity of victim, page 237.

Marital status of victim vs. sex of victim *see* Sex of victim, page 240.

Marital status of victim vs. residence of victim *see* Zone of victim's residence, page 241.

OCCUPATION OF VICTIM

Occupation of victim vs. column inches *see* Column inches, page 203.

Occupation of victim vs. age of murderer *see* Age of murderer, page 225.

Occupation of victim vs. occupation of murderer *see* Occupation of murderer, page 232.

Occupation of victim vs. minimum prison term. The murderers of white collar victims are sentenced to longer prison terms than the murderers of blue collar victims. Examples: 30.1 year mean minimum sentence for killing managerial victims (26 cases); 14.1 year mean minimum for killing service workers (24 cases); 13.0 year mean minimum sentence for killing laborers (23 cases).

This illustrates the contention that the lives of wealthier persons and persons with high occupational prestige are considered more valuable in American jurisprudence than the lives of persons whose income is small and whose occupations carry little prestige.

Occupation of victim vs. weapon used. Laborers are more likely than others to be killed by their murderers' hands. Victims who are service workers are very likely to be murdered with a handgun. Students are more likely than others to be killed by a rifle or shotgun, while professionals have a slim chance of being killed with a rifle or shotgun. Examples: 13 of 58 (22.4%) laborers killed by hands; 4 of 35 (11.4%) students killed by hands; 22 of 46 (47.8%) service workers killed by handgun; 6 of 35 (17.1%) students killed by handgun; 11 of 35 (31.4%) students killed by rifle or shotgun; 1 of 25 (4.0%) professionals killed by rifle or shotgun.

Physical fighting is more common among laborers than other occupational groups because laborers seek to compensate their feelings of class injury by showing others that they have masculine, i.e., fighting ability. Fighting leads to some killings, albeit unintended. This means that killing by hands is mostly the outcome of an intended beating which went too far.

Service workers are not as likely to get involved in fistfights as laborers, not only because service occupations involve many more women, but also because the macho ethic is not as pronounced in service occupations as it is in laboring occupations. In addition, the setting in which service work is done does not lend itself as easily to physical fighting as the settings in which labor is done. Service workers are more often in the presence of persons who carry a knife and who can use it. This is true because service workers frequently come from the black community and because knives are more available in service occupations than in other occupations, for example, in restaurants. Furthermore, knives are easier to conceal in a service occupation than guns and certainly rifles and shotguns.

Students are more often murdered with rifles and shotguns than members of other occupations. Our study involved mostly students from the University of Buffalo, which is located on the border of Buffalo and the suburb of Amherst. During the years 1943–1983 the dormitories now in use were mostly not yet built. Therefore students lived nearby the university on the residential streets in which most people who do have a firearm have a rifle or a shotgun. Thus, students were killed with these weapons as were others living in those same neighborhoods.

Occupation of victim vs. apparent motive. The motive for killing a white collar victim is usually a killing in the course of another crime. Unemployed and student victims are least likely of all occupations to be killed in the course of another crime. Examples: 33 of 49 (67.3%) managerial victims killed in course of other crime; 9 of 13 (69.2%) professional victims killed in course of other crime; 4 of 15 (26.7%) unemployed victims killed in course of other crime; 6 of 26 (23.1%) student victims killed in course of other crime.

The "other crime" is generally robbery. Therefore, those killed in the course of a hold up are almost always store owners or clerks. Consequently the unemployed and students, who have no stores, are unlikely to be killed in such circumstances.

SURVIVORS OF VICTIM

Survivors of victim vs. ethnicity of murderer see Ethnicity of murderer, page 222.

Survivors of victims vs. zone of victim's residence see Residence of victim, page 241.

WEAPON USED

Weapon used vs. column inches see Column inches, page 203.

Weapon used vs. year of murder see Year, page 209.

Weapon used vs. number of murderers *see* Number of murderers, page 219.

Weapon used vs. sex of murderer *see* Sex of murderer, page 227.

Weapon used vs. zone of murderer's residence *see* Zone of murderer's residence, page 229.

Weapon used vs. relationship between murderer and victim *see* Relationship between murderer and victim, page 234.

Weapon used vs. ethnicity of victim *see* Ethnicity of victim, page 237.

Weapon used vs. age of victim *see* Age of victim, page 238.

Weapon used vs. sex of victim *see* Sex of victim, page 240.

Weapon used vs. zone of victim's residence *see* Zone of victim's residence, page 242.

Weapon used vs. occupation of victim *see* Occupation of victim, page 243.

Weapon used vs. minimum prison term. Users of handguns get more prison time than those convicted of murder with other weapons. Users of hands get less time than do other killers. Examples: 18.9 year mean minimum prison term where handgun used (85 cases); 11.1 year mean minimum prison term where hands used (50 cases).

Handguns are used in the course of robberies. Since robber-killers get longer prison sentences than other murderers, this is reflected here. Users of hands are generally white, middle-class, uptown citizens who beat their wives and killed them unintentionally. This is evidently considered more excusable than using a handgun to kill a store owner.

Weapon used vs. apparent motive. Kitchen knives are frequently used when the murderer is motivated by sudden anger and victim precipitation. A rifle or shotgun is often used when the motive is jealousy. Switchblades or stilettoes commonly conclude business dealings. Examples:

32 of 163 (19.6%) murders attributable to sudden anger done with kitchen knife

17 of 75 (22.7%) murders precipitated by victim done with kitchen knife

7 of 187 (3.7%) murders committed in the course of another crime done with kitchen knife

21 of 74 (28.4%) jealousy murders committed with rifle or shotgun

8 of 75 (10.7%) victim precipitated murders committed with rifle or shotgun

20 of 187 (10.7%) murders in course of other crime committed with rifle or shotgun

15 of 49 (30.6%) murders committed due to business dealings done with switchblade or stiletto

0 of 17 organized crime murders done with switchblade or stiletto

Sudden anger and victim precipitation are really the same thing, except that "victim precipitation" is a category applied whenever the offender is not indicted or adjudicated not guilty. Thus, kitchen knives are often the only weapon available to settle a domestic dispute, particularly when no planning has preceded the murder. Jealousy involves heterosexual relationships. It also involves married whites living in the suburbs. Men in these areas often own a rifle or shotgun for hunting or sports purposes.

Murders derived from business dealings generally involve small sums of money or drugs. The poor are most often involved. Since knives are cheaper than guns, the poor are much more likely to carry a knife than a firearm.

MOTIVE

Apparent motive vs. column inches *see* Column inches, page 204.

Apparent motive vs. year of murder *see* Year, page 209.

Apparent motive vs. average temperature of day *see* Temperature, page 216.

Apparent motive vs. number of murderers *see* Number of murderers, page 219.

Apparent motive vs. ethnicity of murderer *see* Ethnicity of murderer, page 222.

Apparent motive vs. age of murderer *see* Age of murderer, page 225.

Apparent motive vs. sex of murderer *see* Sex of murderer, page 227.

Apparent motive vs. zone of murderer's residence *see* Residence of murderer, page 229.

Apparent motive vs. marital status of murderer *see* Marital status of murderer, page 231.

Apparent motive vs. relationship between murderer and victim *see* Relationship between murderer and victim, page 235.

Apparent motive vs. number of victims *see* Number of victims, page 236.

Apparent motive vs. ethnicity of victim *see* Ethnicity of victim, page 238.

Apparent motive vs. age of victim *see* Age of victim, page 239.

Apparent motive vs. sex of victim *see* Sex of victim, page 240.

Apparent motive vs. zone of victim's residence *see* Zone of victim's residence, page 242.

Apparent motive vs. occupation of victim *see* Occupation of victim, page 244.

Apparent motive vs. weapon used *see* Weapon, page 245.

Apparent motive vs. minimum prison term. Murder in the course of another crime draws a stiffer prison sentence than other motives. Murderers who are motivated by sudden anger are given shorter prison terms than other murderers. Examples: 23.9 years mean minimum term for murder in course of other crime (97 cases); 8.3 years mean minimum term for murder due to sudden anger (94 cases).

Murders committed in the course of robbery or rape seem to be much more premeditated than "sudden anger" murders. Moreover, robbery murders frequently victimize store owners whose social class resembles the social class of the judge. "Sudden anger" murders are committed against relatives and friends of the murderer and therefore seem to occur outside of the social environment to which the judge is accustomed.

Apparent motive vs. disposition. Suspects whose victims precipitated their own murders very frequently have their cases dismissed before trial: 25 of 58 (43.1%) victim-precipitated murders dismissed before trial; 19 of 394 (4.8%) all other motives dismissed before trial.

This is evidently true because "victim precipitation" is used to identify "self defense" as the motive for murder.

Apparent motive vs. conviction. Suspects whose victims precipitate their own murders are usually not convicted. Suspects whose apparent motive is another crime or sudden anger are convicted more often than suspects with other motives. Examples: 17 of 38 (44.7%) suspects were convicted whose apparent motive for killing was victim precipitation; 110 of 118 (93.2%) suspects were convicted whose apparent motive for killing was murder in the course of another crime; 112 of 119 (94.1%) suspects were convicted whose apparent motive for killing was sudden anger. See the two paragraphs above.

Apparent motive vs. sentence. Probation is usually given to those convicted of murder whose victims precipitated their own murders. Examples: 12 of 17 (70.6%) victim-precipitated murderers sentenced to probation; 18 of 351 (5.1%) all other motives sentenced to probation.

This is again explained by the use of the term "victim precipitation."

DISPOSITION OF CASE

Disposition of case vs. year of murder *see* Year, page 209.

Disposition of case vs. number of murderers *see* Number of murderers, page 219.

Disposition of case vs. sex of suspect *see* Sex of murderer, page 227.

Disposition of case vs. zone of suspect's residence *see* Residence of murderer, page 230.

Disposition of case vs. sex of victim *see* Sex of victim, page 241.

Disposition of case vs. apparent motive *see* Motive, page 247.

Disposition of case vs. minimum prison term. A murderer convicted by a judge receives much less prison time than a murderer convicted by a jury: 9.6

years mean minimum sentence when trial by judge (165 cases); 21.0 years mean minimum sentence when trial by jury (155 cases).

Judges resent a defendant who uses a jury, rather than the judge. Therefore, a convicted person will receive a longer prison term if he used a jury as the judge avenges himself for being ignored.

Disposition of case vs. conviction of suspect. Judges are more likely to convict a suspect than are juries: 199 of 218 (91.3%) suspects convicted by judge; 188 of 242 (77.7%) suspects convicted by jury.

This is true because judges are generally of a higher social class than murder defendants. Juries will contain a good number of persons of the same social class and race, and therefore exhibit more sympathy for the offender than a judge, who cannot see himself in the situation in which the murderer lives.

Disposition of case vs. sentence. Sentences tend to be more severe for murderers who have been tried by a jury than for murderers who have been tried by a judge. Examples: 21 of 198 (10.6%) murderers sentenced to probation when tried by judge; 7 of 177 (4.0%) murderers sentenced to probation when tried by jury; 0 of 198 murderers sentenced to death when tried by judge; 6 of 177 (3.4%) murderers sentenced to death when tried by jury.

See also Minimum prison term vs. disposition of case, page 249.

CONVICTION OF SUSPECT

Conviction of suspect vs. age of murderer *see* Age of murderer, page 225.

Conviction of suspect vs. apparent motive *see* Motive, page 247.

Conviction of suspect vs. disposition of case *see* Disposition, page 248.

SENTENCE

Sentence vs. column inches *see* Column inches, page 204.

Sentence vs. year of murder *see* Year, page 210.

Sentence vs. ethnicity of murderer *see* Ethnicity of murderer, page 222.

Sentence vs. age of murderer *see* Age of murderer, page 225.

Sentence vs. sex of murderer *see* Sex of murderer, page 228.

Sentence vs. zone of murderer's residence *see* Residence of murderer, page 230.

Sentence vs. marital status of murderer *see* Marital status of murderer, page 232.

Sentence vs. relationship between murderer and victim *see* Relationship between murderer and victim, page 235.

Sentence vs. apparent motive *see* Motive, page 247.

Sentence vs. disposition *see* Disposition, page 248.

LENGTH OF PRISON TERM

Minimum prison term vs. column inches *see* Column inches, page 199.

Minimum prison term vs. number of victims *see* Number of victims, page 236.

Minimum prison term vs. ethnicity of victim *see* Ethnicity of victim, page 237.

Minimum prison term vs. occupation of victim *see* Occupation of victim, page 243.

Minimum prison term vs. weapon used *see* Weapon, page 245.

Minimum prison term vs. apparent motive *see* Motive, page 247.

Minimum prison term vs. disposition of case *see* Disposition, page 248.

Murder Study Data Sheet

I. Demographic Variables

Inches _____

A. Geography of Murder
  1. Date _____
  2. Day of Week _____
  3. Hour of the Day _____
  4. Place: Buffalo _____ Suburb (which) _____
     a. Outdoors
        i. Street _____ (Name of Street) _____
        ii. Other (Specify) _____
     b. Indoors (Address) _____
        i. Private _____
           Where in house? _____
        ii. Public (Type of place, e.g., bar) _____
  5. Zone _____
  6. Average temperature for that day _____
  7. Weather for that day (snow, rain, etc.) _____
  8. Hours of daylight _____
B. Name of murderer(s) _____
   _____
C. Ethnicity of murderer(s)
   1. White _____ 2. Black _____ 3. Native American _____
   4. Hispanic _____ 5. Asian _____ 6. Other _____
D. Age of murderer(s) _____
E. Sex of murderer (s) _____

F. Address of murderer(s) _____
G. Marital status of murderer(s) 1. single _____ 2. married _____
    3. divorced _____ 4. widowed _____
H. Occupation of murderer(s) _____
I. Height and weight of murderer(s) _____
J. Physical or mental disability (specify) _____
K. Prior arrests or convictions? _____
    _____

L. Relationship between murderer(s) and victim(s):
    1. Relative (Murderer) _____ (Victim) _____
    2. Coworker _____
    3. Neighbor _____
    4. Friend _____
    5. Casual acquaintance _____
    6. Stranger _____
    7. Police officer and the like _____
M. Name of Victim(s) _____
    _____

N. Ethnicity of Victim(s)
    1. White _____ 2. Black _____ 3. Native American _____
    4. Hispanic _____ 5. Asian _____ 6. Other _____
O. Age of victim(s) _____
P. Sex of victim(s) _____
Q. Address of victim(s) _____
R. Marital status of victim(s) 1. single _____ 2. married _____
    3. divorced _____ 4. widowed _____
S. Occupation of victim(s) _____
T. Height and weight of victim(s) _____
U. Physical or mental disability (specify) _____
V. Prior arrests or convictions? _____
    _____

W. Survivors _____

II. *Circumstances Surrounding Murder*
    A. Type of weapon used:
        1. Handgun _____ 2. Rifle or shotgun _____ 3. Bomb _____
        4. Kitchen knife _____ 5. Switchblade or stiletto _____
        6. Axe or hatchet _____ 7. Club _____
        8. Icepick _____ 9. Motor vehicle _____ 10. Other _____
    B. Presence of alcohol or other drugs:
        1. Alcohol _____
        2. Drugs (specify) _____
    C. Sexual aspect?
        1. Heterosexual relationship _____
        2. Homosexual relationship _____
    D. Apparent motive for murder
        1. Victim precipitation _____
        2. Other crime (e.g., rape, robbery) _____
        3. Jealousy, infidelity, etc. _____
        4. Drug dealing _____

5. Business dealings _____
6. Organized crime–related _____
7. Gang war _____
8. Racially motivated _____
9. Divorce situation _____
10. Other _____

III. Disposition of Case

A. Dismissed before trial _____
B. Trial by judge _____
C. Trial by jury _____
D. Conviction: Yes _____ No _____
E. Sentence:
  1. Probation _____
  2. Prison term (specify) _____
  3. Death penalty
    a. Executed   (Date) _____
    b. Clemency _____
    c. Sentence reduced (specify) _____
  4. Parole _____
  5. Arrests for new murders? _____
    (If this is the case, start new file for other murder)
F. Has murderer(s) died violently?
  1. Yes, murderer killed self after the act _____
  2. Yes, murderer killed during or soon after commission of act _____
  3. Yes, murderer killed in prison _____
  4. Yes, murderer killed after release from prison _____
    Give brief details _____
  5. No information on death of murderer(s) _____

Notes

2. Who Kills Whom, How, and Why

1. Joseph Cohen, "The Geography of Crime," *The Annals of the American Academy of Political and Social Sciences* 217:29, September 1941.

2. Gerhard Falk, "The Influence of the Seasons on the Crime Rate," *The Journal of Criminal Law, Criminology and Police Science* 43:2, July-August 1952.

3. Marvin Wolfgang, *Patterns in Criminal Homicide*, Philadelphia, University of Pennsylvania Press, 1958.

4. R.E. Park, E.W. Burgess, and R.D. McKenzie, *The City*, Chicago: University of Chicago Press, 1925.

5. Gerhard Falk, "A Sociological Approach to the 'Right-Wrong' Test in Criminal Procedure," *Criminal Law Quarterly* 7:3, November 1964.

3. The Conditions and Dispositions of Homicide

1. Harry Kalven and Hans Zeisel, *The American Jury*, Boston, Little, Brown, 1966, pp. 56–60.

2. *Ibid.*

4. Genocide

1. George Santayana, *Life of Reason I*, "Reason in Common Sense," New York, Scribner's, 1953.

2. Nora Levin, *The Holocaust*, New York, Schocken Books, 1973, and Lucy S. Dawidowicz, *The War Against the Jews*, New York, Holt, Rinehart and Winston, 1975.

3. John Phillip Jones, ed., "Leopold von Ranke," *The Syracuse Scholar* Vol. 9, No. 1, 1988.

4. Martin Gilbert, *The Holocaust*, New York, Hill and Wang, 1979, p. 33.

5. *Ibid.*, p. 87.

6. *Ibid.*, p. 113.

7. *Ibid.*, p. 141.

8. *Ibid.*, p. 188.

9. *Ibid.*, p. 226.

10. Robert Payne, *The Life and Death of Adolf Hitler*, New York, Praeger Publishers, 1973, pp. 471–472.

11. Willard Allen Fletcher, "Einsatzgruppen" in *The Holocaust*, New York, Garland Publishing, Vol. 10, 1982.

12. *Ibid.*, pp. 131–132.

13. Gilbert, *op. cit.*, p. 248.

14. *Die Zeit* No. 31, August 5, 1988, p. 24.

15. Jocehn von Lang and Claus Sybill, eds., *Eichmann Interrogated*, New York, Farrar, Strauss and Giroux, 1983, p. 77.

16. *The Trial of the Major War Criminals* as published in *Nazi Conspiracy and Aggression*, Washington, D.C., Government Printing Office, 15 vols., 1951–1952.

17. Levin, *op. cit.*, pp. 311–313.

18. Henry Friedlander, "The Final Solution," in *The Holocaust*, Vol. 12, New York, Garland Publishing, 1982, p. 33.

19. *Ibid.* p. 91.

20. Gilbert, *op. cit.*, p. 442.

21. *Encyclopedia Americana*, Vol. 29, 1951.

22. Bruno Bettelheim, *Surviving*, New York, Alfred A. Knopf, 1979, p. 60.

23. *Ibid.*

24. Saul S. Friedman, *AMCHA, An Oral Testament of the Holocaust*, 1979, Washington, D.C., University Press of America, p. 261.

25. Helen Fein, *Accounting for Genocide*, New York, Free Press, 1979, p. 3.

26. Abraham H. Hartunian, *A Memoir of the Armenian Genocide*, trans. from the original Armenian manuscripts, Boston, Beacon Press, 1972.

27. *Ibid.*, p. 77.

28. *Ibid.*

29. Hubert G. Locke, ed., *Exile in the Fatherland*, New York, Wm. B. Eerdmans, 1986, p. viii.

30. Richard G. Hovannisian, *The Armenian Genocide in Perspective*, New Brunswick, Transaction Books, 1986, p. 91.

31. *Ibid.*, p. 86.

32. Fein, *op. cit.*, pp. 1–10.

33. Fein, *op. cit.*, p. 10.

34. Everett C. Hughes, "Good People and Dirty Work," *Social Problems* Vol. 10, No. 1, Summer 1962.

35. Carl D. Evans, "The Church's False Witness Against the Jews," *The Christian Century* May 5, 1982, pp. 530–532.

36. *Documents of Vatican II*, "Non-Christians," the Vatican, pp. 664–665.

37. Russell Thornton, *American Indian Holocaust and Survival*, Norman, University of Oklahoma Press, 1980, p. 107.

38. Rex Alan Smith, *Moon of Popping Trees*, Lincoln, University of Nebraska Press, 1975, pp. 179–195.

39. Hughes, *op. cit.*, p. 4.

5. *Serial Killings and Mass Murder*

1. Donald H.J. Herman, Helen L. Morrison, Yvonne S. Sor, Julie A. Norman and David M. Neff, "People of the State of Illinois vs. John Gacy: The Functioning of the Insanity Defense at the Limits of the Criminal Law." *The West Virginia Law Review* V. 86, pp. 1169–1273, Summer, 1984.

2. Gerhard Falk, "A Sociological Approach to the 'Right-Wrong' Test in Criminal Procedure," *The Criminal Law Quarterly* Vol. 7, No. 3, November 1964.

3. Herman, et. al., *op. cit.*, p. 1184.

4. Herman, et. al., *op. cit.*, p. 1186.

5. Gerhard Falk, "The Public Image of the Sex Offender," *Mental Hygiene* Vol. 48, No. 4, October 1964.

6. *Chicago Tribune*, March 1, 1980, p. 2, column 5.

7. Mark Thompson, "Ramirez Faces 60 New Charges," *The Los Angeles Daily Journal* Vol. 98, September 30, 1985, p. 22.

8. Marcia Chambers, *New York Times*, Friday, May 7, 1985, Sec. I, p. 21.

9. Ronald Holmes and James D. DeBurger, "Profiles in Terror: The Serial Murderer," *Federal Probation* Vol. 49, September 1985, p. 32.

10. Gerold Frank, *The Boston Strangler*, New York, New Amsterdam Library, 1967, pp. 355–357.

11. Elliott Leyton, *Compulsive Killers: The Story of Modern Multiple Murder*, New York, Washington News Books, 1986, p. 141.

12. *Ibid.*, pp. 146–147.

13. Joachim Fest, *Hitler*, New York, Vintage Books, 1975; John Toland, *Adolf Hitler*, Garden City, N.Y., Doubleday, 1976.

14. Peter Hernon, *A Terrible Thunder: The Story of the New Orleans Sniper*, Garden City, New York, Doubleday, 1978.

15. Stephen Winn and David Merrill, *Ted Bundy: The Killer Next Door*, New York, Bantam Books, 1980; Richard W. Larsen, *Bundy: The Deliberate Stranger*, Englewood Cliffs, N.J., Prentice Hall, 1980.

16. Stephen G. Michaud and Hugh Aynesworth, *The Only Living Witness*, New York, New American Library, 1983, pp. 44–45.

17. Jack Levin and James Alan Fox, *Mass Murder*, New York, Plenum Press, 1985, pp. 229–230.

18. Ronald Holmes and James DeBurger, *Serial Murder*, Newbury Park, California, Sage Publications, 1987, pp. 128–129.

19. B.L. Danto, J. Bruhns, and A.H. Kutscher, *The Human Side of Homicide*, New York, Columbia University Press, 1982, p. 14.

20. Holmes and DeBurger, *Federal Probation, op. cit.*, pp. 21–22.

21. *New York Times*, April 14, 1988, Sec. I, p. 28.

22. *New York Times*, April 16, 1988, p. 7.

23. *New York Times*, March 27, 1988, p. 5.

24. *New York Times*, January 31, 1988, p. 24.

25. *New York Times*, January 3, 1988, p. 1.

26. Marc Goldstein, "Multiple Slayings in Nation's Recent History," *New York Times*, July 19, 1984; Part I, p. 124.

27. Fest, *op. cit.*

28. Levin and Fox, *op. cit.*

29. *Buffalo News*, Sunday, February 21, 1988.

30. Associated Press, February 16, 1988.

31. *Buffalo News*, December 29, 1987, p. 1.

32. *New York Times*, January 1, 1988, p. 32.

33. *Buffalo News*, May 23, 1989, p. 1.

34. *Time*, December 21, 1987, p. 30.

35. *New York Times*, July 18, 1984, p. 1.

36. *New York Times*, July 20, 1984, Sec. II, p. 5.

37. Donald Treiman, *Occupational Prestige in Comparative Perspective*, New York, The Academic Press, 1977.

38. Holmes and DeBurger, *Federal Probation, op. cit.*, pp. 22–23.

6. Assassination for Money

1. Will Durant, *The Age of Faith*, New York, Simon and Schuster, 1950, p. 262.

2. *Ibid.*, p. 310.

3. Task Force on Organized Crime, *Organized Crime*, Washington, D.C., U.S. Government Printing Office, 1976.

4. Roy Rowan, "The Fifty Biggest Mafia Bosses," *Fortune* Vol. 114, No. 11, November 10, 1986.

5. Howard Abadinsky, *Organized Crime*, Chicago, Nelson-Hall, 1986, p. 255.

6. Rowan, *op. cit.*, pp. 24–38; Anonymous, *Life*, September 1, 1967, pp. 15–103; *New York Times*, January 14, 1987, p. B5.

7. Bill Richards and Alex Kotlowitz, "Judge Finds 3 Corporate Officials Guilty of Murder," *Wall Street Journal*, June 17, 1985, p. 2.

8. Howard Abadinsky, *The Mafia in America*, New York, Praeger Publishers, 1981, p. 99.

9. Virgil W. Peterson, *The Mob*, Ottawa, Illinois, Green Hill Publishers, 1983, pp. 231–323.

10. *Ibid.*, pp. 318–319.

11. *New York Times*, June 29, 1988, p. 1.

12. *Buffalo News*, April 14, 1985, p. A-11.

13. *New York Times*, January 14, 1987, p. B4.

14. *U.S. News & World Report* October 6, 1986, p. 23.

15. Jimmy Fellner, *Harper's Magazine*, Vol. 276, No. 58, February 9, 1988, pp. 58–59.

16. *New York Times*, August 9, 1987, p. 1.

17. Life, *op. cit.*, p. 103.

18. *New York Times*, May 25, 1988, I, 5:1; June 4, 1988, I, 9:6; June 18, 1988, I, 31, 3; June 29, 1988, I, 1:1.

19. Gus Tyler, *Organized Crime in America*, Ann Arbor, University of Michigan Press, 1962, p. 230.

20. Nicholas Pileggi, *Wise Guy*, New York, Simon and Schuster, 1985, p. 119.

21. Tyler, *op. cit.*, p. 231.

22. James Cook, "The Invisible Enterprise," *Forbes Magazine*, September 29, 1980, pp. 60–74.

7. Assassination for a Cause

1. James W. Clarke, *American Assassins: The Darker Side of Politics*, Princeton, Princeton University Press, 1982, pp. 4–5.

2. *Ibid.*, p. 9.

3. Gerhard Falk, "A Sociological Approach to the 'Right-Wrong' Test in Criminal Procedure," *The Criminal Law Quarterly* Vol. 7, No. 3, November 1964.

4. Clarke, *op. cit.*

5. Selig Adler, "The Operation on President McKinley," *Scientific American* Vol. CCIII, March 1963, pp. 118–130.

6. Clarke, *op. cit.*, p. 76.

7. Clarke, *op. cit.*, p. 141.

8. Craig Unger, "John Lennon's Killer: The Nowhere Man," *New York*, Vol. 14, June 22, 1981, pp. 30–32.

9. Clarke, *op. cit.*, p. 124.

10. *New York Times*, April 1, 1981, p. A19.

11. Stanford M. Lyman, *The Seven Deadly Sins*, New York, St. Martin's Press, 1978.

12. *Ibid.*, p. 185.

13. Leo Tolstoy, *War and Peace* (Louise and Aylmer Maude, trans.), New York, W.W. Norton, 1966.

14. *Ibid.*, p. 1335.

15. Clarke, *op. cit.*, pp. 242–243.

16. Clarke, *op. cit.*, p. 257.

17. *Sacramento Bee*, September 10, 1975, p. Al.
18. Clarke, *op. cit.*, p. 155.
19. Clarke, *op. cit.*, p. 163.
20. Clarke, *op. cit.*, p. 165.
21. Clarke, *op. cit.*, pp. 232–237.
22. William Shakespeare, *Julius Caesar*, Act 3, Scene 2.

8. Murder at Random: Terror for a "Cause"

1. Charles Krauthammer, "It's Simply Murder," *The Washington Post National Weekly Edition*, December 31, 1984, p. 1.
2. B.F. Woods, "Terrorism: The Continuing Crisis," *The Police Chief* Vol. 48, 1981, p. 52.
3. The Committee on Internal Security, United States House of Representatives, *Terrorism*, U.S. Government Printing Office, Washington, D.C., 1974.
4. "Closing in on the Pan Am Bombers," *U.S. News and World Report* May 22, 1989.
5. John Cooley, ABC News, Television Program, May 19, 1989.
6. "Narrowing the Suspects List," *Time* April 24, 1989, p. 40.
7. "A Christmas Tragedy, *Newsweek* Vol. CXIII, No. 1, January 2, 1989, p. 14.
8. Noel O'Sullivan, *Terrorism, Ideology and Revolution*, Boulder, Col., Westview Press, 1986, pp. 80–85.
9. Benjamin Netanyahu, ed., *International Terrorism: Challenge and Response*, the Jonathan Institute, Jerusalem, 1981, p. 55.
10. Brian Jenkins and Janera Johnson, *International Terrorism: A Chronology*, Santa Monica, California, the Rand Corporation, 1975.
11. James M. Poland, *Understanding Terrorism*, Englewood Cliffs, N.J., Prentice Hall, 1988, p. 163.
12. "Security: The Invisible Bomb," *Newsweek* Vol. CXIII, No. 1, January 2, 1989, p. 20.
13. *Ibid.*, p. 163.
14. Janera Johnson, *International Terrorism and World Security*, New York, John Wiley & Sons, 1974, pp. 35–49.
15. David C. Rappaport, "Messianic Sanctions for Terror," *Comparative Politics* Vol. 20, No. 2, January 1988, p. 197.
16. *Ibid.*, pp. 200–207.
17. J. Becker, *Hitler's Children*, Philadelphia, J.B. Lippincott, 1977.
18. Gerhard Spoerl, "Klopfzeichen aus dem Knast," *Die Zeit* Vol. 44, No. 17, April 29, 1989, p. 4.
19. Gerhard Falk, "Terror as Politics: The German Case," *The International Review of History and Political Science* Vol. XX, No. 4, November 1983, pp. 22–32.
20. I. Fetcher und G. Rohrmoser, *Ideologien und Strategien*, Opladen, Westdeutscher Verlag, GmbH., 1981.
21. *Ibid.*, p. 45.
22. *Ibid.*, p. 45.
23. *Ibid.*, p. 17.
24. Karl Marx, *Capital*, New York, The Modern Library, 1936.
25. Andre Morois, *A History of England*, New York, Grove Press, 1960, p. 348.
26. "Quis Custodiet Ipsos Custodes?" *The Economist* Vol. 308, No. 7567, September 10, 1988, p. 70.
27. "No End to Ulster's Killings," *The Economist* Vol. 306, No. 7542, March 19, 1988, p. 62.

28. "Brotherly Hate," *The Economist* Vol. 307, No. 7556, June 25, 1988, pp. 19, 20 and 22.

29. Andrew Phillips, "Welsh Nationalist," *McLean's* Vol. 101, No. 51, December 12, 1988, p. 50.

30. Serge Schmemann, "Bomb Wounds 18 in Durban Store," *New York Times,* September 2, 1988, p. Al.

31. "North Korean Admits Putting Bomb on Plane," *New York Times,* March 5, 1989, p. A5.

32. J.G. Stratton, "The Terrorist Act of Hostage Taking: A View of Violence and the Perpetrators," *The Journal of Political Science Administration* Vol. 6, No. 1, 1978.

33. M. Cherif Bassiouni, "Terrorism, Law Enforcement, and the Mass Media: Perspectives, Problems, Proposals," *The Journal of Criminal Law and Criminology* Vol. 72, No. 1, Spring 1981, p. 1.

34. Bassiouni, *op. cit.,* p. 14.

35. *Ibid.,* pp. 17–18.

36. *New York Times,* March 19, 1977, p. 33.

37. Woods, *op. cit.,* p. 52.

38. *New York Times,* October 8, 1985, p. 1; October 11, 1985, p. 1; October 13, 1985, p. 1; October 14, 1985, p. 1.

39. *New York Times,* I, January 16, 1988, p. 1.

40. *New York Times,* I, December 22, 1988, p. 14.

41. Laura Shapiro, "Satanic Fury," *Newsweek* Vol. 113, No. 27, February 27, 1989, p. 37.

42. *New York Times,* October 13, 1989, p. 1.

43. William J. Casey, "International Terrorism: Potent Challenge to American Intelligence," *Vital Speeches* Vol. LI, No. 23, September 15, 1985, 713–716.

44. Steven Emerson, "Secret Warriors," *New York Times Magazine,* November 13, 1988, pp. 68–78.

45. "Terror Alert," *U.S. News and World Report* Vol. 106, No. 18, May 8, 1989, p. 18.

9. Murder by Death

1. *New York Times,* August 9, 1987, p. 22.

2. Clinton T. Duffy and Al Hirshberg, *88 Men and Two Women,* Garden City, New York, Doubleday, 1962.

3. Colin Turnbull, "Death by Decree," *Natural History* Vol. LXXXVII, No. 5, May 1978, pp. 50–66.

4. Stephen H. Gettinger, *Sentenced to Die,* New York, Macmillan, 1979, pp. 89–90.

5. *Ibid.,* p. 90.

6. Lewis E. Lawes, *Life and Death in Sing Sing,* New York, Garden City Publishing, 1928, pp. 170–171 & 188–190.

7. *Texas Monthly,* February 1983, pp. 100–105.

8. *Time,* December 20, 1982, pp. 28–29.

9. Gettinger, *op. cit.,* p. 91.

10. William McAllen Green, "An Ancient Debate on Capital Punishment," *The Classical Journal* Vol. 24, January 1929, pp. 267–275.

11. Caesare Beccaria, *Essay on Crimes and Punishments,* trans. Henry Paolucci, Indianapolis, Bobbs Merrill, 1963.

12. *The Buffalo News* "Election Could Provide Boost to Death Penalty," September 26, 1988, p. All.

13. Nathan Ausubel, *The Book of Jewish Knowledge*, New York, Crown, 1964, p. 153 and p. 389.

14. National Interreligious Task Force on Criminal Justice, *Capital Punishment: What the Religious Community Says*, New York, n.d.

15. Isaac Ehrlich, "The Deterrent Effect of Capital Punishment: A Question of Life or Death," *American Economic Review* Vol. 65, p. 397, 1975.

16. Vincent M. Scramuzza and Paul L. MacKendrick, *The Ancient World*, New York, Henry Holt and Company, 1958, pp. 509–511.

17. "Uusque tandem, Catilina, abutere patientam nostram?" "How long, Catilina, will you abuse our patience?" is a famous passage from that well known event. (Tr. the author.)

18. Green, *op. cit.*, p. 52.

19. Ernest van den Haag, *Punishing Criminals*, New York, Basic Books, 1975.

20. Dane Archer and Rosemary Gartner, *Violence & Crime in Cross National Perspective*, New Haven, Yale University Press, 1984, p. 133.

21. American Broadcasting Co., telecast, September 1988.

22. Immanuel Kant, *The Metaphysical Elements of Justice* (John Ladd, trans.), New York, Bobbs-Merrill, 1965, p. 102.

23. Immanuel Kant, *Fundamental Principles of the Metaphysics of Morals* (T.K. Abbott, trans.), London, Longmans, Green, 1873. This is a translation of Kant's *Metaphisik der Sitten*. Kant's rather extreme position in this matter is thoroughly discussed in H. Seeger, *Die Strafrechtstheorie Kants und seiner Nachfolger (The Penal Law Theories of Kant and His Successors)*, and in Igor Primorac, *Prestup I Kazna (Transgression and Punishment)*. Unfortunately, neither of these books has been rendered into English.

24. Ernest van den Haag, "Could Successful Rehabilitation Reduce the Crime Rate?" *Journal of Criminal Law and Criminology* Vol. 73, 1022–1035.

25. David Margolick, "25 Wrongfully Executed in the U.S., Study Finds," *New York Times*, November 14, 1985, p. A19.

26. Isadore Zimmerman, *Punishment Without Crime*, New York, Manor Publishing, 1973.

27. *New York Times*, October 6, 1980, Sect. B, p. 3.

28. *Oakland Tribune*, March 6, 1981, p. A2.

29. Gerhard Falk, "Violence and the American Police," *The International Review of History and Political Science* Vol. 23, No. 4, November 1986, pp. 23–34.

30. *New York Times*, January 19, 1984, p. B9.

31. *Philadelphia Daily News*, March 7, 1986, p. 9.

32. "The Ordeal of Larry Hicks," *Playboy*, May 1981, p. 66.

33. Hugo Adam Bedau and Michael L. Radelet, "Miscarriages of Justice in Potentially Capital Cases," *The Stanford Law Review* Vol. 40, No. 1, November 1987, pp. 91–172.

34. *Buffalo News*, November 17, 1985, p. A-5.

35. M. Dwayne Smith, "Patterns of Discrimination in Assessments of the Death Penalty: The Case of Louisiana," *The Journal of Criminal Justice* Vol. 15, 1987, pp. 279–286.

36. Charles Lucas, *Recueil des debats des Assembles Legislative de la France sur la question de la peine de mort*, Paris, 1831, Part I, p. 38.

37. William Bowers and Glenn Pierce, "Deterrence or Brutalization: What Is the Effect of Executions?" *Crime and Delinquency* Vol. 26, 1980, pp. 453–484.

38. John Ortiz Smylka, "The Human Impact of Capital Punishment: Interviews with Families on Death Row," *The Journal of Criminal Justice* Vol. 15, No. 4, 1987, pp. 331–347.

39. *Ibid.*, p. 340.

40. *Atlanta Journal and Constitution*, August 13, 1978.

41. E.P. Evans, *The Criminal Prosecution and Capital Punishment of Animals*, London, 1906, quoted in Arthur Koestler, *Reflections on Hanging* (see note 55).

42. *Wilkerson vs. Utah*, 1878, 99 U.S. 130.
43. *In re Kemmler*, 136 U.S. 436, 1890.
44. *In re Kemmler*, 136 U.S. 436, 1890.
45. Constitution of the United States.
46. *Trop vs. Dulles*, 356 U.S. 86, 1958.
47. *International Review of Public Opinion* Vol. II, No. 3, 1967, p. 84.
48. *Witherspoon vs. Illinois*, 391 U.S. 510.
49. *Lockhart vs. McCree*, 106 S. Ct. 1758 (1986).
50. *Furman vs. Georgia*, 408 U.S. 235, 1972, p. 242.
51. *Buffalo News*, April 23, 1987, p. All.
52. *Gregg vs. Georgia*, 428 U.S. 153.
53. Georgia Code Par. 27-2534.1.
54. *Coker vs. Georgia*, 433 U.S. 583, 1977.
55. *Godfrey vs. Georgia*, 446 U.S. 420.
56. *Woodson vs. North Carolina*, 428 U.S. 280 (1976).
57. *Ibid.*, p. 305.
58. *Buffalo News*, April 22, 1987, p. A-3.
59. *New York Times*, July 8, 1988, Sec. II, page 20.
60. *New York Times*, June 30, 1988, Sec. 1, p. 17.
61. U.S. Department of Justice, Bureau of Justice Statistics, *Sourcebook of Criminal Justice Statistics, 1989*, Washington, United States Government Printing Office, 1989, pp. 662–667.
62. Arthur Koestler, *Bricks to Babel*, New York, Random House, 1980.

10. Murder Now and Then

1. United States Department of Justice, Federal Bureau of Investigation *Uniform Crime Report*, Washington, D.C., July 10, 1989, p. 52.
2. *Ibid.*
3. *Ibid.* (UCR errors corrected by author.)
4. Marvin Wolfgang and Franco Ferracuti, *The Subculture of Violence*, London, Tavistock, 1967.
5. Nina Baym, *The Scarlet Letter: A Reading*. Boston, Twayne Publishers, 1986, p. 45.
6. Ernst Troeltsch, *Die Soziallehren der Christlichen Kirchen und Gruppen* (1911), has been translated into English as *The Social Teachings of the Christian Churches* by Olive Wyon. New York, Harper Torchbooks, 1960, p. 611.
7. Troeltsch, *op. cit.*, p. 619. This was of course not a Calvinistic invention. Jacob Burckhardt had already shown that the duality between individualism and human consciousness as a member of a people had developed in Renaissance Italy and was derived from the teachings of St. Augustine. *See* Jackob Burckhardt, *The Civilization of the Renaissance in Italy* (S.G.C. Middlemore, trans.), London, Phaidon Publishers, 1950, p. 81., and in *De coelestia hierarchia* written in the 6th century by Dyonisius the Aeropagite. This can be found in Mary Douglas, *Purity and Danger, An Analysis of Concepts of Pollution and Taboo*, London, Routledge and Keegan Paul, 1966.
8. Gerhard Lenski, *The Religious Factor*, New York, Doubleday, 1961, p. 90.
9. Carl N. Degler, *Out of Our Past*, New Yorker, Harper & Row, 1959, p. 16.
10. E. Digby Baltzell, *Puritan Boston and Quaker Philadelphia*, New York, the Free Press, 1979, p. 134.
11. Frederick Jackson Turner, *The Frontier of American History*, New York, Henry Holt, 1921.
12. Robert A. Caro, *The Years of Lyndon Johnson: The Path to Power*, New York, Alfred A. Knopf, 1983, pp. 11–18.

13. *Ibid.*, p. 18.

14. Degler, *op. cit.*, p. 191.

15. U.S. Department of Justice, *Uniform Crime Reports*, 1989, p. 325.

16. *Ibid.*, p. 325.

17. Konrad Lorenz, *On Aggression*, London, Methuen, 1966.

18. N.J. Felipe and Robert Sommer, "Invasions of Personal Space," *Social Problems* Vol. 14, 1966, pp. 206–214.

19. R. Ardrey, *The Territorial Imperative*, New York, Dell Books, 1966. *See also* J.D. Fisher and D. Byrne, "Too Close for Comfort: Sex Differences in Response to Invasions of Personal Space," *The Journal of Personality and Social Psychology* Vol. 32, 1975, pp. 15–21.

20. Henry Gleitman, *Psychology*, New York, W.W. Norton, 1986, p. 345.

21. *World Almanac*, New York, Pharos Books, 1988, p. 532.

22. *Ibid.*, pp. 572–589.

23. Kenneth Tardiff and Elliott M. Gross, "Homicide in New York City," *Bulletin of the New York Academy of Medicine* Vol. 62, No. 5, June 1986, p. 416.

24. See the study by Robert Sennett and Jonathan Cobb, *The Hidden Injuries of Class*, New York, Random House, 1972; also, James S. Coleman and Lee Rainwater, *Social Standing in America*, New York, Basic Books, 1978, and David Whitman and Jeannye Thornton, "A Nation Apart," *U.S. News and World Report*, March 17, 1986, pp. 18–21.

25. Gerhard Falk, "Status Differences and the Frustration-Aggression Hypothesis," *The International Journal of Social Psychiatry* Vol. 5, No. 3, Winter 1959.

26. Falk, *op. cit.*, p. 215. Obviously, the least desirable areas of both cities had the most homicide.

27. H.C. Brearly, *Homicide in the United States*, Chapel Hill, University of North Carolina Press, 1932.

28. Andrew F. Henry and James F. Short, Jr., *Suicide and Homicide*, Glencoe, Ill., Free Press, 1954.

29. *Ibid.*, p. 82.

30. *Ibid.*, p. 96.

31. World Almanac, 1988, *op. cit.*, p. 86.

32. Otto Pollak, *The Criminality of Women*, Philadelphia, University of Pennsylvania Press, 1950.

33. Falk, *op. cit.*, p. 220.

34. George B. Vold and Thomas J. Bernard, *Theoretical Criminology*, New York, Oxford University Press, 1986, p. 138.

35. Steven F. Messner (1), "Societal Development, Social Equality and Homicide," *Social Forces* Vol. 61, 1982, pp. 225–240. Steven F. Messner (2), "Income Inequality and Murder Rates: Some Cross National Findings," *Comparative Social Research* Vol. 3, 1980, pp. 185–198; John Braithwaite and Valerie Braithwaite (3), "The Effect of Income Inequality and Social Democracy on Homicides: A Cross National Comparison," *The British Journal of Criminology* Vol. 20, 1980, pp. 45–53; John Braithwaite (4), *Inequality, Crime and Public Policy*, Routledge and Keegan Paul, London, 1979; Marvin D. Krohn (5), "Inequality, Unemployment and Crime," *Sociological Quarterly* Vol. 17, 1976, pp. 303–333; (6) Lyn McDonald, *Sociology of Law and Order*, London, Faber and Faber, 1976.

36. Judith Blau and Peter Blau, "The Cost of Inequality: Metropolitan Structure and Violent Crime," *American Sociological Review*, Vol. 47, 1982, pp. 114–129.

37. Tardiff and Gross, *op. cit.*, pp. 413–425.

38. *Ibid.*, p. 415.

39. *Ibid.*, p. 424.

40. Stuart Palmer, *The Psychology of Murder*, New York, Thomas Y. Crowell, 1960.

41. *Ibid.*, p. 248.

42. *Ibid.*, p. 248.

43. Murray Straus, "Domestic Violence and Homicide Antecedents," *Bulletin of the New York Academy of Medicine* Vol. 62, No. 5, June 1986.

44. Richard Gelles, *An Exploratory Study of Intra-Family Violence*, Durham, N.H., 1973 (unpublished Ph.D. dissertation).

45. Ed Magnuson, "Child Abuse: The Ultimate Betrayal," *Time*, September 5, 1983, p. 21.

46. Samuel G. Freedman, "When Parents Kill: The Story of Shawn," *New York Times*, September 2, 1983, p. B1.

47. Magnuson, *op. cit.*, p. 22.

11. *"Logos"*

1. *Historical Statistics of the United States, Colonial Times to 1970*, pp. 58 and 63; *Statistical Abstracts of the United States*, 1984, p. 78.

2. Gerhard Falk, "The Contribution of the Alcohol Culture to Alcoholism in America," *The British Journal of Addiction* Vol. 65, No. 2, May 1970.

3. Kathleen J. Ferraro and John M. Johnson, "How Women Experience Battering: The Process of Victimization," *Social Problems* Vol. 30, No. 3, February 1983, pp. 325–335.

4. Bruno Bettelheim, "Eichmann: The System, the Victims," *The New Republic*, June 15, 1963, p. 33.

5. Hannah Arendt, *Eichmann in Jerusalem: A Report on the Banality of Evil*, New York, Viking Press, 1963.

6. *Ibid.*, pp. 23–33.

7. *Ibid.*, p. 25.

8. *Ibid.*, p. 269.

9. Gerhard Falk, "'Sado-Masochism' and Popular Western Culture," in: *S & M: Studies in Sado-Masochism*, Thomas S. Weinberg and G.W. Levi Kamel, eds., Buffalo, Prometheus Books, 1983.

10. Stephen J. Pfohl, "The 'Discovery' of Child Abuse," *Social Problems* Vol. 24, No. 3, February 1977, pp. 315–321.

11. *Ibid.*, p. 41.

12. *Ibid.*, p. 47.

13. Ronald S. Linsky and Murray Straus, *Social Stress in the United States*, Dover, Mass., Auburn House, 1986, p. 78.

14. *Ibid.*, pp. 72–73, 81–82.

15. *Ibid.*, p. 76.

16. Franklin E. Zimring, *The Citizen's Guide to Gun Control*, New York, Macmillan, 1987, p. 79.

17. *Ibid.*, p. 79.

18. Marvin Wolfgang, *Patterns in Criminal Homicide*, Philadelphia, University of Pennsylvania Press, 1958.

19. James D. Wright, Peter H. Rossi and Kathleen Daly, *Under the Gun: Weapons, Crime and Violence in America*, New York, Aldine, 1983.

20. Viktor E. Frankl, *Man's Search for Meaning* (Ilse Lasch, trans.), New York, Washington Square Press, 1963.

21. *Ibid.*, p. 173.

22. Raoul Naroll, *The Moral Order*, Beverly Hills, Calif., Sage Publications, 1983, pp. 392–395.

23. Celia S. Heller, *On the Edge of Destruction*, New York, Columbia University Press, 1977.

24. *Ibid.*, p. 74.

25. H.H. Gerth and C. Wright Mills, *From Max Weber: Essays in Sociology*, New York, Oxford University Press, 1958, p. 405.

26. Heller, *op. cit.*, p. 62.

27. *Ibid.*, p. 150.

28. Mark Zborowski and Elizabeth Herzog, *Life Is with People*, New York, International Universities Press, 1952. This is the report of a committee of anthropologists under the chairmanship of Ruth Benedict and Margaret Mead who collected information from East European Jewish refugees during World War II. The result is a detailed description of the Eastern European Jewish community as it existed before 1940.

29. Edwin H. Sutherland, *White Collar Crime*, New York, Dryden Press, 1949.

30. Ferdinand Tonnies, *Community and Society (Gemeinschaft und Gesellschaft)*, Charles P. Loomis, trans., New York, American Book, 1940.

31. *Geist der Neuzeit*, Leipzig, Hans Buske Verlag, 1935.

32. Georg Simmel, *Conflict* (Kurt H. Wolff, trans.), Glencoe, Ill., Free Press, 1955, pp. 83–84.

33. Alvin Toffler, *Future Shock*, New York, Random House, 1970.

34. *Ibid.*, p. 92.

35. James A. Michener, *Kent State*, New York, Random House, 1971, p. 341.

36. *Ibid.*, p. 442.

37. *Ibid.*, p. 446.

38. *Ibid.*, p. 455.

39. *Ibid.*, p. 460.

40. *Time*, Vol. 132, No. 17, October 24, 1988, p. 34.

41. Martin Buber, *The I and the Thou*, New York, Charles Scribner's Sons, 1958. We are using the word you, rather than "thou," which is an unfortunate misinterpretation of Buber's original work, *Ich und Du*, as it appeared in German in 1923.

42. George H. Mead, *Mind, Self and Society*, (Charles W. Morris, ed.) Chicago, University of Chicago Press, 1934.

43. *Ibid.*, p. 164.

44. *Ibid.*, p. 137.

Appendix

1. For more information on this, see any introductory statistics text.

2. Tests used to indicate strength of relationship or the percent of variance of one category that could be explained by another were, depending on the type of data, multiple regression analysis, Pearsonian and partial correlation, analysis of variance, and chi-square test. For more information on these, see Lester Guest's *Beginning Statistics* (New York, Thomas Y. Crowell, 1967).

3. Levels of significance for all featured covariances are less than .1 for measures of strength of relationship derived from the tests mentioned in discussion of the second selection criterion.

4. It should be noted, for example, that Wilbanks' study, *Murder in Miami* (University Press of America, 1984), which was done in a metropolitan area with substantially different characteristics as the instant study, draws many of the same conclusions as the study of murder in Buffalo.

5. That is, the single value of age of murderer which would give you the least possible error between your prediction and reality.

6. Betty Friedan, *The Feminine Mystique*, New York, Norton, 1963.

7. Note that in two high-column-inch relationship categories (police and coworker), women are insignificantly represented.

8. See Gerhard Lenski, *The Religious Factor*, New York, Doubleday, 1961.

9. See Gerhard Falk, "The Influence of the Seasons on the Crime Rate," *The Journal of Criminal Law, Criminology and Police Science* Vol. 43, No. 2, July-August 1952.

10. *Ibid.*

11. A brief note regarding use of the "mean year" statistic is in order here, since its meaning is not intuitively obvious (as is, for example, mean column inches of newspaper coverage). The "mean year" statistic in this category is used as a succinct way of showing trends over the course of time. One could, for example, compare the number of murders in the near suburbs for the 1940s, 1950s, 1960s, 1970s, and 1980s to the number of murders downtown for each said decade, and thereby show that the number is increasing faster in the near suburbs than downtown. The briefer way to do the same thing, however, is simply to calculate the mean year of murder for each category. In this instance, the mean year for murders committed in the near suburbs is 1973, while the mean year for murders committed downtown is 1967. This means that, on the average, murders committed in the near suburbs were committed more recently than murders committed downtown. In other words, where a murder occurred in Erie County in, say, 1950, there was a poor chance that it occurred in the near suburbs. Where a murder occurred in Erie County in 1980, there was a much better chance that it occurred in the near suburbs.

Bibliography

Articles

Adler, Selig. "The Operation on President McKinley." *Scientific American* **CCIII**, March 1963.

Bassiouni, M. Cherif. "Terrorism, Law Enforcement and the Mass Media: Perspectives, Problems, Proposals." *The Journal of Criminal Law and Criminology* **72**, No. 1, 1981.

Bedau, Hugo Adam, and Michael L. Radelet. "Miscarriages of Justice in Potentially Capital Cases." *The Stanford Law Review* **40**, No. 1, November 1987.

Bettelheim, Bruno. "Eichmann: The System, the Victims." *The New Republic.* June 15, 1963.

Blau, Judith, and Peter Blau. "The Cost of Inequality: Metropolitan Structure and Violent Crime." *The American Sociological Review* **47**, 1982.

Bowers, William, and Glenn Pierce. "Deterrence or Brutalization: What Is the Effect of Executions?" *Crime and Delinquency* **26**, 1980.

Braithwaite, John, and Valerie Braithwaite. "The Effect of Income Inequality and Social Democracy on Homicides: A Cross National Comparison." *The British Journal of Criminology* **20**, 1980.

Cohen, Joseph. "The Geography of Crime." *The Annals of the American Academy of Political and Social Sciences* **217**:29, September 1941.

Cook, James. "The Invisible Enterprise." *Forbes Magazine.* September 29, 1980.

Ehrlich, Isaac. "The Deterrent Effect of Capital Punishment: A Question of Life or Death." *American Economic Review* **65**, 1975.

Evans, Carl D., "The Church's False Witness Against the Jews." *The Christian Century.* May 5, 1982.

Falk, Gerhard. "A Sociological Approach to the 'Right-Wrong' Test in Criminal Procedure." *The Criminal Law Quarterly* **7**, No. 3, November 1964.

_____. "The Public Image of the Sex Offender." *Mental Hygiene* **48**, No. 4, October 1964.

_____. "'Sado-Masochism' and Popular Western Culture." in *S & M: Studies in Sado-Masochism.* Thomas S. Weinberg and G.W. Levi Kamel, eds. Buffalo, N.Y.: Prometheus Books, 1983.

_____. "Status Differences and the Frustration-Aggression Hypothesis." *The International Journal of Social Psychiatry* **5**, No. 3, Winter 1959.

_____. "The Influence of the Seasons on the Crime Rate." *The Journal of Criminal Law, Criminology and Police Science* **43**:2, July-August 1952.

_____. "The Contribution of the Alcohol Culture to Alcoholism in America." *The British Journal of Addiction* **65**, No. 2, May 1970.

_____. "Terror as Politics: The German Case." *The International Review of History and Political Science* **XX**, No. 4, November 1983, pp. 22–32.

_____. "Violence and the American Police." *The International Review of History and Political Science* **23**, No. 4, November 1986.

Felipe, N.J., and Robert Sommer. "Invasions of Personal Space." *Social Problems* **14**, 1966.

Ferraro, Kathleen J., and John M. Johnson. "How Women Experience Battering: The Process of Victimization." *Social Problems* **30**, No. 3, February 1983.

Fisher, Jeffrey D., and D. Byrne. "Too Close for Comfort: Sex Differences in Response to Invasions of Personal Space." *The Journal of Personality and Social Psychology* **32**, July, 1975.

Freedman, Samuel G. "When Parents Kill: The Story of Shawn." *New York Times.* September 2, 1983.

Goldstein, Marc. "Multiple Slayings in Nation's Recent History." *New York Times.* July 19, 1984.

Green, William McAllen. "An Ancient Debate on Capital Punishment." *The Classical Journal* **24**, January 1929.

Herman, Donald H.J., Helen L. Morrison, Yvonne S. Sor, Julie A. Norman and David M. Neff. "People of the State of Illinois vs. John Gacy: The Functioning of the Insanity Defense at the Limits of the Criminal Law." *The West Virginia Law Review* **86**, Summer 1984.

Holmes, Ronald, and James D. DeBurger. "Profiles in Terror: The Serial Murderer." *Federal Probation* **49**, September 1985.

Hughes, Everett C. "Good People and Dirty Work." *Social Problems* **10**, No. 1, Summer 1962.

International Review of Public Opinion **II**, No. 3, 1967.

Jones, John Phillip, ed. "Leopold von Ranke." *The Syracuse Scholar* **9**, No. 1, 1988.

Krauthammer, Charles. "It's Simply Murder." *The Washington Post National Weekly Edition.* December 31, 1984, p. 1.

Krohn, Marvin D. "Inequality, Unemployment and Crime." *Sociological Quarterly* **17**, 1976.

Magnuson, Ed. "Child Abuse: The Ultimate Betrayal." *Time.* September 5, 1983.

Margolick, David. "25 Wrongfully Executed in the U.S., Study Finds." *New York Times.* November 14, 1985.

Messner, Steven F. "Societal Development, Social Equality and Homicide." *Social Forces* **61**, 1982.

_____. "Income Inequality and Murder Rates: Some Cross National Findings." *Comparative Social Research* **3**, 1980.

Pfohl, Stephen J. "The 'Discovery' of Child Abuse." *Social Problems* **24**, No. 3, February 1977.

Phillips, Andrew. "Welsch Nationalists." *McLean's* **101**, No. 51, December 12, 1988.

Rappaport, David C. "Messianic Sanctions for Terror." *Comparative Politics* **20**, No. 2, January 1988.

Richards, Bill, and Alex Kotlowitz. "Judge Finds 3 Corporate Officials Guilty of Murder." *The Wall Street Journal.* June 17, 1985.

Rowan, Roy. "The Fifty Biggest Mafia Bosses." *Fortune* **114**, No. 11, November 10, 1986.

Schmemann, Serge. "Bomb Wounds Eighteen in Durban Store." *New York Times.* September 2, 1988, p. A-1.

Shapiro, Laura. "Satanic Fury." *Newsweek* **113**, No. 27, February 27, 1989.

Smith, M. Dwayne. "Patterns of Discrimination in Assessments of the Death Penalty: The Case of Louisiana." *The Journal of Criminal Justice* **15**, 1987.

Smylka, John Ortiz. "The Human Impact of Capital Punishment: Interviews with Families on Death Row." *The Journal of Criminal Justice* **15**, No. 4, 1987.

Spoerl, Gerhard. "Klopfzeichen aus dem Knast." *Die Zeit* **44**, No. 17, April 29, 1989.

Stratton, J.G. "The Terrorist Act of Hostage Taking: A View of Violence and the Perpetrators." *The Journal of Political Science Administration* **6**, No. 1, 1978.

Straus, Murray. "Domestic Violence and Homicide Antecedents." *Bulletin of the New York Academy of Medicine* **62**, No. 5, June 1986.
Tardiff, Kenneth, and Elliott M. Gross. "Homicide in New York City." *Bulletin of the New York Academy of Medicine* **62**, No. 5, June 1986.
Thompson, Mark. "Ramirez Faces 60 New Charges." *The Los Angeles Daily Journal* **98**, September 30, 1985.
Turnbull, Colin. "Death by Decree." *Natural History* **LXXXVII**, No. 5, May 1978.
Unger, Craig. "John Lennon's Killer: The Nowhere Man." *New York* **14**, June 22, 1981.
van den Haag, Ernest. "Could Successful Rehabilitation Reduce the Crime Rate?" *Journal of Criminal Law and Criminology* **73**, No. 3, Fall 1982.
Whitman, David, and Jeannye Thornton. "A Nation Apart." *U.S. News and World Report.* March 17, 1986.
Woods, B.F. "Terrorism: The Continuing Crisis." *The Police Chief* **48**, 1981, p. 52.

Books

Abadinsky, Howard. *Organized Crime.* Chicago: Nelson-Hall, 1986.
————. *The Mafia in America.* New York: Praeger, 1981.
Archer, Dane, and Rosemary Gartner. *Violence & Crime in Cross National Perspective.* New Haven: Yale University Press, 1984.
Ardrey, R. *The Territorial Imperative.* New York: Dell, 1966.
Arendt, Hannah. *Eichmann in Jerusalem: A Report on the Banality of Evil.* New York: Viking, 1963.
Ausubel, Nathan. *The Book of Jewish Knowledge.* New York, Crown, 1964.
Baltzell, E. Digby. *Puritan Boston and Quaker Philadelphia.* New York: Free Press, 1979.
Baym, Nina. *The Scarlet Letter: A Reading.* Boston: Twayne, 1986.
Beccaria, Caesare. *Essay on Crimes and Punishments.* (Henry Paolucci, trans.) Indianapolis: Bobbs-Merrill, 1963.
Becker, Jay. *Hitler's Children.* Philadelphia: J.B. Lippincott, 1977.
Bettelheim, Bruno. *Surviving.* New York: Alfred A. Knopf, 1979.
Braithwaite, John. *Inequality, Crime and Public Policy.* London: Routledge and Keegan Paul, 1979.
Brearly, H.C. *Homicide in the United States.* Chapel Hill: University of North Carolina Press, 1932.
Buber, Martin. *The I and the Thou.* New York: Charles Scribner's Sons, 1958.
Burckhardt, Jacob. *The Civilization of the Renaissance in Italy.* (S.G.C. Middlemore, trans.) London: Phaidon, 1950.
Caro, Robert A. *The Years of Lyndon Johnson: The Path to Power.* New York: Alfred A. Knopf, 1983.
Clarke, James W. *American Assassins: The Darker Side of Politics.* Princeton: Princeton University Press, 1982.
Coleman, James S., and Lee Rainwater. *Social Standing in America.* New York: Basic Books, 1978.
Danto, B.L., J. Bruhns, and A.H. Kutscher. *The Human Side of Homicide.* New York: Columbia University Press, 1982.
Dawidowicz, Lucy S. *The War Against the Jews.* New York: Holt, Rinehart and Winston, 1975.
Degler, Carl N. *Out of Our Past.* New York: Harper & Row, 1959.
Douglas, Mary. *Purity and Danger, An Analysis of Concepts of Pollution and Taboo.* London: Routledge and Keegan Paul, 1966.

Duffy, Clinton T., and Al Hirshberg. *88 Men and Two Women*. Garden City, New York: Doubleday, 1962.

Durant, Will. *The Age of Faith*. New York: Simon and Schuster, 1950.

Evans, E.P. *The Criminal Prosecution and Capital Punishment of Animals*. London, 1906: quoted in Arthur Koestler, *Reflections on Hanging*.

Fein, Helen. *Accounting for Genocide*. New York: Free Press, 1979.

Fest, Joachim. *Hitler*. New York: Vintage Books, 1975.

Fetcher, Isadore, and G. Rohrmoser. *Ideologien und Strategien*. Opladen, Germany: Westdeutscher, 1981.

Fletcher, Willard Allen. *The "Einsatzgruppen" in the Holocaust* Vol. 10. New York: Garland, 1982.

Frank, Gerold. *The Boston Strangler*. New York: New Amsterdam Library, 1967.

Frankl, Viktor E. *Man's Search for Meaning*. (Ilse Lasch, trans.) New York: Washington Square Press, 1963.

Friedlander, Henry. *The Holocaust: The Final Solution* Vol. 12. New York: Garland, 1982.

Friedman, Saul S. *AMCHA, An Oral Testament of the Holocaust*. Washington, D.C.: University Press of America, 1979.

Gelles, Richard. *An Exploratory Study of Intra-Family Violence*. Durham, N.H.: unpublished Ph.D. dissertation, 1973.

Gerth, H.H., and C. Wright Mills. *From Max Weber: Essays in Sociology*. New York: Oxford University Press, 1958.

Gettinger, Stephen H. *Sentenced to Die*. New York: Macmillan, 1979.

Gilbert, Martin. *The Holocaust*. New York: Hill and Wang, 1979.

Gleitman, Henry. *Psychology*. New York: W.W. Norton, 1986.

Hartunian, Abraham H. *A Memoir of the Armenian Genocide Translated from the Original Armenian Manuscripts*. Boston: Beacon Press, 1972.

Haskell, Martin R., and Lewis Yablonsky. *Juvenile Delinquency*. Chicago: Rand McNally, 1974.

Heller, Celia S. *On the Edge of Destruction*. New York: Columbia University Press, 1977.

Henry, Andrew F., and James F. Short, Jr. *Suicide and Homicide*. Glencoe, Ill.: Free Press, 1954.

Hernon, Peter. *A Terrible Thunder: The Story of the New Orleans Sniper*. Garden City, N.Y.: Doubleday, 1978.

Historical Statistics of the United States, Colonial Times to 1970. U.S. Bureau of the Census, Washington, D.C.: U.S. Government Printing Office, 1975.

Homes, Ronald, and James DeBurger. *Serial Murder*. Newbury Park, Calif.: Sage, 1987.

Hovannisian, Richard G. *The Armenian Genocide in Perspective*. New Brunswick, N.J.: Transaction Books, 1986.

International School of Disarmament and Research on Conflicts. *International Terrorism and World Security*. New York: John Wiley & Sons, 1975.

Jenkins, Brian and Janera Johnson. *International Terrorism: A Chronology*. Santa Monica, Calif.: Rand Corp., 1975.

Kalven, Harry, and Hans Zeisel. *The American Jury*. Boston: Little, Brown, 1966.

Kant, Immanuel. *Fundamental Principles of the Metaphysics of Morals*. (T.K. Abbott, trans.) London: Longmans, Gree, 1873.

_____. *The Metaphysical Elements of Justice*. (John Ladd, trans) New York: Bobbs-Merrill, 1965.

Koestler, Arthur. *Bricks to Babel*. New York: Random House, 1980.

Larsen, Richard W. *Bundy: The Deliberate Stranger*. Englewood Cliffs, N.J.: Prentice Hall, 1980.

Lawes, Lewis E. *Life and Death in Sing Sing*. New York: Garden City, 1928.

Lenski, Gerhard. *The Religious Factor.* New York: Doubleday, 1961.

Levin, Jack, and James Alan Fox. *Mass Murder.* New York: Plenum Press, 1985.

Levin, Nora. *The Holocaust.* New York: Schocken, 1973.

Leyton, Elliott. *Compulsive Killers: The Story of Modern Multiple Murder.* New York: Washington News Books, 1986.

Linsky, Ronald S., and Murray Straus. *Social Stress in the United States.* Dover, Mass.: Auburn House, 1986.

Locke, Ed. *Exile in the Fatherland.* New York: William B. Eerdmans, 1986.

Lorenz, Konrad. *On Aggression.* London: Methuen, 1966.

Lucas, Charles. *Recueil des debats des Assembles Legislative de la France sur la question de la peine de mort.* Paris, 1831.

Lyman, Stanford M. *The Seven Deadly Sins.* New York: St. Martin's Press, 1978.

Marx, Karl. *Capital.* New York: Modern Library, 1936.

McDonald, Lyn. *Sociology of Law and Order.* London: Faber and Faber, 1976.

Mead, George H. *Mind, Self and Society.* (Charles W. Morris, ed.) Chicago: University of Chicago Press, 1934.

Michaud, Stephen G., and Hugh Aynesworth. *The Only Living Witness.* New York: New American Library, 1983.

Michener, James A. *Kent State.* New York: Random House, 1971.

Morois, Andre. *A History of England.* New York: Grove Press, 1960.

Naroll, Raoul. *The Moral Order.* Beverly Hills, Calif.: Sage, 1983.

National Interreligious Task Force on Criminal Justice. *Capital Punishment: What the Religious Community Says.* New York: n.d.

Netanyahu, Benjamin. *International Terrorism: Challenge and Response.* Jerusalem: Jonathan Institute, 1981.

O'Sullivan, Noel. *Terrorism, Ideology and Revolution.* Boulder, Col.: Westview Press, 1986.

Palmer, Stuart. *The Psychology of Murder.* New York: Thomas Y. Crowell, 1960.

Park, R.E., E.W. Burgess, and R.D. McKenzie. *The City.* Chicago: University of Chicago Press, 1925.

Payne, Robert. *The Life and Death of Adolf Hitler.* New York: Praeger, 1973.

Peterson, Virgil W. *The Mob.* Ottawa, Ill.: Green Hill, 1983.

Pileggi, Nicholas. *Wise Guy.* New York: Simon and Schuster, 1985.

Poland, James M. *Understanding Terrorism.* Englewood Cliffs, N.J.: Prentice Hall, 1988.

Pollak, Otto. *The Criminality of Women.* Philadelphia: University of Pennsylvania Press, 1950.

Primorac, Igor. *Prestup I. Kazna.* n.p., n.d.

Santayana, George. *Life of Reason: Reason in Common Sense.* New York: Scribner's, 1953.

Scramuzza, Vincent M., and Paul L. MacKendrick. *The Ancient World.* New York: Henry Holt, 1958.

Seeger, H. *Die Strafrechtstheorie Kants und seiner Nachfolger.* Tübingen, Germany: H. Laupp, 1892.

Sennett, Robert, and Jonathan Cobb. *The Hidden Injuries of Class.* New York: Random House, 1972.

Simmel, Georg. *Conflict.* (Kurt H. Wolff, trans.) Glencoe, Ill.: Free Press, 1955.

Smith, Rex Alan. *Moon of Popping Trees.* Lincoln: University of Nebraska Press, 1975.

Sutherland, Edwin H. *White Collar Crime.* New York: Dryden, 1949.

Thornton, Russell. *American Indian Holocaust and Survival.* Norman: University of Oklahoma Press, 1980.

Toffler, Alvin. *Future Shock.* New York: Random House, 1970.

Toland, John. *Adolf Hitler.* Garden City, N.Y.: Doubleday, 1976.

Tolstoy, Leo. *War and Peace.* (Louise and Aylmer Maude, trans.) New York: W.W. Norton, 1966.

Tonnies, Ferdinand. *Community and Society (Gemeinschaft und Gesellschaft)* (Charles P. Loomis, trans.) New York: American, 1940.

_____. *Geist der Neuzeit.* Leipzig: Hans Buske Verlag, 1935.

Treiman, Donald. *Occupational Prestige in Comparative Perspective.* New York: Academic Press, 1977.

Troeltsch, Ernst. *Die Soziallehren der Christlichen Kirchen und Gruppen* (1911). Translated into English as *The Social Teachings of the Christian Churches* by Olive Wyon. New York: Harper Torchbooks, 1960.

Turner, Frederick Jackson. *The Frontier of American History.* New York: Henry Holt, 1921.

Tyler, Gus. *Organized Crime in America.* Ann Arbor: University of Michigan Press, 1962.

United States Department of Commerce, United States Bureau of the Census. *Statistical Abstracts of the United States,* Washington, D.C.: U.S. Government Printing Office, 1984, 1985, 1986, 1987.

United States Department of Justice. *Sourcebook of Criminal Justice Statistics.* Washington, D.C., 1989.

United States Department of Justice, Federal Bureau of Investigation. *Uniform Crime Reports.* Washington, D.C., 1989.

United States Department of Justice, Task Force on Organized Crime. *Organized Crime.* Washington, D.C.: U.S. Government Printing Office, 1976.

United States Department of Justice. The Trial of the Major War Criminals as published in: *Nazi Conspiracy and Aggression.* Washington, D.C.: Government Printing Office, 15 vols., 1951–1952.

van den Haag, Ernest. *Punishing Criminals.* New York: Basic Books, 1975.

The Vatican. *Documents of the Vatican II.*

Vold, George B., and Thomas J. Bernard. *Theoretical Criminology,* New York: Oxford University Press, 1986.

von Lang, John, and Claus Sybill, eds. *Eichmann Interrogated.* New York: Farrar, Strauss and Giroux, 1983.

Winn, Stephen, and David Merrill. *Ted Bundy: The Killer Next Door.* New York: Bantam Books, 1980.

Wolfgang, Marvin. *Patterns in Criminal Homicide.* Philadelphia: University of Pennsylvania Press, 1958.

Wolfgang, Marvin, and Franco Ferracuti. *The Subculture of Violence.* London: Tavistock, 1967.

World Almanac. New York: Pharos Books, 1988.

Wright, James D., Peter H. Rossi, and Kathleen Daly. *Under the Gun: Weapons, Crime and Violence in America.* New York: Aldine, 1983.

Zborowski, Mark, and Elizabeth Herzog. *Life Is with People.* New York: International Universities Press, 1952.

Zimmerman, Isadore. *Punishment Without Crime.* New York: Manor Publishing, 1973.

Zimring, Franklin E. *The Citizen's Guide to Gun Control.* New York: Macmillan, 1987.

Newspapers, Television, and Popular Magazines

American Broadcasting Company, Telecast, September 1988.

Associated Press

Atlanta Journal and Constitution

Buffalo Courier-Express

Buffalo News
Chicago Tribune
Die Zeit
Economist
Harper's Magazine
Life
New York Times
Newsweek
Oakland Tribune
Philadelphia Daily News
Playboy
Sacramento Bee
Texas Monthly
Time
U.S. News & World Report

Case Law and Statutes

Coker vs. Georgia, 433 U.S. 583 (1977)
Constitution of the United States
Furman vs. Georgia, 408 U.S. 235 (1972)
Georgia Code
Godfrey vs. Georgia, 446 U.S. 420
Gregg vs. Georgia, 428 U.S. 153
In re Kemmler, 136 U.S. 436 (1890)
Lockhart vs. McCree, 106 S. Ct. 1758 (1986)
Trop vs. Dulles, 356 U.S. 86 (1958)
Woodson vs. North Carolina, 428 U.S. 280 (1976)

Index